The spotlight on Rumiko Takahashi's career began in 1978 when she won an honorable mention in Shogakukan's annual New Comic Artist Contest for *Those Selfish Aliens*. Later that same year, her boy-meets-alien comedy series, *Urusei Yatsura*, was serialized in *Weekly Shonen Sunday*. This phenomenally successful manga series was adapted into anime format and spawned a TV series and half a dozen theatrical-release movies, all incredibly popular in their own right. Takahashi followed up the success of her debut series with one blockbuster hit after another—*Maison Ikkoku* ran from 1980 to 1987, *Ranma ½* from 1987 to 1996, and *Inuyasha* from 1996 to 2008. Other notable works include *Mermaid Saga*, *Rumic Theater*, and *One-Pound Gospel*.

Takahashi won the prestigious Shogakukan Manga Award twice in her career, once for *Urusei Yatsura* in 1981 and the second time for *Inuyasha* in 2002. A majority of the Takahashi canon has been adapted into other media such as anime, live-action TV series, and film. Takahashi's manga, as well as the other formats her work has been adapted into, have continued to delight generations of fans around the world. Distinguished by her wonderfully endearing characters, Takahashi's work adeptly incorporates a wide variety of elements such as comedy, romance, fantasy, and martial arts. While her series are difficult to pin down into one simple genre, the signature style she has created has come to be known as the "Rumic World." Rumiko Takahashi is an artist who truly represents the very best from the world of manga.

RIN-NE
VOLUME 8
Shonen Sunday Edition

STORY AND ART BY
RUMIKO TAKAHASHI

© 2009 Rumiko TAKAHASHI/Shogakukan
All rights reserved.
Original Japanese edition "KYOUKAI NO RINNE"
published by SHOGAKUKAN Inc.

Translation/Christine Dashiell
Touch-up Art & Lettering/Evan Waldinger
Design/Yukiko Whitley
Editor/Mike Montesa

Printed in Canada

Published by VIZ Media, LLC
P.O. Box 77010
San Francisco, CA 94107

10 9 8 7 6 5 4 3 2 1
First printing, March 2012

www.viz.com

WWW.SHONENSUNDAY.COM

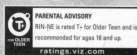

RIN-NE

Story and Art by
Rumiko Takahashi

RIN-NE

Characters

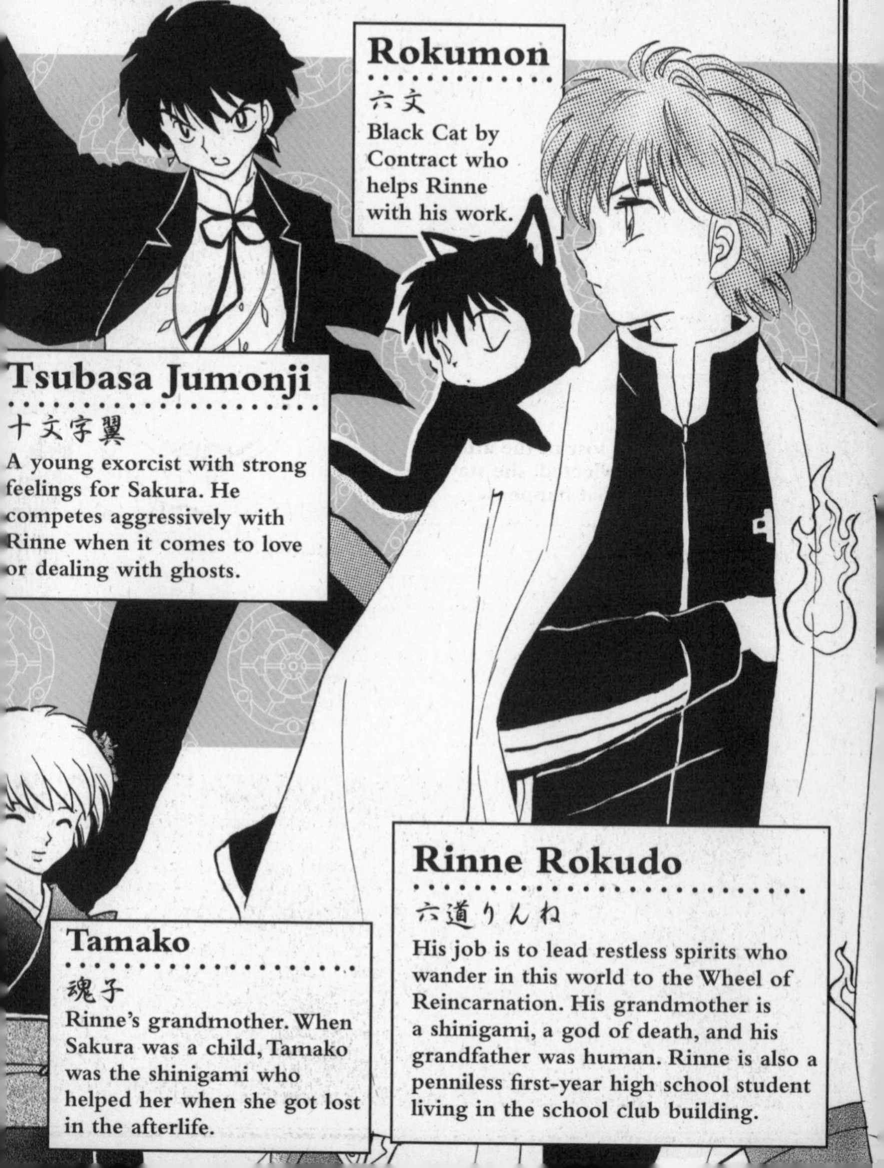

Rokumon

六文

Black Cat by Contract who helps Rinne with his work.

Tsubasa Jumonji

十文字翼

A young exorcist with strong feelings for Sakura. He competes aggressively with Rinne when it comes to love or dealing with ghosts.

Rinne Rokudo

六道りんね

His job is to lead restless spirits who wander in this world to the Wheel of Reincarnation. His grandmother is a shinigami, a god of death, and his grandfather was human. Rinne is also a penniless first-year high school student living in the school club building.

Tamako

魂子

Rinne's grandmother. When Sakura was a child, Tamako was the shinigami who helped her when she got lost in the afterlife.

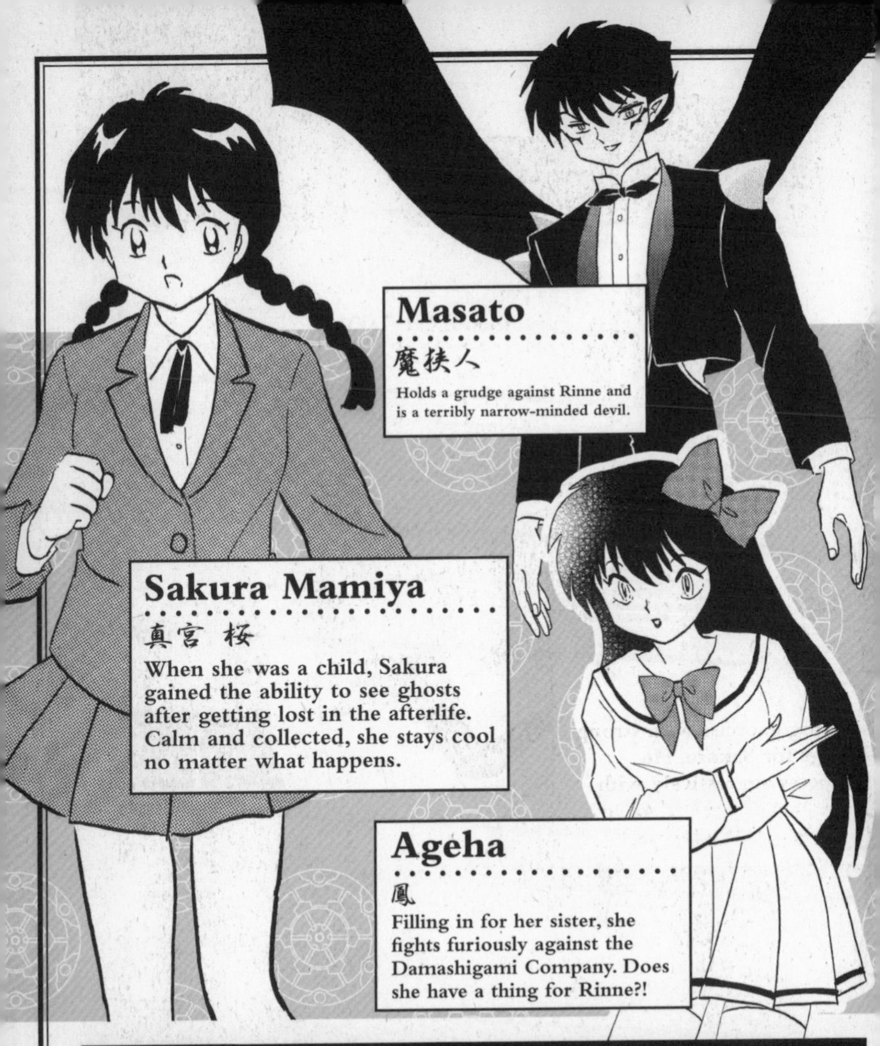

Masato

魔狭人

Holds a grudge against Rinne and is a terribly narrow-minded devil.

Sakura Mamiya

真宮 桜

When she was a child, Sakura gained the ability to see ghosts after getting lost in the afterlife. Calm and collected, she stays cool no matter what happens.

Ageha

鳳

Filling in for her sister, she fights furiously against the Damashigami Company. Does she have a thing for Rinne?!

The Story So Far

Together, Sakura, the girl who can see ghosts, and Rinne the shinigami (sort of) spend their days helping spirits that can't pass on reach the afterlife, and deal with all kinds of strange phenomena at their school.

Ghosts have never haunted Sakura's house, but when they start showing up in her room she goes to Rinne for help. Despite Jumonji and Ageha's jealous interference, Rinne manages a perfect solution to Sakura's problem.

Between this incident, the strange goings on at a festival, and dealing with the curse of some mischievous cat spirits, Rinne's shinigami duties are keeping him busy!

Contents

Chapter 69: Homestay Training......7

Chapter 70: The Story Behind the Alligator Woman......25

Chapter 71: Chibi's Memories......43

Chapter 72: Introduction to an Evil Spirit......61

Chapter 73: Supervisory Liability......79

Chapter 74: Party of Five, This Way......97

Chapter 75: The Friendly Square......115

Chapter 76: The Curse of the Kitchen Counter......133

Chapter 77: The Strangling Scarf......151

Chapter 78: The Present......169

CHAPTER 69: HOMESTAY TRAINING

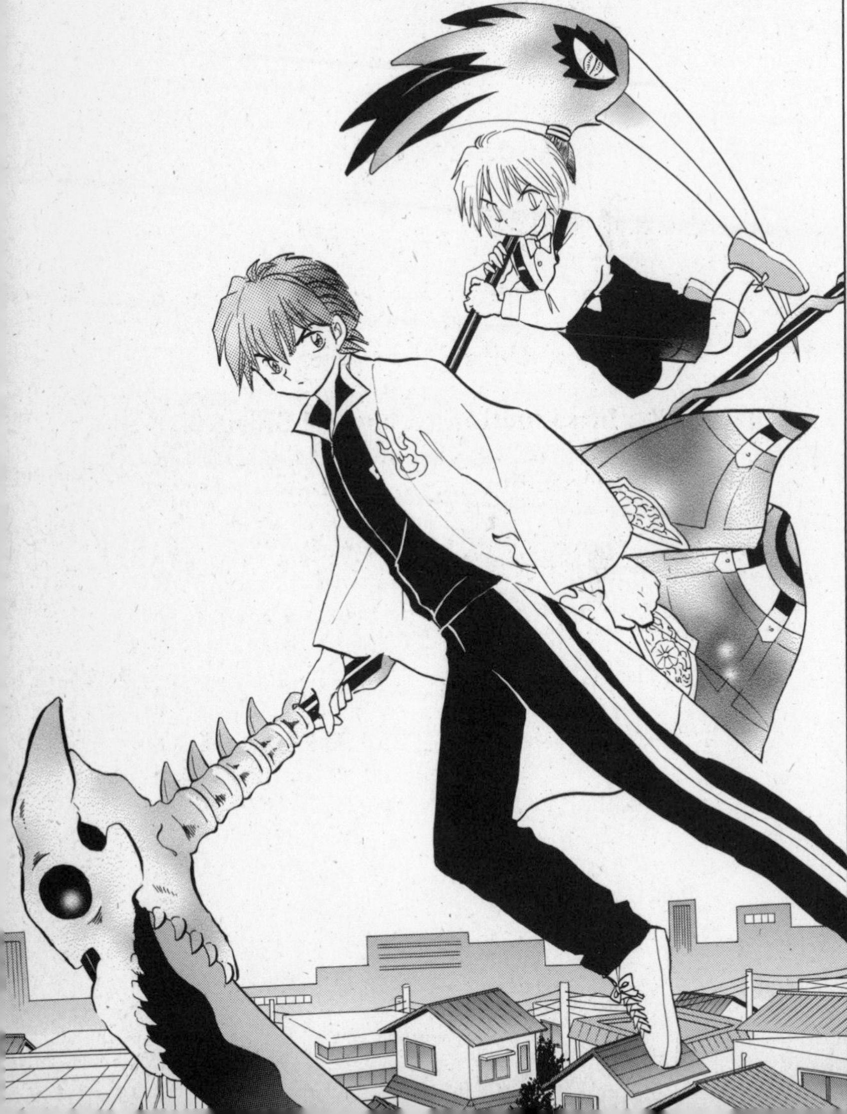

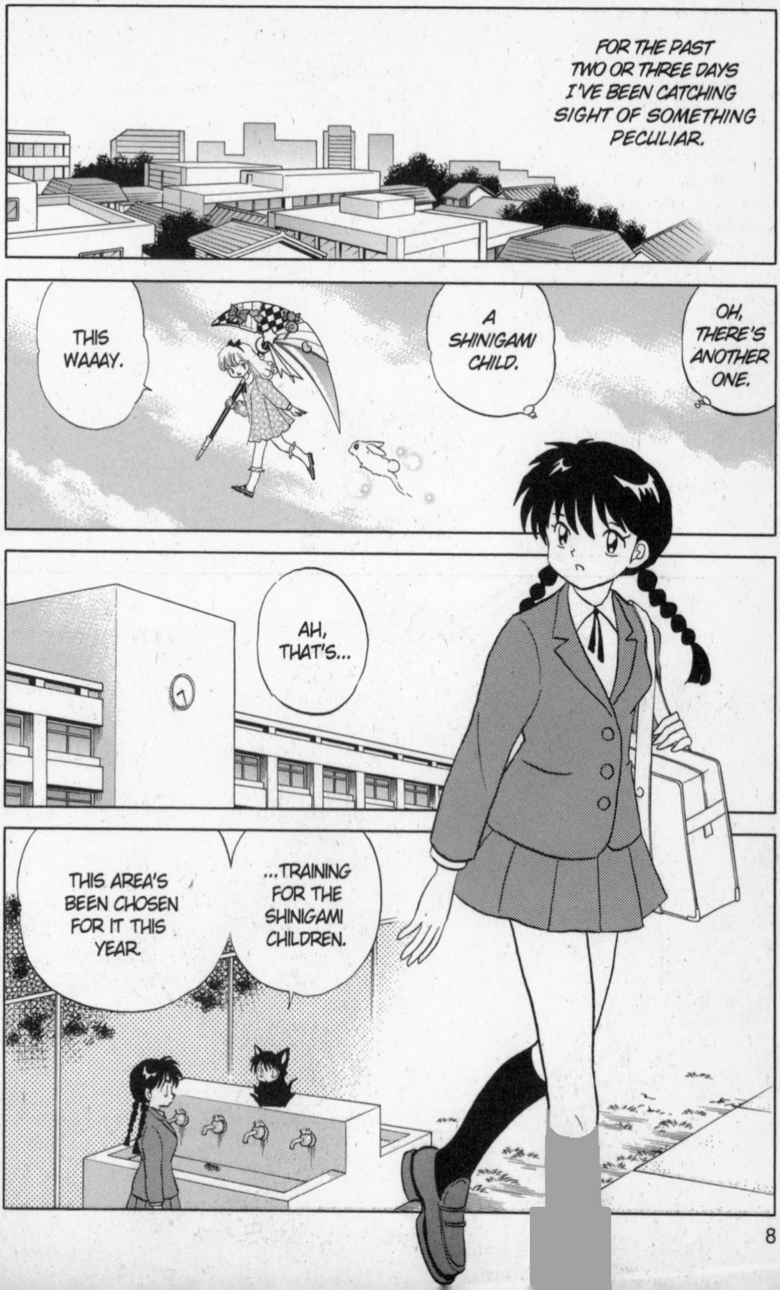
FOR THE PAST TWO OR THREE DAYS I'VE BEEN CATCHING SIGHT OF SOMETHING PECULIAR.
OH, THERE'S ANOTHER ONE.
A SHINIGAMI CHILD.
THIS WAAAY.
AH, THAT'S...
...TRAINING FOR THE SHINIGAMI CHILDREN.
THIS AREA'S BEEN CHOSEN FOR IT THIS YEAR.

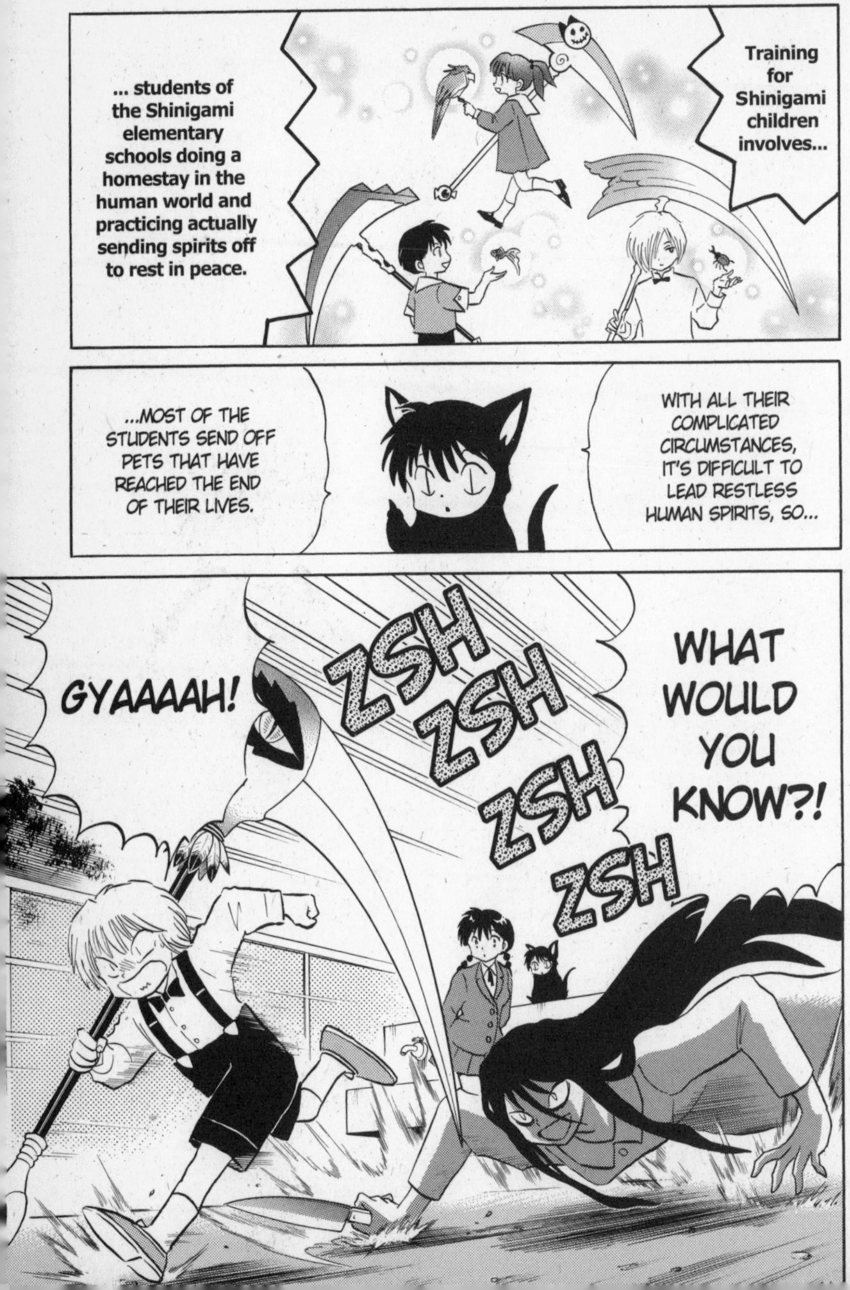
Training for Shinigami children involves...
... students of the Shinigami elementary schools doing a homestay in the human world and practicing actually sending spirits off to rest in peace.
WITH ALL THEIR COMPLICATED CIRCUMSTANCES, IT'S DIFFICULT TO LEAD RESTLESS HUMAN SPIRITS, SO...
...MOST OF THE STUDENTS SEND OFF PETS THAT HAVE REACHED THE END OF THEIR LIVES.
WHAT WOULD YOU KNOW?!
ZSH
ZSH
ZSH
ZSH
GYAAAAH!

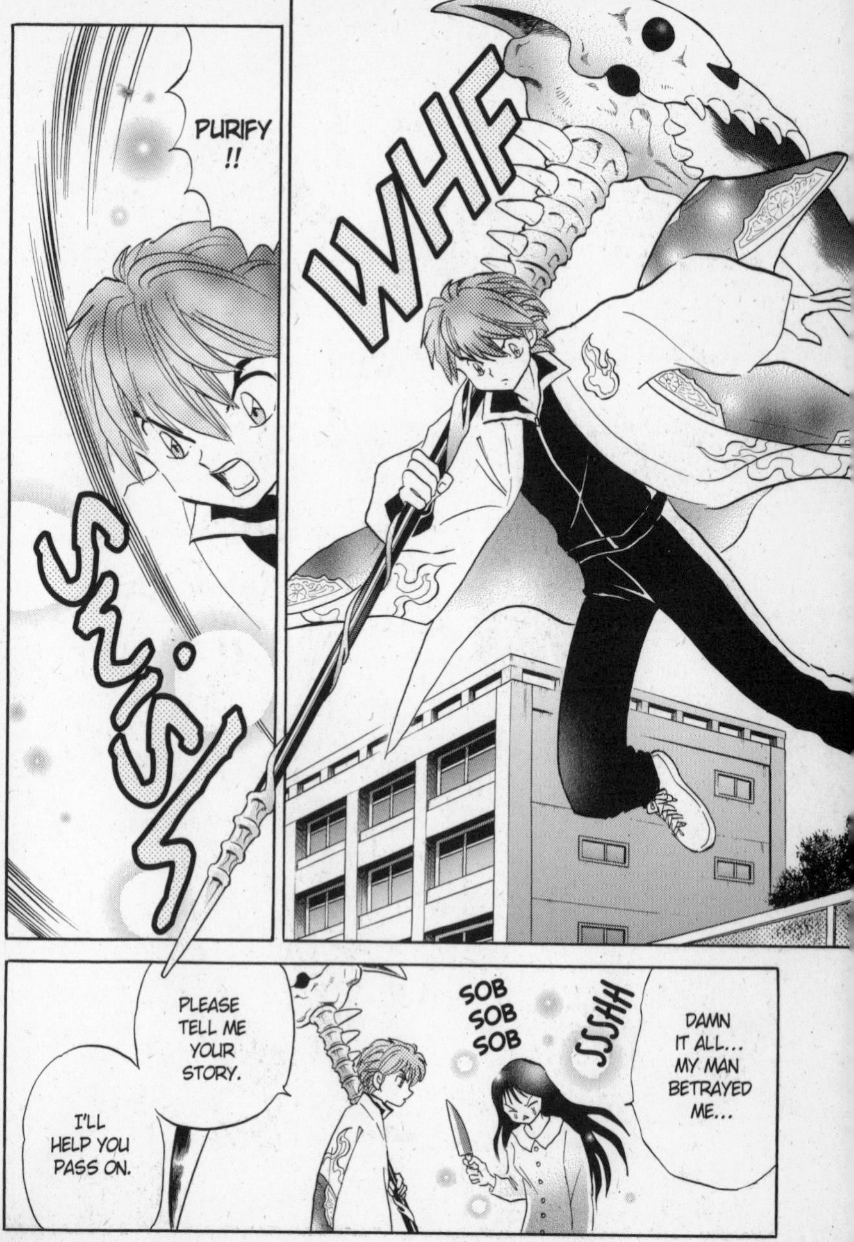
WHF
PURIFY !!
SWISH
DAMN IT ALL... MY MAN BETRAYED ME...
SSSHH
SOB SOB SOB
PLEASE TELL ME YOUR STORY.
I'LL HELP YOU PASS ON.

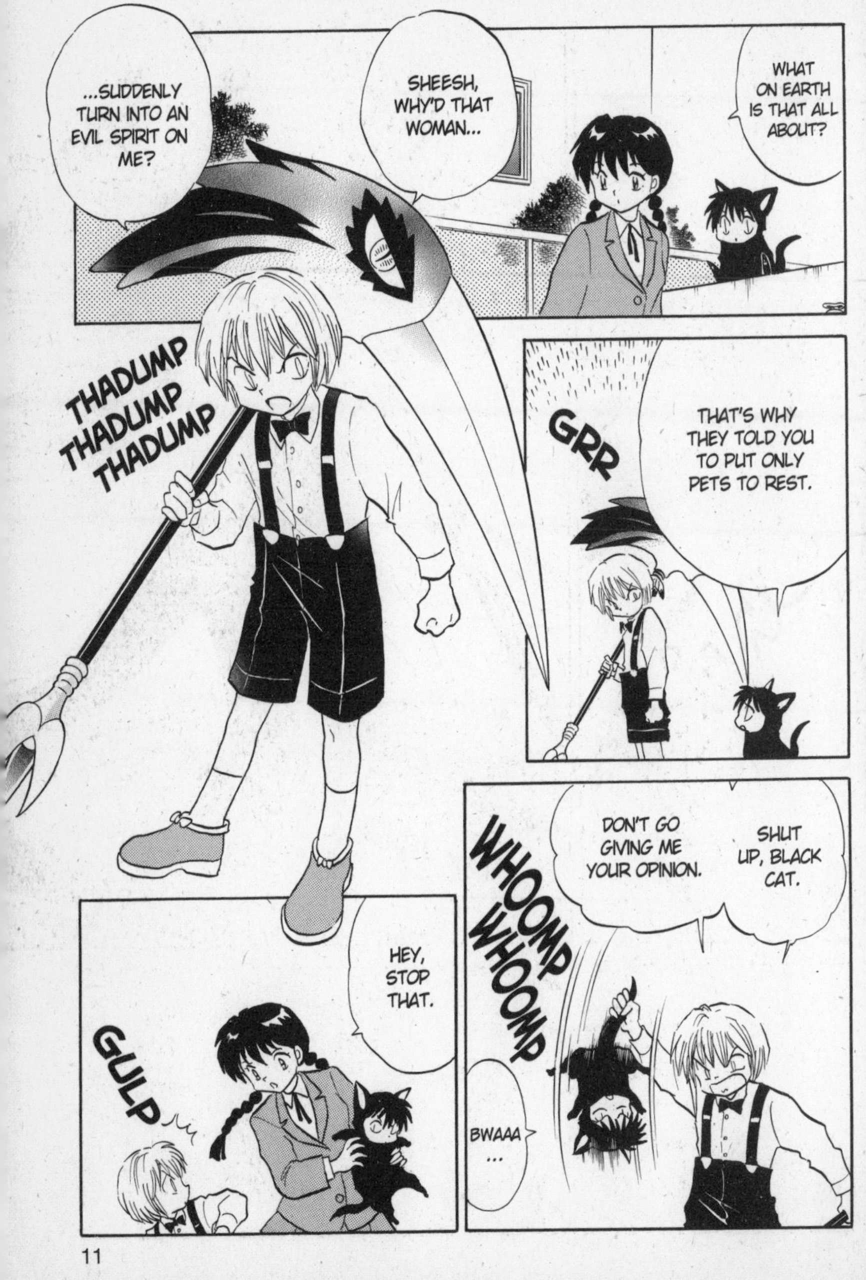
WHAT ON EARTH IS THAT ALL ABOUT?
SHEESH, WHY'D THAT WOMAN...
...SUDDENLY TURN INTO AN EVIL SPIRIT ON ME?
GRR
THAT'S WHY THEY TOLD YOU TO PUT ONLY PETS TO REST.
THADUMP THADUMP THADUMP
SHUT UP, BLACK CAT.
DON'T GO GIVING ME YOUR OPINION.
WHOOMP WHOOMP
BWAAA ...
HEY, STOP THAT.
GULP

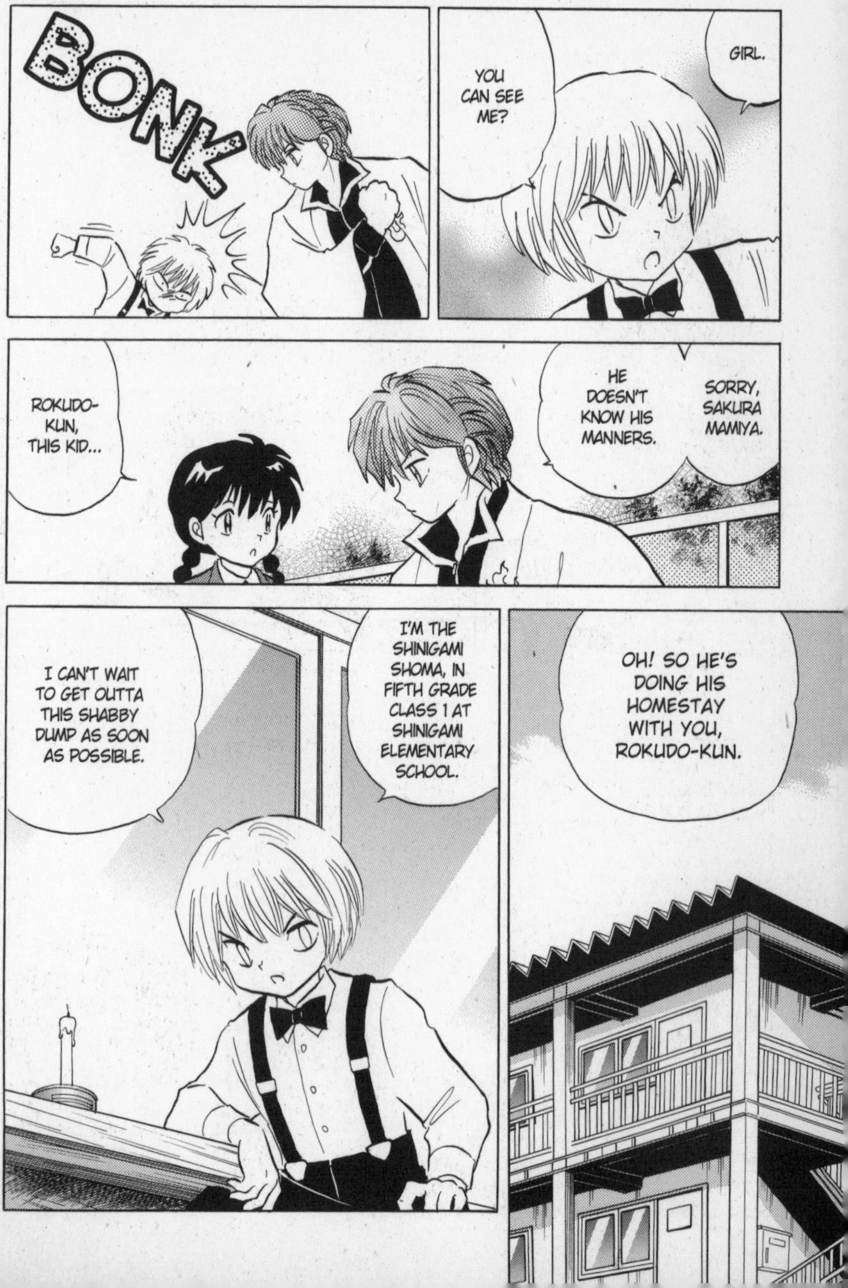
GIRL.
YOU CAN SEE ME?
BONK
SORRY, SAKURA MAMIYA.
HE DOESN'T KNOW HIS MANNERS.
ROKUDO-KUN, THIS KID...
OH! SO HE'S DOING HIS HOMESTAY WITH YOU, ROKUDO-KUN.
I'M THE SHINIGAMI SHOMA, IN FIFTH GRADE CLASS 1 AT SHINIGAMI ELEMENTARY SCHOOL.
I CAN'T WAIT TO GET OUTTA THIS SHABBY DUMP AS SOON AS POSSIBLE.

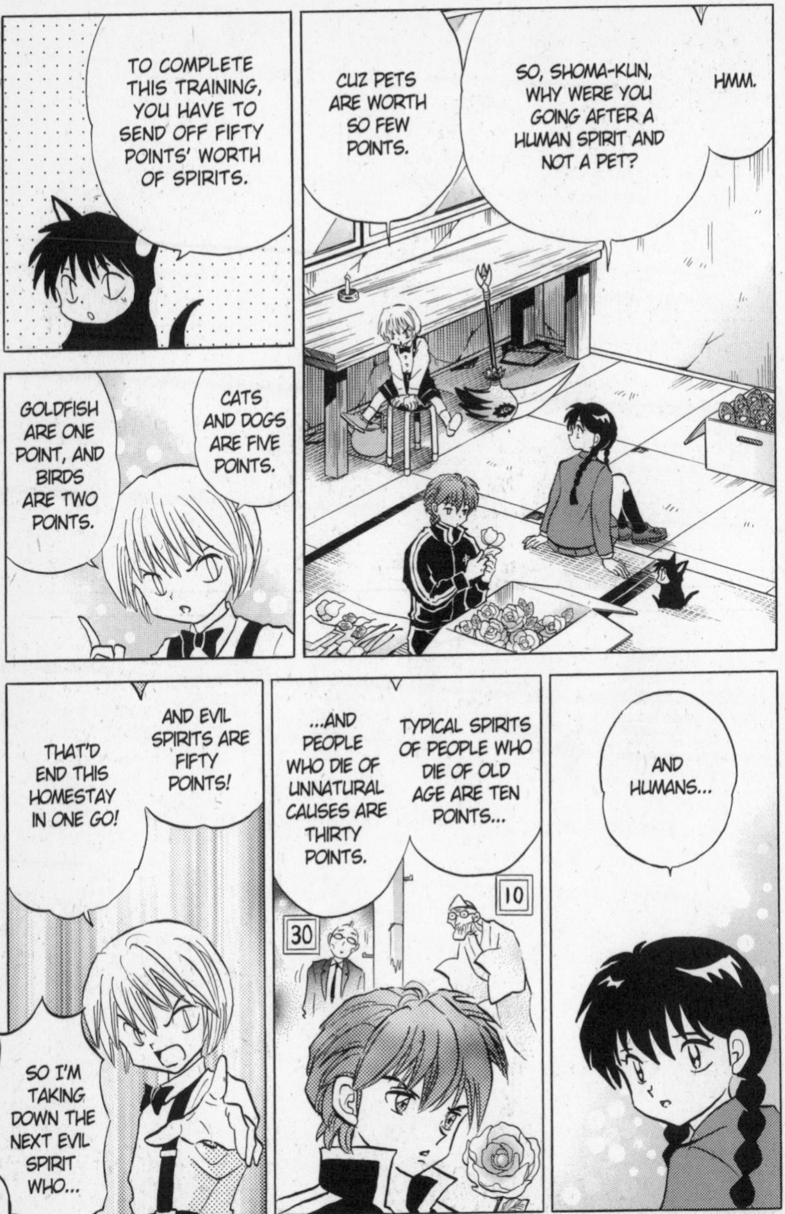
HMM.
SO, SHOMA-KUN, WHY WERE YOU GOING AFTER A HUMAN SPIRIT AND NOT A PET?
CUZ PETS ARE WORTH SO FEW POINTS.
TO COMPLETE THIS TRAINING, YOU HAVE TO SEND OFF FIFTY POINTS' WORTH OF SPIRITS.
CATS AND DOGS ARE FIVE POINTS.
GOLDFISH ARE ONE POINT, AND BIRDS ARE TWO POINTS.
AND HUMANS...
TYPICAL SPIRITS OF PEOPLE WHO DIE OF OLD AGE ARE TEN POINTS...
...AND PEOPLE WHO DIE OF UNNATURAL CAUSES ARE THIRTY POINTS.
10
30
AND EVIL SPIRITS ARE FIFTY POINTS!
THAT'D END THIS HOMESTAY IN ONE GO!
SO I'M TAKING DOWN THE NEXT EVIL SPIRIT WHO...

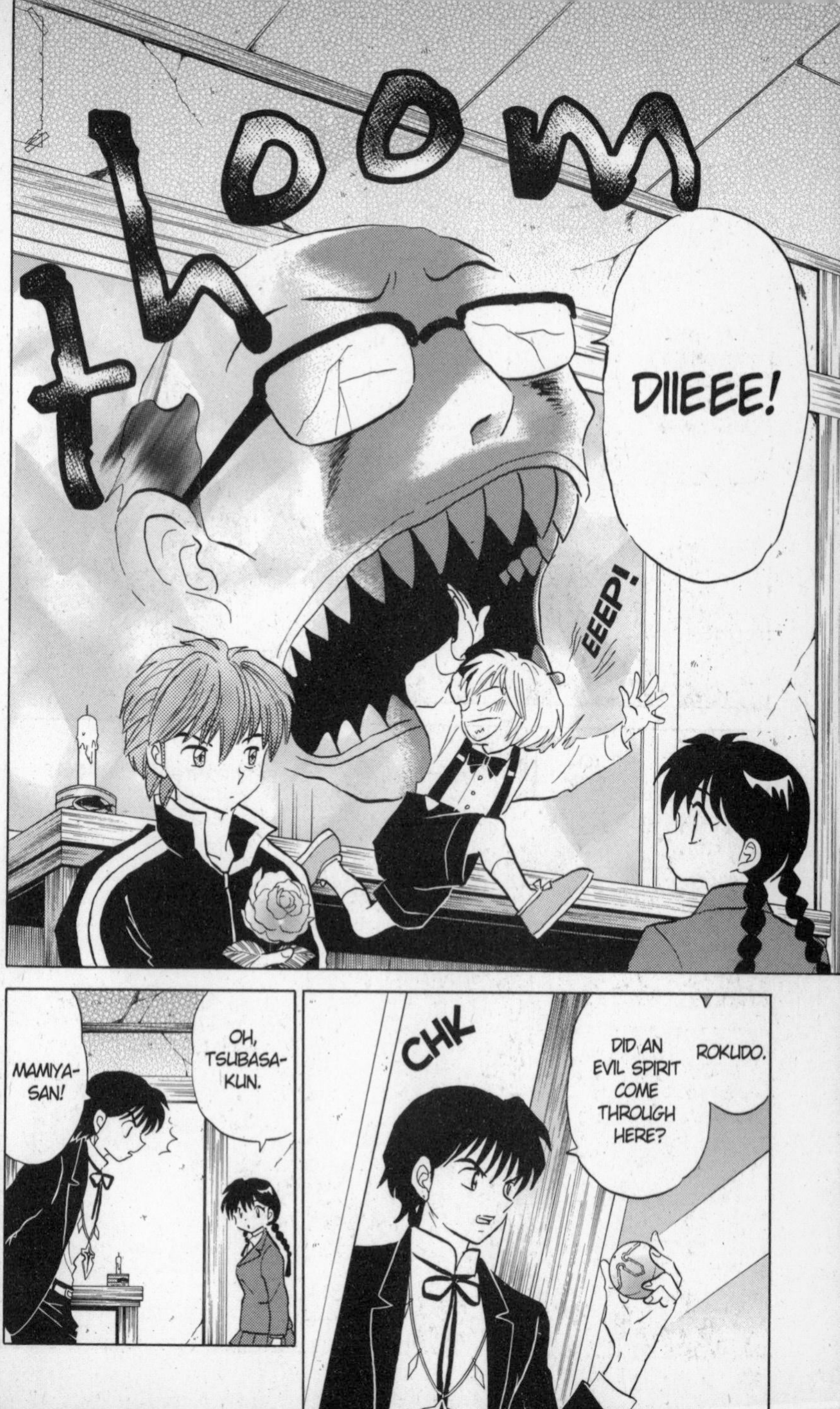
thoom
DIIEEE!
EEEP!
ROKUDO.
DID AN EVIL SPIRIT COME THROUGH HERE?
CHK
OH, TSUBASA-KUN.
MAMIYA-SAN!

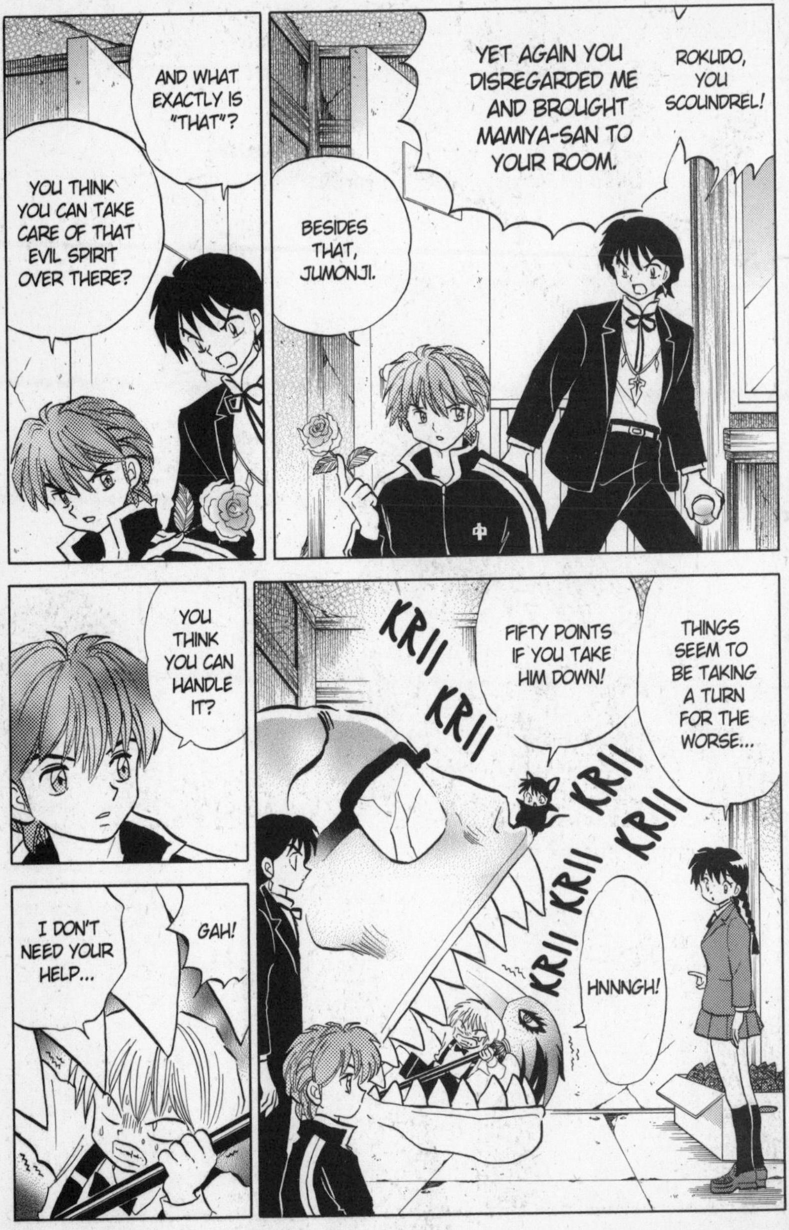
ROKUDO, YOU SCOUNDREL!
YET AGAIN YOU DISREGARDED ME AND BROUGHT MAMIYA-SAN TO YOUR ROOM.
BESIDES THAT, JUMONJI.
AND WHAT EXACTLY IS "THAT"?
YOU THINK YOU CAN TAKE CARE OF THAT EVIL SPIRIT OVER THERE?
THINGS SEEM TO BE TAKING A TURN FOR THE WORSE...
FIFTY POINTS IF YOU TAKE HIM DOWN!
KRII KRII
KRII KRII
KRII KRII KRII
HNNNGH!
YOU THINK YOU CAN HANDLE IT?
GAH!
I DON'T NEED YOUR HELP...

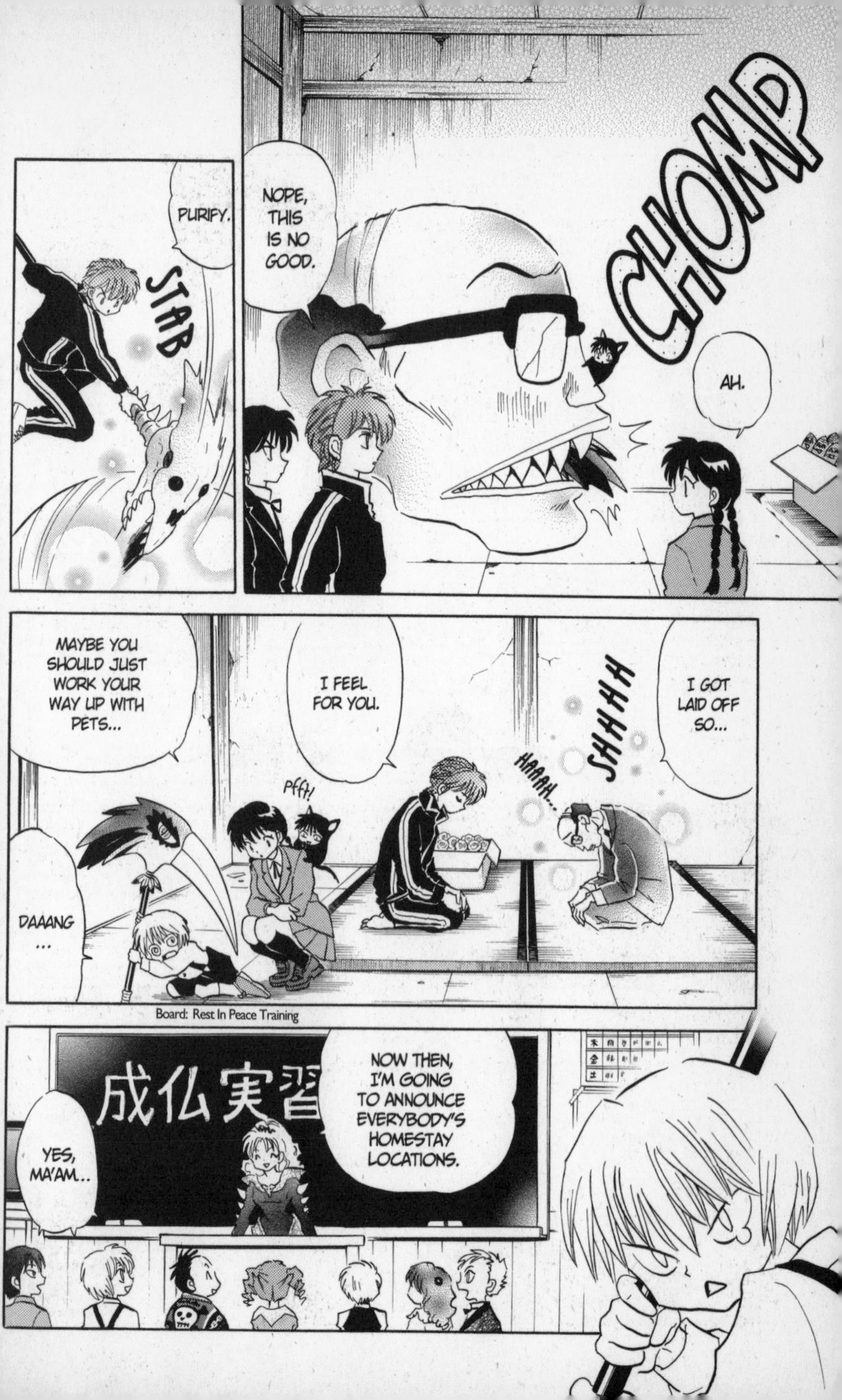
CHOMP
AH.
NOPE, THIS IS NO GOOD.
PURIFY.
STAB
I GOT LAID OFF SO...
SHHHHH
HAAAH...
I FEEL FOR YOU.
MAYBE YOU SHOULD JUST WORK YOUR WAY UP WITH PETS...
Pfft!
DAAANG ...
Board: Rest In Peace Training
成仏実習
NOW THEN, I'M GOING TO ANNOUNCE EVERYBODY'S HOMESTAY LOCATIONS.
YES, MA'AM...

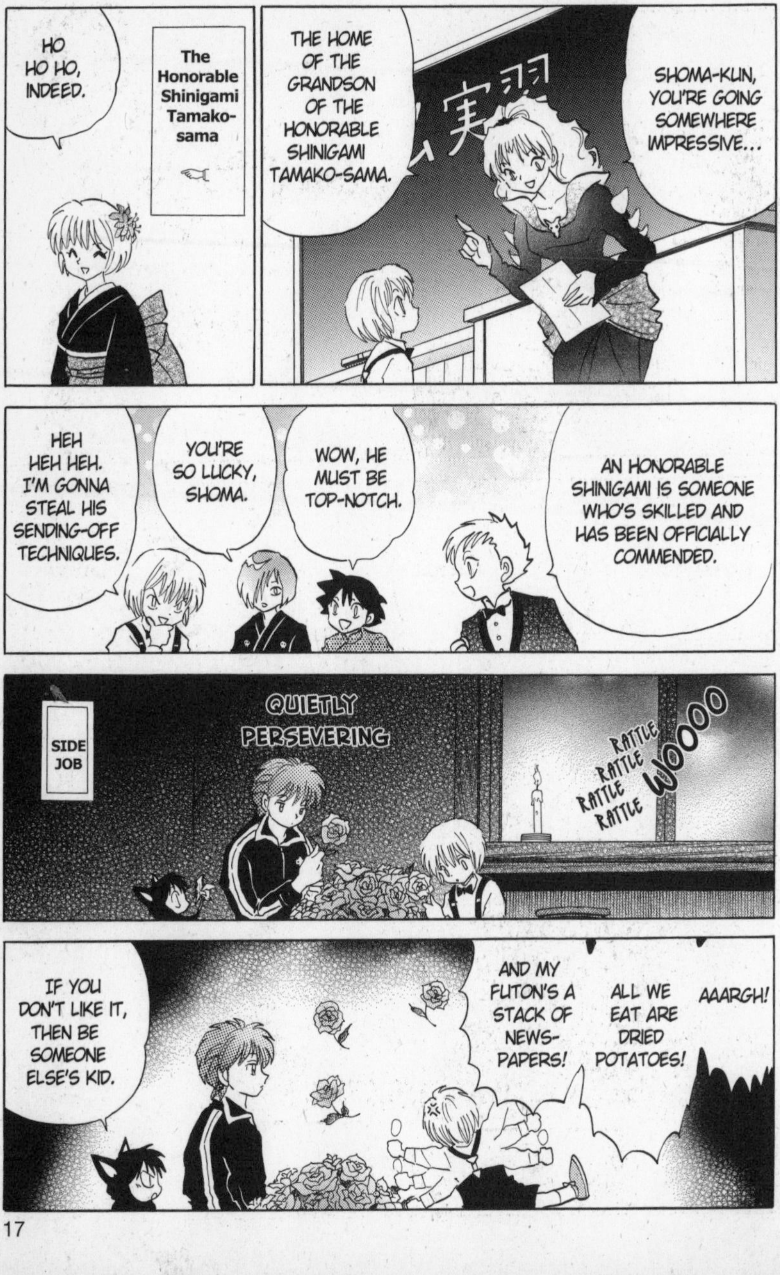
SHOMA-KUN, YOU'RE GOING SOMEWHERE IMPRESSIVE...
THE HOME OF THE GRANDSON OF THE HONORABLE SHINIGAMI TAMAKO-SAMA.
The Honorable Shinigami Tamako-sama
HO HO HO, INDEED.
AN HONORABLE SHINIGAMI IS SOMEONE WHO'S SKILLED AND HAS BEEN OFFICIALLY COMMENDED.
WOW, HE MUST BE TOP-NOTCH.
YOU'RE SO LUCKY, SHOMA.
HEH HEH HEH. I'M GONNA STEAL HIS SENDING-OFF TECHNIQUES.
WOOOO
RATTLE RATTLE RATTLE RATTLE
QUIETLY PERSEVERING
SIDE JOB
AAARGH!
ALL WE EAT ARE DRIED POTATOES!
AND MY FUTON'S A STACK OF NEWS-PAPERS!
IF YOU DON'T LIKE IT, THEN BE SOMEONE ELSE'S KID.

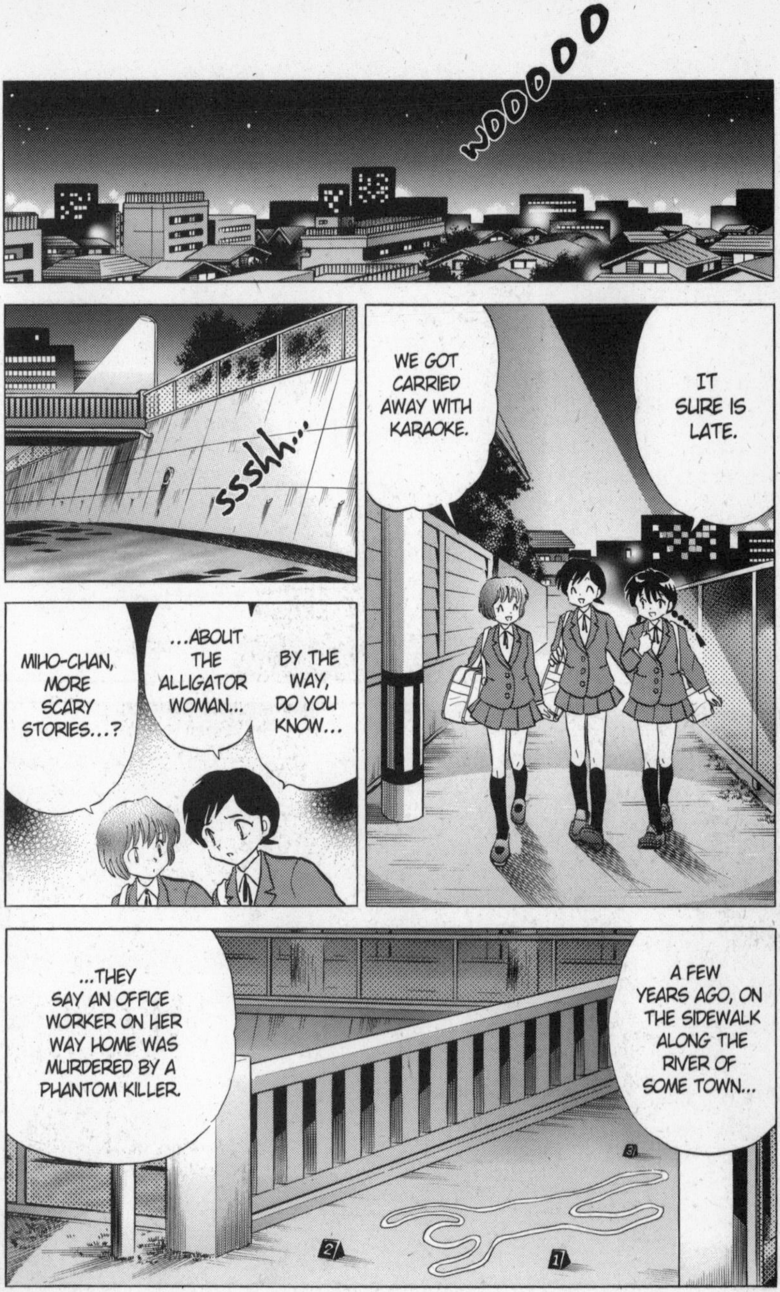
WDDDDD
IT SURE IS LATE.
WE GOT CARRIED AWAY WITH KARAOKE.
ssshh...
BY THE WAY, DO YOU KNOW...
...ABOUT THE ALLIGATOR WOMAN...
MIHO-CHAN, MORE SCARY STORIES...?
A FEW YEARS AGO, ON THE SIDEWALK ALONG THE RIVER OF SOME TOWN...
...THEY SAY AN OFFICE WORKER ON HER WAY HOME WAS MURDERED BY A PHANTOM KILLER.

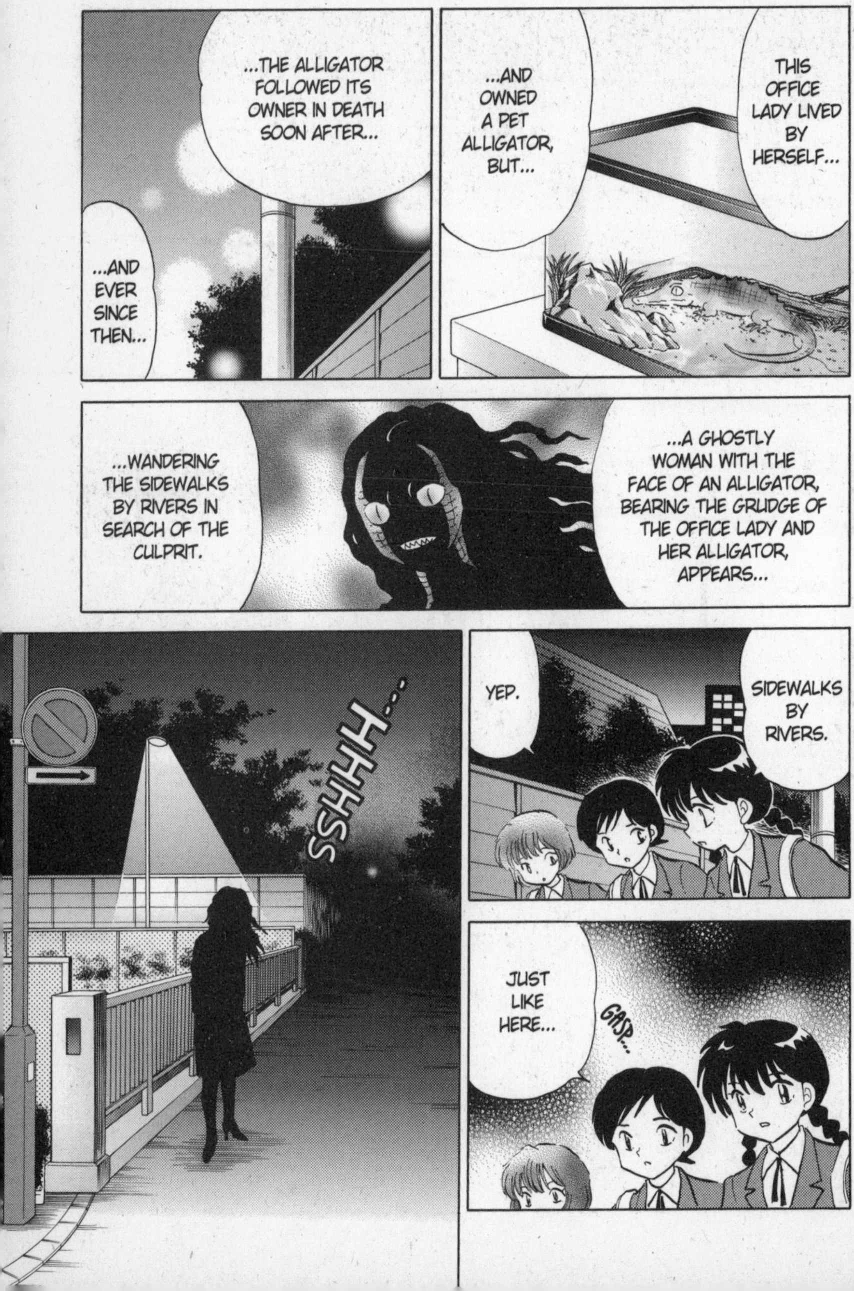
THIS OFFICE LADY LIVED BY HERSELF...
...AND OWNED A PET ALLIGATOR, BUT...
...THE ALLIGATOR FOLLOWED ITS OWNER IN DEATH SOON AFTER...
...AND EVER SINCE THEN...
...A GHOSTLY WOMAN WITH THE FACE OF AN ALLIGATOR, BEARING THE GRUDGE OF THE OFFICE LADY AND HER ALLIGATOR, APPEARS...
...WANDERING THE SIDEWALKS BY RIVERS IN SEARCH OF THE CULPRIT.
SIDEWALKS BY RIVERS.
YEP.
JUST LIKE HERE...
GASP...
SSHHH...

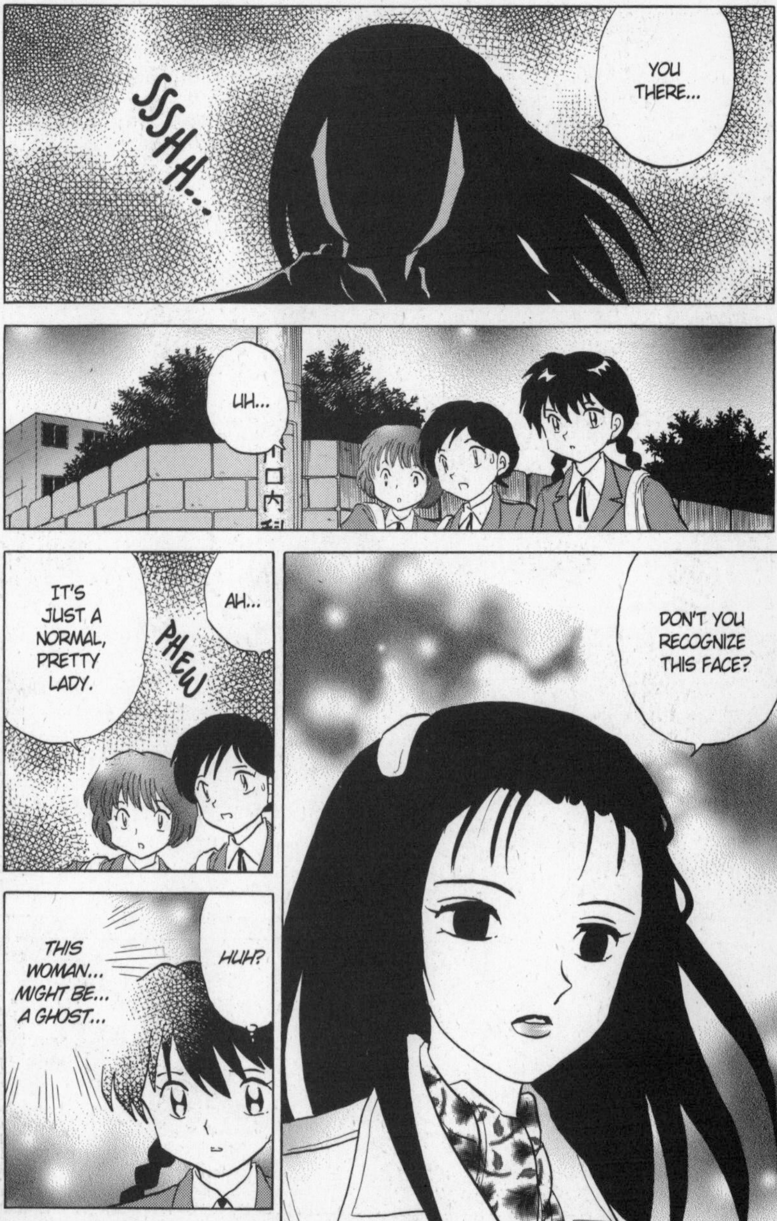
YOU THERE...
SSSHH...
UH...
DON'T YOU RECOGNIZE THIS FACE?
AH...
PHEW
IT'S JUST A NORMAL, PRETTY LADY.
HUH?
THIS WOMAN... MIGHT BE... A GHOST...

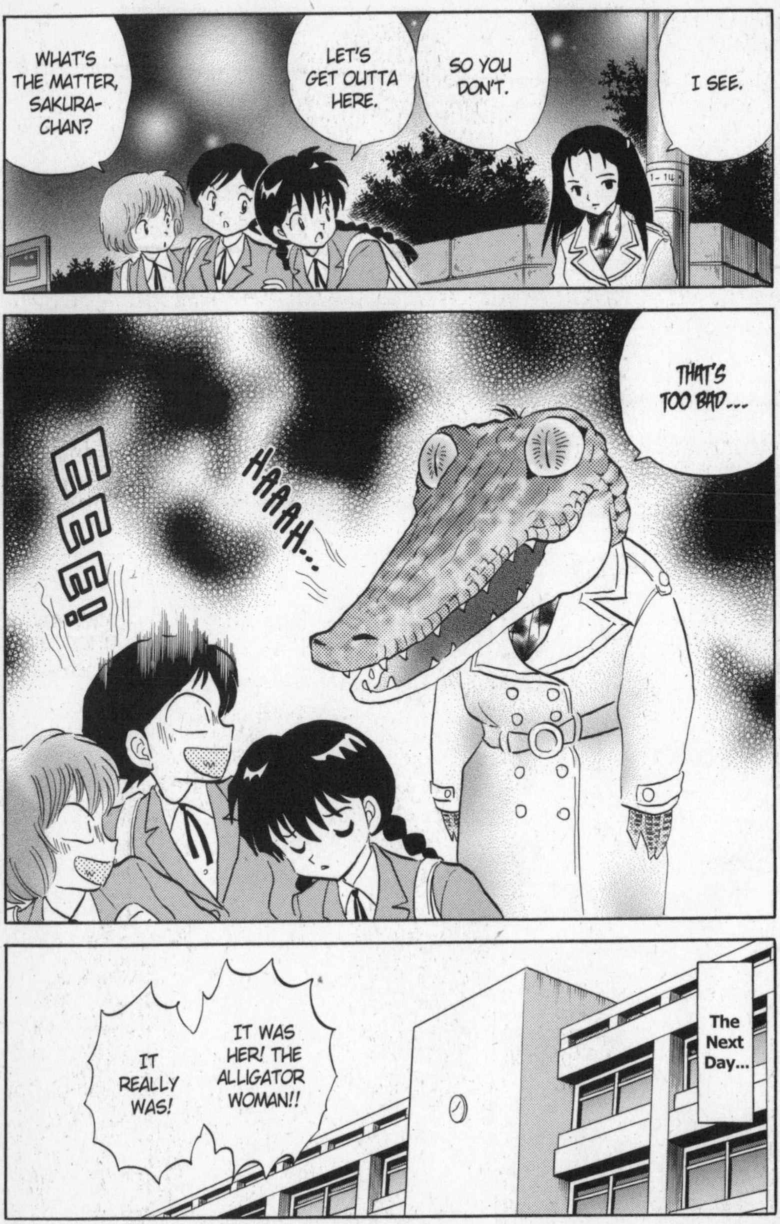
I SEE.
SO YOU DON'T.
LET'S GET OUTTA HERE.
WHAT'S THE MATTER, SAKURA-CHAN?
THAT'S TOO BAD...
HAAAAH...
EEEE!
The Next Day...
IT WAS HER! THE ALLIGATOR WOMAN!!
IT REALLY WAS!

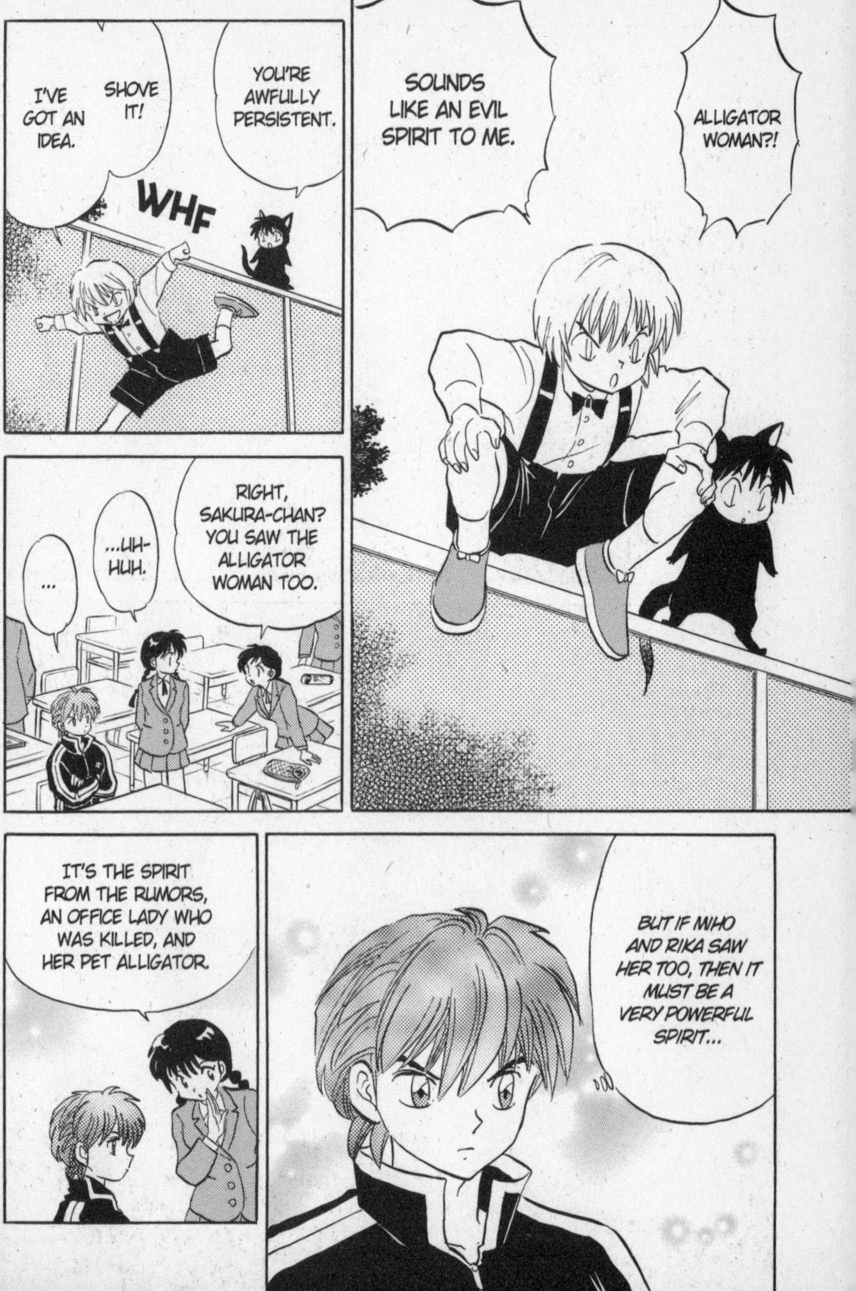
ALLIGATOR WOMAN?!
SOUNDS LIKE AN EVIL SPIRIT TO ME.
YOU'RE AWFULLY PERSISTENT.
SHOVE IT!
I'VE GOT AN IDEA.
WHF
RIGHT, SAKURA-CHAN? YOU SAW THE ALLIGATOR WOMAN TOO.
...UH-HUH.
...
BUT IF MIHO AND RIKA SAW HER TOO, THEN IT MUST BE A VERY POWERFUL SPIRIT...
IT'S THE SPIRIT FROM THE RUMORS, AN OFFICE LADY WHO WAS KILLED, AND HER PET ALLIGATOR.

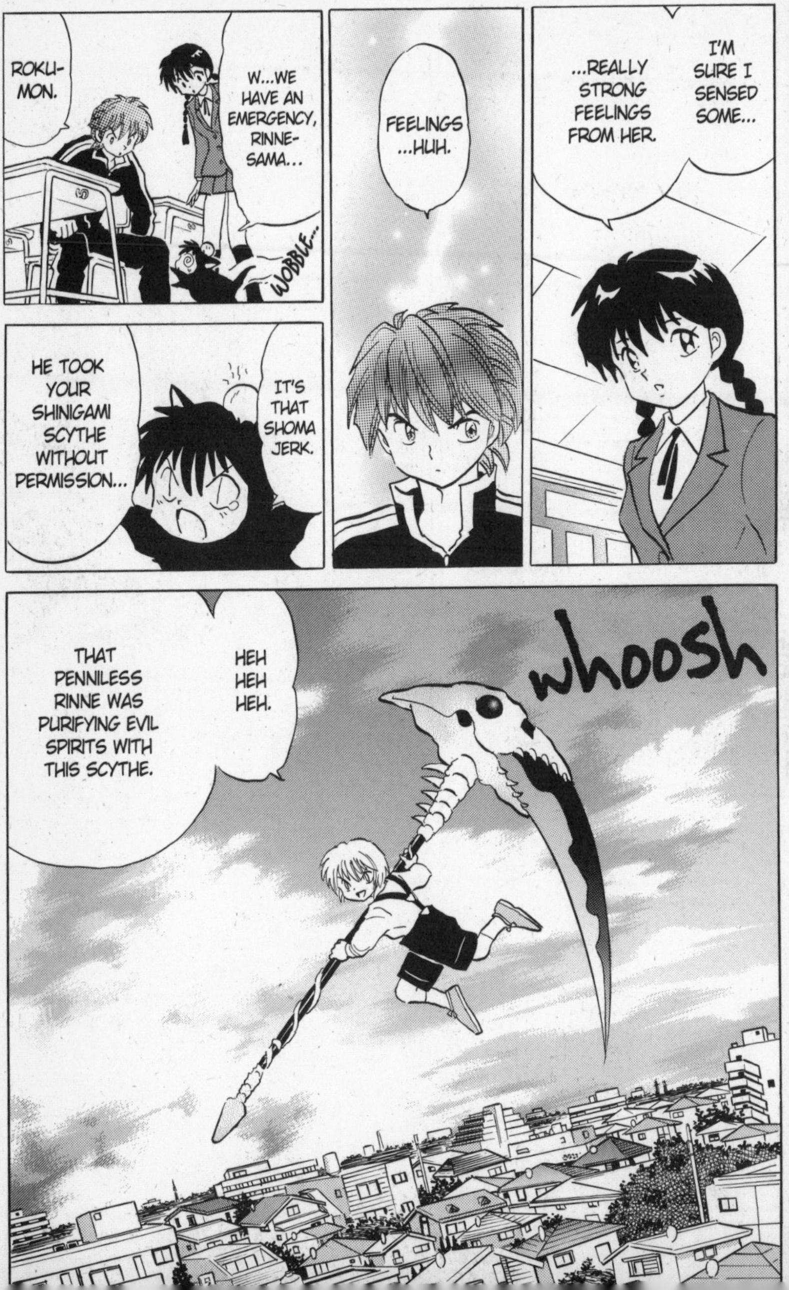
I'M SURE I SENSED SOME...
...REALLY STRONG FEELINGS FROM HER.
FEELINGS ...HUH.
W...WE HAVE AN EMERGENCY, RINNE-SAMA...
ROKU-MON.
WOBBLE...
IT'S THAT SHOMA JERK.
HE TOOK YOUR SHINIGAMI SCYTHE WITHOUT PERMISSION...
whoosh
HEH HEH HEH.
THAT PENNILESS RINNE WAS PURIFYING EVIL SPIRITS WITH THIS SCYTHE.

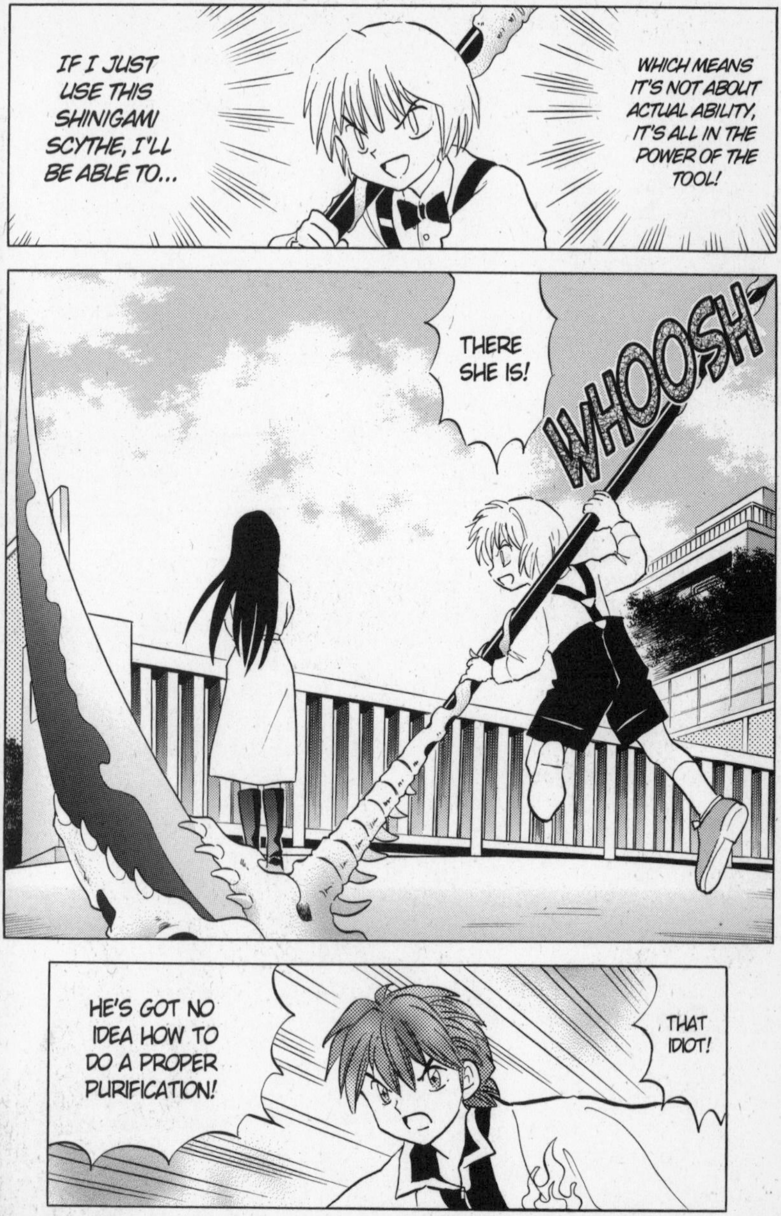
WHICH MEANS IT'S NOT ABOUT ACTUAL ABILITY, IT'S ALL IN THE POWER OF THE TOOL!
IF I JUST USE THIS SHINIGAMI SCYTHE, I'LL BE ABLE TO...
WHOOSH
THERE SHE IS!
THAT IDIOT!
HE'S GOT NO IDEA HOW TO DO A PROPER PURIFICATION!

CHAPTER 70: THE STORY BEHIND THE ALLIGATOR WOMAN

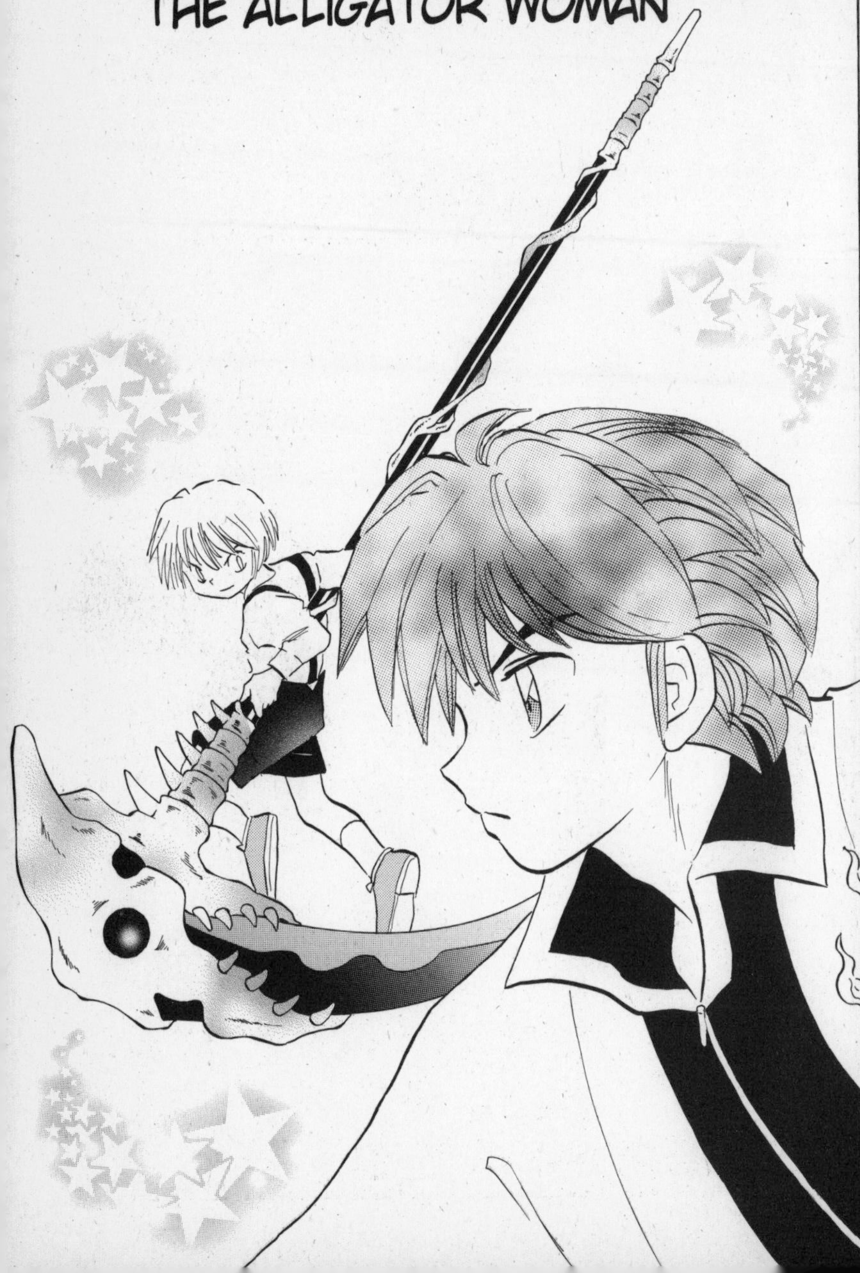

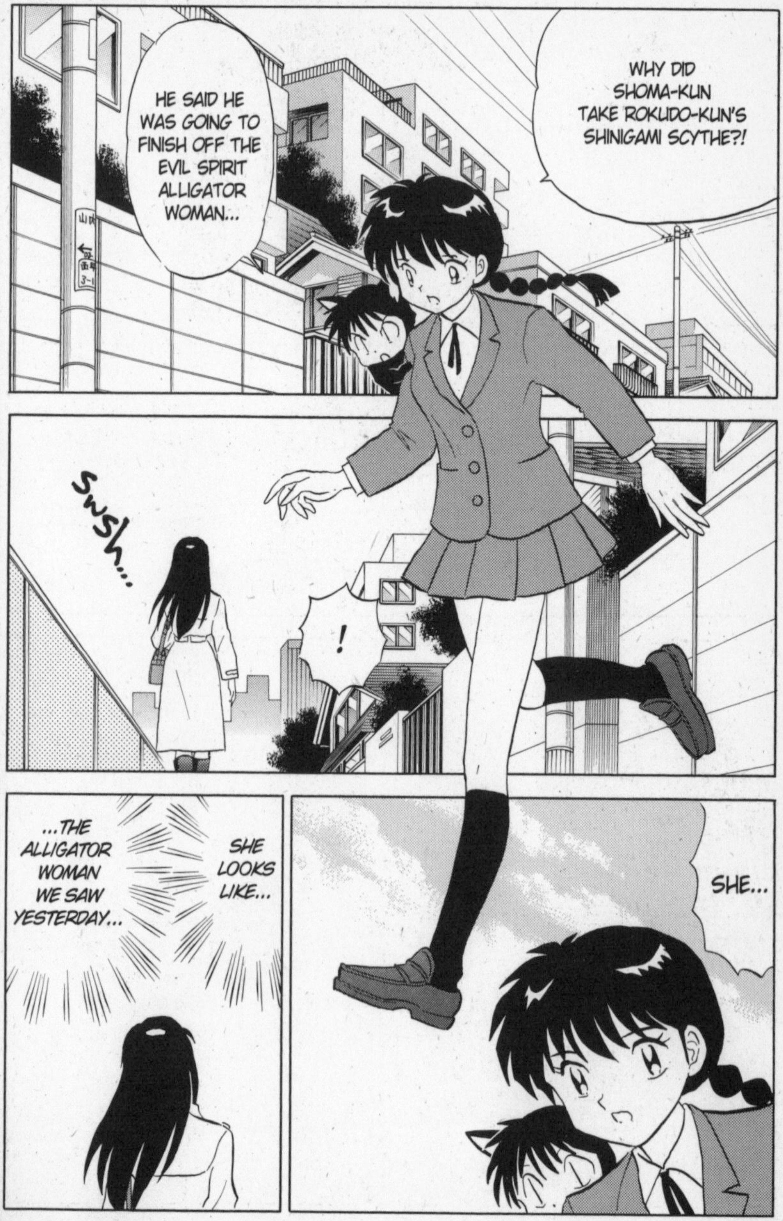
WHY DID SHOMA-KUN TAKE ROKUDO-KUN'S SHINIGAMI SCYTHE?!
HE SAID HE WAS GOING TO FINISH OFF THE EVIL SPIRIT ALLIGATOR WOMAN...
SWSH...
!
SHE...
SHE LOOKS LIKE...
...THE ALLIGATOR WOMAN WE SAW YESTERDAY...

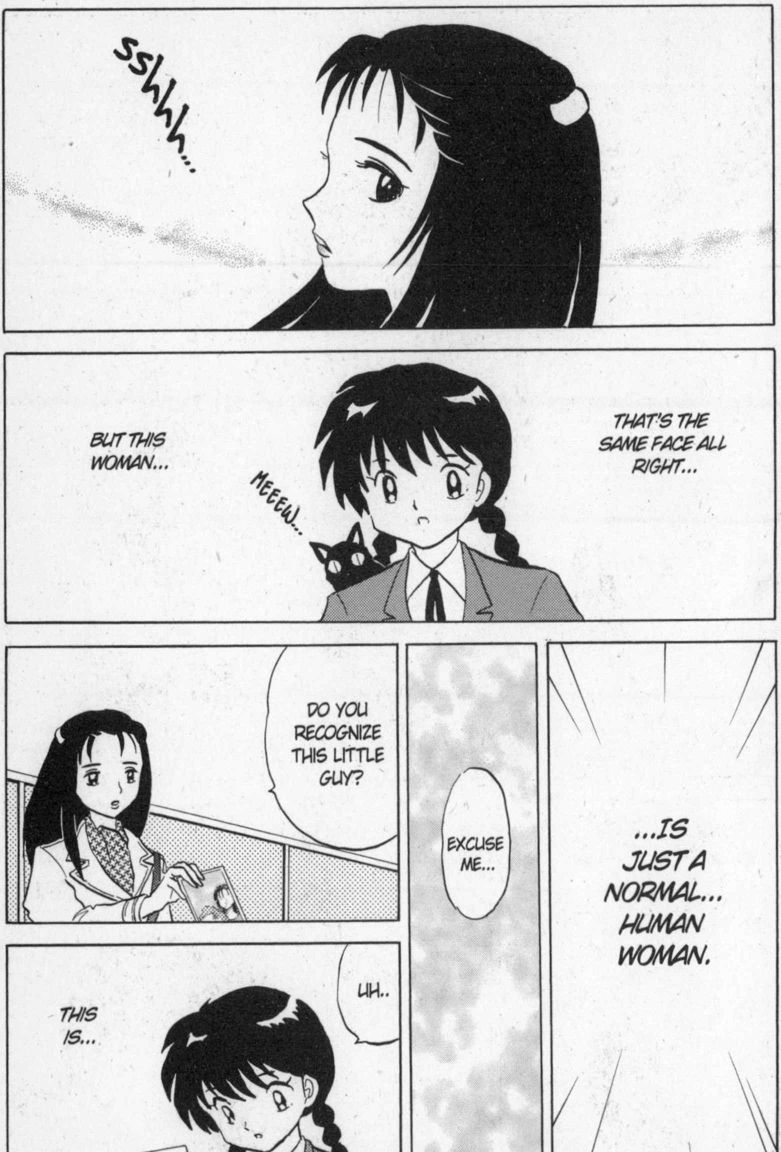
sshhh...
THAT'S THE SAME FACE ALL RIGHT...
MEEEW...
BUT THIS WOMAN...
...IS JUST A NORMAL... HUMAN WOMAN.
EXCUSE ME...
DO YOU RECOGNIZE THIS LITTLE GUY?
UH..
THIS IS...

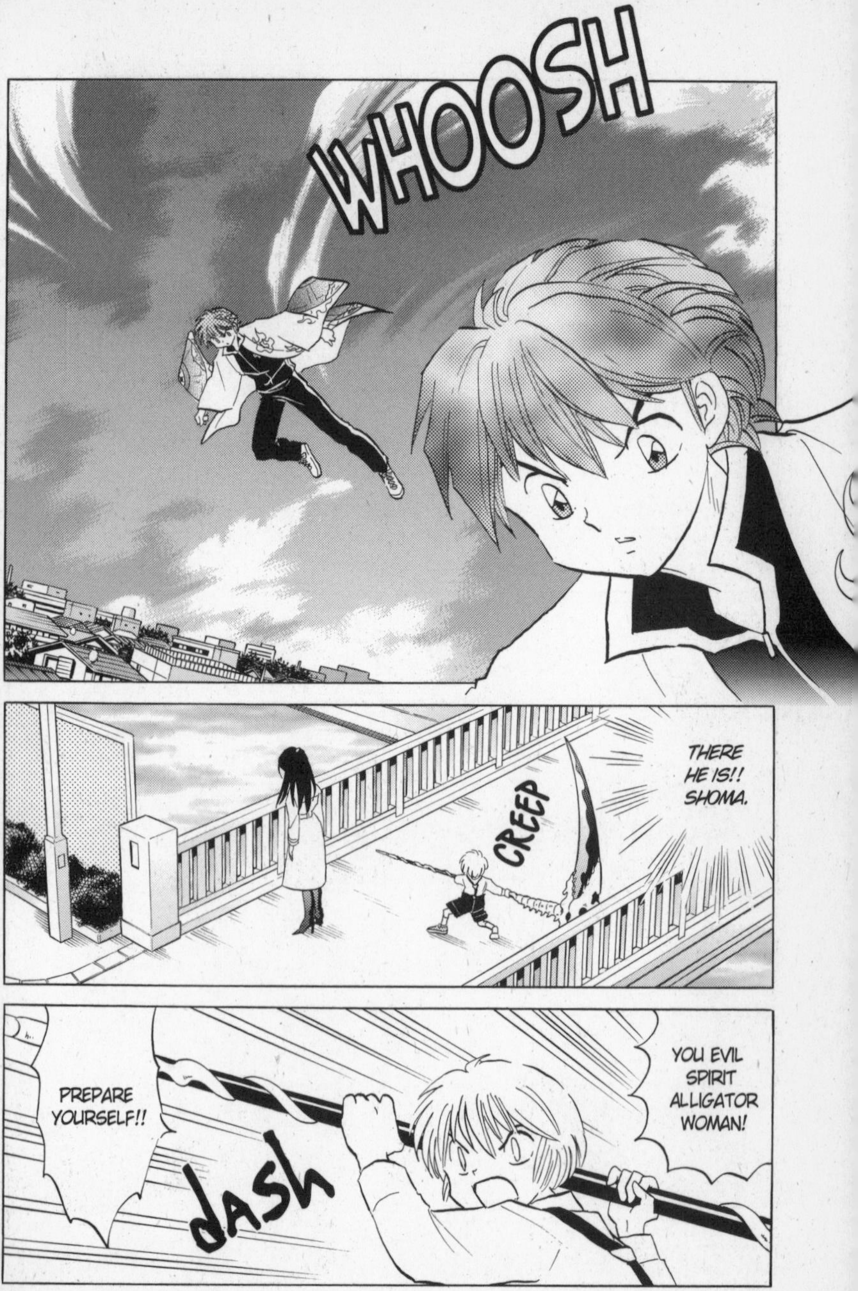
WHOOSH
THERE HE IS!! SHOMA.
CREEP
YOU EVIL SPIRIT ALLIGATOR WOMAN!
PREPARE YOURSELF!!
dash

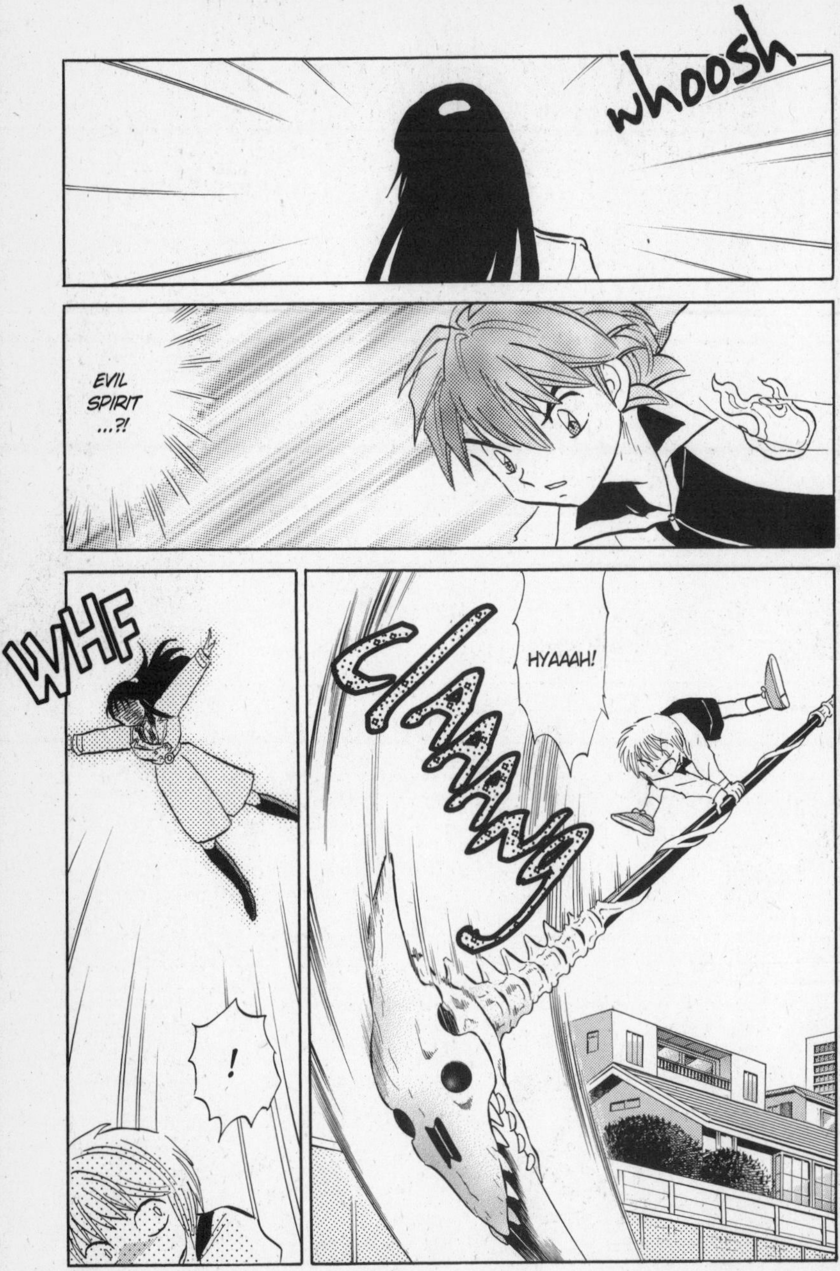
whoosh
EVIL SPIRIT ...?!
HYAAAH!
WHF
!

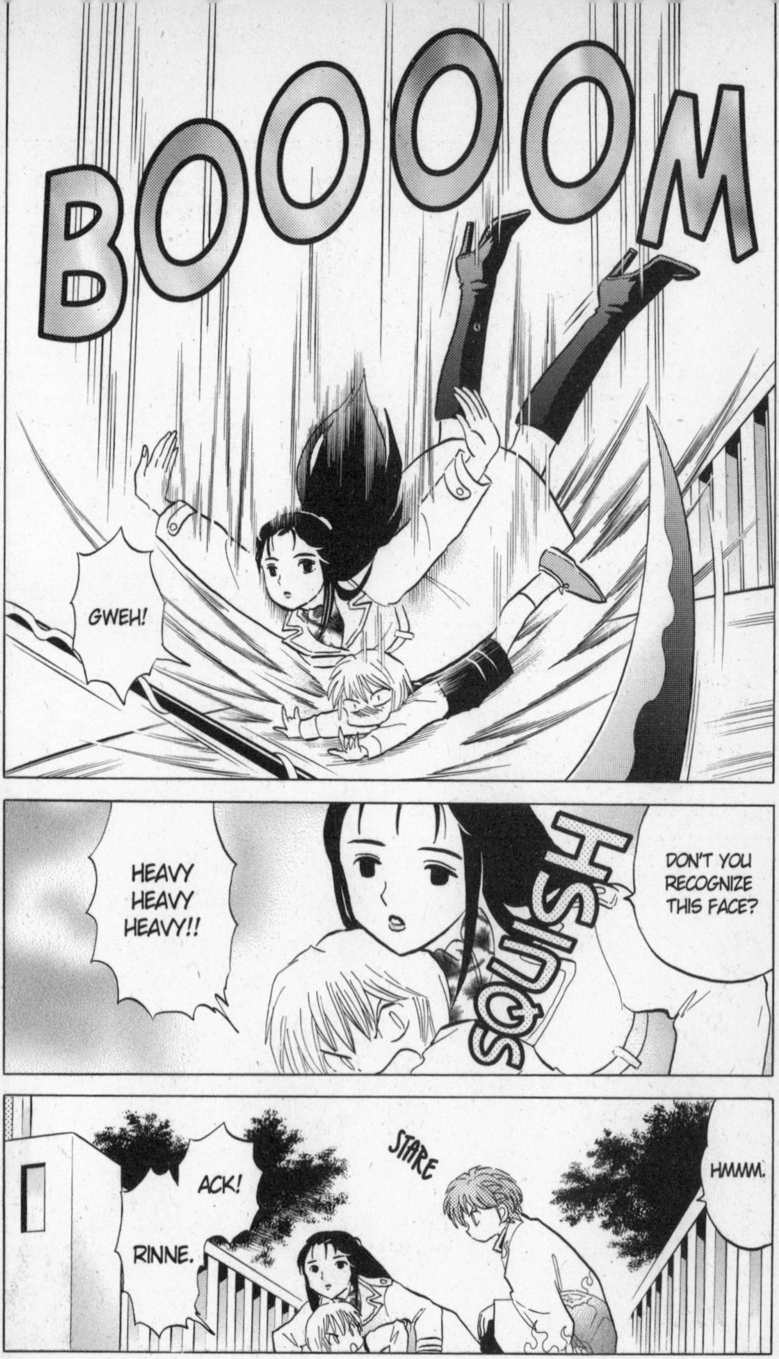
BOOOOM
GWEH!
DON'T YOU RECOGNIZE THIS FACE?
SQUISH
HEAVY HEAVY HEAVY!!
HMMM.
STARE
ACK!
RINNE.

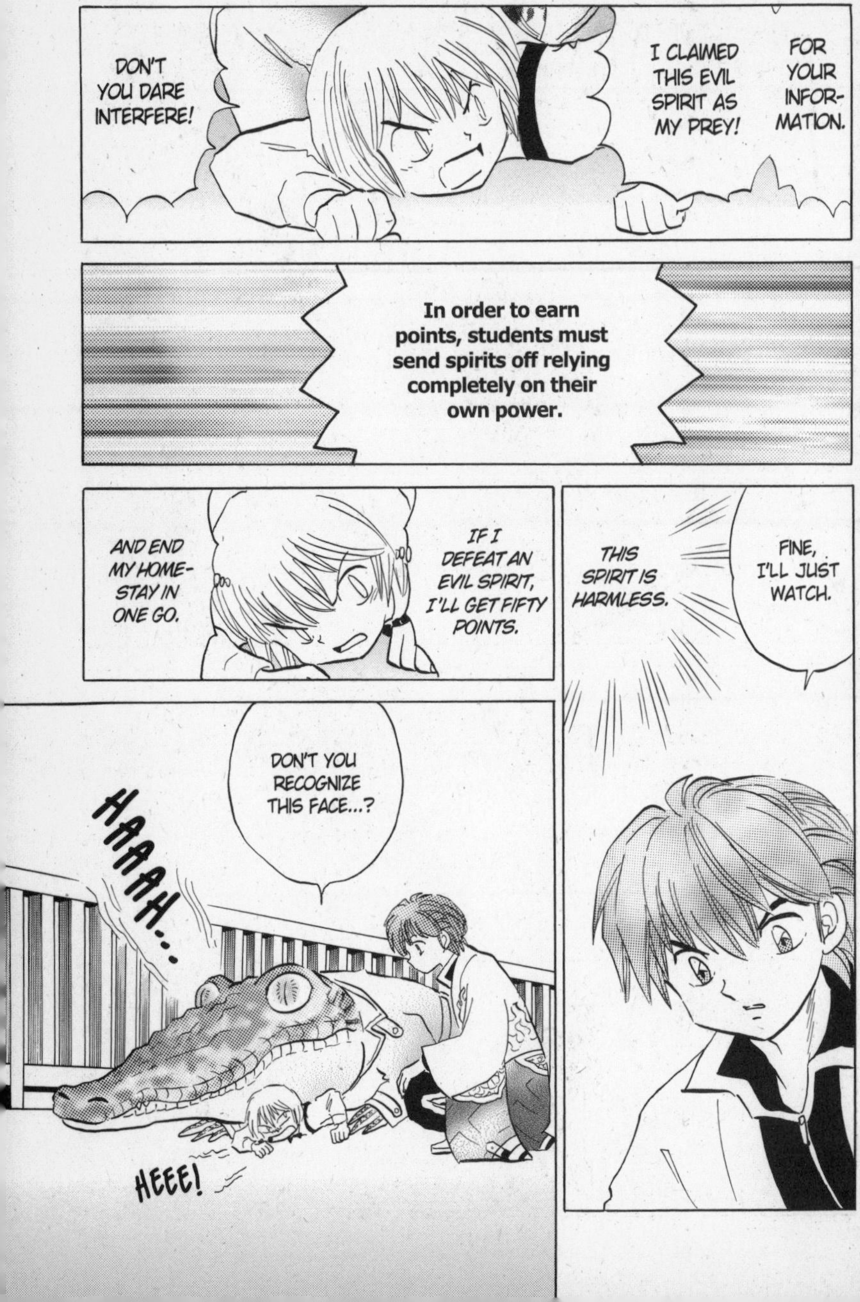
FOR YOUR INFOR-MATION.
I CLAIMED THIS EVIL SPIRIT AS MY PREY!
DON'T YOU DARE INTERFERE!
In order to earn points, students must send spirits off relying completely on their own power.
FINE, I'LL JUST WATCH.
THIS SPIRIT IS HARMLESS.
IF I DEFEAT AN EVIL SPIRIT, I'LL GET FIFTY POINTS.
AND END MY HOME-STAY IN ONE GO.
DON'T YOU RECOGNIZE THIS FACE...?
HAAAAH...
HEEE!

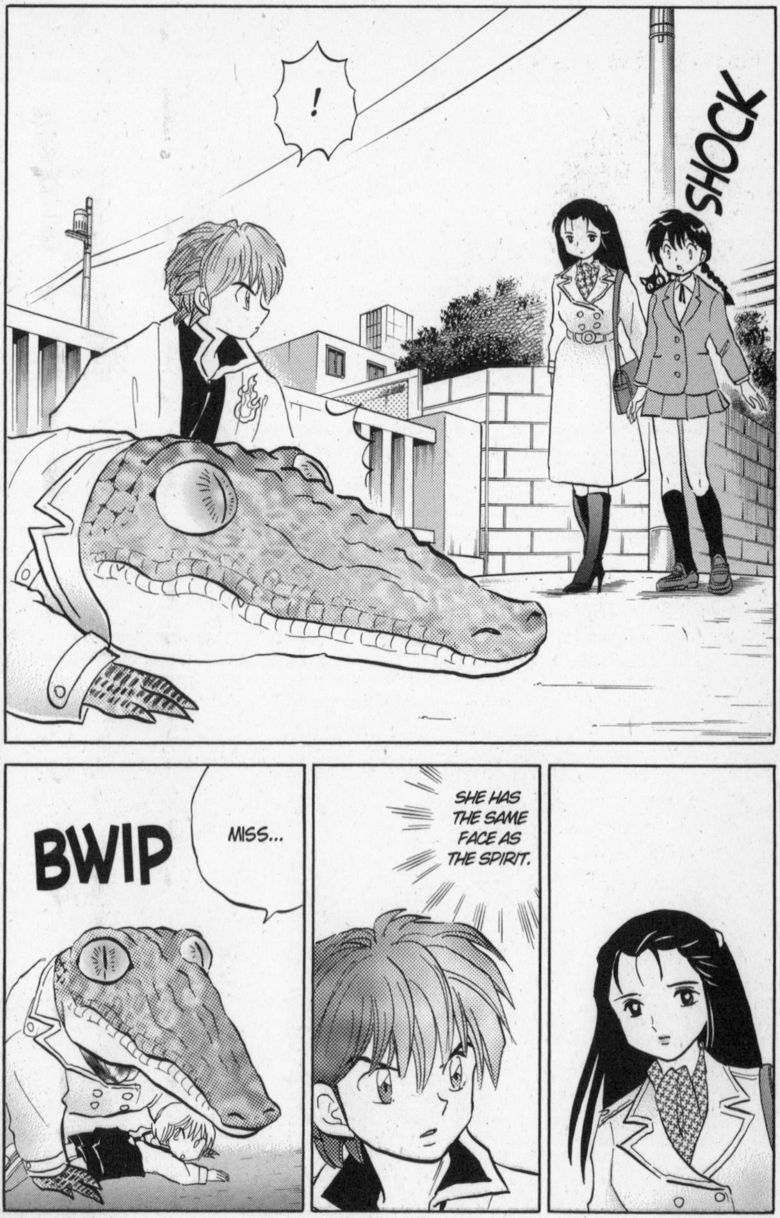

SHOCK
!
SHE HAS THE SAME FACE AS THE SPIRIT.
MISS...
BWIP

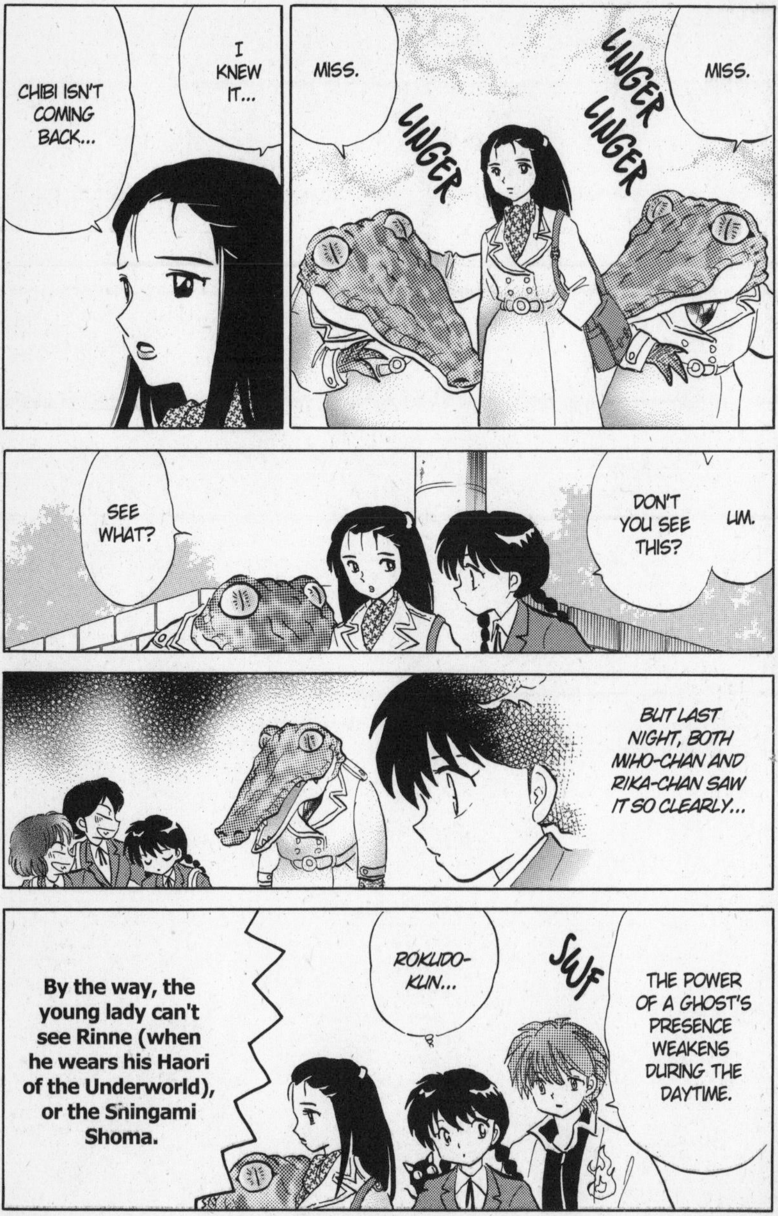
MISS.
LINGER LINGER
LINGER
MISS.
I KNEW IT...
CHIBI ISN'T COMING BACK...
UM.
DON'T YOU SEE THIS?
SEE WHAT?
BUT LAST NIGHT, BOTH MIHO-CHAN AND RIKA-CHAN SAW IT SO CLEARLY...
THE POWER OF A GHOST'S PRESENCE WEAKENS DURING THE DAYTIME.
SWF
ROKUDO-KUN...
By the way, the young lady can't see Rinne (when he wears his Haori of the Underworld), or the Shingami Shoma.

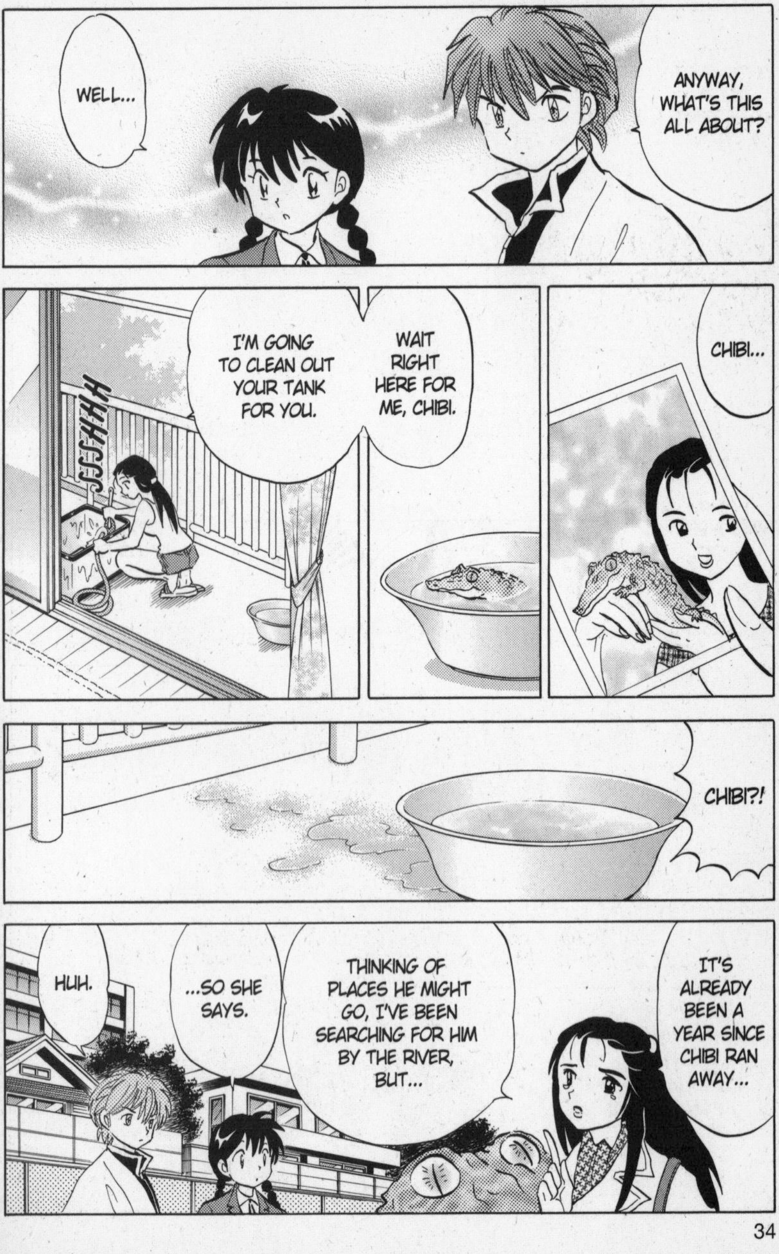
ANYWAY, WHAT'S THIS ALL ABOUT?
WELL...
CHIBI...
I'M GOING TO CLEAN OUT YOUR TANK FOR YOU. WAIT RIGHT HERE FOR ME, CHIBI.
SSSHHHH
CHIBI?!
IT'S ALREADY BEEN A YEAR SINCE CHIBI RAN AWAY...
THINKING OF PLACES HE MIGHT GO, I'VE BEEN SEARCHING FOR HIM BY THE RIVER, BUT...
...SO SHE SAYS.
HUH.

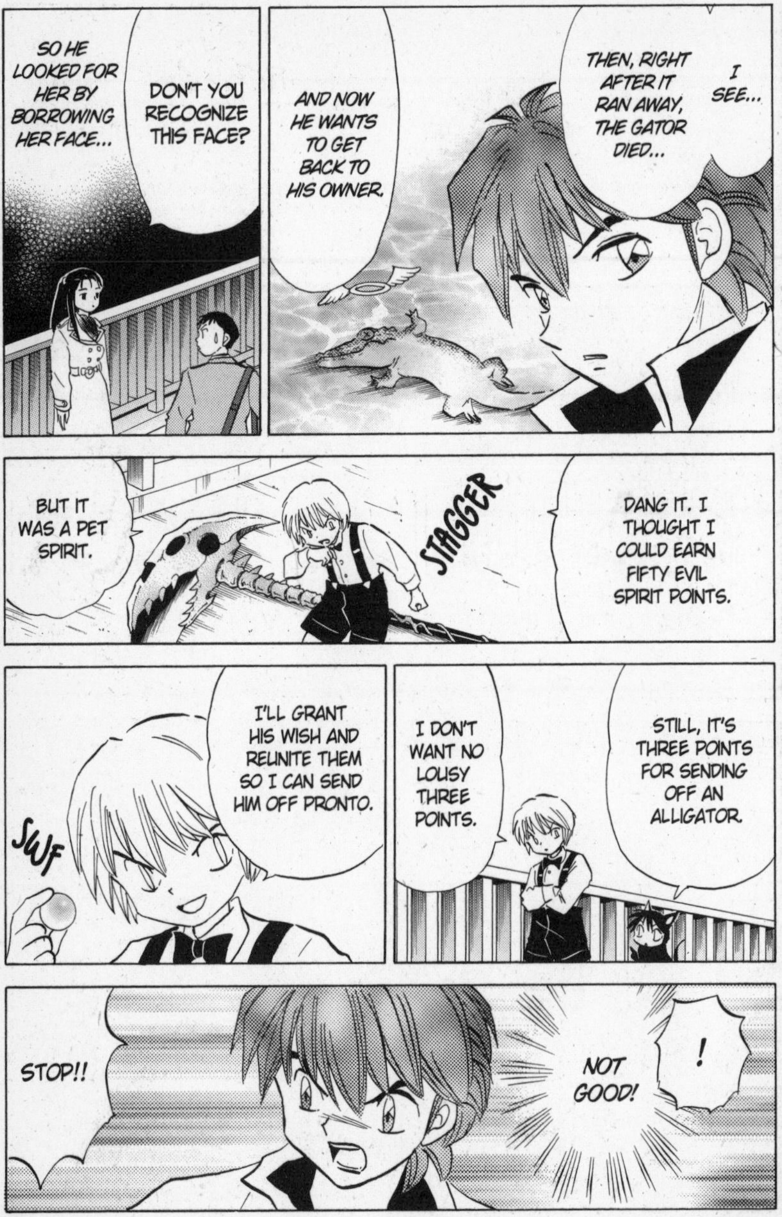
I SEE...
THEN, RIGHT AFTER IT RAN AWAY, THE GATOR DIED...
AND NOW HE WANTS TO GET BACK TO HIS OWNER.
DON'T YOU RECOGNIZE THIS FACE?
SO HE LOOKED FOR HER BY BORROWING HER FACE...
DANG IT. I THOUGHT I COULD EARN FIFTY EVIL SPIRIT POINTS.
STAGGER
BUT IT WAS A PET SPIRIT.
STILL, IT'S THREE POINTS FOR SENDING OFF AN ALLIGATOR.
I DON'T WANT NO LOUSY THREE POINTS.
I'LL GRANT HIS WISH AND REUNITE THEM SO I CAN SEND HIM OFF PRONTO.
SWF
!
NOT GOOD!
STOP!!

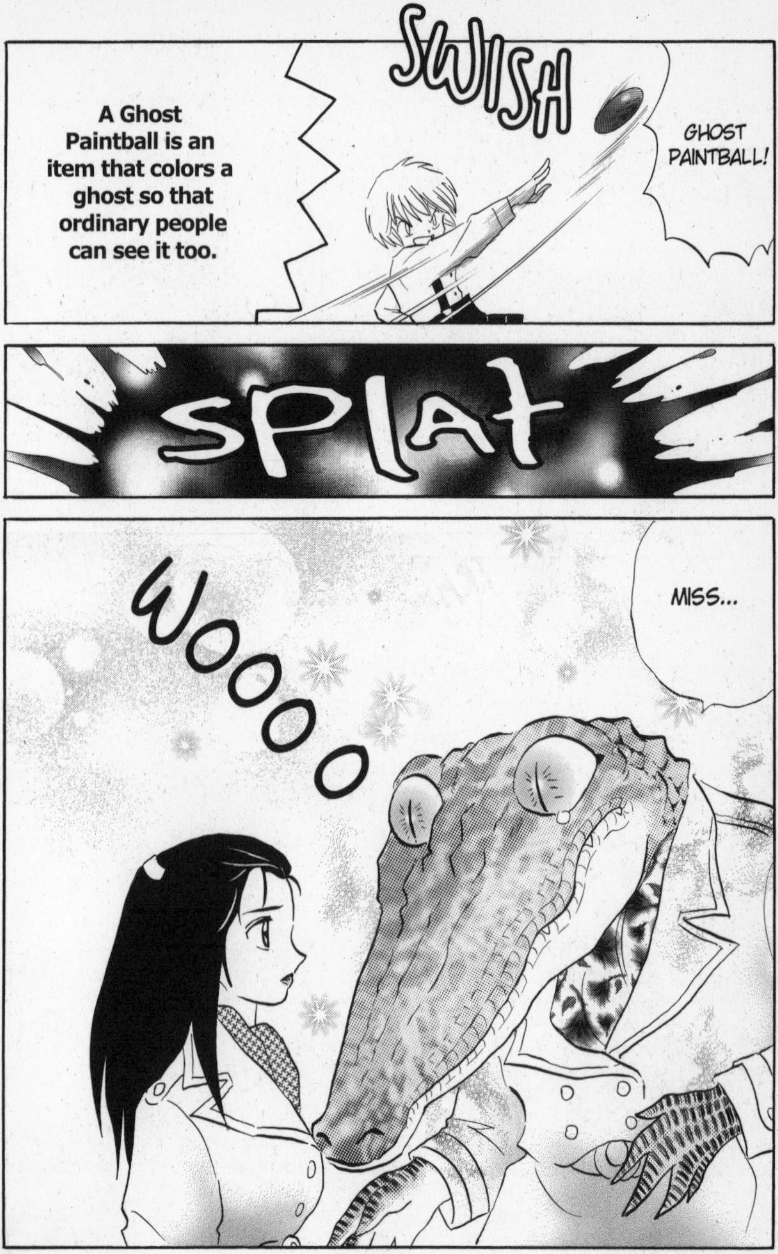
GHOST PAINTBALL!
SWISH
A Ghost Paintball is an item that colors a ghost so that ordinary people can see it too.
SPLAT
MISS...
WOOOOO

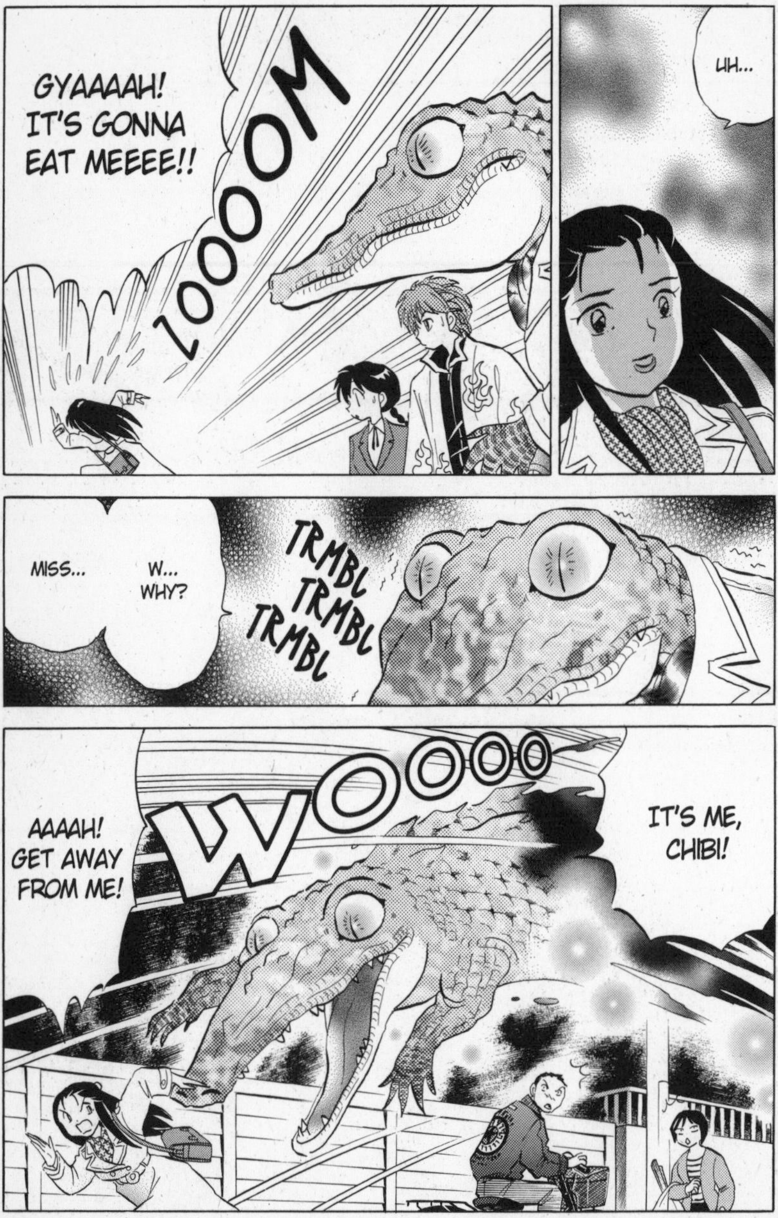
UH...
ZOOOOM
GYAAAAH! IT'S GONNA EAT MEEEE!!
TRMBL TRMBL TRMBL
MISS... W... WHY?
IT'S ME, CHIBI!
WOOOO
AAAAH! GET AWAY FROM ME!

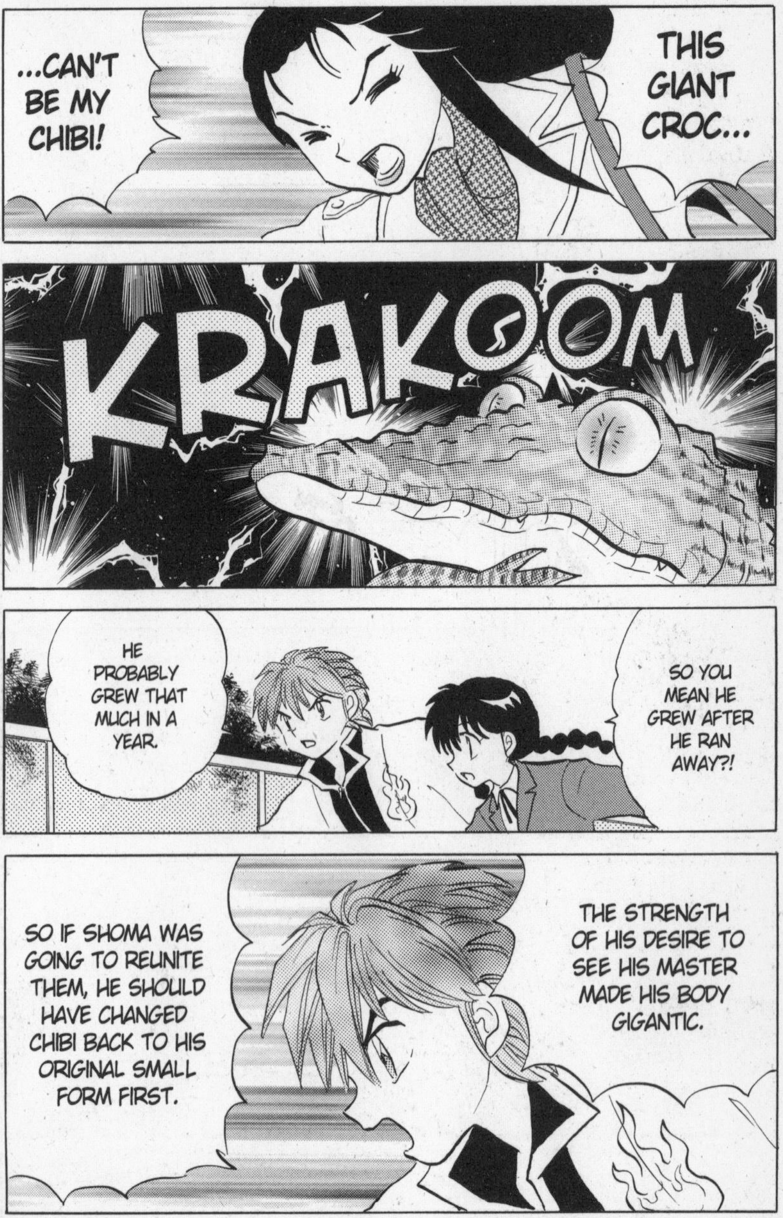
THIS GIANT CROC...
...CAN'T BE MY CHIBI!
KRAKOOM
SO YOU MEAN HE GREW AFTER HE RAN AWAY?!
HE PROBABLY GREW THAT MUCH IN A YEAR.
THE STRENGTH OF HIS DESIRE TO SEE HIS MASTER MADE HIS BODY GIGANTIC.
SO IF SHOMA WAS GOING TO REUNITE THEM, HE SHOULD HAVE CHANGED CHIBI BACK TO HIS ORIGINAL SMALL FORM FIRST.

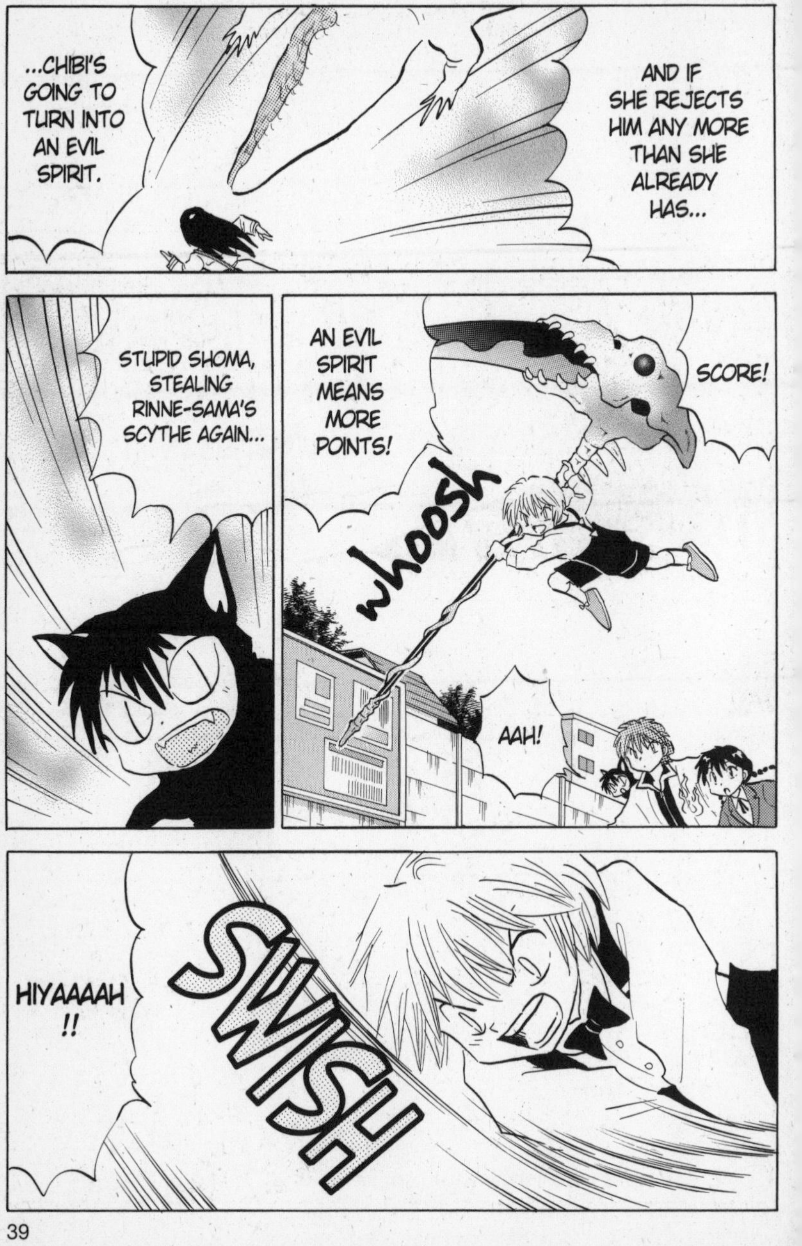
AND IF SHE REJECTS HIM ANY MORE THAN SHE ALREADY HAS...
...CHIBI'S GOING TO TURN INTO AN EVIL SPIRIT.
SCORE!
AN EVIL SPIRIT MEANS MORE POINTS!
whoosh
AAH!
STUPID SHOMA, STEALING RINNE-SAMA'S SCYTHE AGAIN...
SWISH
HIYAAAAH!!

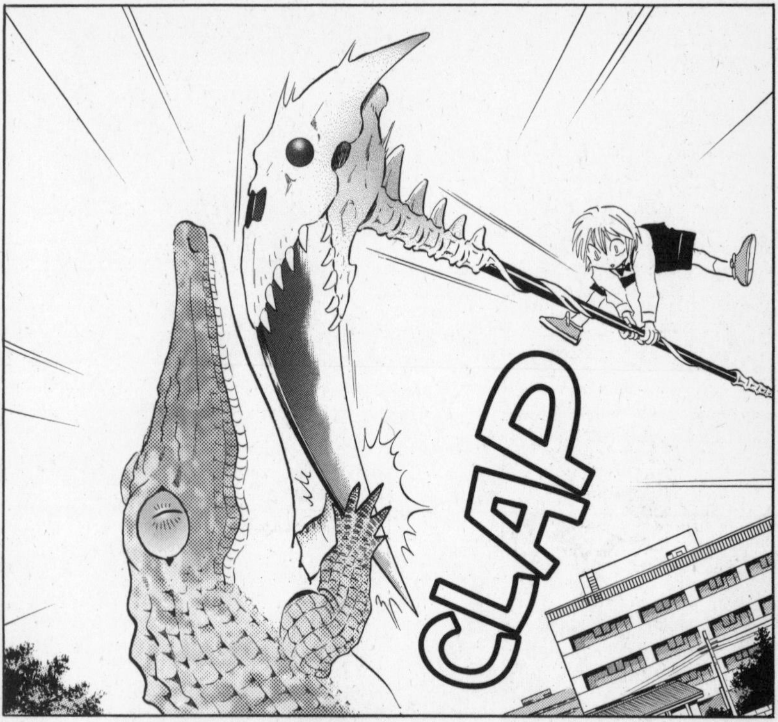
CLAP

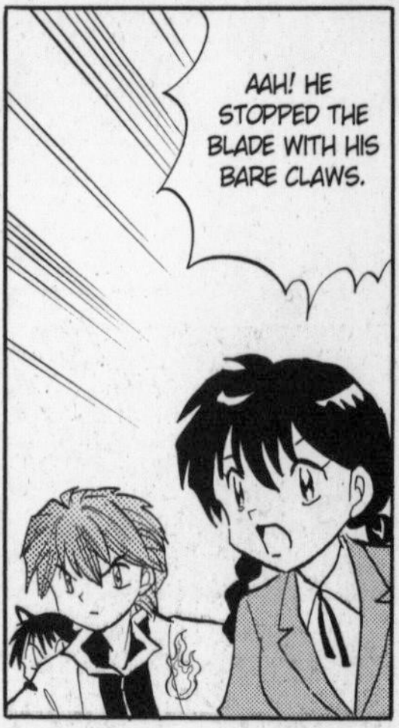
AAH! HE STOPPED THE BLADE WITH HIS BARE CLAWS.

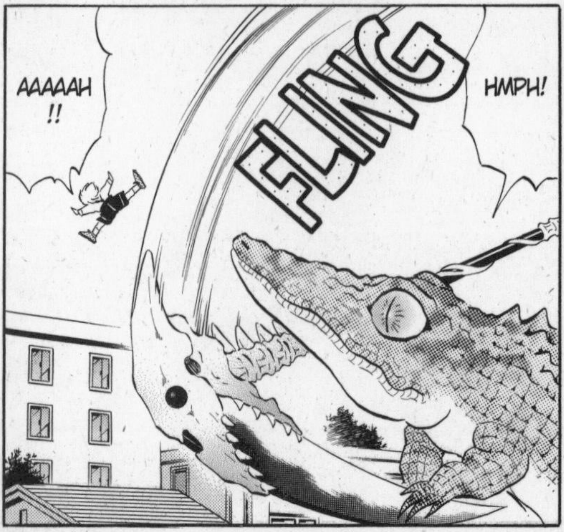
HMPH!
FLING
AAAAAH !!

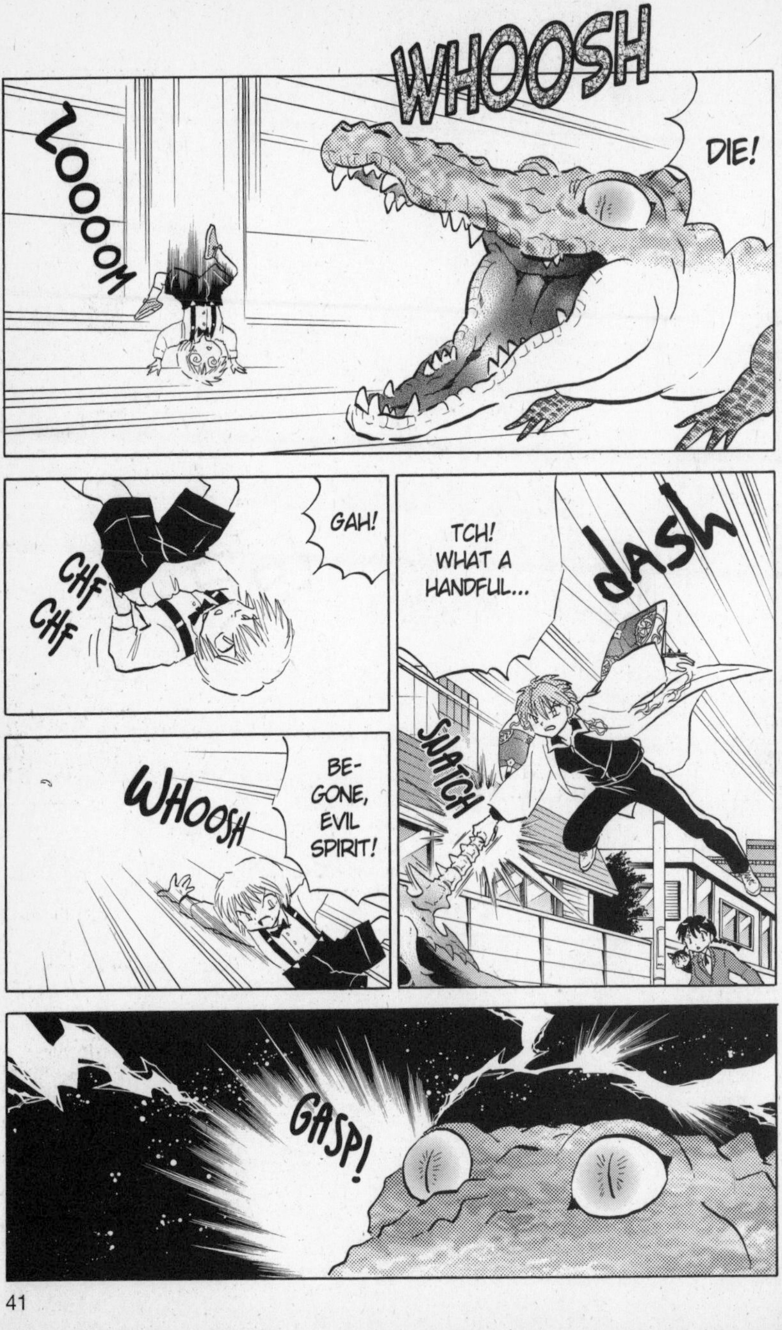
WHOOSH
DIE!
ZOOOOM
dash
TCH! WHAT A HANDFUL...
SNATCH
GAH!
CHF CHF
BE-GONE, EVIL SPIRIT!
WHOOSH
GASP!

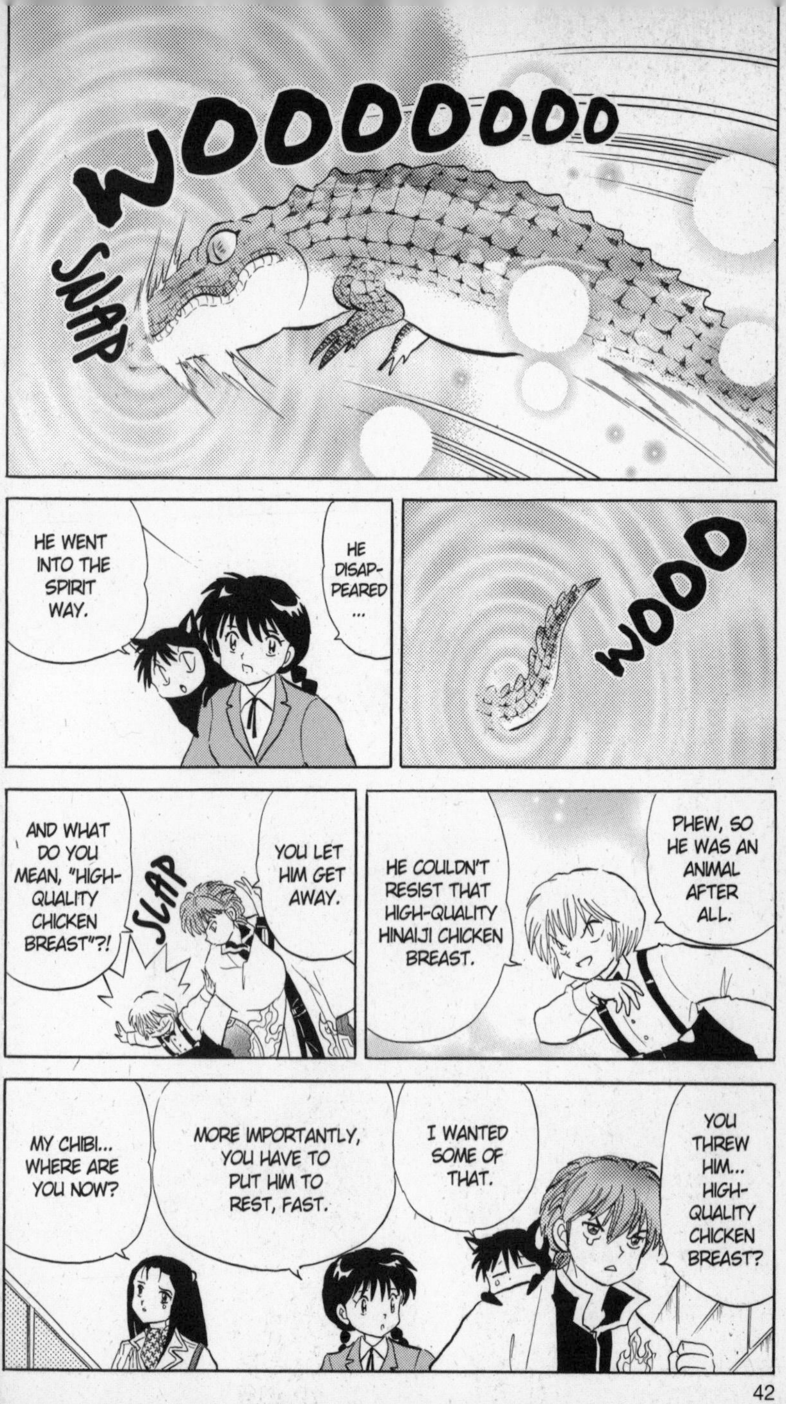
WOOOOOOD
SNAP
WOOD
HE DISAPPEARED...
HE WENT INTO THE SPIRIT WAY.
PHEW, SO HE WAS AN ANIMAL AFTER ALL.
HE COULDN'T RESIST THAT HIGH-QUALITY HINAIJI CHICKEN BREAST.
YOU LET HIM GET AWAY.
SLAP
AND WHAT DO YOU MEAN, "HIGH-QUALITY CHICKEN BREAST"?!
YOU THREW HIM... HIGH-QUALITY CHICKEN BREAST?
I WANTED SOME OF THAT.
MORE IMPORTANTLY, YOU HAVE TO PUT HIM TO REST, FAST.
MY CHIBI... WHERE ARE YOU NOW?

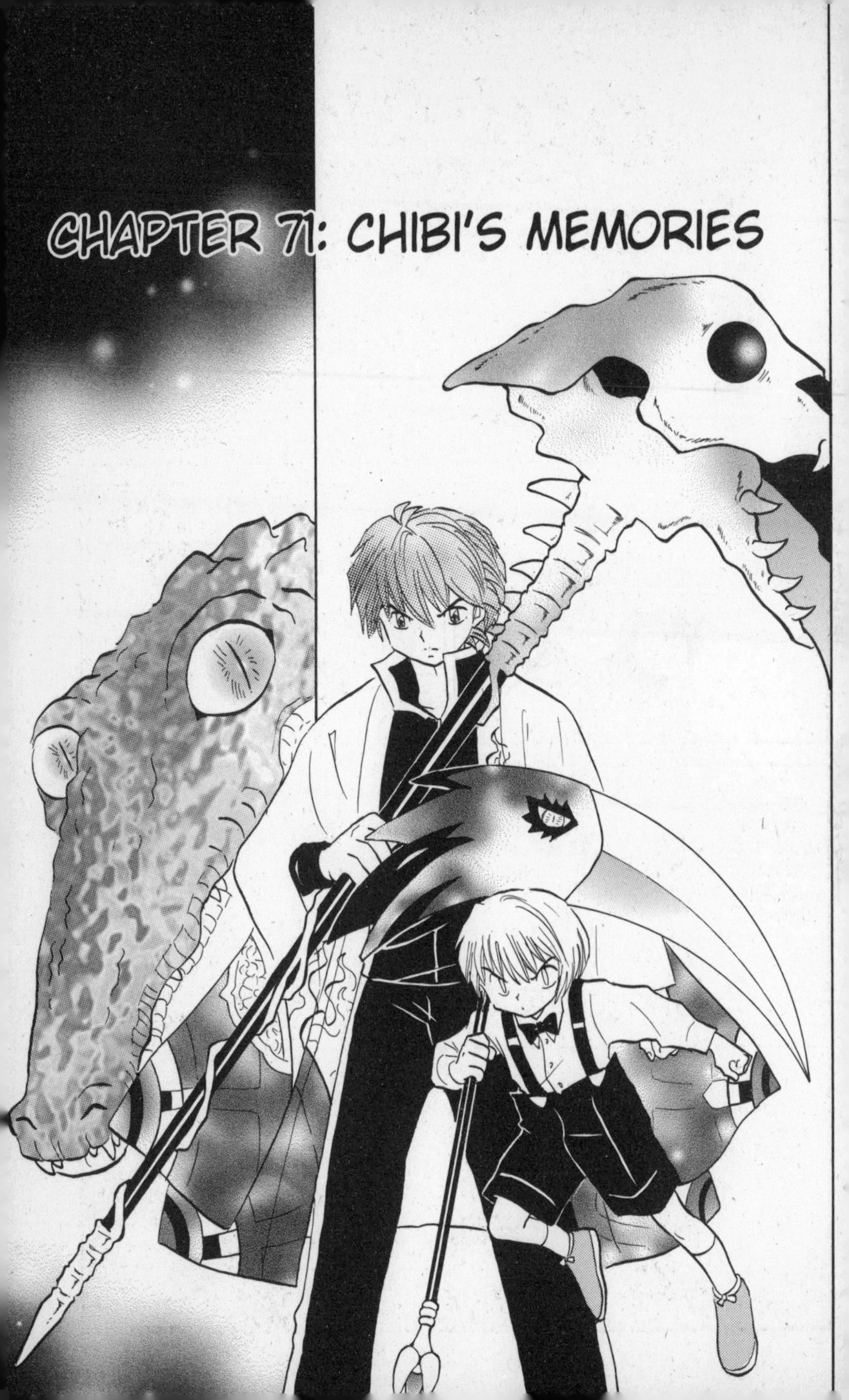
CHAPTER 71: CHIBI'S MEMORIES

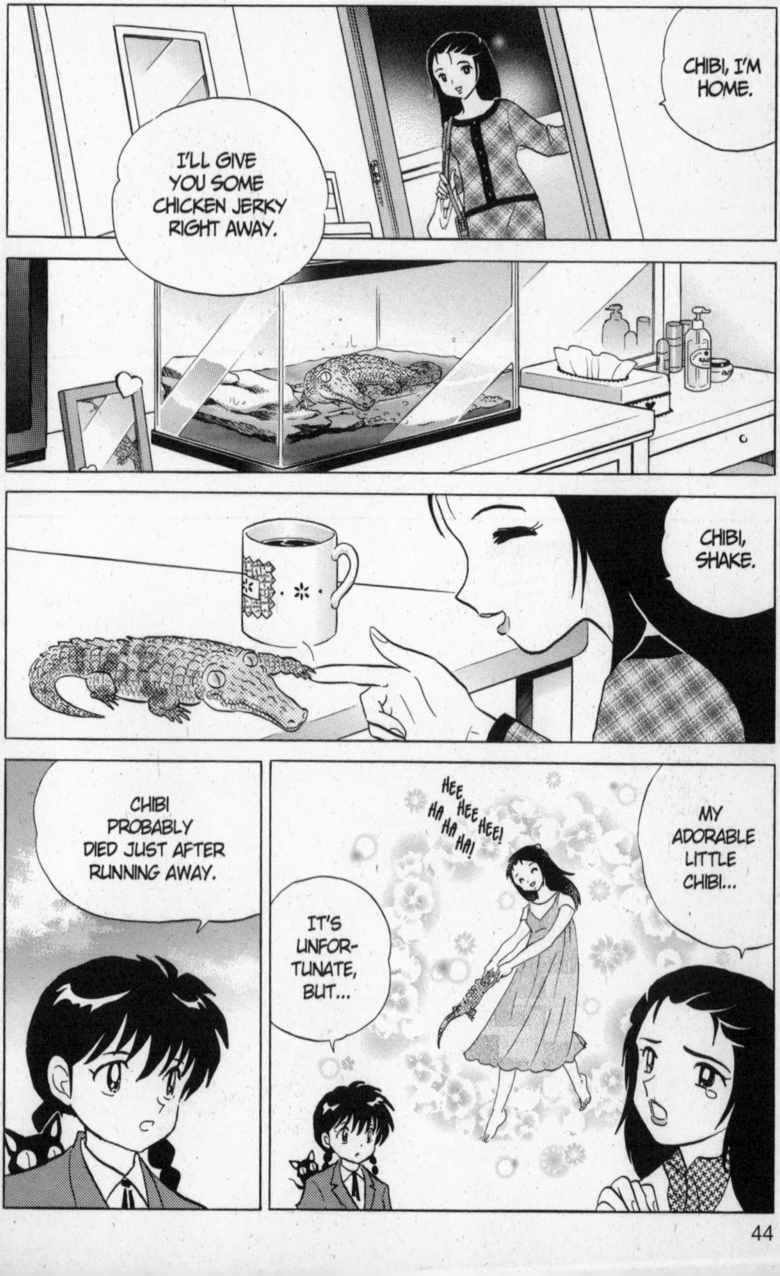
CHIBI, I'M HOME.
I'LL GIVE YOU SOME CHICKEN JERKY RIGHT AWAY.
CHIBI, SHAKE.
MY ADORABLE LITTLE CHIBI...
HEE HEE HEE! HA HA HA!
IT'S UNFOR-TUNATE, BUT...
CHIBI PROBABLY DIED JUST AFTER RUNNING AWAY.

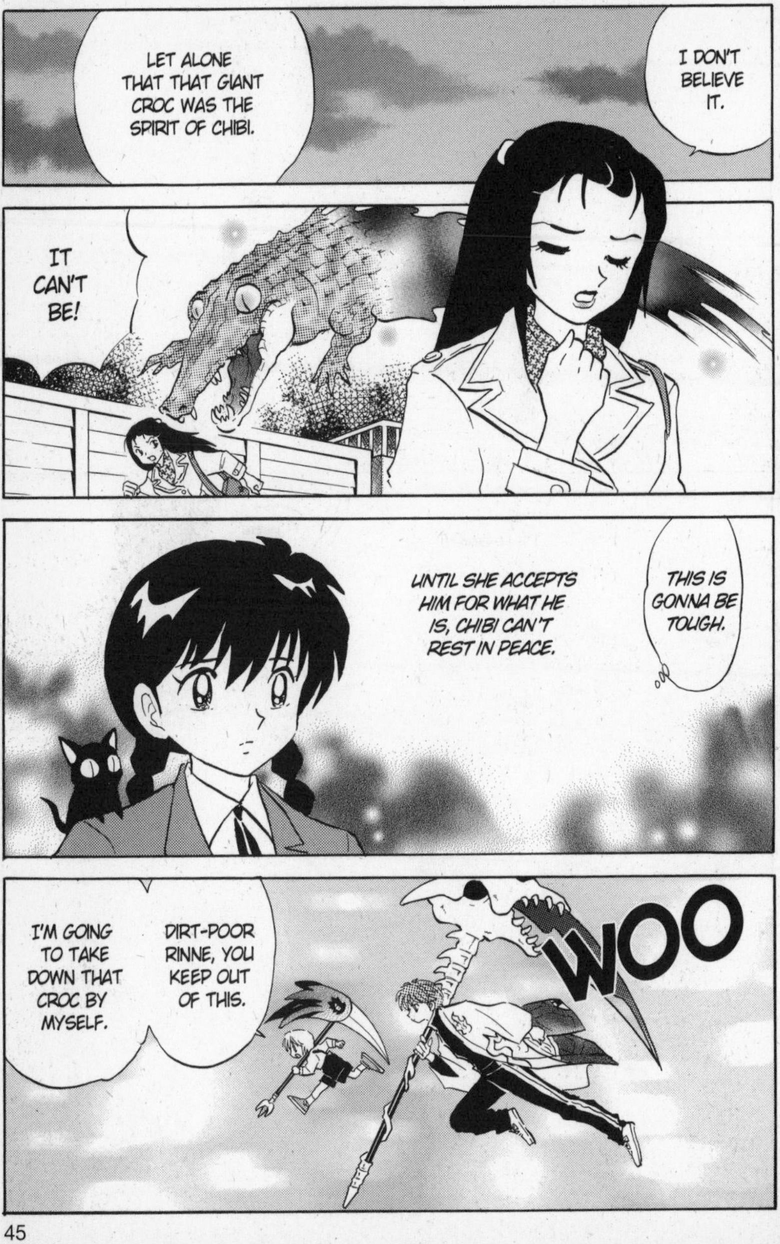
I DON'T BELIEVE IT.
LET ALONE THAT THAT GIANT CROC WAS THE SPIRIT OF CHIBI.
IT CAN'T BE!
THIS IS GONNA BE TOUGH.
UNTIL SHE ACCEPTS HIM FOR WHAT HE IS, CHIBI CAN'T REST IN PEACE.
WOO
DIRT-POOR RINNE, YOU KEEP OUT OF THIS.
I'M GOING TO TAKE DOWN THAT CROC BY MYSELF.

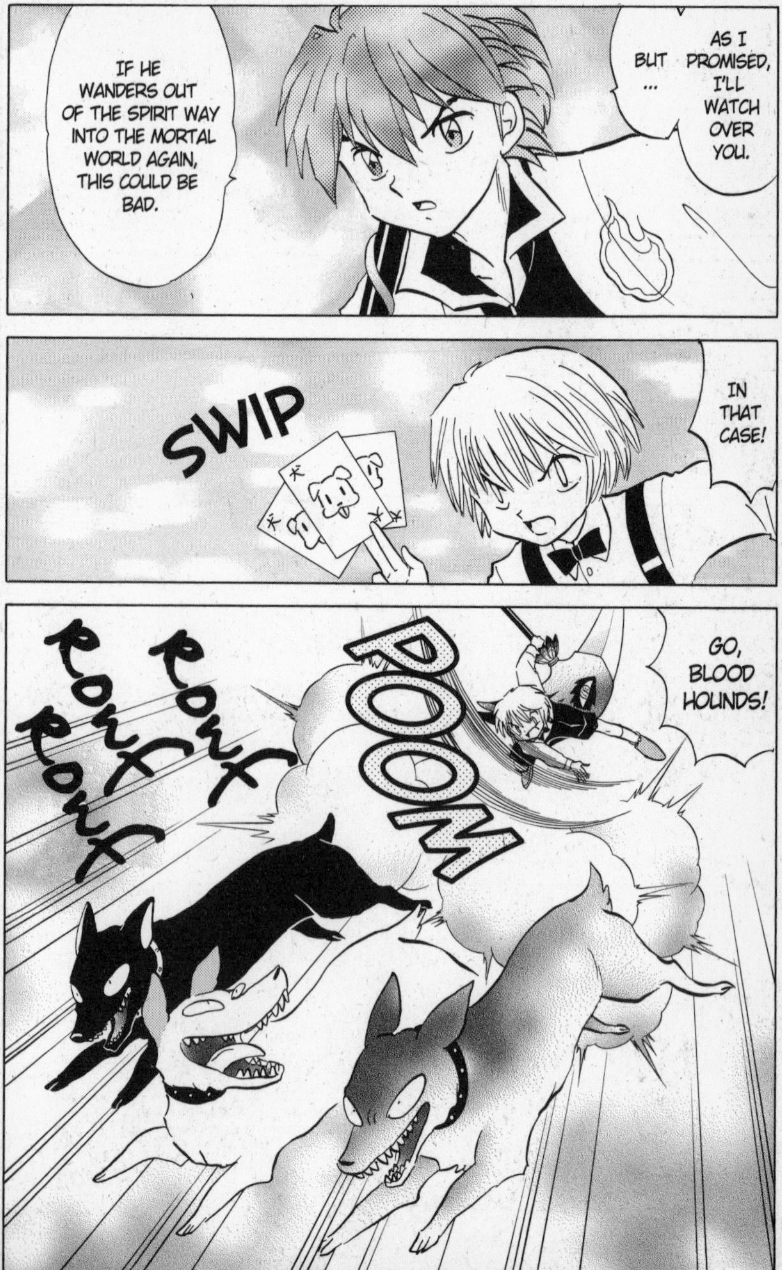
AS I PROMISED, I'LL WATCH OVER YOU.
BUT ...
IF HE WANDERS OUT OF THE SPIRIT WAY INTO THE MORTAL WORLD AGAIN, THIS COULD BE BAD.
IN THAT CASE!
SWIP
GO, BLOOD HOUNDS!
POOM
ROWF
ROWF
ROWF

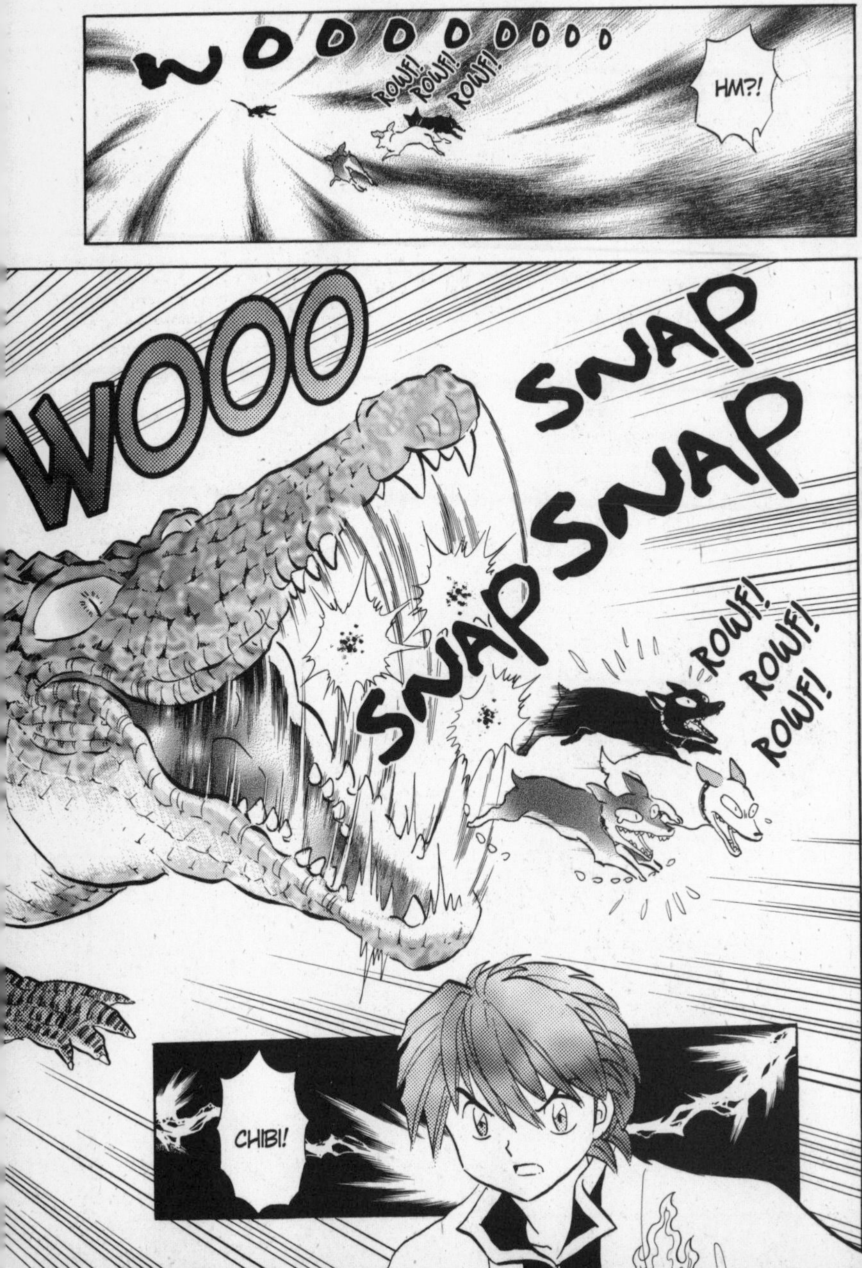
HM?!
WOOOOOOOOO
ROWF! ROWF! ROWF!
WOOO
SNAP SNAP SNAP
ROWF! ROWF! ROWF!
CHIBI!

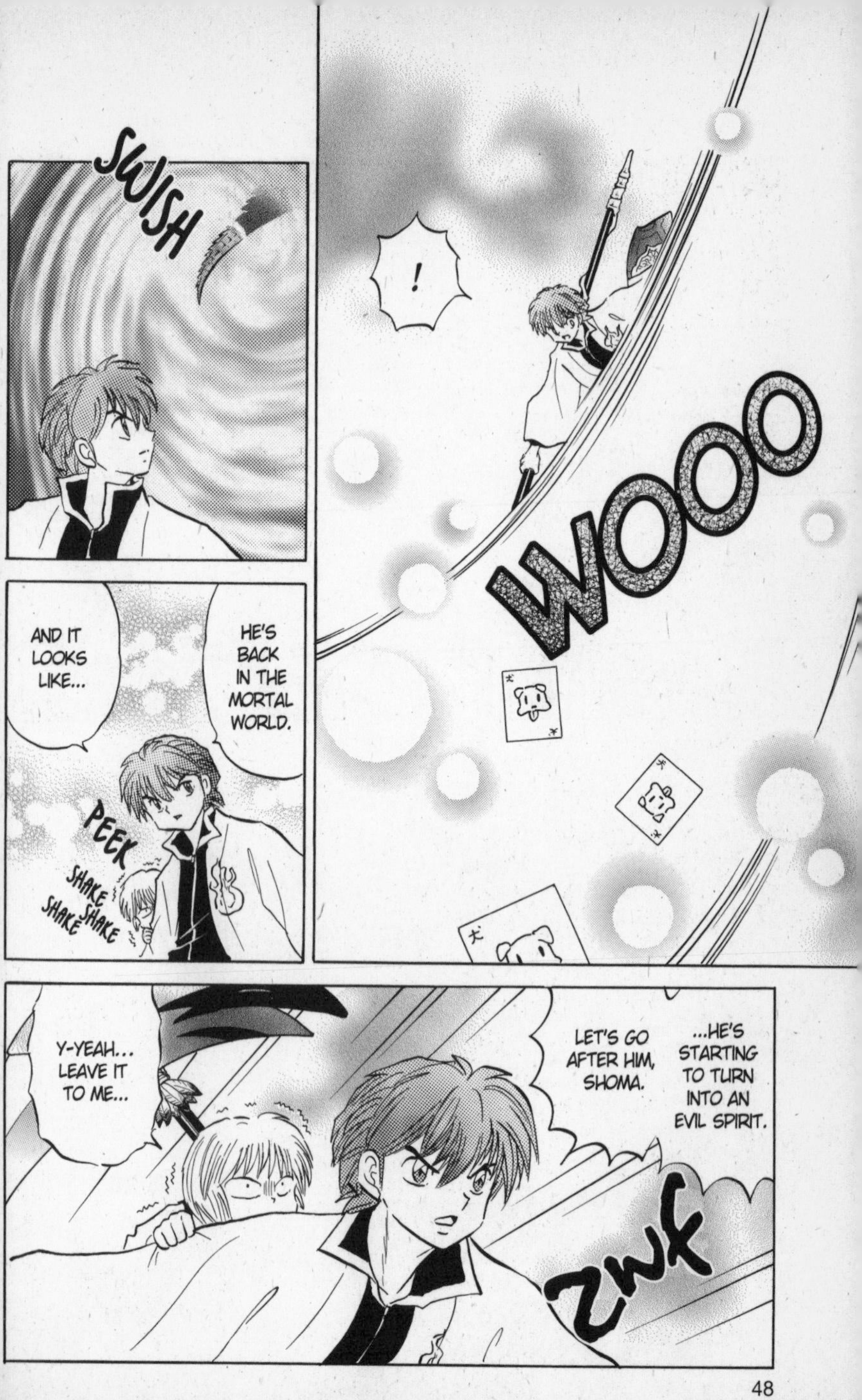
!
WOOO
SWISH
HE'S BACK IN THE MORTAL WORLD.
AND IT LOOKS LIKE...
PEEK
SHAKE SHAKE SHAKE
...HE'S STARTING TO TURN INTO AN EVIL SPIRIT.
LET'S GO AFTER HIM, SHOMA.
ZWF
Y-YEAH... LEAVE IT TO ME...

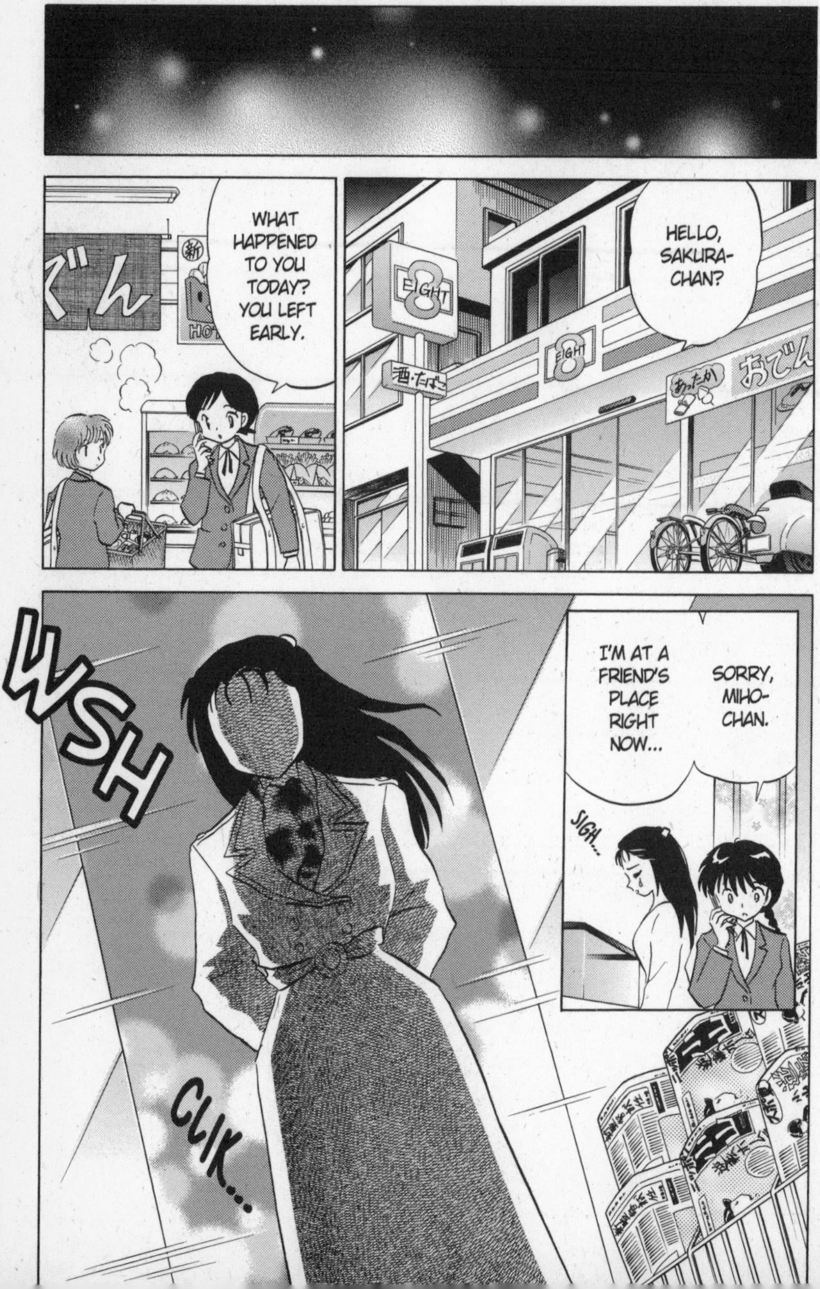
HELLO, SAKURA-CHAN?
WHAT HAPPENED TO YOU TODAY? YOU LEFT EARLY.
SORRY, MIHO-CHAN.
I'M AT A FRIEND'S PLACE RIGHT NOW...
SIGH...
WSH
CLIK...

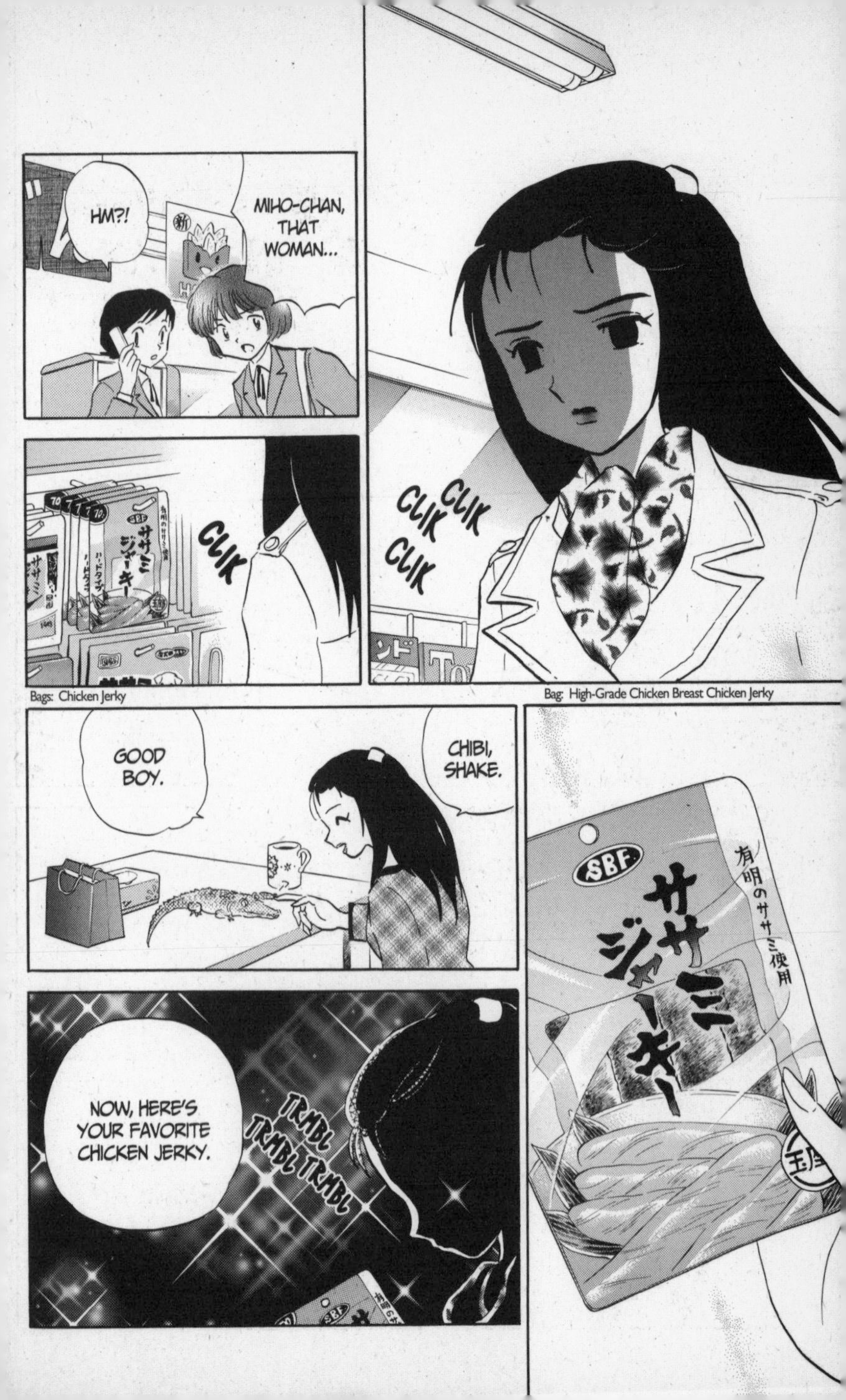
CLIK
CLIK
CLIK
MIHO-CHAN, THAT WOMAN...
HM?!
CLIK
Bag: High-Grade Chicken Breast Chicken Jerky
Bags: Chicken Jerky
SBF
ササミジャーキー
有明のササミ使用
CHIBI, SHAKE.
GOOD BOY.
NOW, HERE'S YOUR FAVORITE CHICKEN JERKY.
TRMBL TRMBL TRMBL

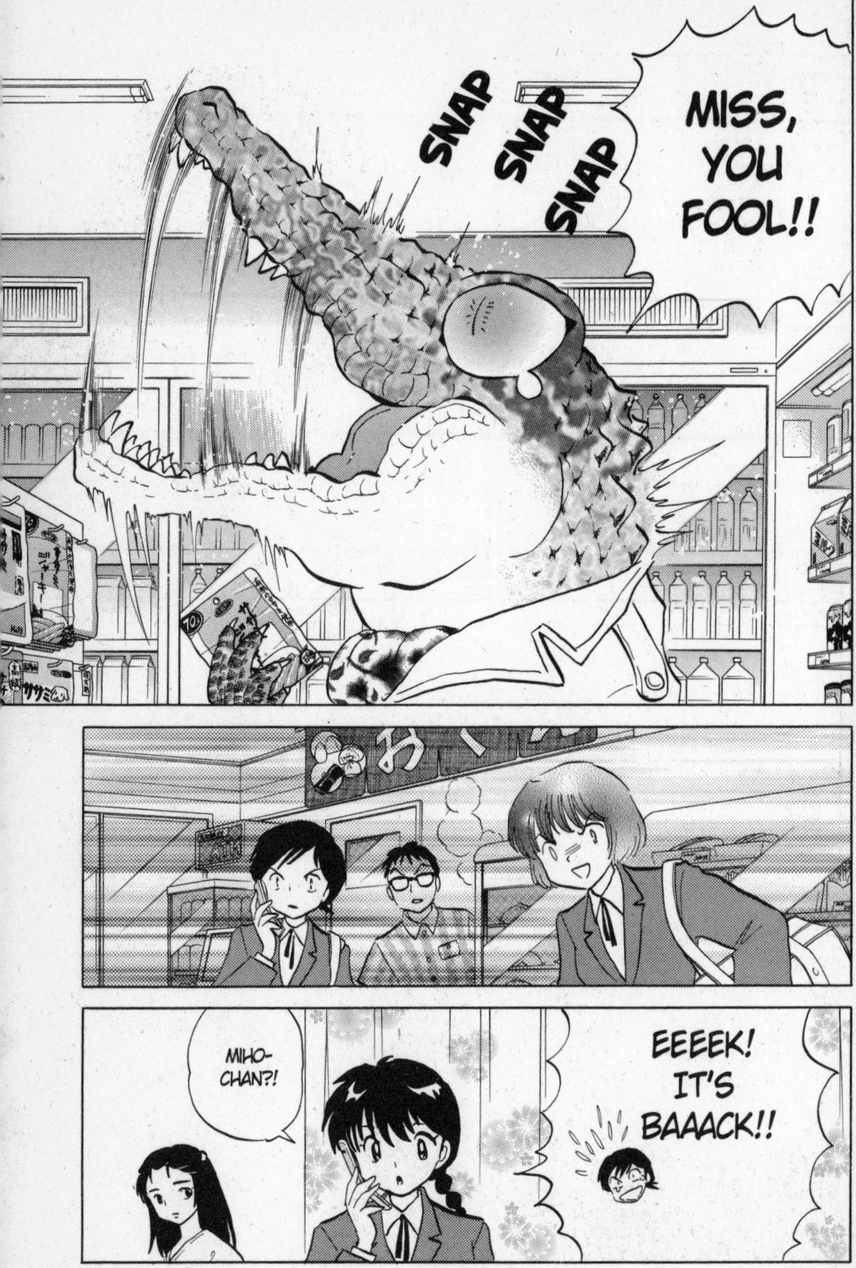
MISS, YOU FOOL!!
SNAP
SNAP
SNAP
EEEEK! IT'S BAAACK!!
MIHO-CHAN?!

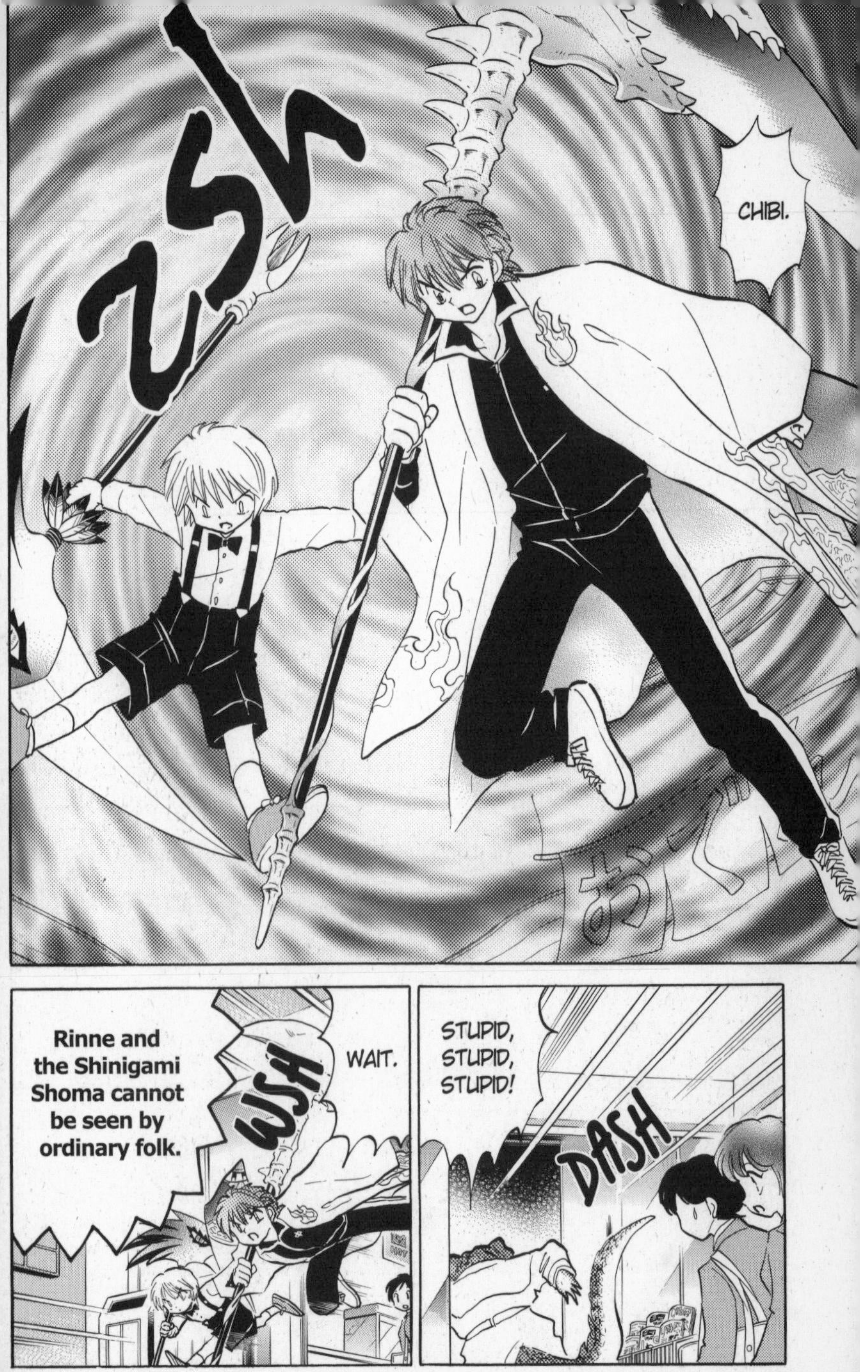
CHIBI.
ZSH
STUPID, STUPID, STUPID!
DASH
WAIT.
WSH
Rinne and the Shinigami Shoma cannot be seen by ordinary folk.

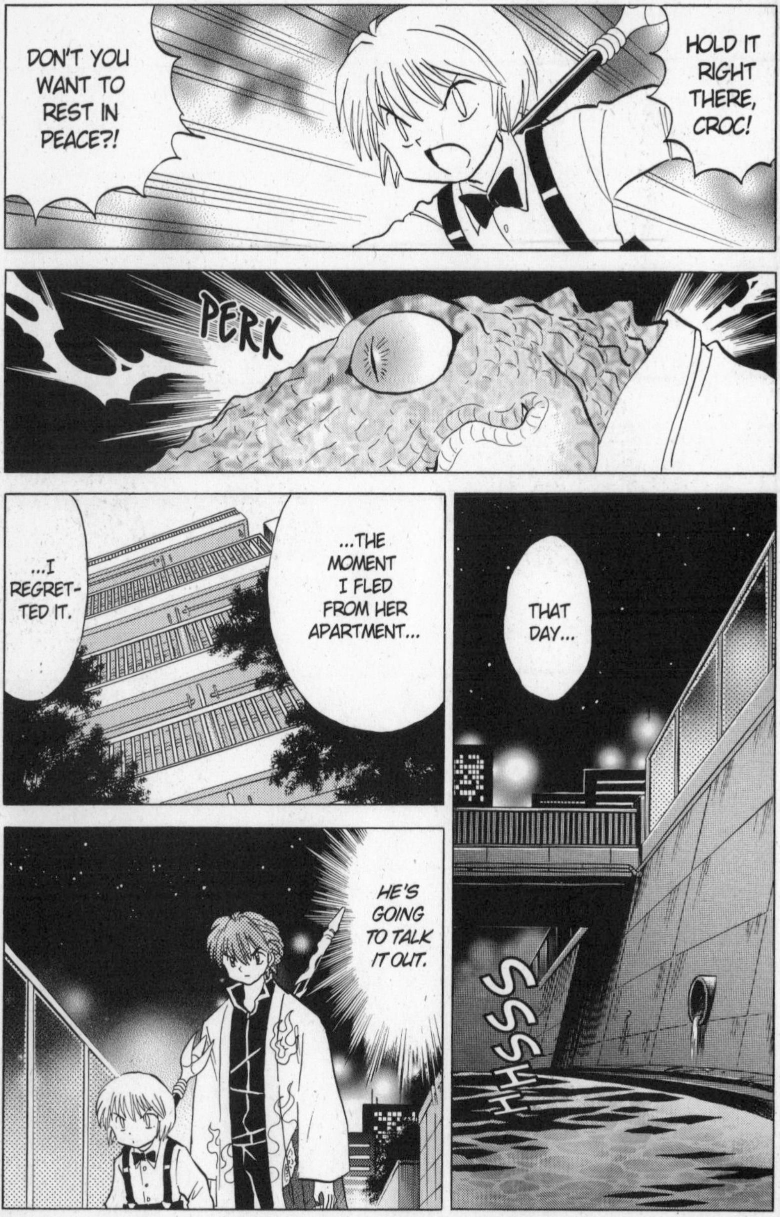
HOLD IT RIGHT THERE, CROC!
DON'T YOU WANT TO REST IN PEACE?!
PERK
THAT DAY...
SSSHHH
...THE MOMENT I FLED FROM HER APARTMENT...
...I REGRET-TED IT.
HE'S GOING TO TALK IT OUT.

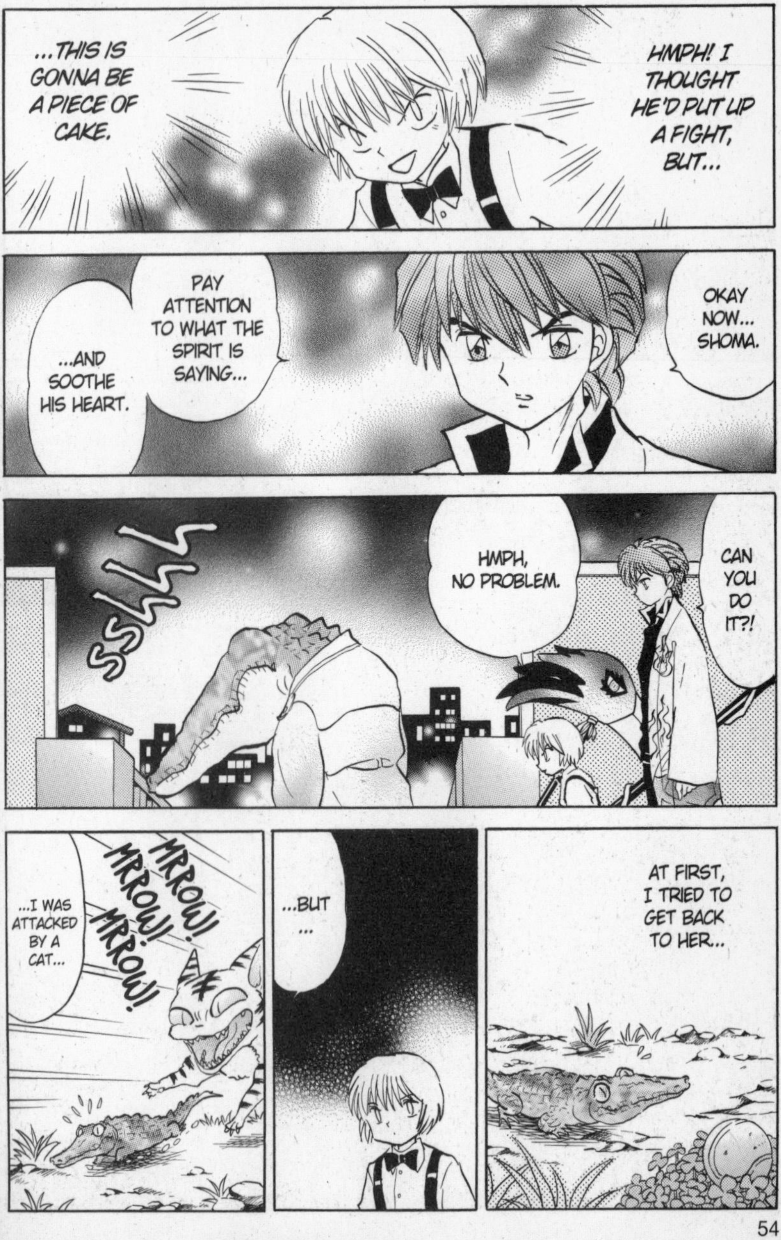
HMPH! I THOUGHT HE'D PUT UP A FIGHT, BUT...
...THIS IS GONNA BE A PIECE OF CAKE.
OKAY NOW... SHOMA.
PAY ATTENTION TO WHAT THE SPIRIT IS SAYING...
...AND SOOTHE HIS HEART.
CAN YOU DO IT?!
HMPH, NO PROBLEM.
SSSS
AT FIRST, I TRIED TO GET BACK TO HER...
...BUT ...
MRROW!! MRROW!! MRROW!!
...I WAS ATTACKED BY A CAT...

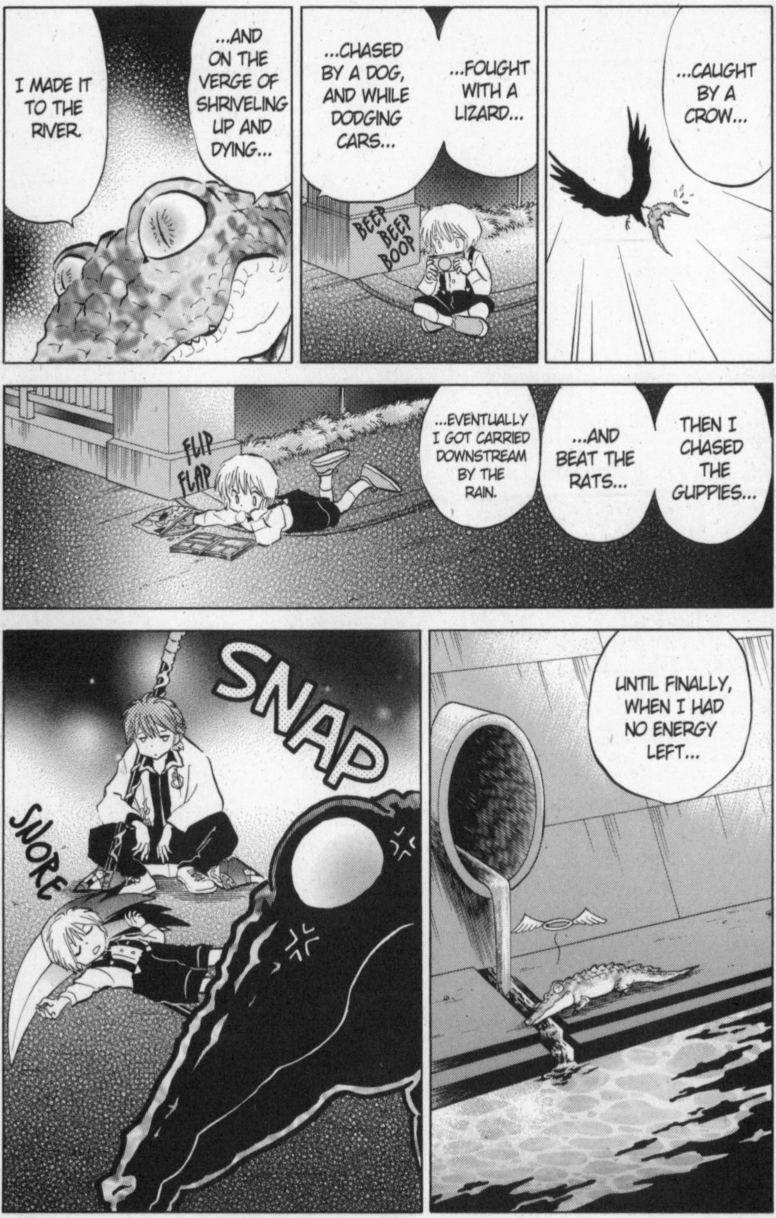
...CAUGHT BY A CROW...
...FOUGHT WITH A LIZARD...
...CHASED BY A DOG, AND WHILE DODGING CARS...
BEEP BEEP BOOP
...AND ON THE VERGE OF SHRIVELING UP AND DYING...
I MADE IT TO THE RIVER.
THEN I CHASED THE GUPPIES...
...AND BEAT THE RATS...
...EVENTUALLY I GOT CARRIED DOWNSTREAM BY THE RAIN.
FLIP FLAP
UNTIL FINALLY, WHEN I HAD NO ENERGY LEFT...
SNAP
SNORE

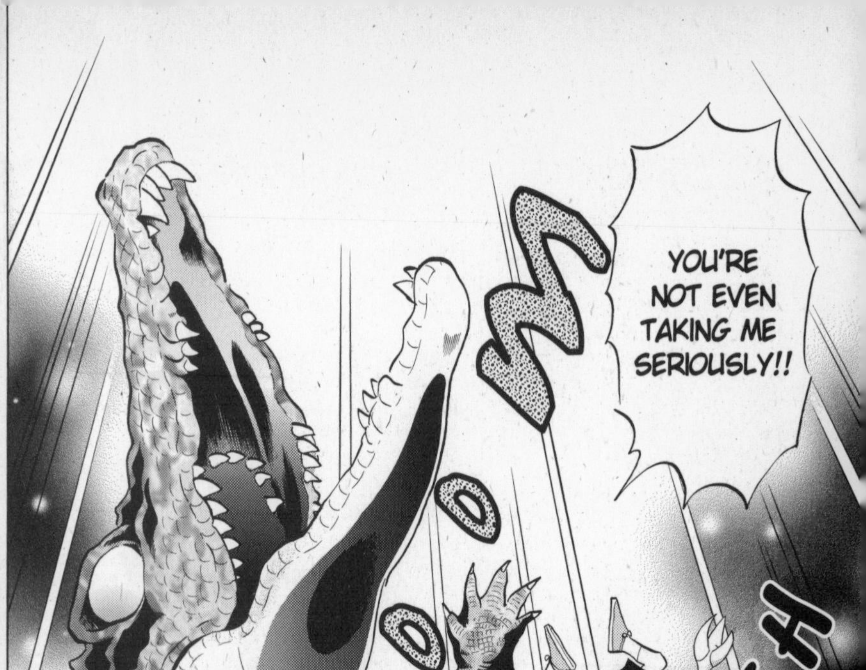
YOU'RE NOT EVEN TAKING ME SERIOUSLY!!
KA-KRASH
GOOOOM

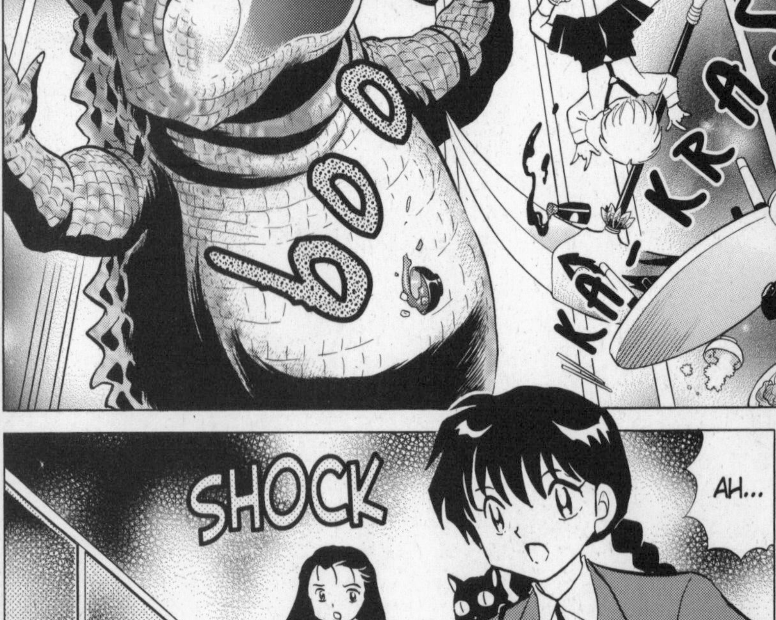
AH...
SHOCK

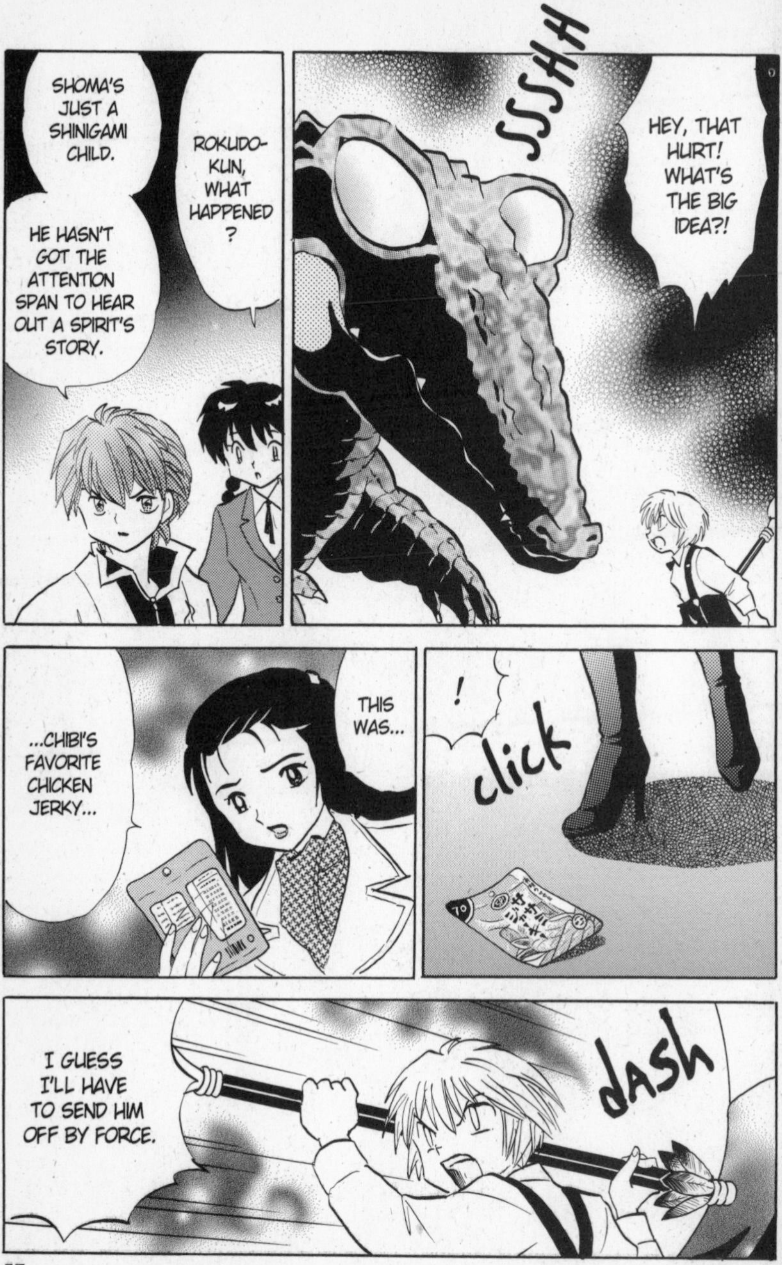
SSSHH
HEY, THAT HURT! WHAT'S THE BIG IDEA?!
ROKUDO-KUN, WHAT HAPPENED?
SHOMA'S JUST A SHINIGAMI CHILD.
HE HASN'T GOT THE ATTENTION SPAN TO HEAR OUT A SPIRIT'S STORY.
!
click
THIS WAS...
...CHIBI'S FAVORITE CHICKEN JERKY...
dash
I GUESS I'LL HAVE TO SEND HIM OFF BY FORCE.

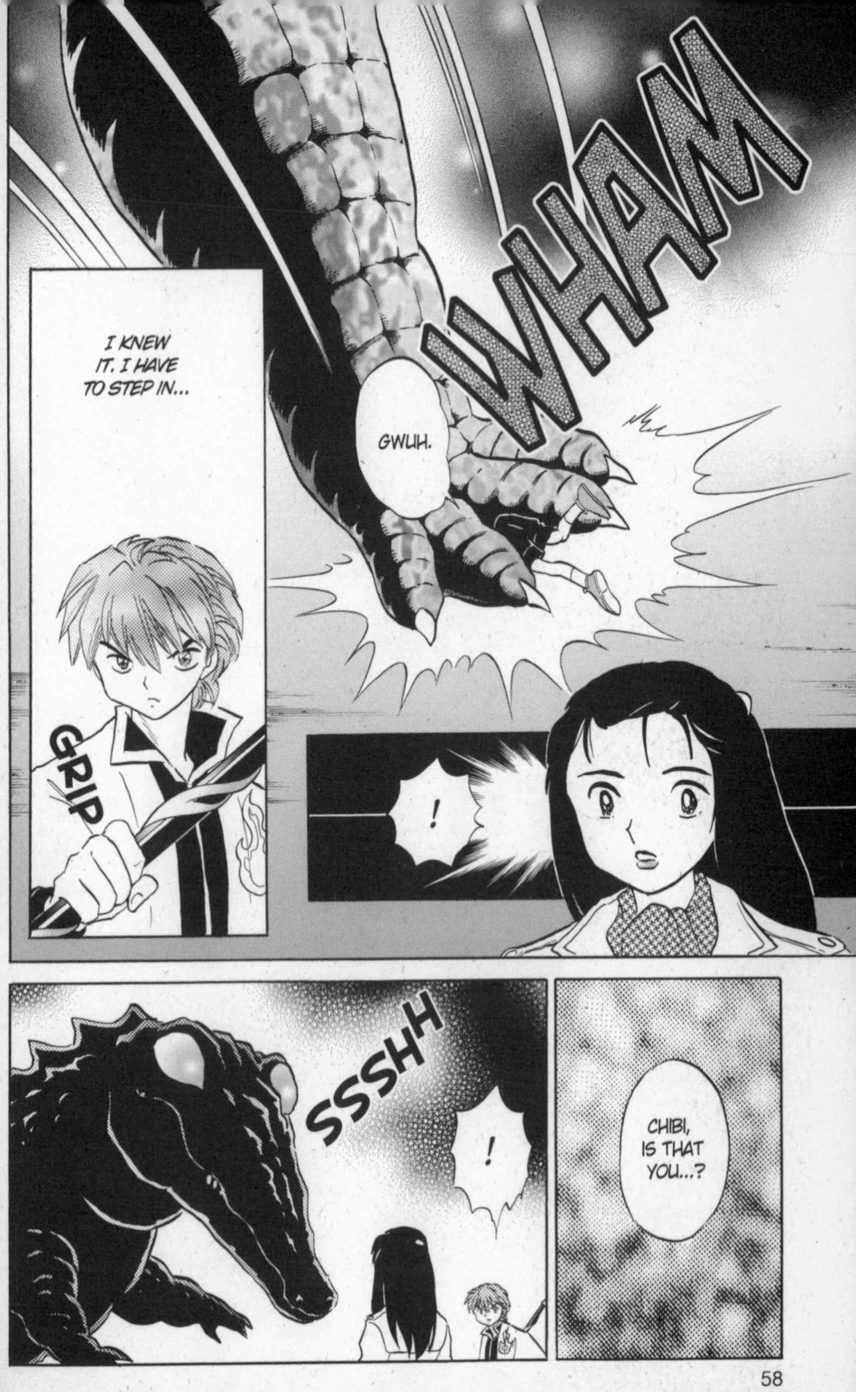
WHAM
GWUH.
!
I KNEW IT. I HAVE TO STEP IN...
GRIP
CHIBI, IS THAT YOU...?
SSSHH
!

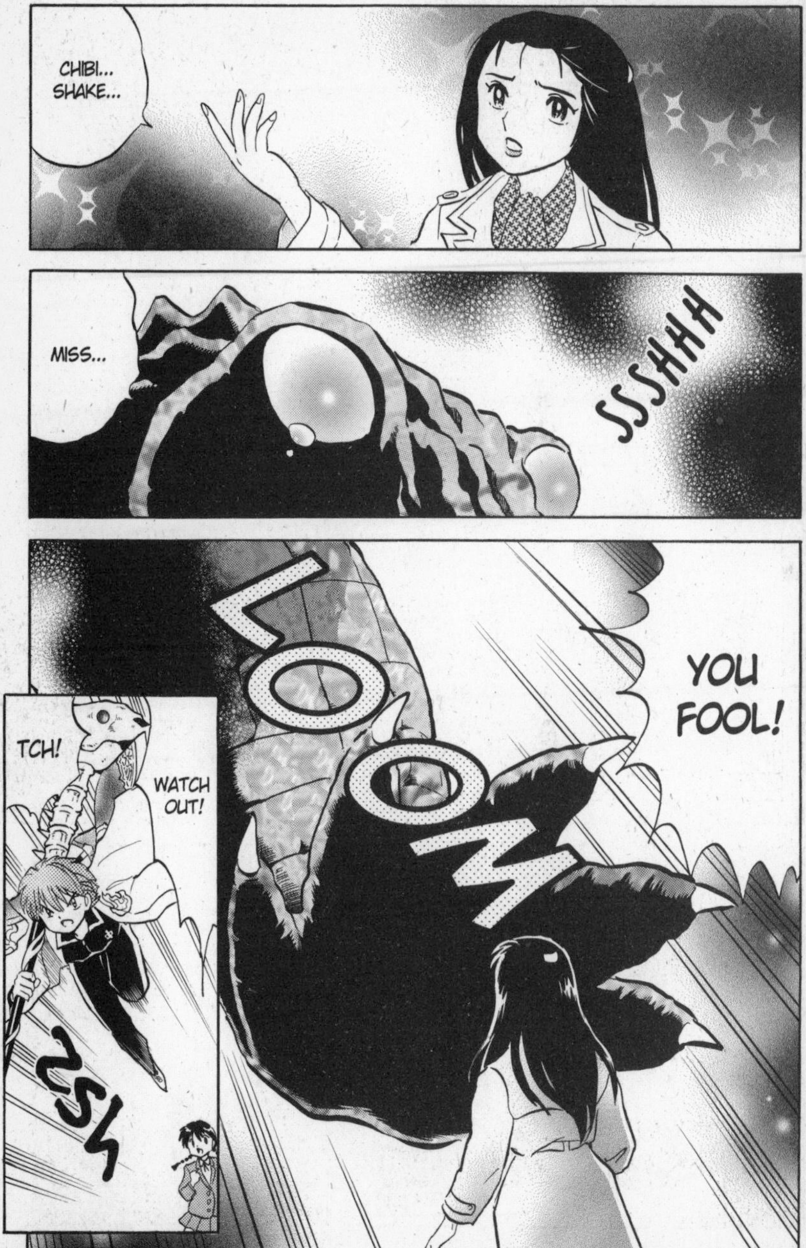
CHIBI... SHAKE...
MISS...
SSSHHH
YOU FOOL!
LOOOM
TCH!
WATCH OUT!
ZSH

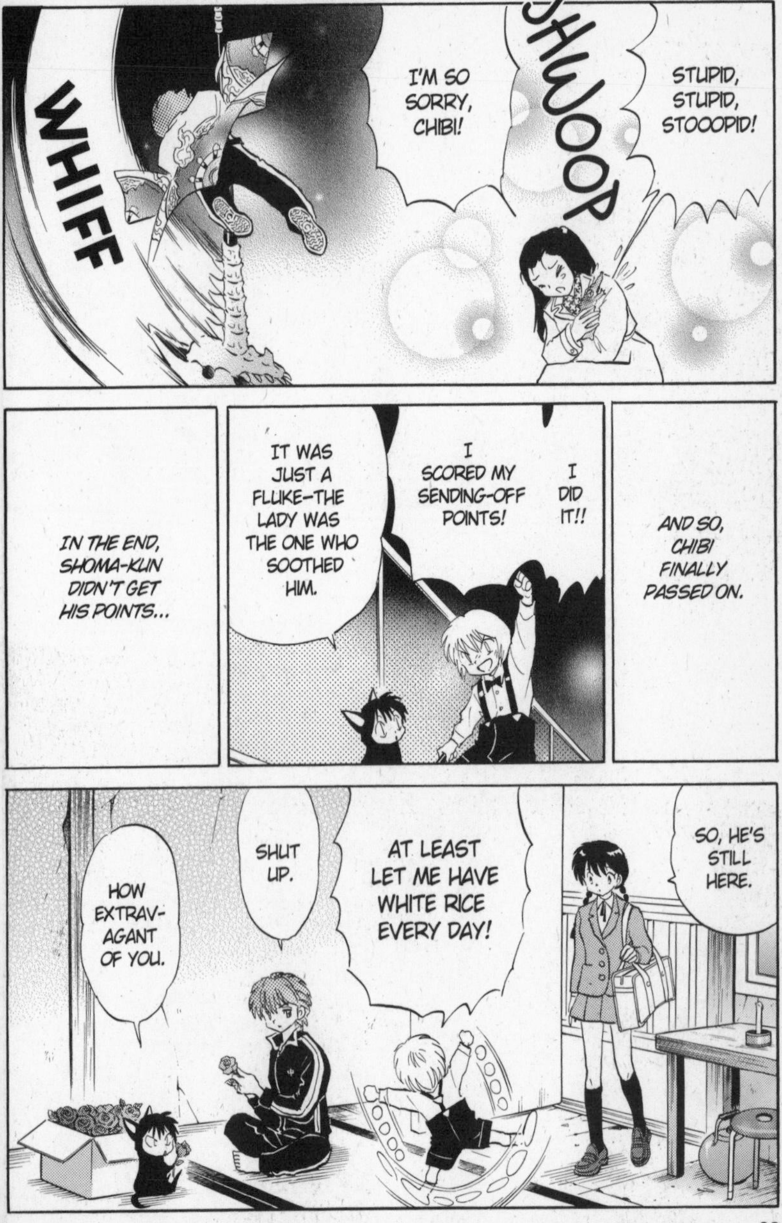
STUPID, STUPID, STOOOPID!
SHWOOP
I'M SO SORRY, CHIBI!
WHIFF
AND SO, CHIBI FINALLY PASSED ON.
I DID IT!!
I SCORED MY SENDING-OFF POINTS!
IT WAS JUST A FLUKE—THE LADY WAS THE ONE WHO SOOTHED HIM.
IN THE END, SHOMA-KUN DIDN'T GET HIS POINTS...
SO, HE'S STILL HERE.
AT LEAST LET ME HAVE WHITE RICE EVERY DAY!
SHUT UP.
HOW EXTRAV-AGANT OF YOU.

CHAPTER 72: INTRODUCTION TO AN EVIL SPIRIT

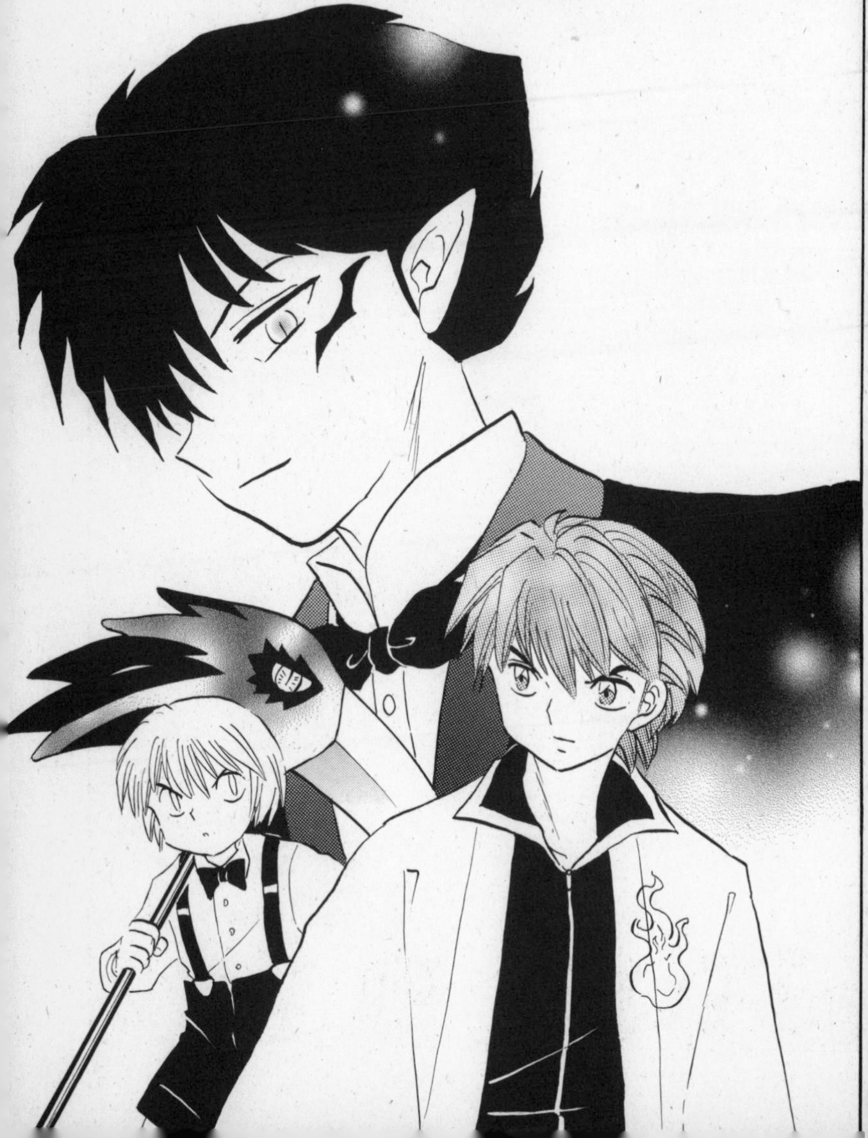

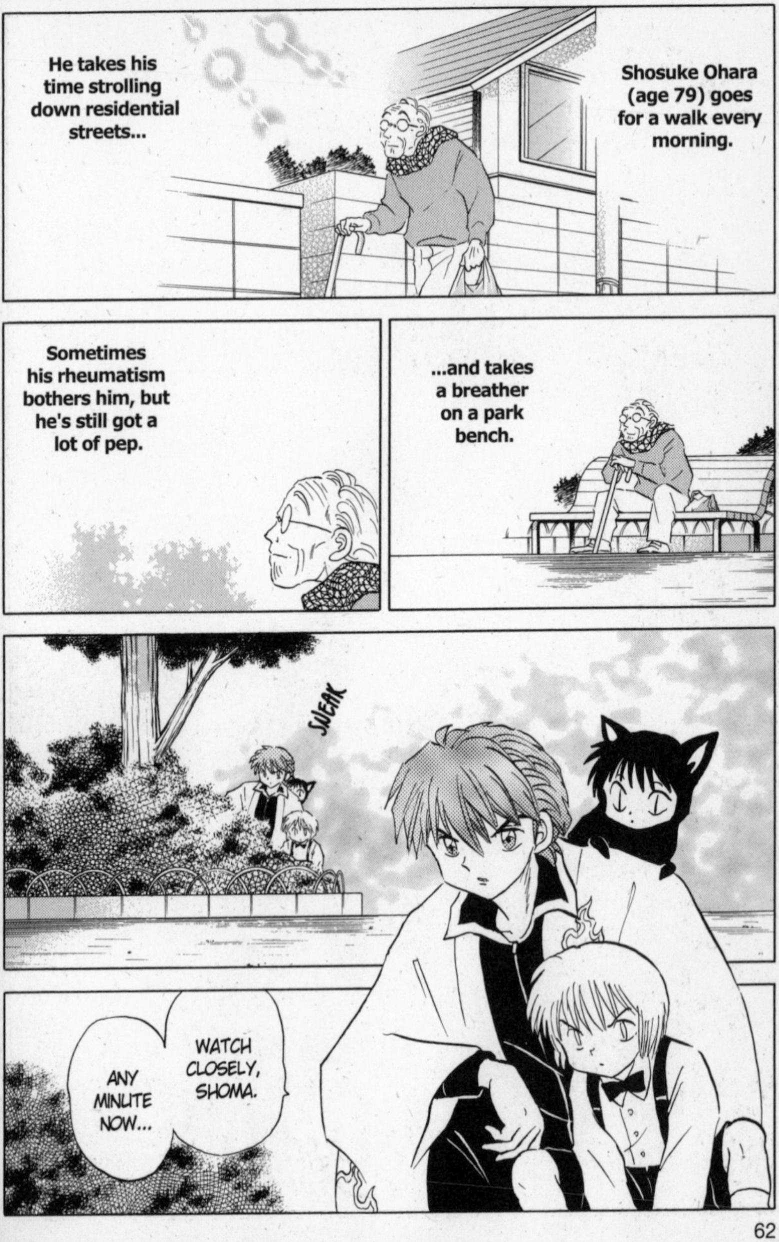
Shosuke Ohara (age 79) goes for a walk every morning.
He takes his time strolling down residential streets...
...and takes a breather on a park bench.
Sometimes his rheumatism bothers him, but he's still got a lot of pep.
SNEAK
WATCH CLOSELY, SHOMA.
ANY MINUTE NOW...

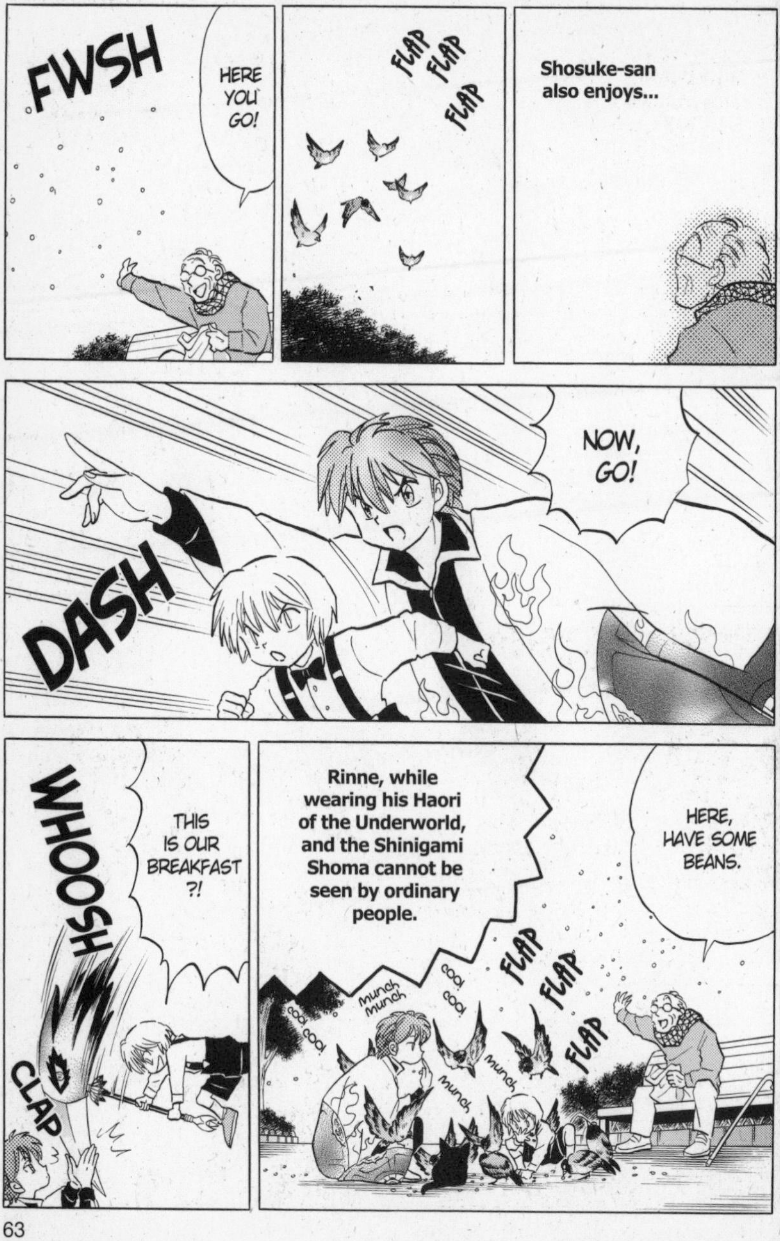
Shosuke-san also enjoys...
FLAP FLAP FLAP
HERE YOU GO!
FWSH
NOW, GO!
DASH
HERE, HAVE SOME BEANS.
Rinne, while wearing his Haori of the Underworld, and the Shinigami Shoma cannot be seen by ordinary people.
FLAP FLAP FLAP
coo! coo!
Munch Munch
coo! coo!
munch munch
THIS IS OUR BREAKFAST ?!
WHOOOSH
CLAP

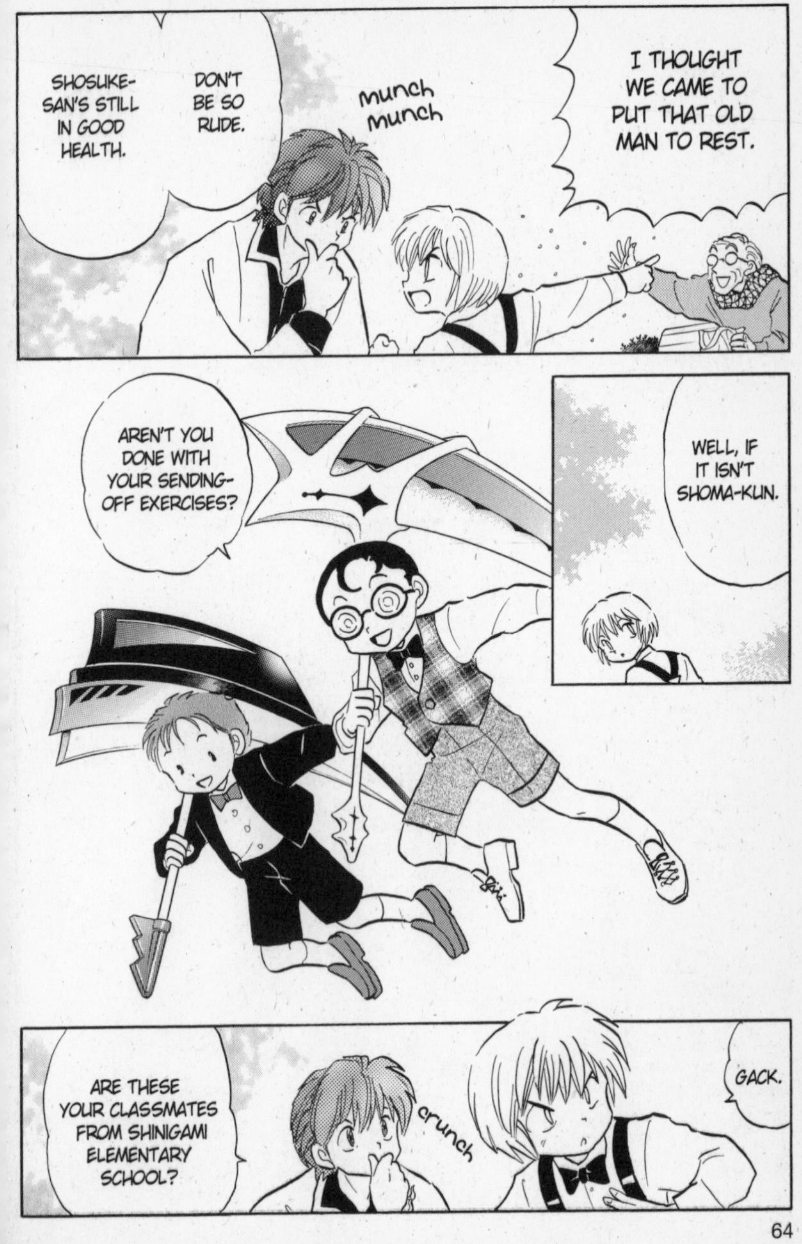
I THOUGHT WE CAME TO PUT THAT OLD MAN TO REST.
munch munch
DON'T BE SO RUDE.
SHOSUKE-SAN'S STILL IN GOOD HEALTH.
WELL, IF IT ISN'T SHOMA-KUN.
AREN'T YOU DONE WITH YOUR SENDING-OFF EXERCISES?
GACK.
crunch
ARE THESE YOUR CLASSMATES FROM SHINIGAMI ELEMENTARY SCHOOL?

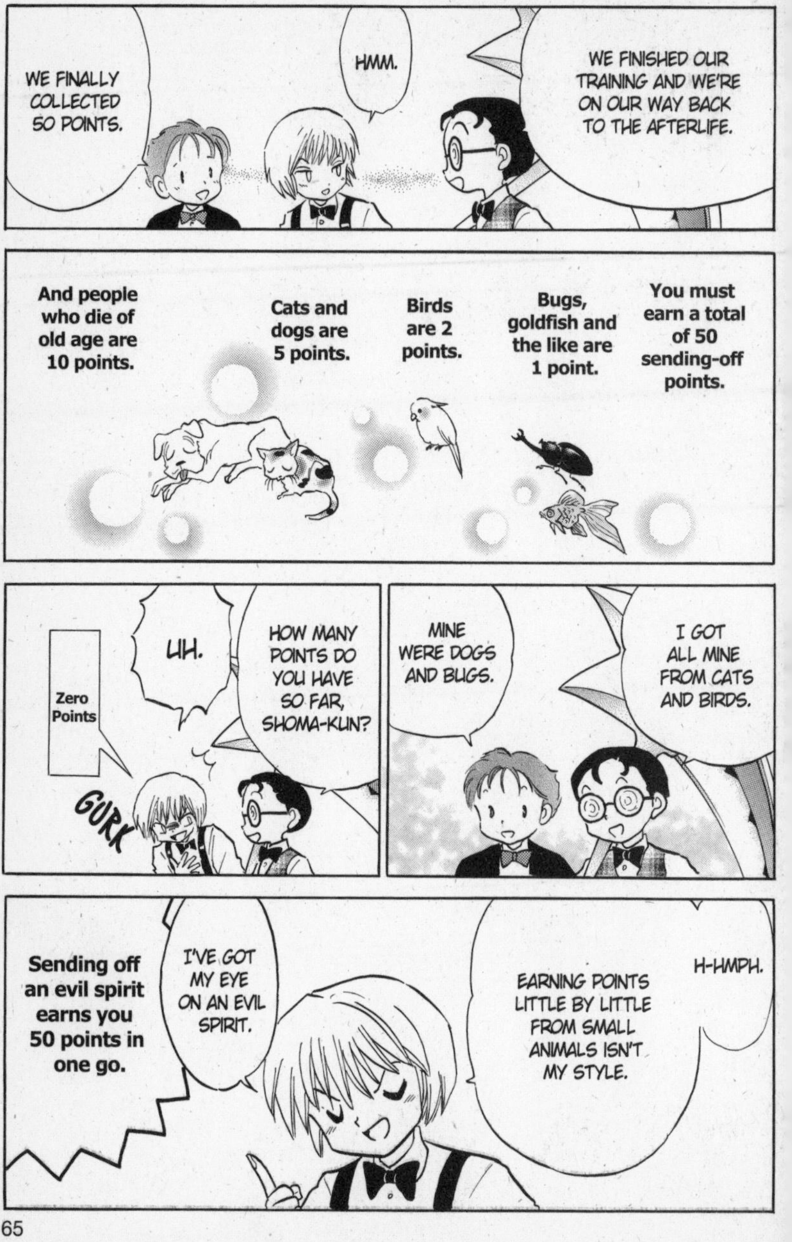
WE FINISHED OUR TRAINING AND WE'RE ON OUR WAY BACK TO THE AFTERLIFE.
HMM.
WE FINALLY COLLECTED 50 POINTS.
You must earn a total of 50 sending-off points.
Bugs, goldfish and the like are 1 point.
Birds are 2 points.
Cats and dogs are 5 points.
And people who die of old age are 10 points.
I GOT ALL MINE FROM CATS AND BIRDS.
MINE WERE DOGS AND BUGS.
HOW MANY POINTS DO YOU HAVE SO FAR, SHOMA-KUN?
UH.
Zero Points
GURK
H-HMPH.
EARNING POINTS LITTLE BY LITTLE FROM SMALL ANIMALS ISN'T MY STYLE.
I'VE GOT MY EYE ON AN EVIL SPIRIT.
Sending off an evil spirit earns you 50 points in one go.

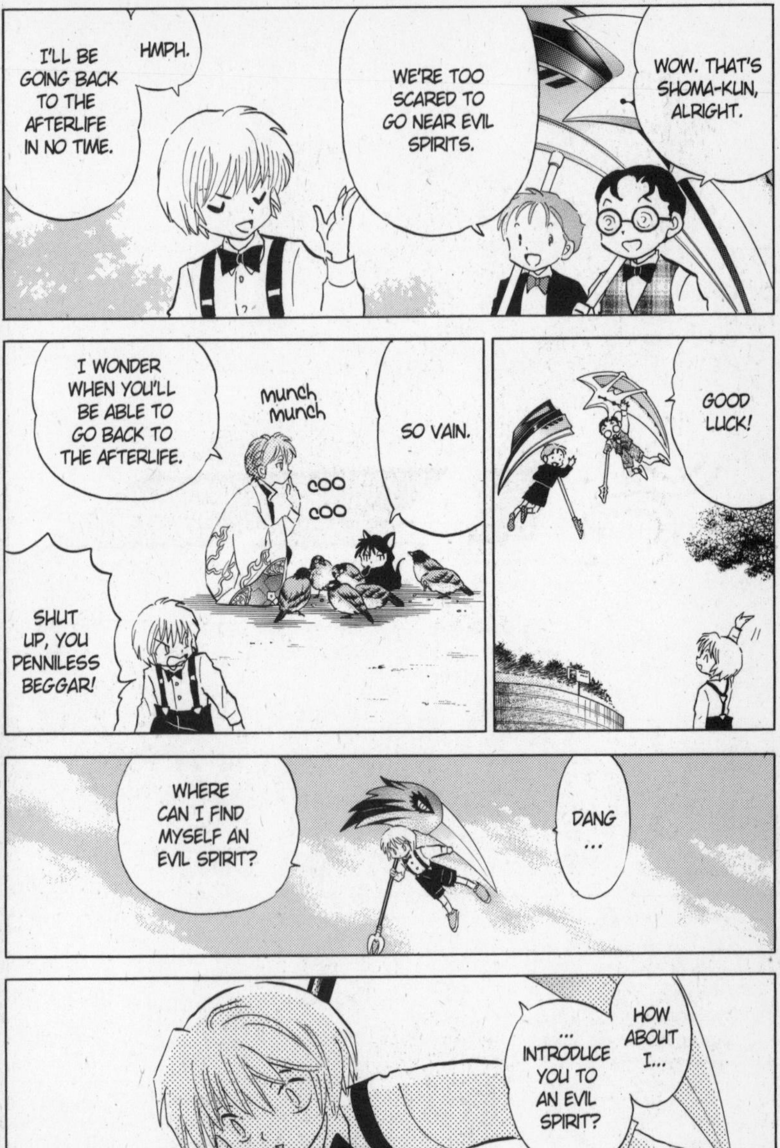
WOW. THAT'S SHOMA-KUN, ALRIGHT.
WE'RE TOO SCARED TO GO NEAR EVIL SPIRITS.
HMPH.
I'LL BE GOING BACK TO THE AFTERLIFE IN NO TIME.
GOOD LUCK!
SO VAIN.
munch munch
COO COO
I WONDER WHEN YOU'LL BE ABLE TO GO BACK TO THE AFTERLIFE.
SHUT UP, YOU PENNILESS BEGGAR!
DANG ...
WHERE CAN I FIND MYSELF AN EVIL SPIRIT?
HOW ABOUT I...
... INTRODUCE YOU TO AN EVIL SPIRIT?

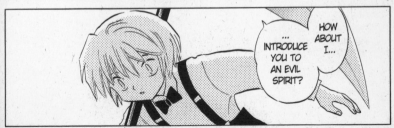

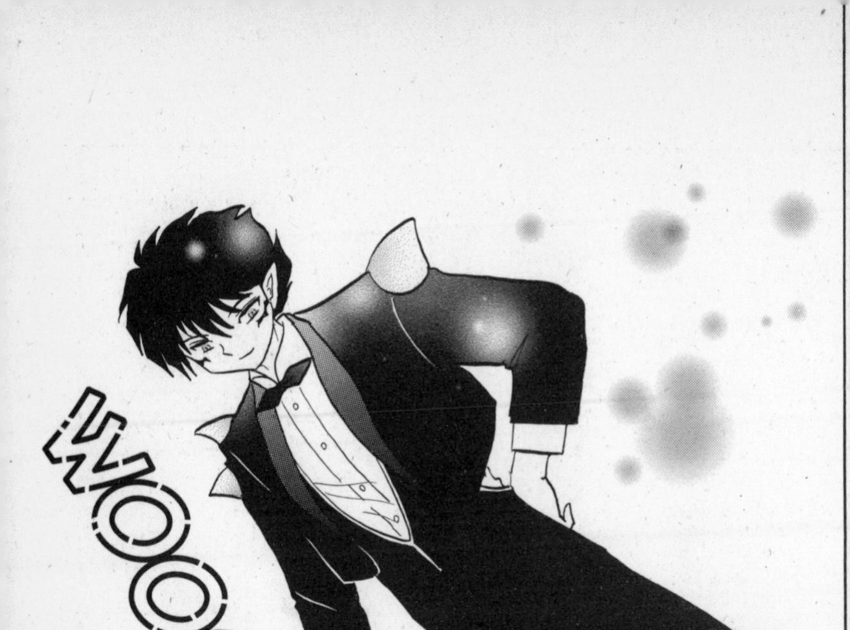
WOOOO

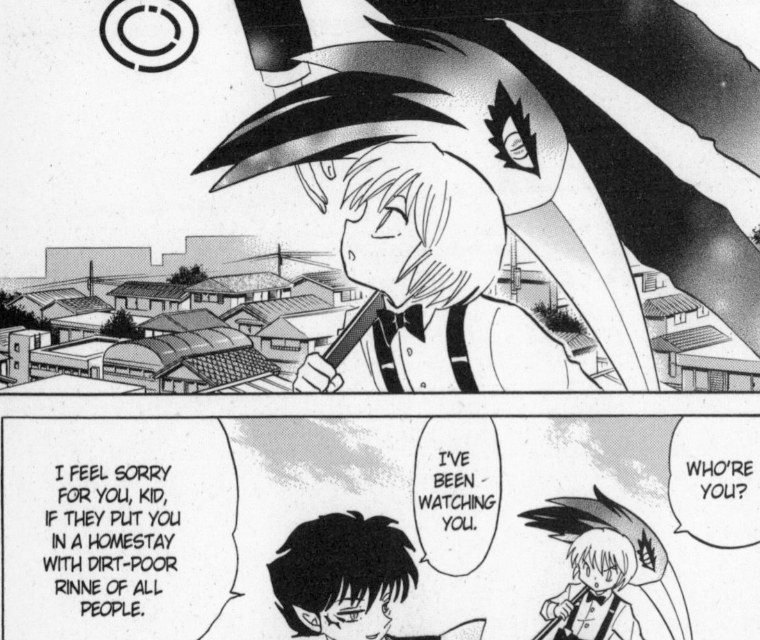
WHO'RE YOU?
I'VE BEEN WATCHING YOU.
I FEEL SORRY FOR YOU, KID, IF THEY PUT YOU IN A HOMESTAY WITH DIRT-POOR RINNE OF ALL PEOPLE.

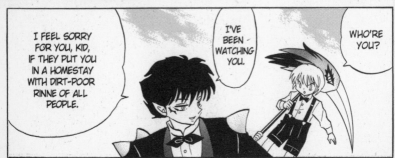

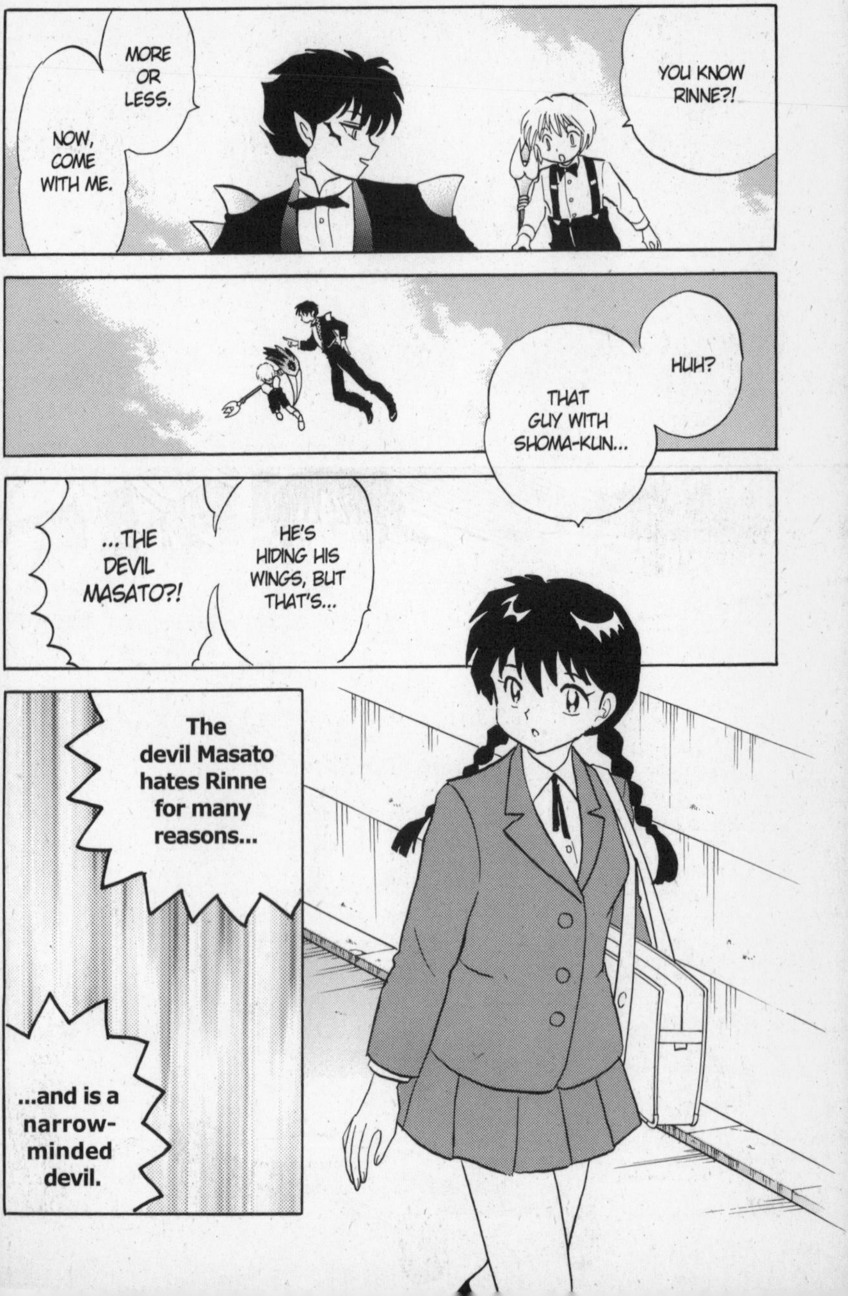
YOU KNOW RINNE?!
MORE OR LESS.
NOW, COME WITH ME.
HUH?
THAT GUY WITH SHOMA-KUN...
HE'S HIDING HIS WINGS, BUT THAT'S...
...THE DEVIL MASATO?!
The devil Masato hates Rinne for many reasons...
...and is a narrow-minded devil.

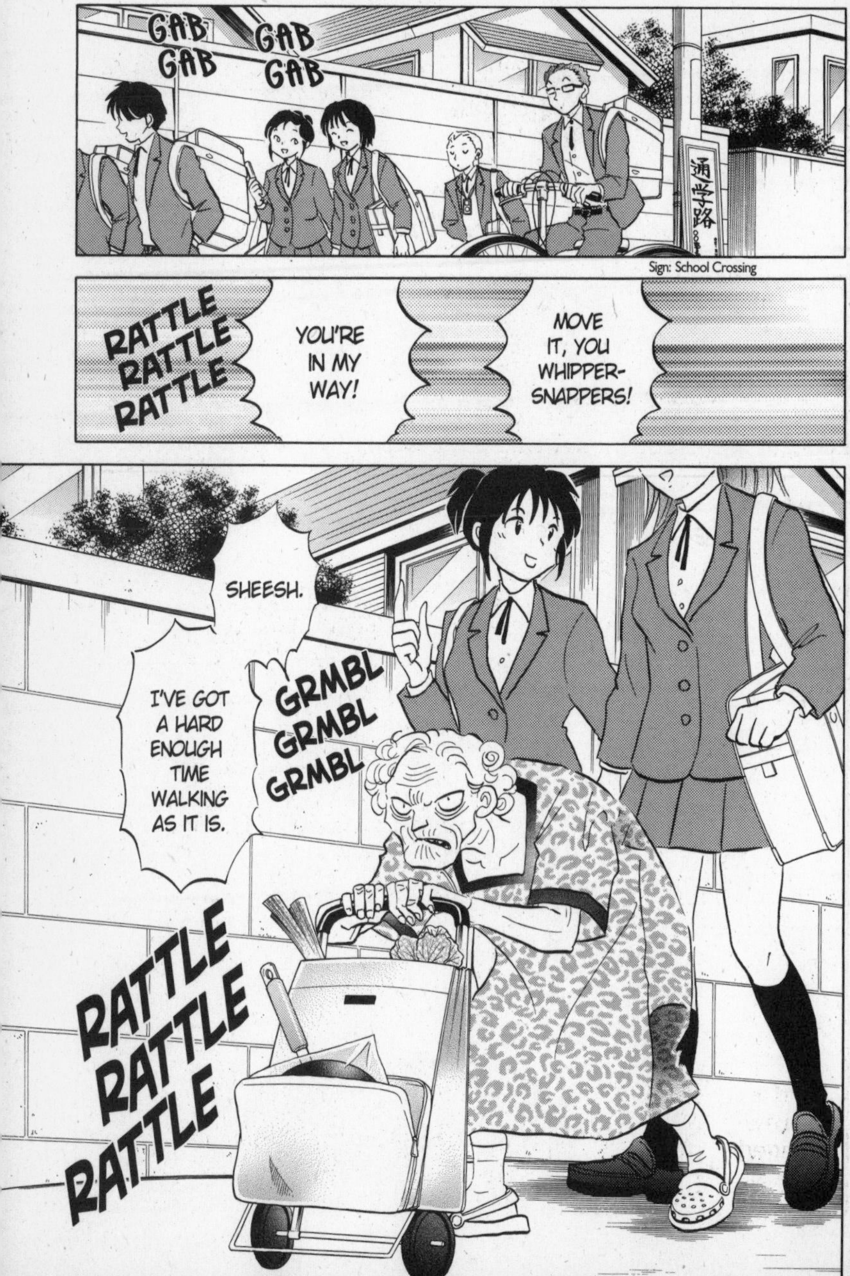
GAB GAB
GAB GAB
通学路
MOVE IT, YOU WHIPPER-SNAPPERS!
YOU'RE IN MY WAY!
RATTLE RATTLE RATTLE
SHEESH.
GRMBL GRMBL GRMBL
I'VE GOT A HARD ENOUGH TIME WALKING AS IT IS.
RATTLE RATTLE RATTLE
Sign: School Crossing

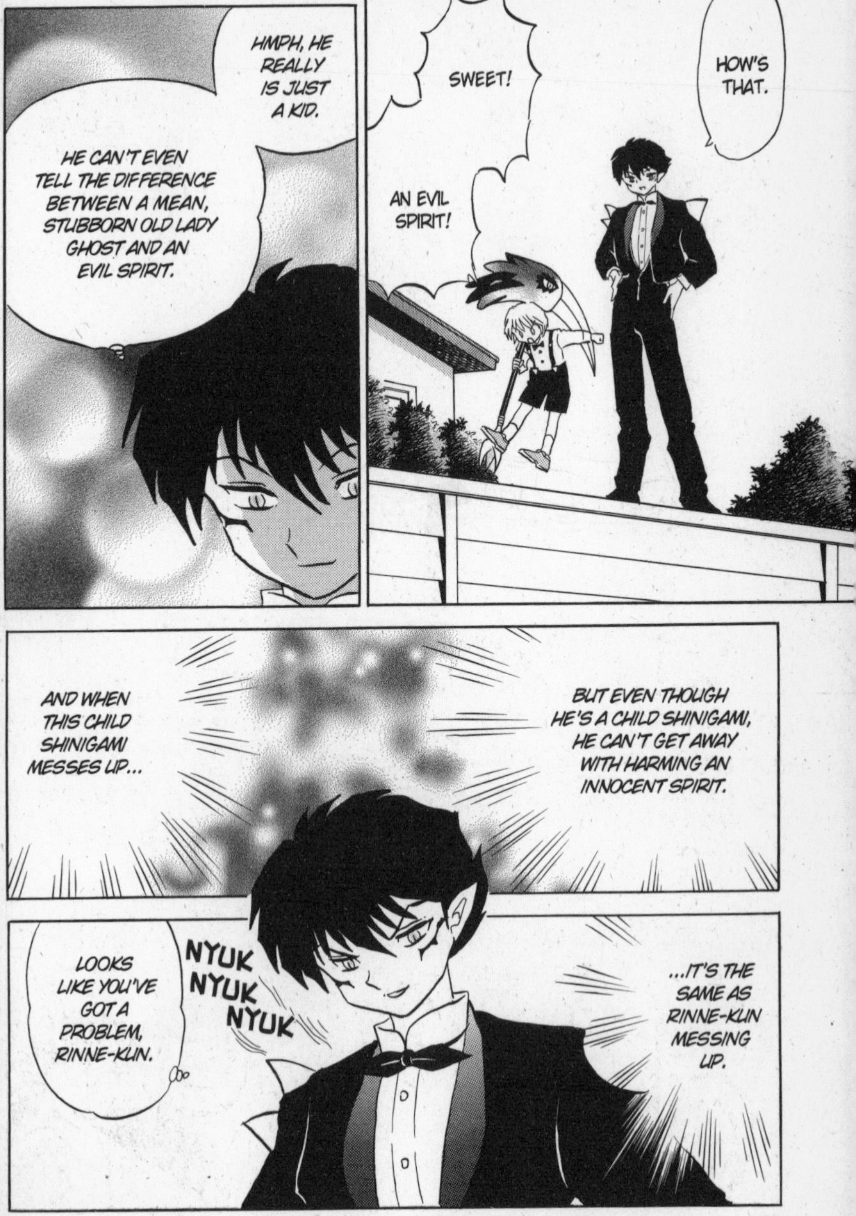
HOW'S THAT.
SWEET!
AN EVIL SPIRIT!
HMPH, HE REALLY IS JUST A KID.
HE CAN'T EVEN TELL THE DIFFERENCE BETWEEN A MEAN, STUBBORN OLD LADY GHOST AND AN EVIL SPIRIT.
BUT EVEN THOUGH HE'S A CHILD SHINIGAMI, HE CAN'T GET AWAY WITH HARMING AN INNOCENT SPIRIT.
AND WHEN THIS CHILD SHINIGAMI MESSES UP...
...IT'S THE SAME AS RINNE-KUN MESSING UP.
NYUK NYUK NYUK
LOOKS LIKE YOU'VE GOT A PROBLEM, RINNE-KUN.

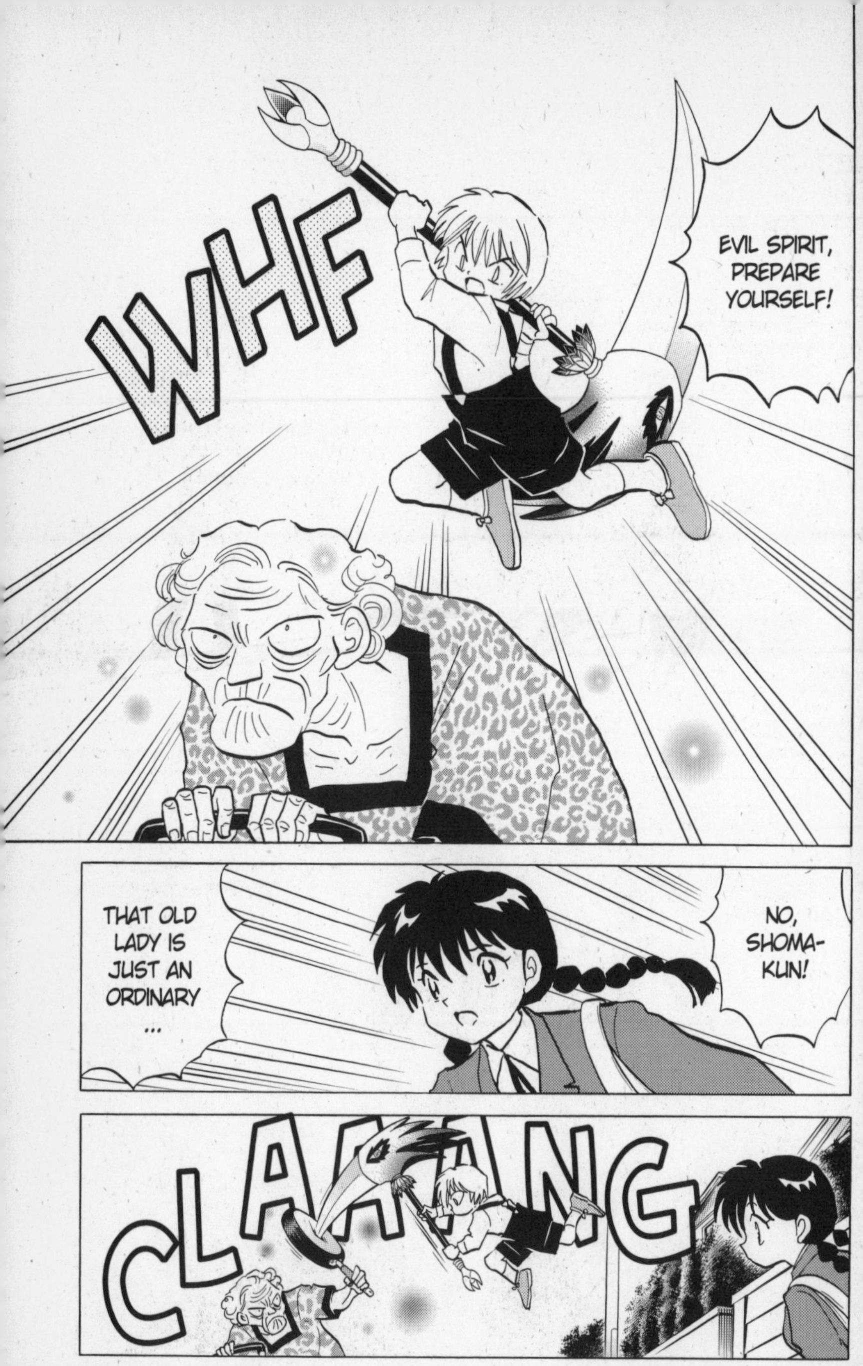
WHF
EVIL SPIRIT, PREPARE YOURSELF!
NO, SHOMA-KUN!
THAT OLD LADY IS JUST AN ORDINARY ...
CLAAANG

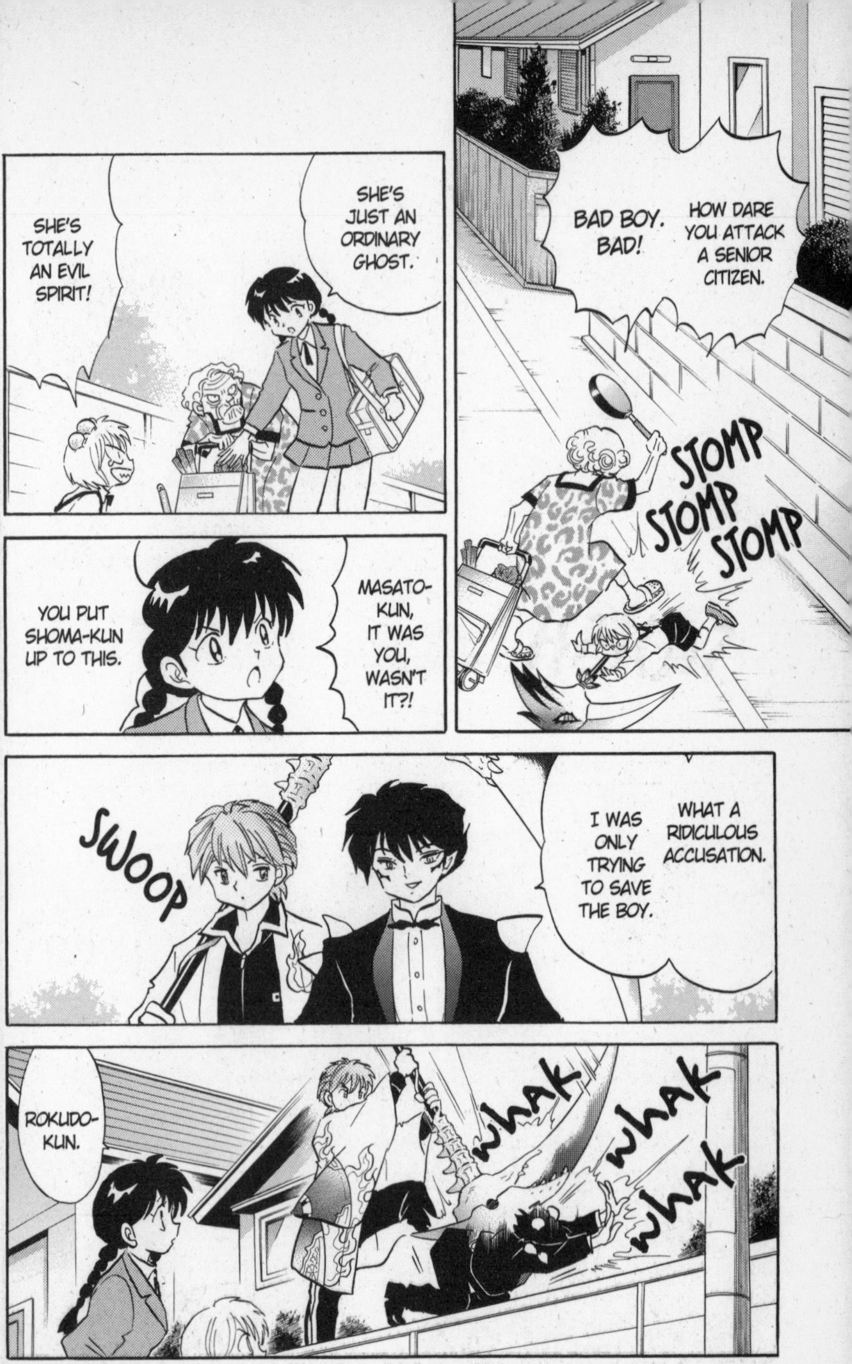
HOW DARE YOU ATTACK A SENIOR CITIZEN.
BAD BOY. BAD!
STOMP STOMP STOMP
SHE'S JUST AN ORDINARY GHOST.
SHE'S TOTALLY AN EVIL SPIRIT!
MASATO-KUN, IT WAS YOU, WASN'T IT?!
YOU PUT SHOMA-KUN UP TO THIS.
WHAT A RIDICULOUS ACCUSATION.
I WAS ONLY TRYING TO SAVE THE BOY.
SWOOP
whak whak whak
ROKUDO-KUN.

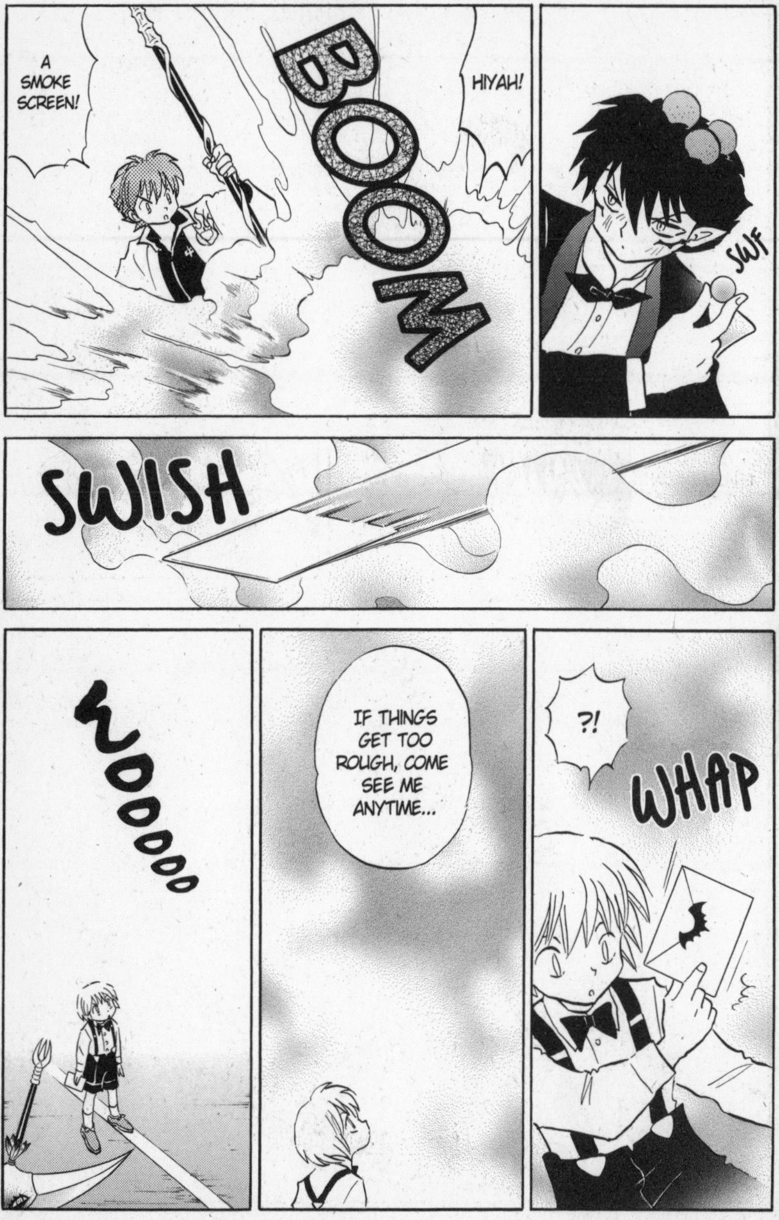
SWF
HIYAH!
BOOM
A SMOKE SCREEN!
SWISH
?!
WHAP
IF THINGS GET TOO ROUGH, COME SEE ME ANYTIME...
WOOOOOO

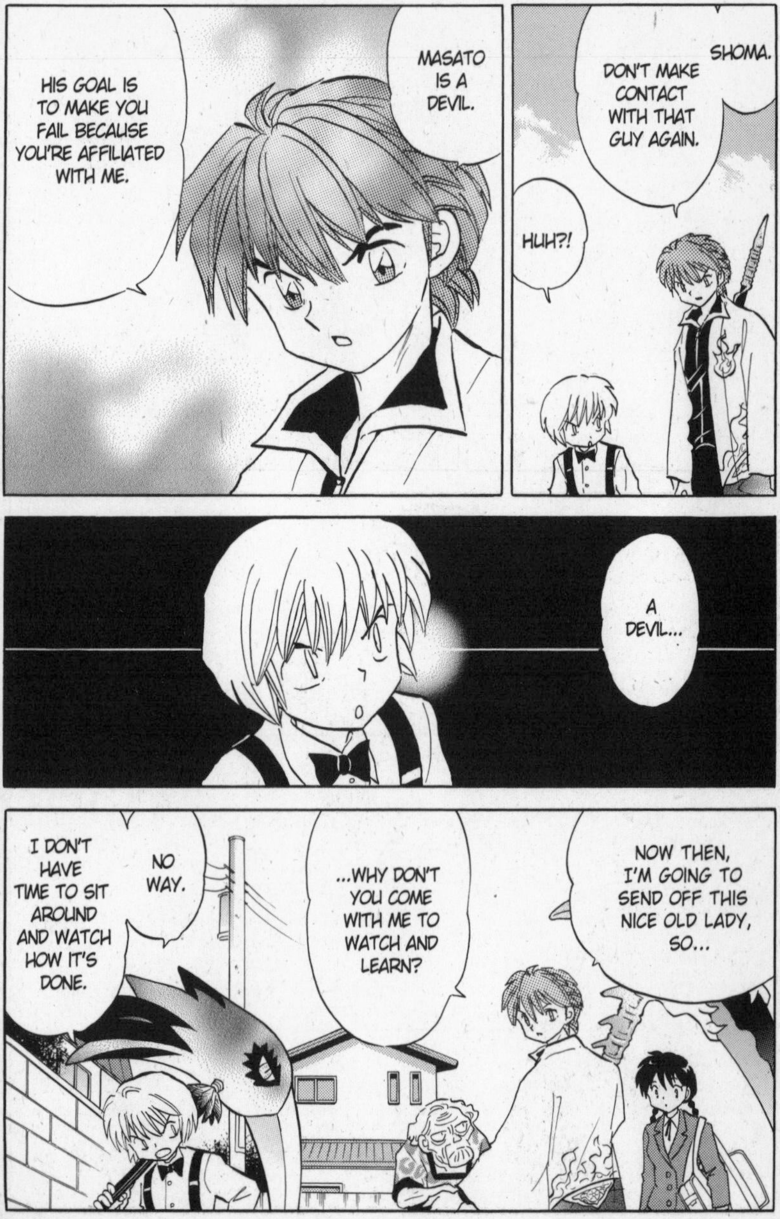
SHOMA.
DON'T MAKE CONTACT WITH THAT GUY AGAIN.
HUH?!
MASATO IS A DEVIL.
HIS GOAL IS TO MAKE YOU FAIL BECAUSE YOU'RE AFFILIATED WITH ME.
A DEVIL...
NOW THEN, I'M GOING TO SEND OFF THIS NICE OLD LADY, SO...
...WHY DON'T YOU COME WITH ME TO WATCH AND LEARN?
NO WAY.
I DON'T HAVE TIME TO SIT AROUND AND WATCH HOW IT'S DONE.

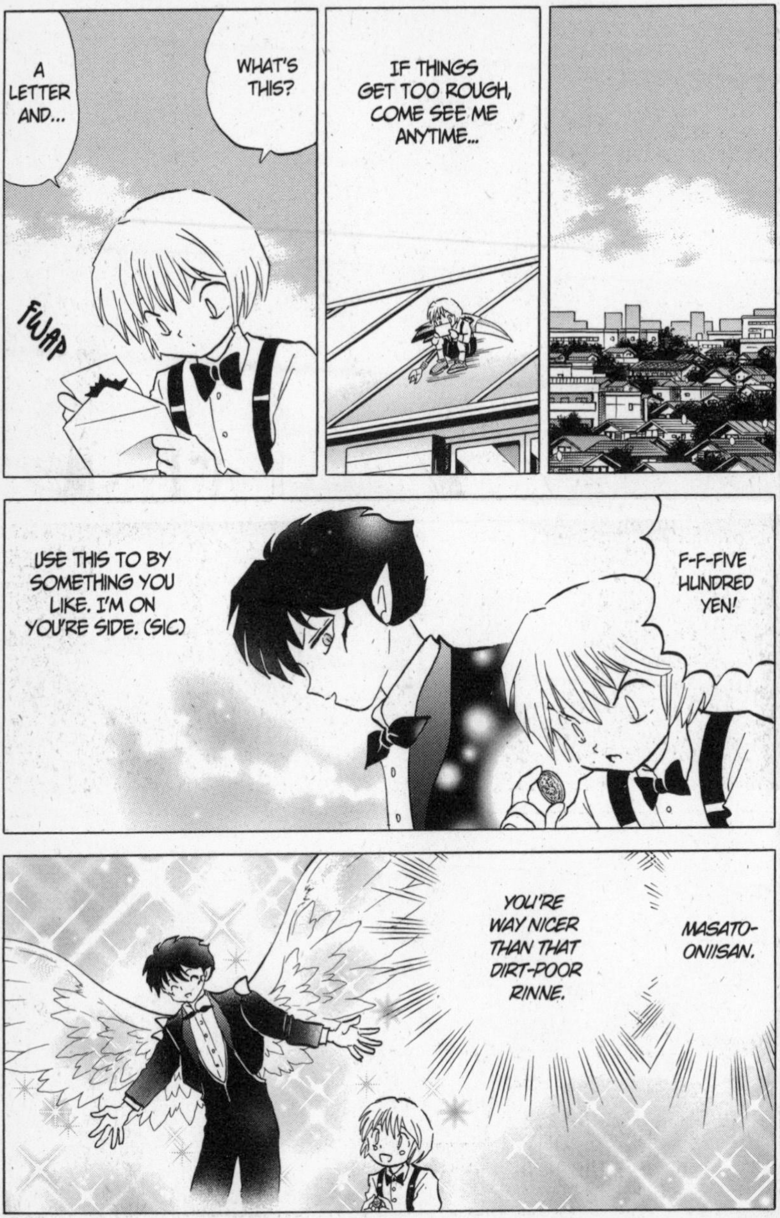
IF THINGS GET TOO ROUGH, COME SEE ME ANYTIME...
WHAT'S THIS?
A LETTER AND...
FWAP
F-F-FIVE HUNDRED YEN!
USE THIS TO BY SOMETHING YOU LIKE. I'M ON YOU'RE SIDE. (SIC)
MASATO-ONIISAN.
YOU'RE WAY NICER THAN THAT DIRT-POOR RINNE.

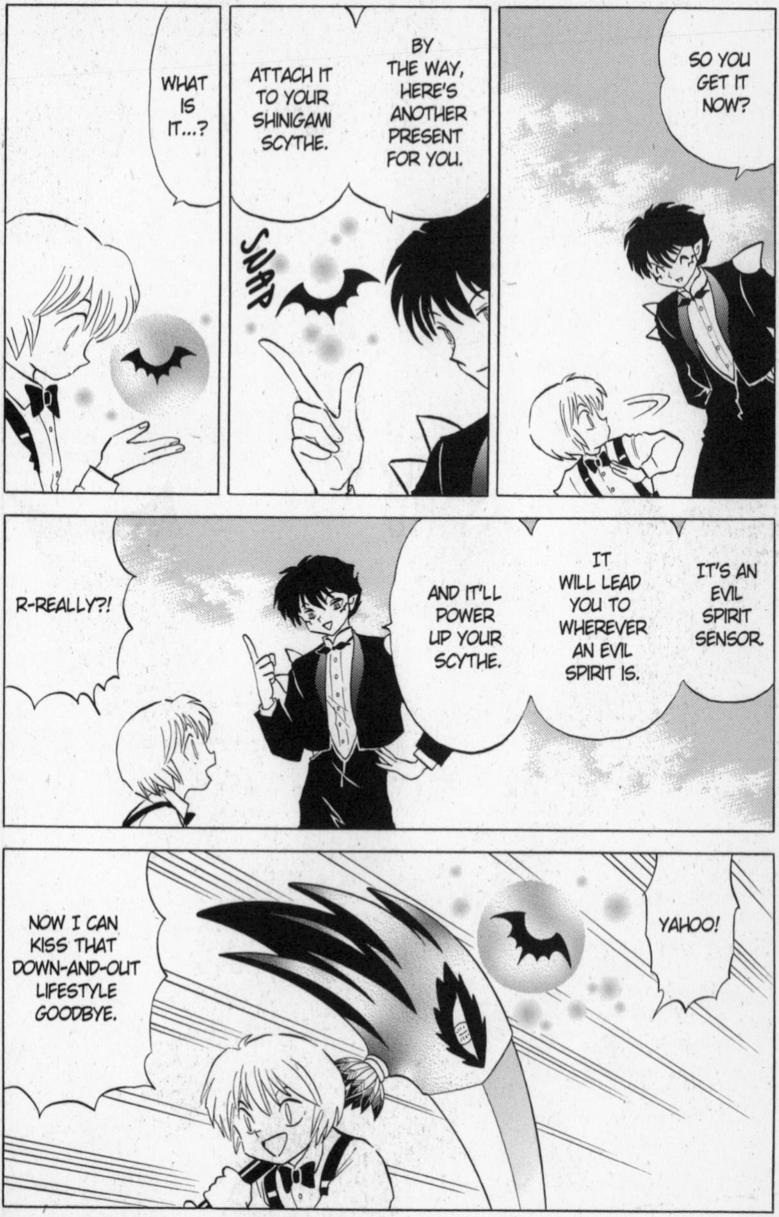
SO YOU GET IT NOW?
BY THE WAY, HERE'S ANOTHER PRESENT FOR YOU.
ATTACH IT TO YOUR SHINIGAMI SCYTHE.
SNAP
WHAT IS IT...?
IT'S AN EVIL SPIRIT SENSOR.
IT WILL LEAD YOU TO WHEREVER AN EVIL SPIRIT IS.
AND IT'LL POWER UP YOUR SCYTHE.
R-REALLY?!
YAHOO!
NOW I CAN KISS THAT DOWN-AND-OUT LIFESTYLE GOODBYE.

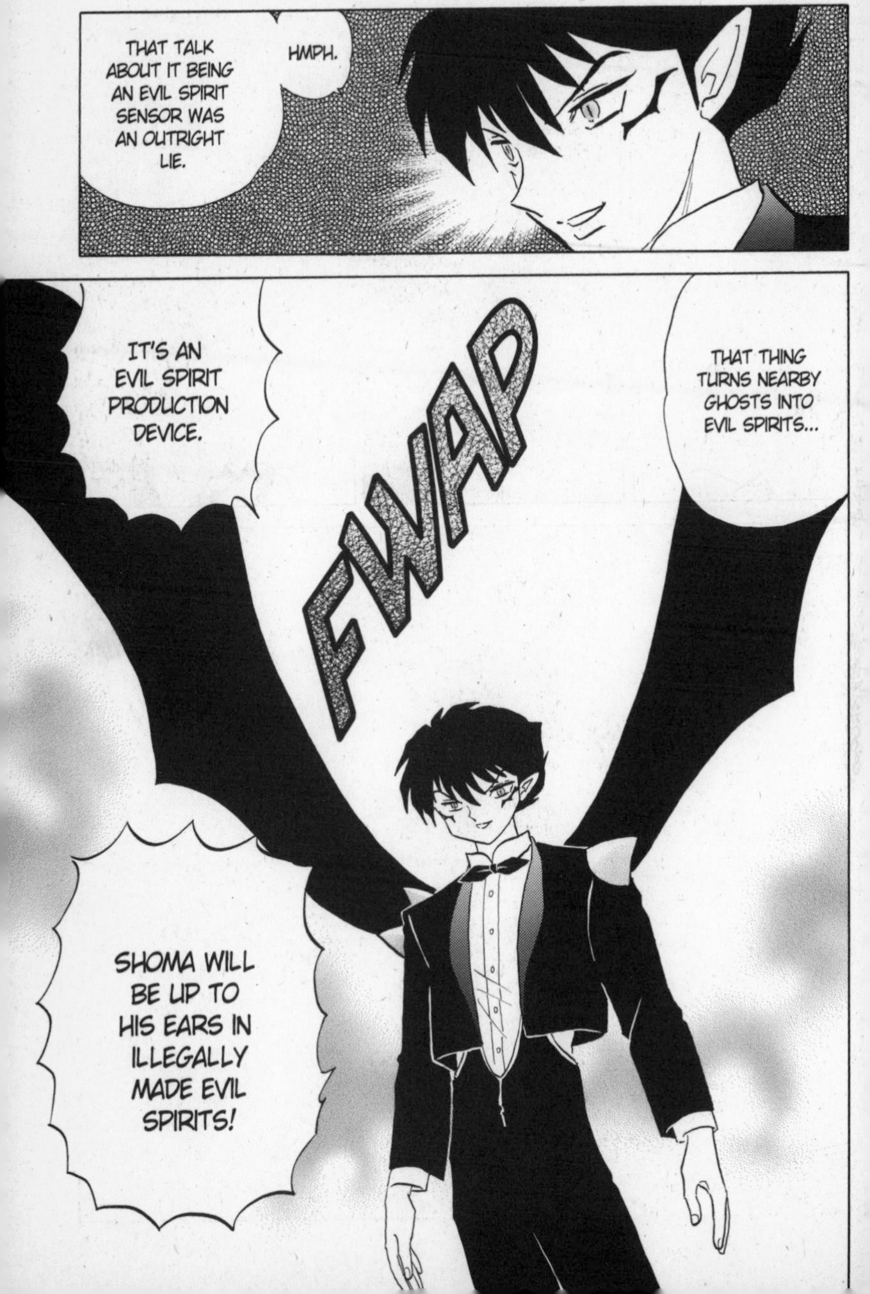
HMPH.
THAT TALK ABOUT IT BEING AN EVIL SPIRIT SENSOR WAS AN OUTRIGHT LIE.
THAT THING TURNS NEARBY GHOSTS INTO EVIL SPIRITS...
IT'S AN EVIL SPIRIT PRODUCTION DEVICE.
FWAP
SHOMA WILL BE UP TO HIS EARS IN ILLEGALLY MADE EVIL SPIRITS!

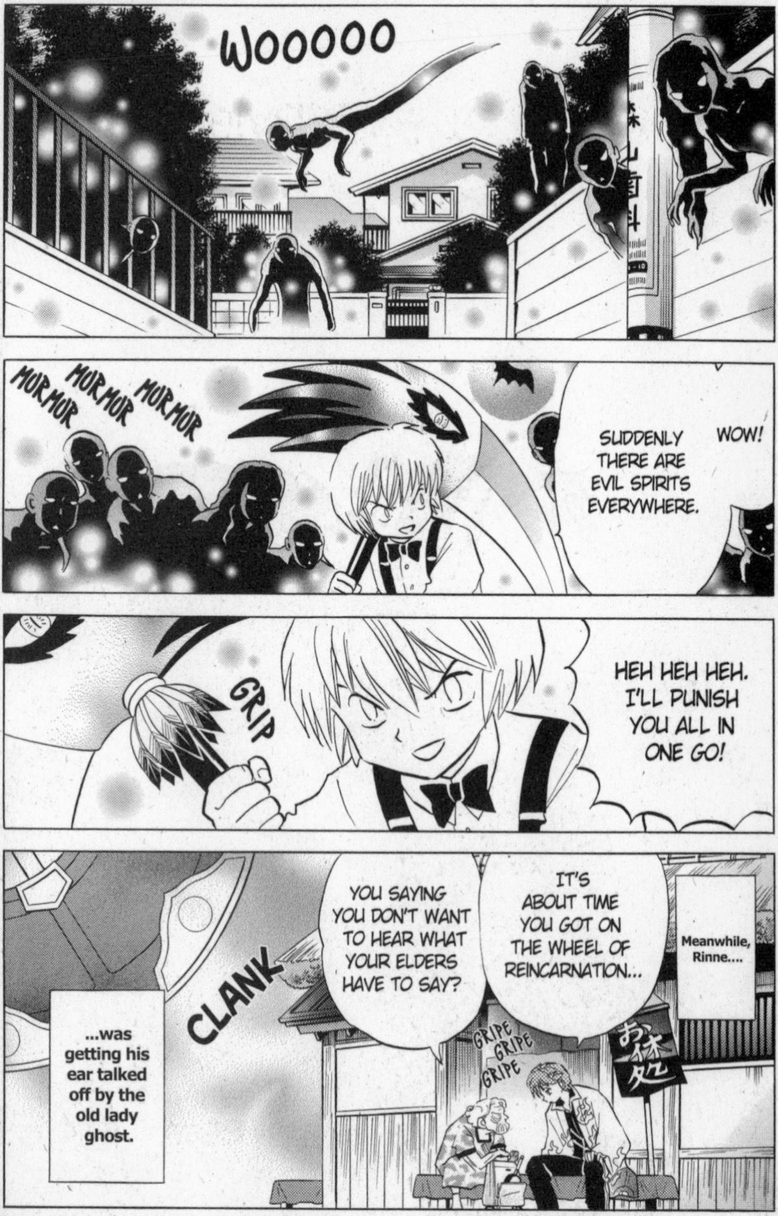
WOOOOO
WOW!
SUDDENLY THERE ARE EVIL SPIRITS EVERYWHERE.
MORMOR MORMOR MORMOR
HEH HEH HEH. I'LL PUNISH YOU ALL IN ONE GO!
GRIP
Meanwhile, Rinne....
IT'S ABOUT TIME YOU GOT ON THE WHEEL OF REINCARNATION...
YOU SAYING YOU DON'T WANT TO HEAR WHAT YOUR ELDERS HAVE TO SAY?
CLANK
GRIPE GRIPE GRIPE
お休処
...was getting his ear talked off by the old lady ghost.

CHAPTER 73: SUPERVISORY LIABILITY

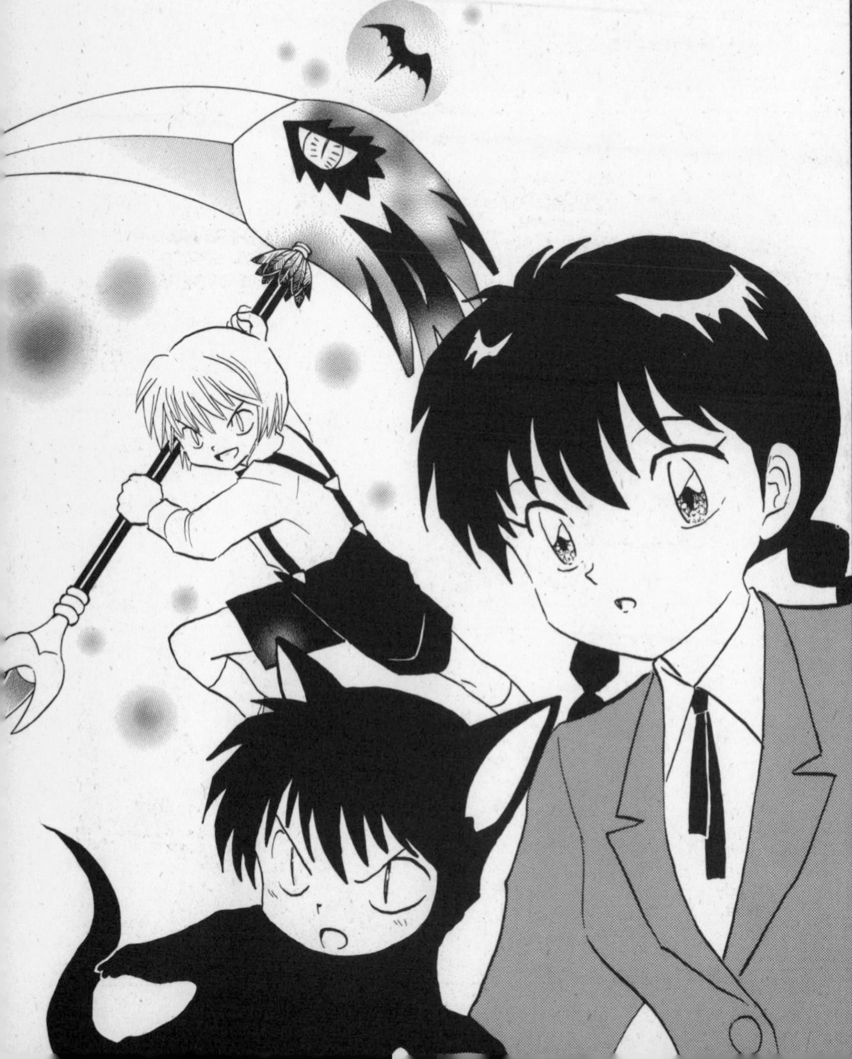

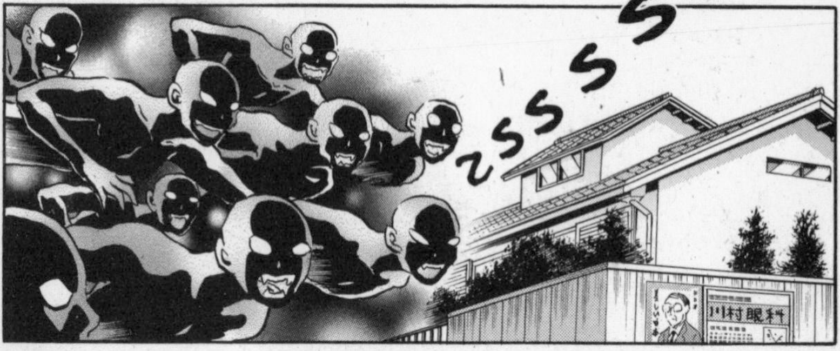
ZSSSSS
川村眼科

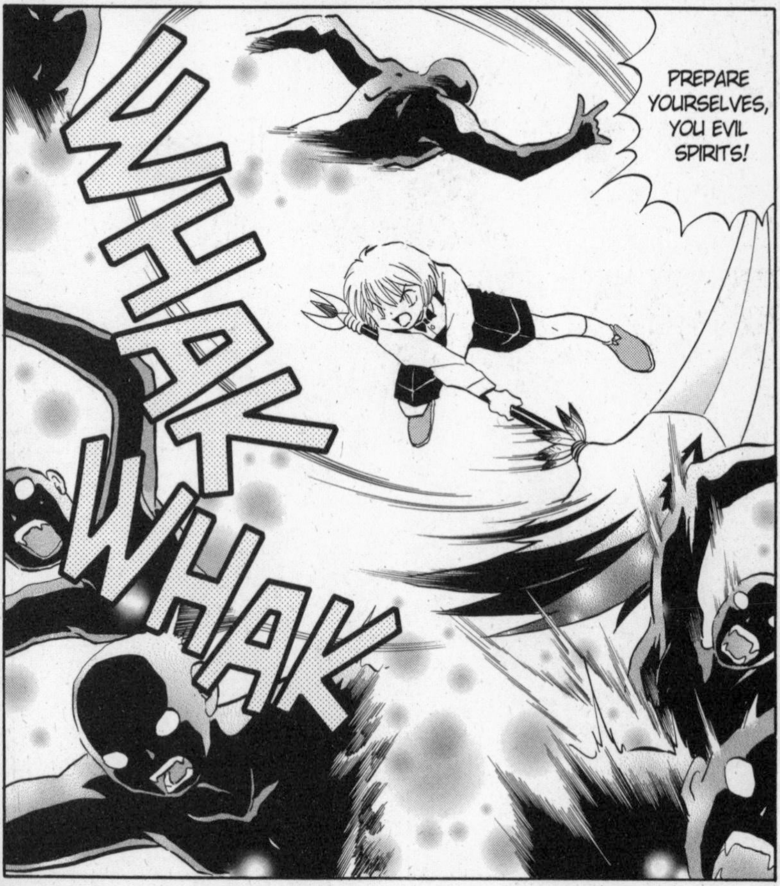
PREPARE YOURSELVES, YOU EVIL SPIRITS!
WHAK WHAK

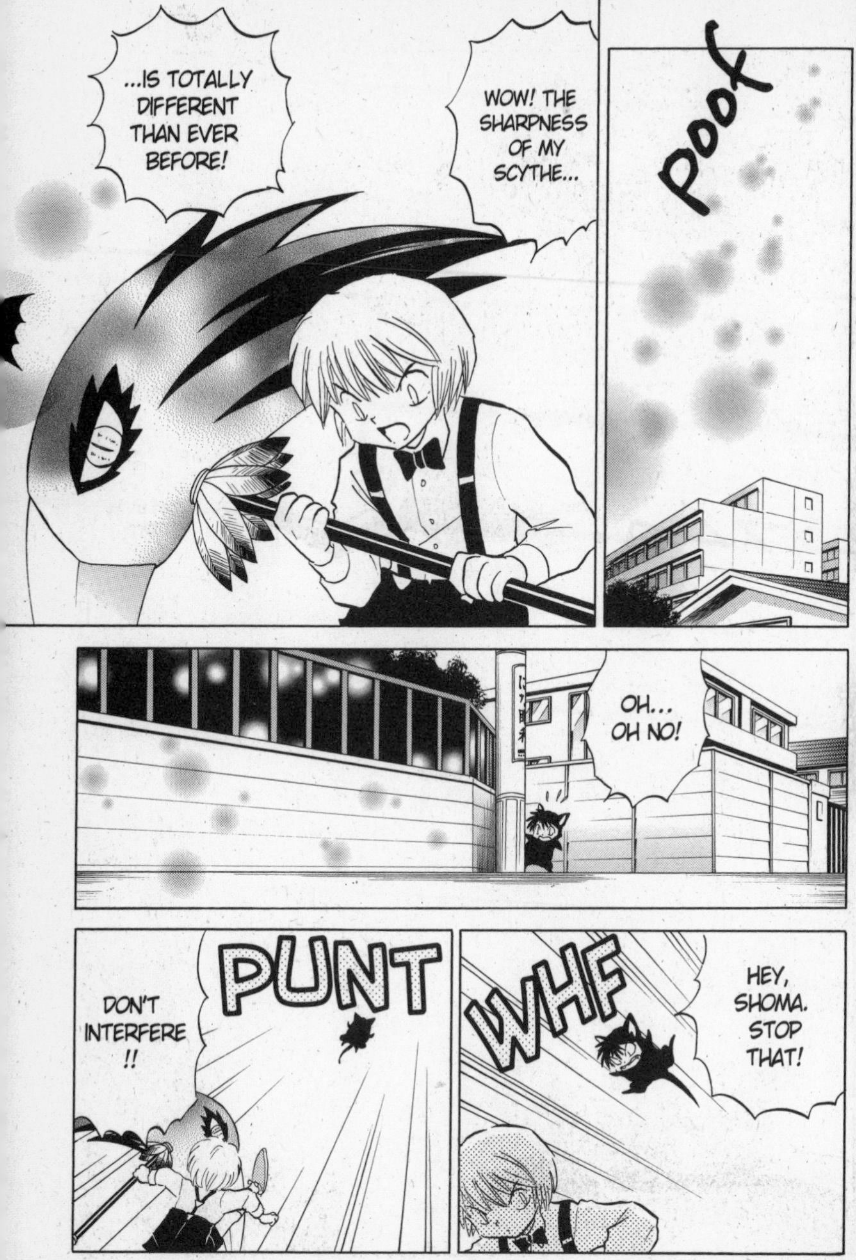
POOF
WOW! THE SHARPNESS OF MY SCYTHE...
...IS TOTALLY DIFFERENT THAN EVER BEFORE!
OH... OH NO!
WHF
HEY, SHOMA. STOP THAT!
PUNT
DON'T INTERFERE !!

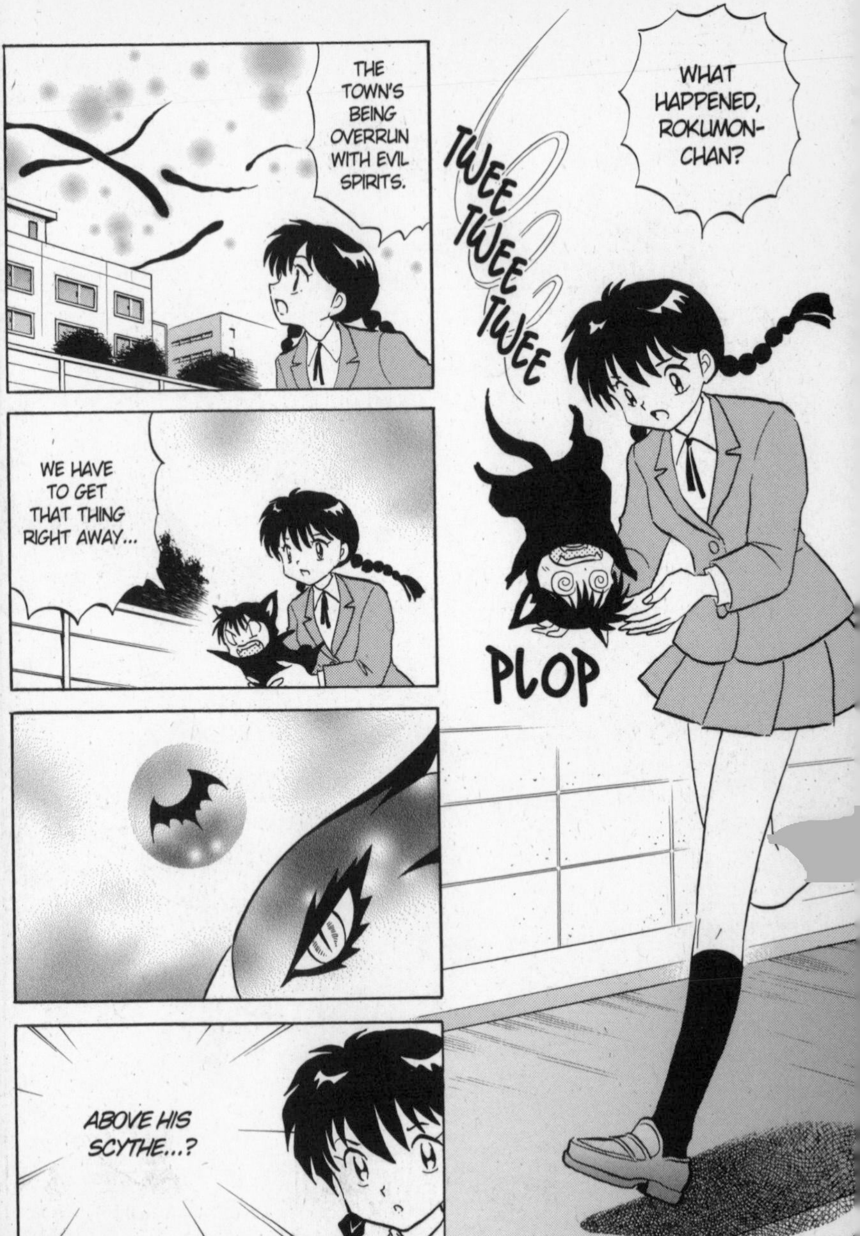
WHAT HAPPENED, ROKUMON-CHAN?
TWEE TWEE TWEE
PLOP
THE TOWN'S BEING OVERRUN WITH EVIL SPIRITS.
WE HAVE TO GET THAT THING RIGHT AWAY...
ABOVE HIS SCYTHE...?

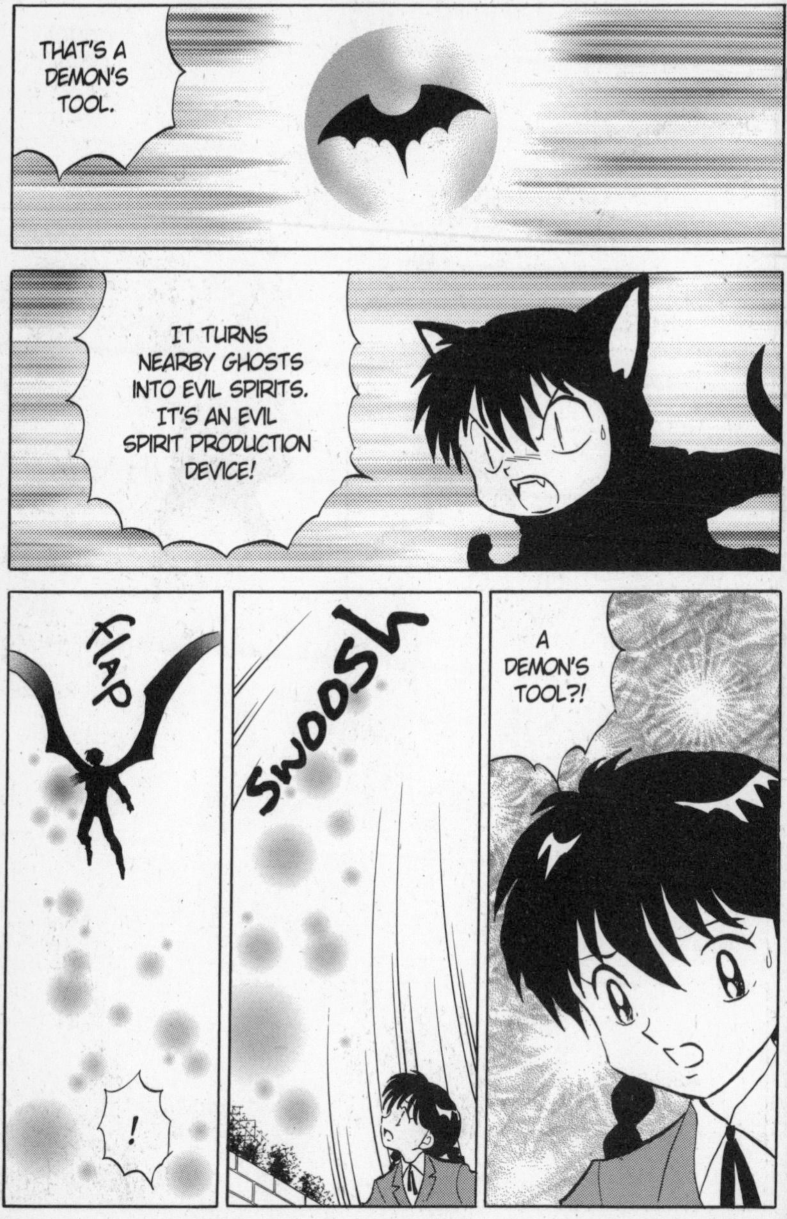
THAT'S A DEMON'S TOOL.
IT TURNS NEARBY GHOSTS INTO EVIL SPIRITS. IT'S AN EVIL SPIRIT PRODUCTION DEVICE!
A DEMON'S TOOL?!
SWOOSH
FLAP
!

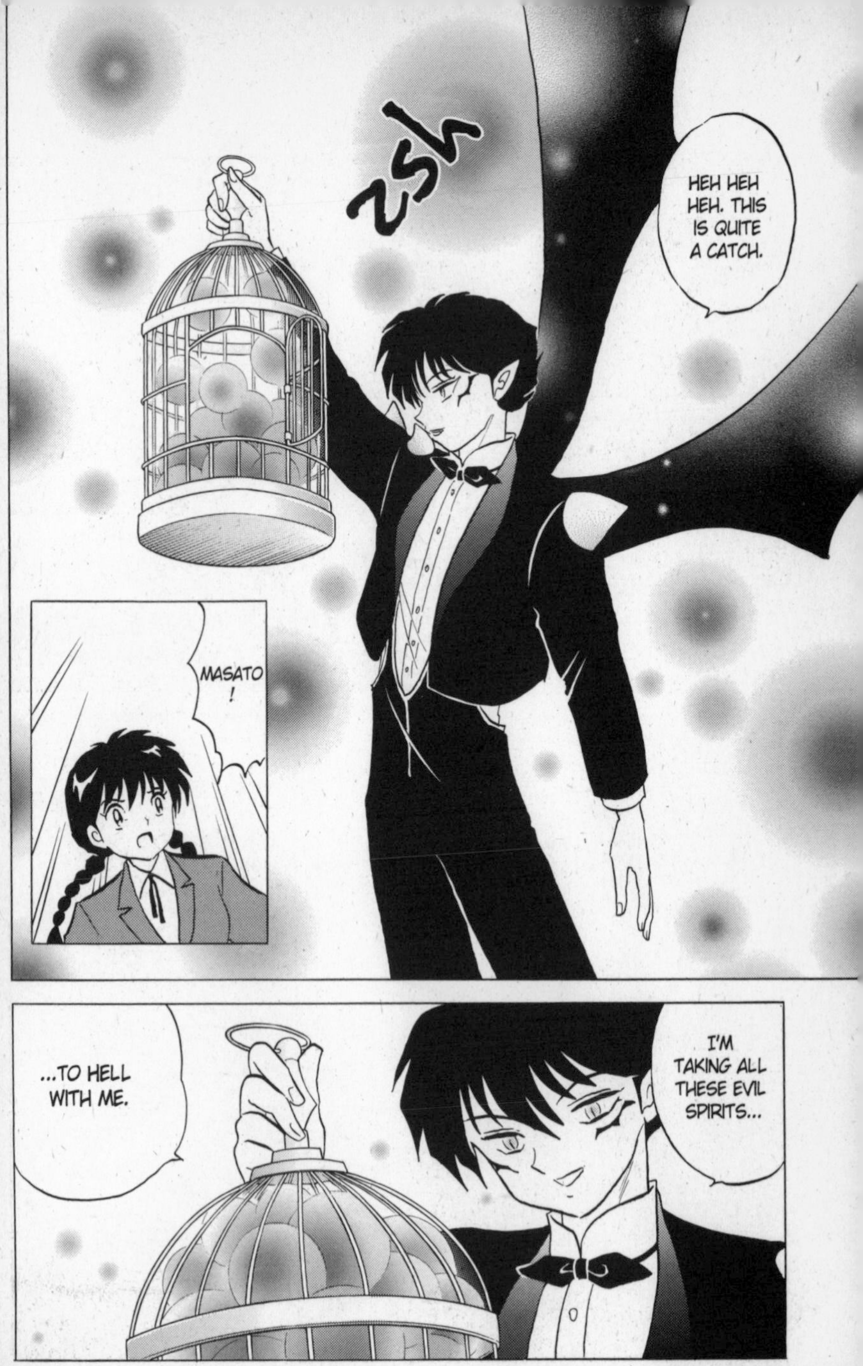
zsh
HEH HEH HEH. THIS IS QUITE A CATCH.
MASATO!
I'M TAKING ALL THESE EVIL SPIRITS...
...TO HELL WITH ME.

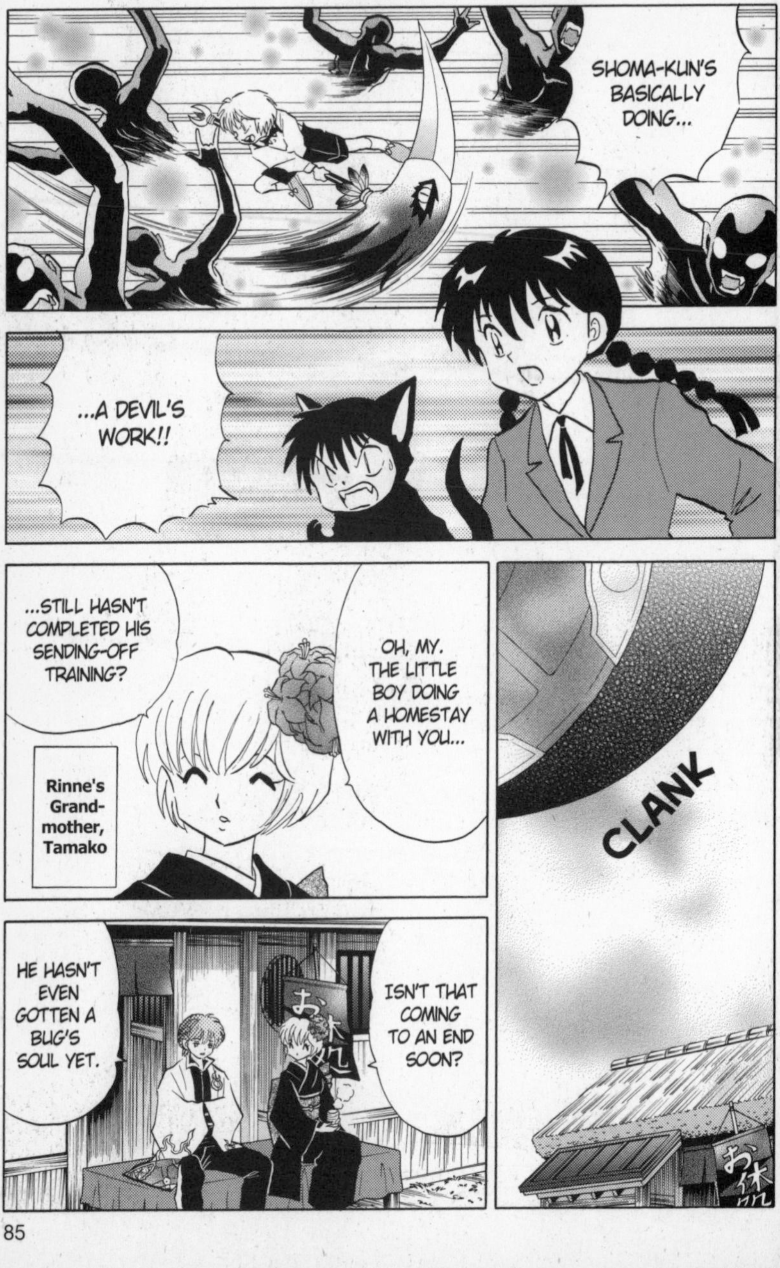
SHOMA-KUN'S BASICALLY DOING...
...A DEVIL'S WORK!!
CLANK
OH, MY. THE LITTLE BOY DOING A HOMESTAY WITH YOU...
...STILL HASN'T COMPLETED HIS SENDING-OFF TRAINING?
Rinne's Grand-mother, Tamako
ISN'T THAT COMING TO AN END SOON?
HE HASN'T EVEN GOTTEN A BUG'S SOUL YET.

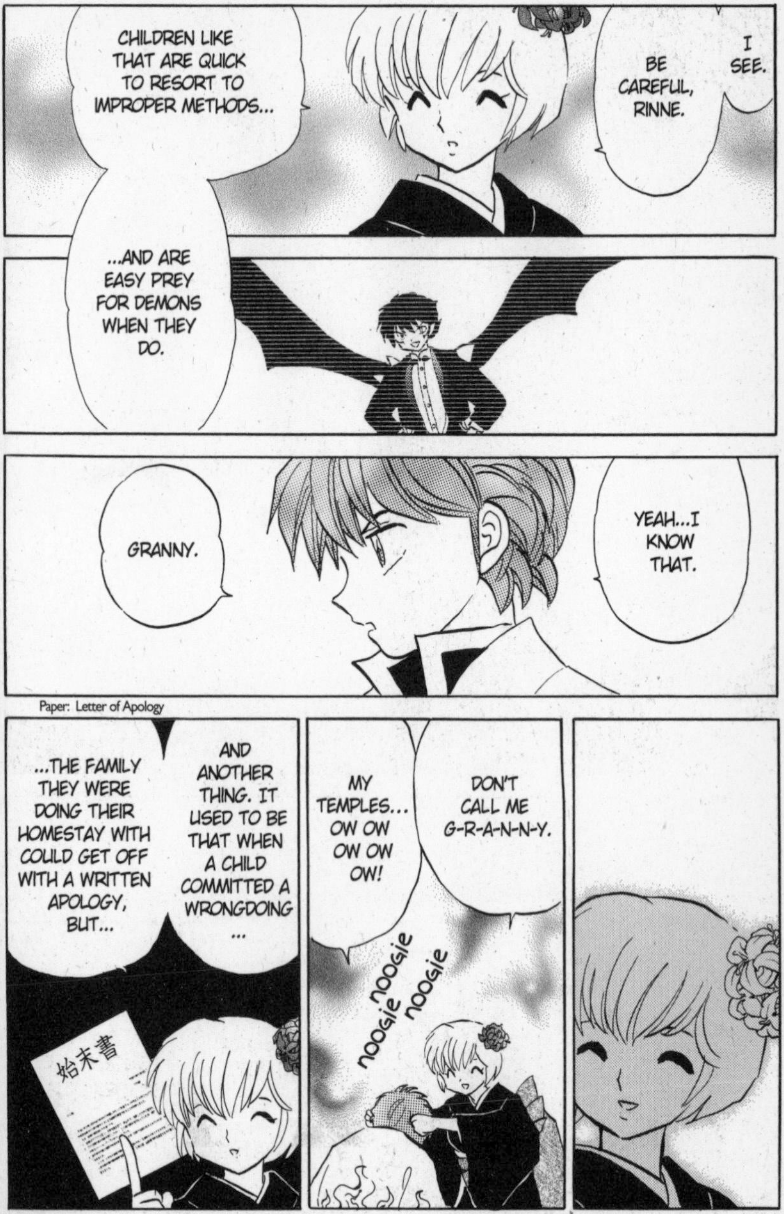
I SEE.
BE CAREFUL, RINNE.
CHILDREN LIKE THAT ARE QUICK TO RESORT TO IMPROPER METHODS...
...AND ARE EASY PREY FOR DEMONS WHEN THEY DO.
YEAH...I KNOW THAT.
GRANNY.
DON'T CALL ME G-R-A-N-N-Y.
MY TEMPLES... OW OW OW OW OW!
NOOGIE NOOGIE NOOGIE
AND ANOTHER THING. IT USED TO BE THAT WHEN A CHILD COMMITTED A WRONGDOING...
...THE FAMILY THEY WERE DOING THEIR HOMESTAY WITH COULD GET OFF WITH A WRITTEN APOLOGY, BUT...
始末書
Paper: Letter of Apology

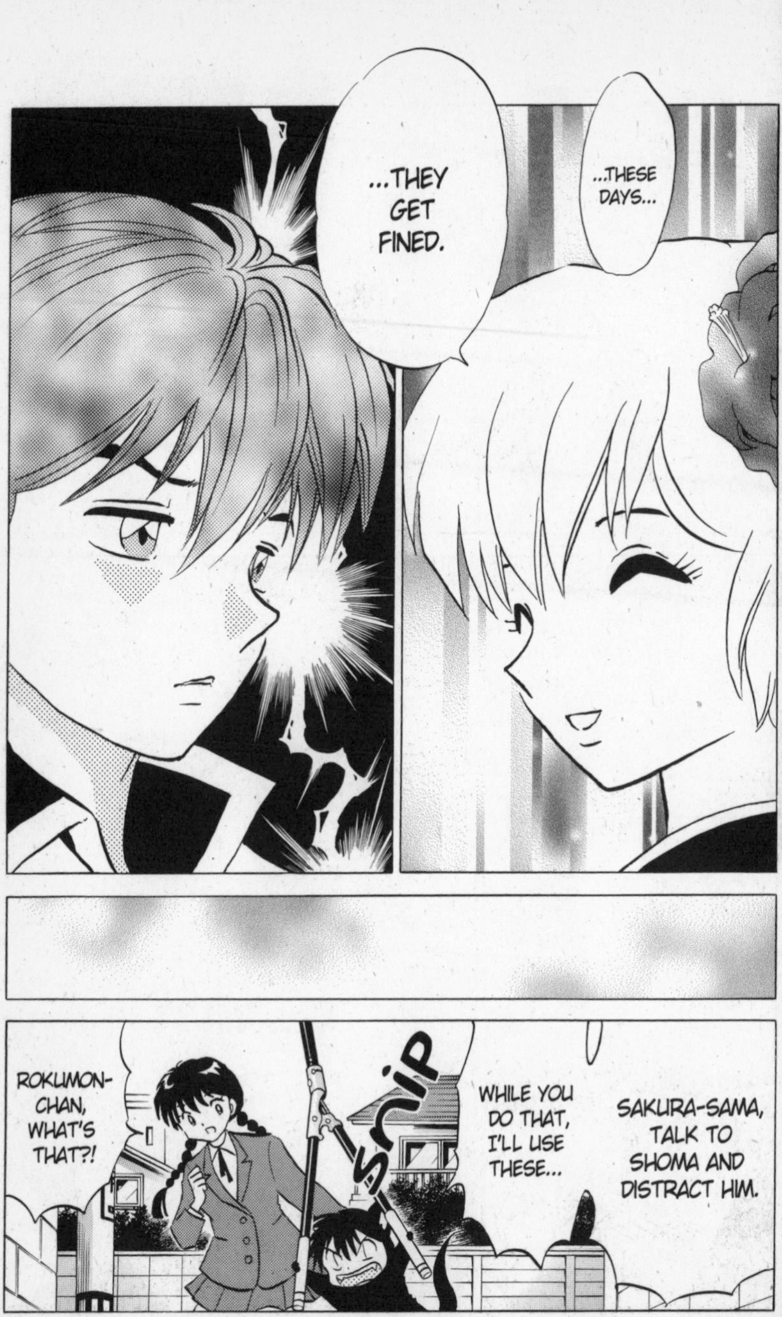
...THESE DAYS...
...THEY GET FINED.
SAKURA-SAMA, TALK TO SHOMA AND DISTRACT HIM.
WHILE YOU DO THAT, I'LL USE THESE...
SNIP
ROKUMON-CHAN, WHAT'S THAT?!

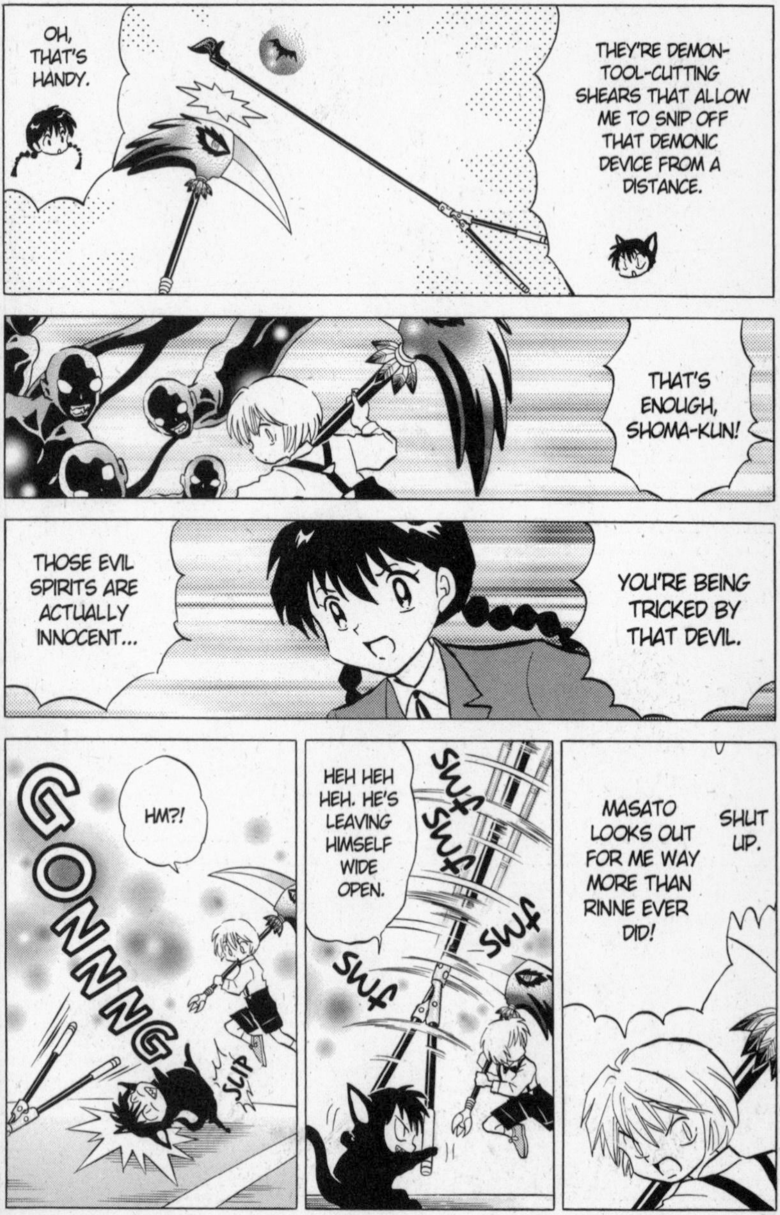
THEY'RE DEMON-TOOL-CUTTING SHEARS THAT ALLOW ME TO SNIP OFF THAT DEMONIC DEVICE FROM A DISTANCE.
OH, THAT'S HANDY.
THAT'S ENOUGH, SHOMA-KUN!
THOSE EVIL SPIRITS ARE ACTUALLY INNOCENT...
YOU'RE BEING TRICKED BY THAT DEVIL.
MASATO LOOKS OUT FOR ME WAY MORE THAN RINNE EVER DID!
SHUT UP.
SWF SWF
SWF
HEH HEH HEH. HE'S LEAVING HIMSELF WIDE OPEN.
SWF
HM?!
GONNNG
SLIP

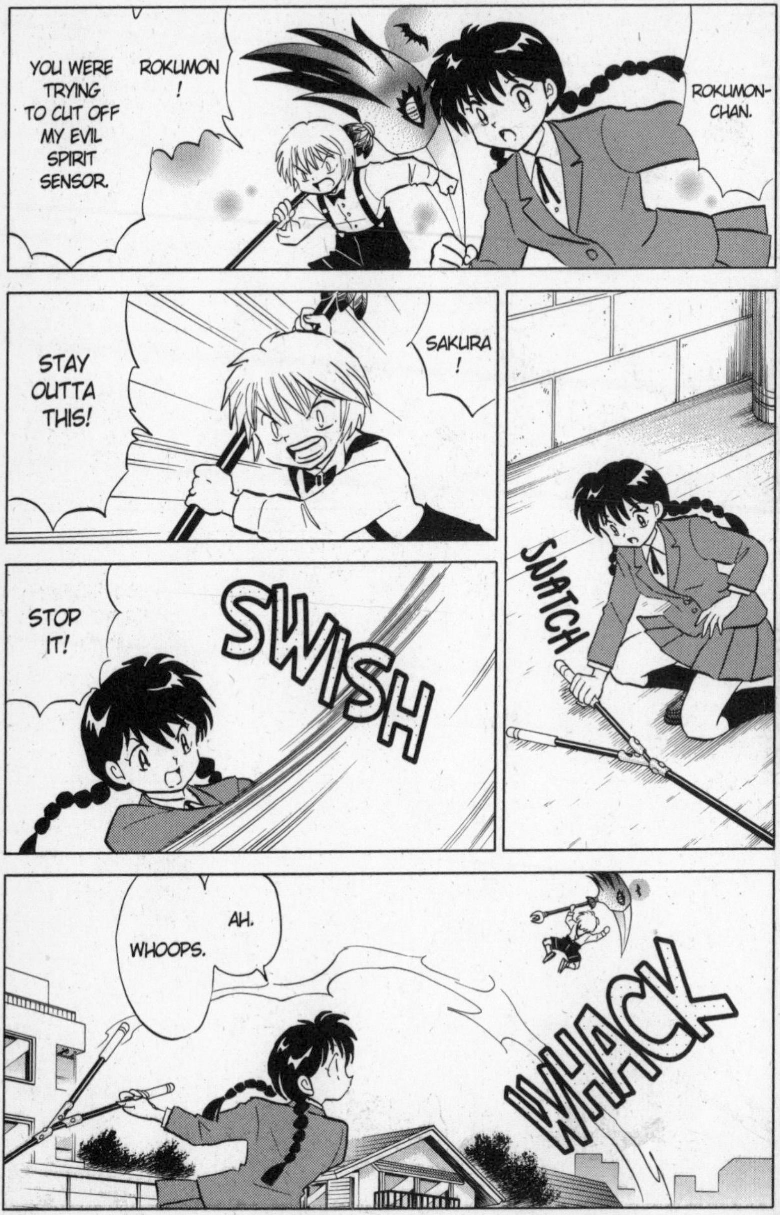
ROKUMON-CHAN.
ROKUMON!
YOU WERE TRYING TO CUT OFF MY EVIL SPIRIT SENSOR.
SNATCH
SAKURA!
STAY OUTTA THIS!
SWISH
STOP IT!
WHACK
AH. WHOOPS.

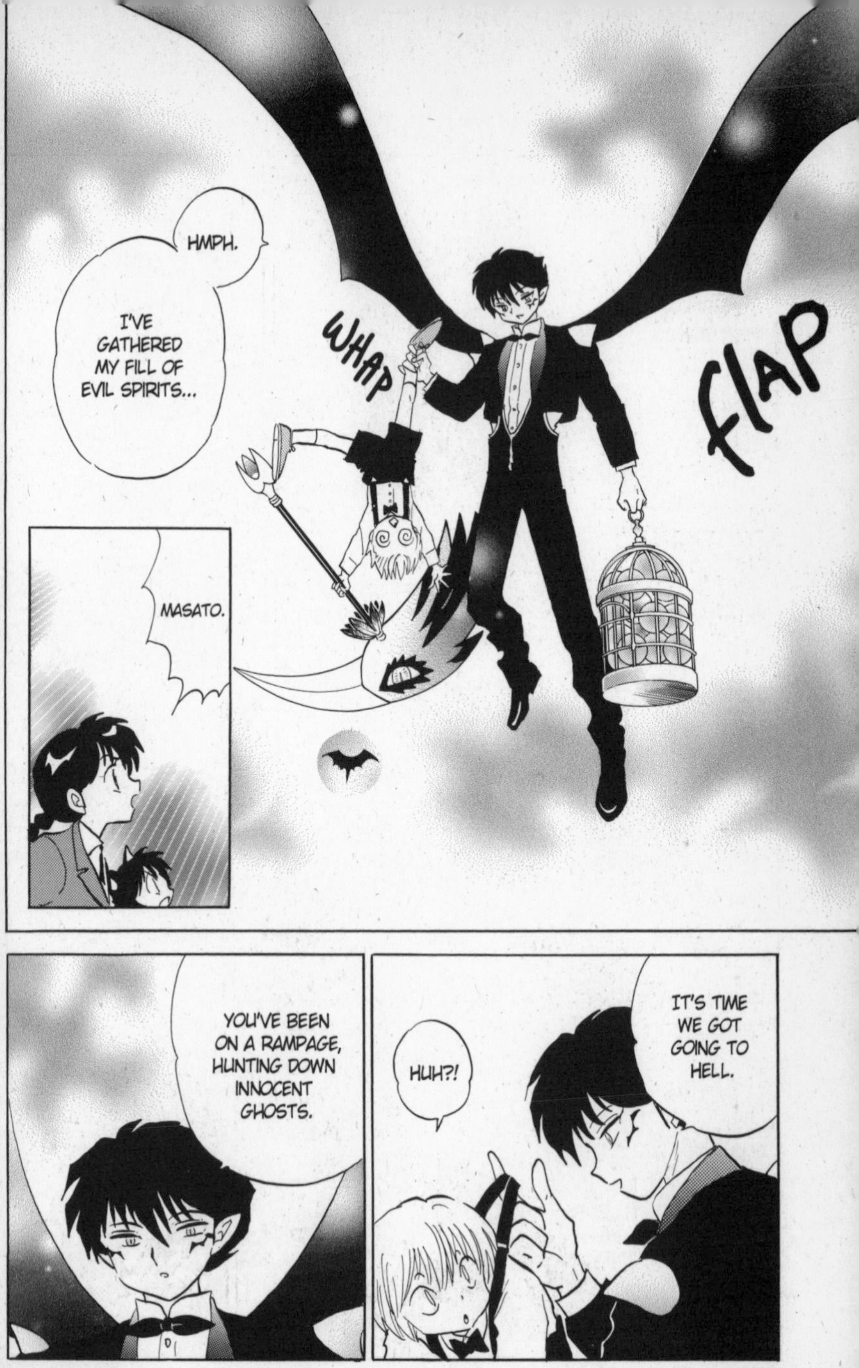
FLAP
WHAP
HMPH.
I'VE GATHERED MY FILL OF EVIL SPIRITS...
MASATO.
IT'S TIME WE GOT GOING TO HELL.
HUH?!
YOU'VE BEEN ON A RAMPAGE, HUNTING DOWN INNOCENT GHOSTS.

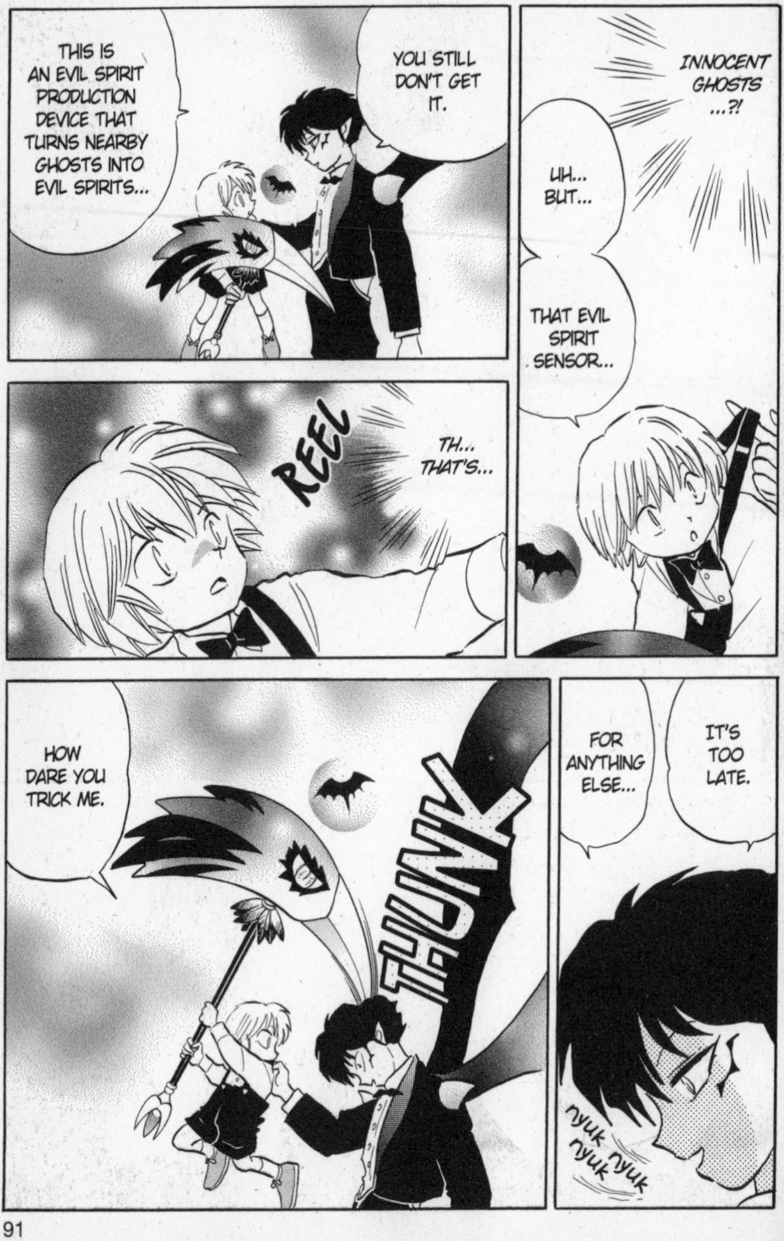
INNOCENT GHOSTS ...?!
UH... BUT...
THAT EVIL SPIRIT SENSOR...
YOU STILL DON'T GET IT.
THIS IS AN EVIL SPIRIT PRODUCTION DEVICE THAT TURNS NEARBY GHOSTS INTO EVIL SPIRITS...
TH... THAT'S...
REEL
IT'S TOO LATE.
FOR ANYTHING ELSE...
nyuk nyuk
nyuk nyuk
HOW DARE YOU TRICK ME.
THUNK

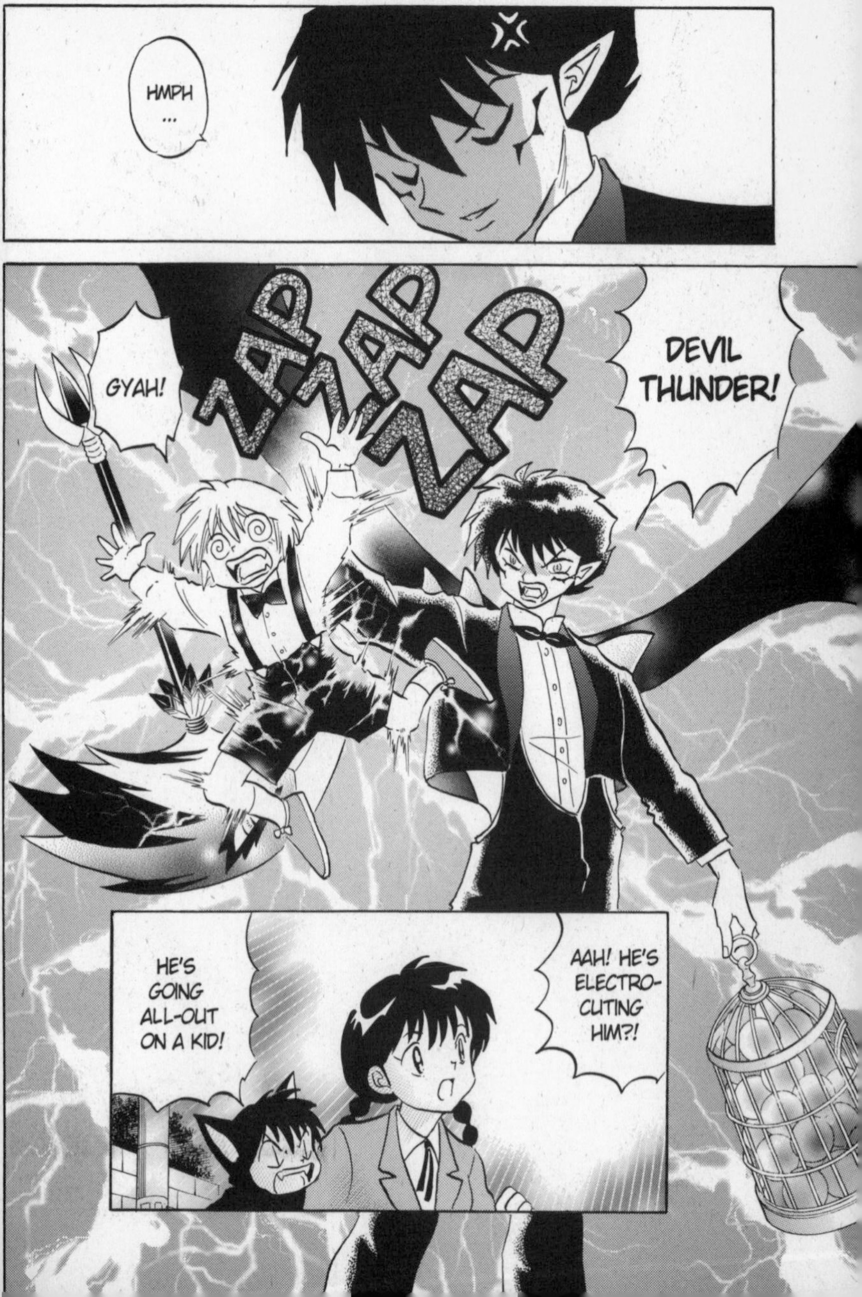
HMPH ...
DEVIL THUNDER!
ZAP ZAP ZAP
GYAH!
AAH! HE'S ELECTRO-CUTING HIM?!
HE'S GOING ALL-OUT ON A KID!

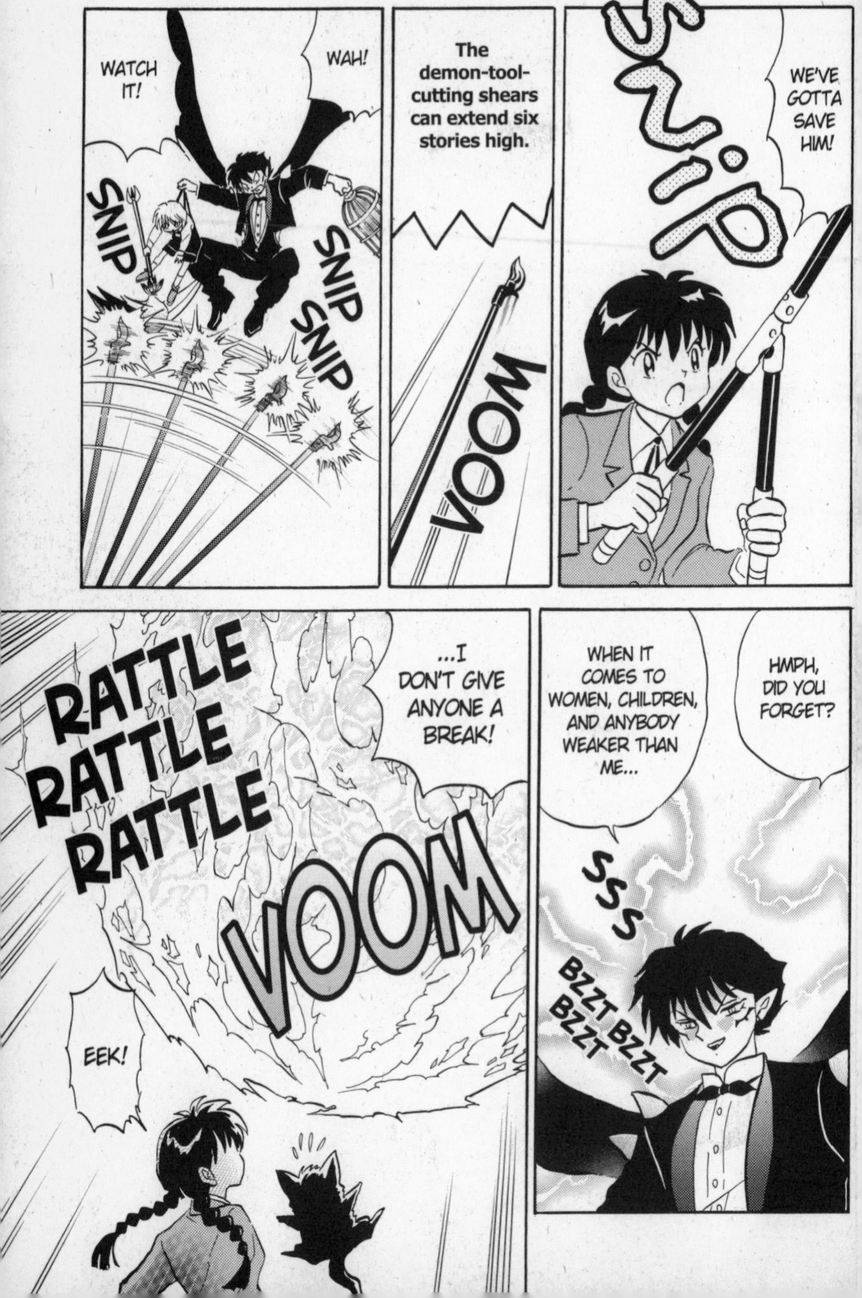
SNIP
WE'VE GOTTA SAVE HIM!
The demon-tool-cutting shears can extend six stories high.
VOOM
WAH!
WATCH IT!
SNIP
SNIP
SNIP SNIP
HMPH, DID YOU FORGET?
WHEN IT COMES TO WOMEN, CHILDREN, AND ANYBODY WEAKER THAN ME...
SSS
BZZT BZZT BZZT
...I DON'T GIVE ANYONE A BREAK!
RATTLE RATTLE RATTLE
VOOM
EEK!

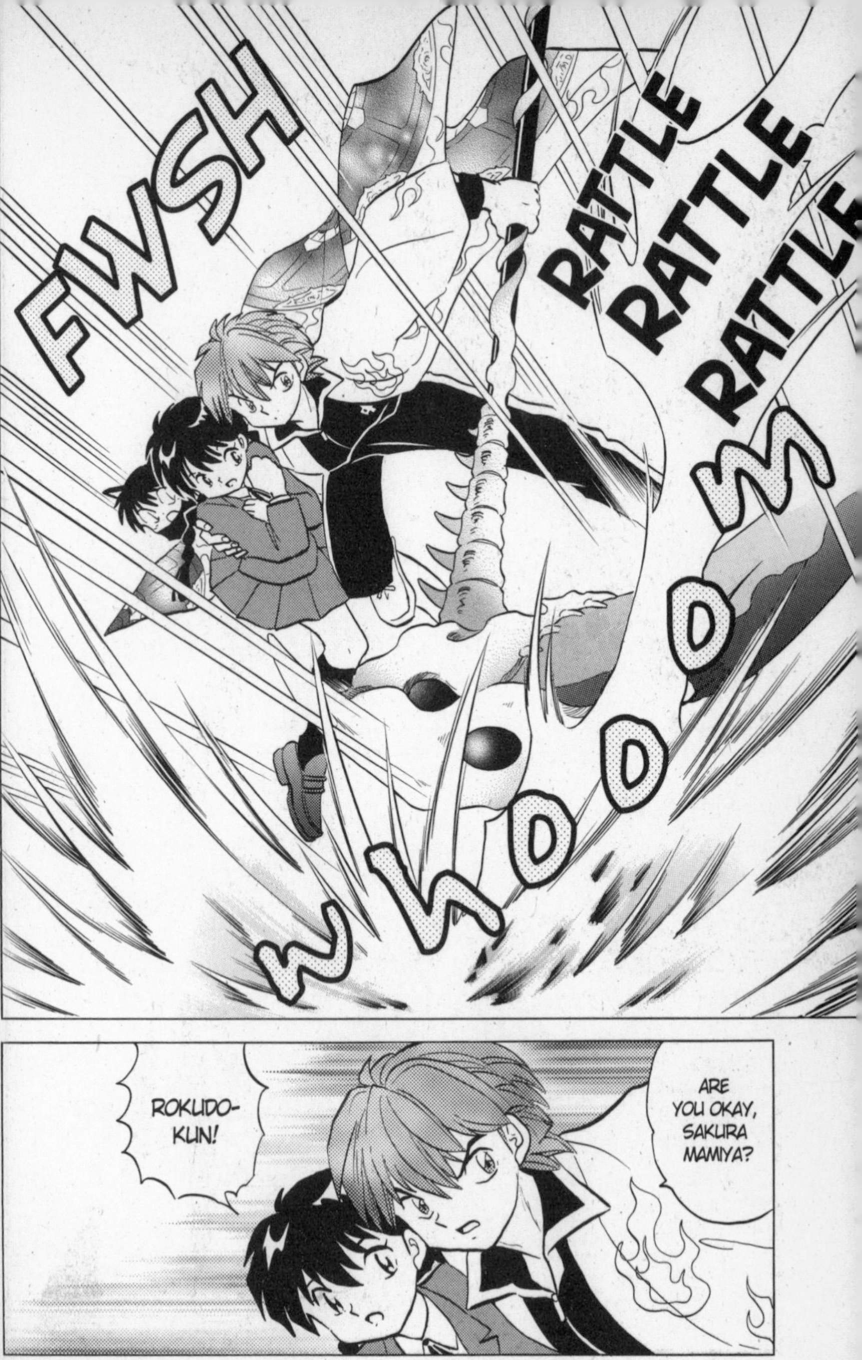
RATTLE RATTLE RATTLE
FWSH
WHOOOOM
ARE YOU OKAY, SAKURA MAMIYA?
ROKUDO-KUN!

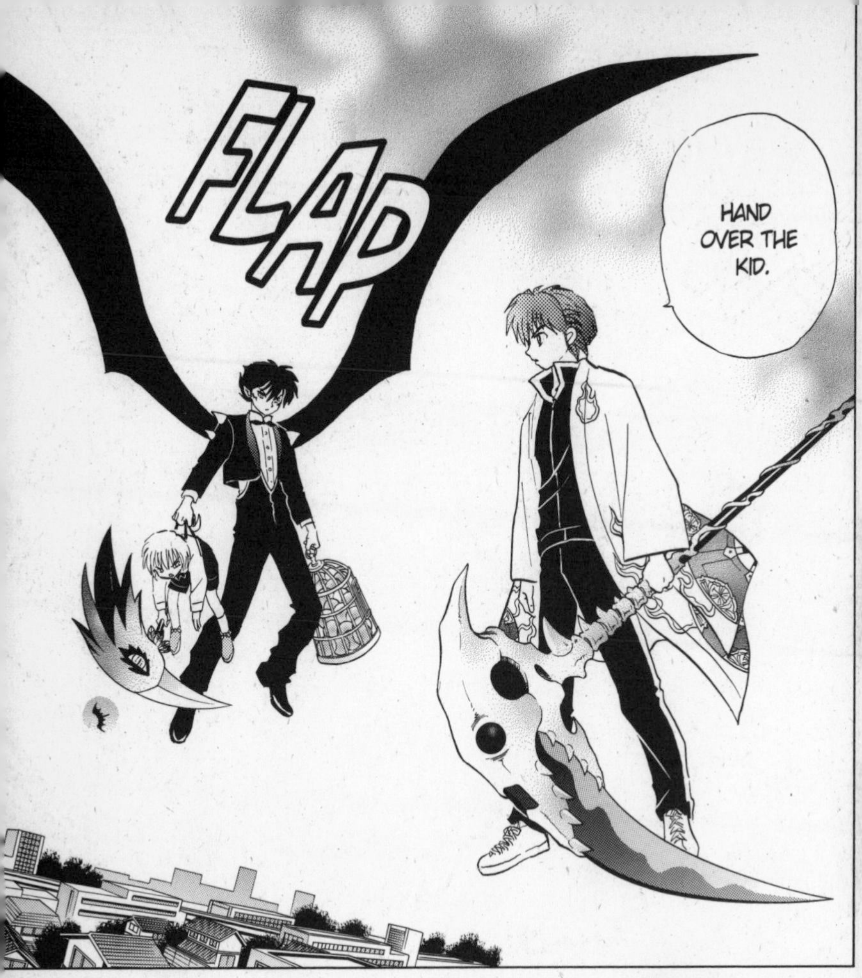
HAND OVER THE KID.
FLAP

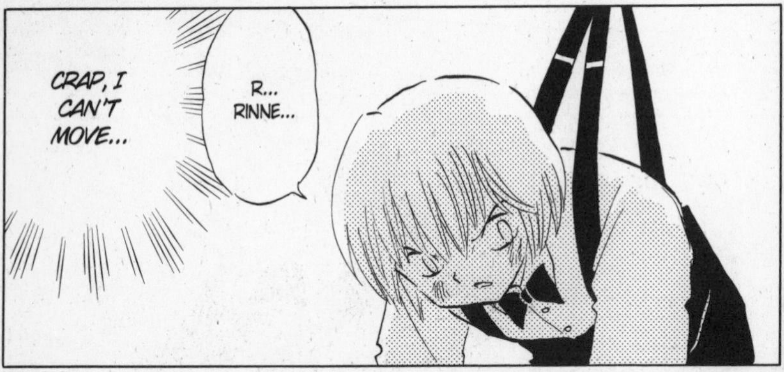
R... RINNE...
CRAP, I CAN'T MOVE...

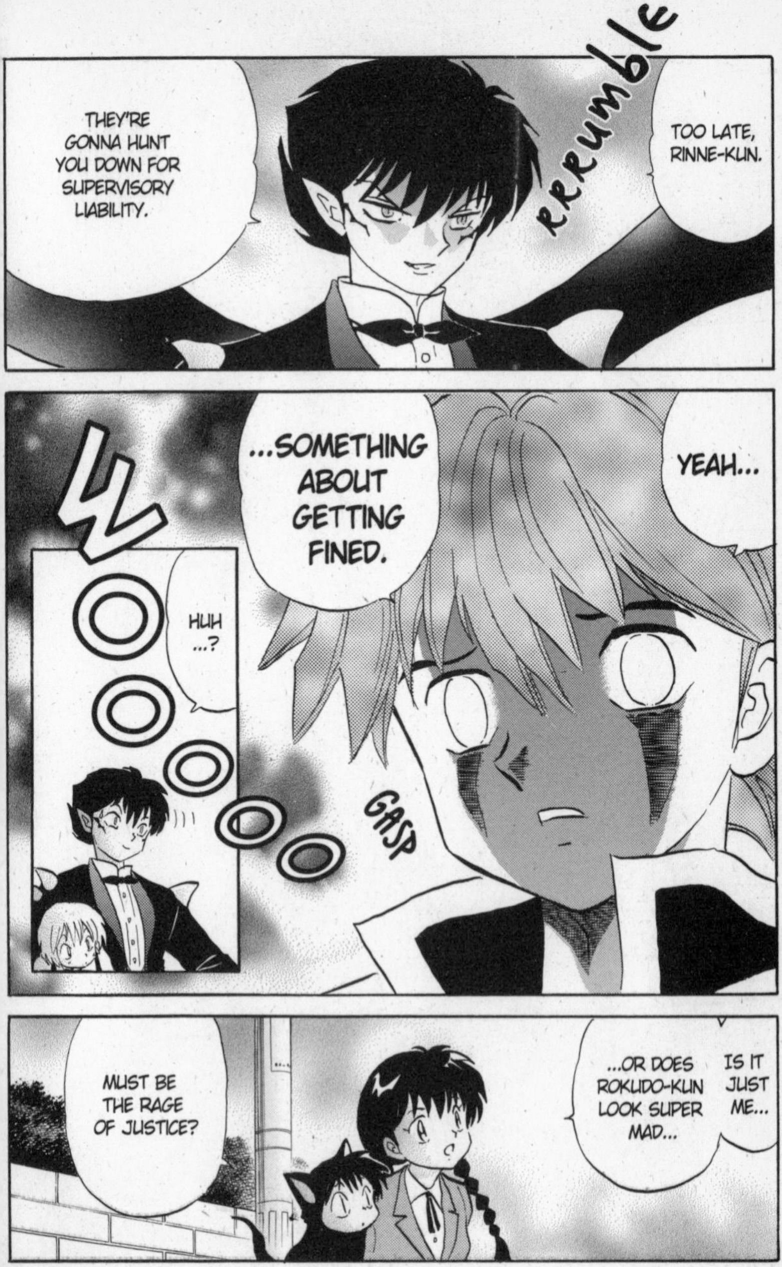
TOO LATE, RINNE-KUN.
RRRUMBLE
THEY'RE GONNA HUNT YOU DOWN FOR SUPERVISORY LIABILITY.
YEAH...
...SOMETHING ABOUT GETTING FINED.
GASP
WOOOOO
HUH ...?
IS IT JUST ME...
...OR DOES ROKUDO-KUN LOOK SUPER MAD...
MUST BE THE RAGE OF JUSTICE?

CHAPTER 74: PARTY OF FIVE, THIS WAY

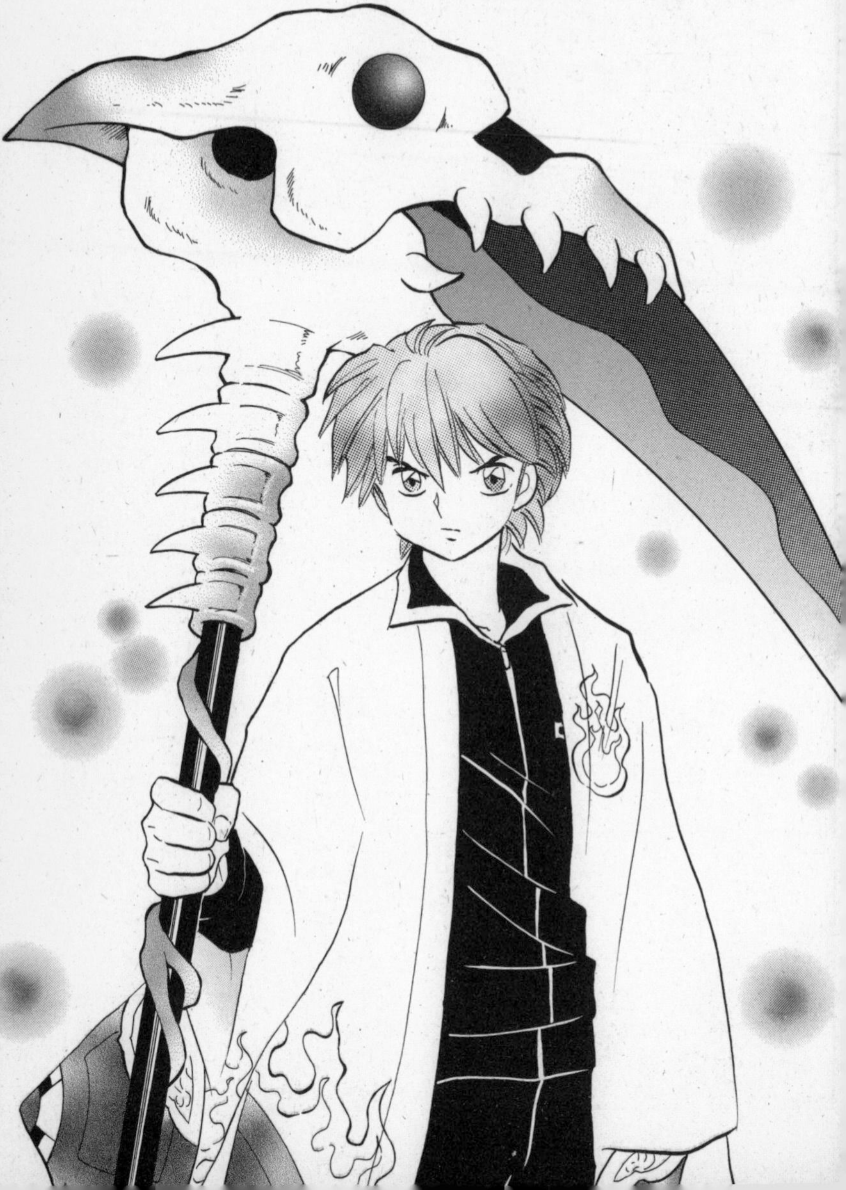

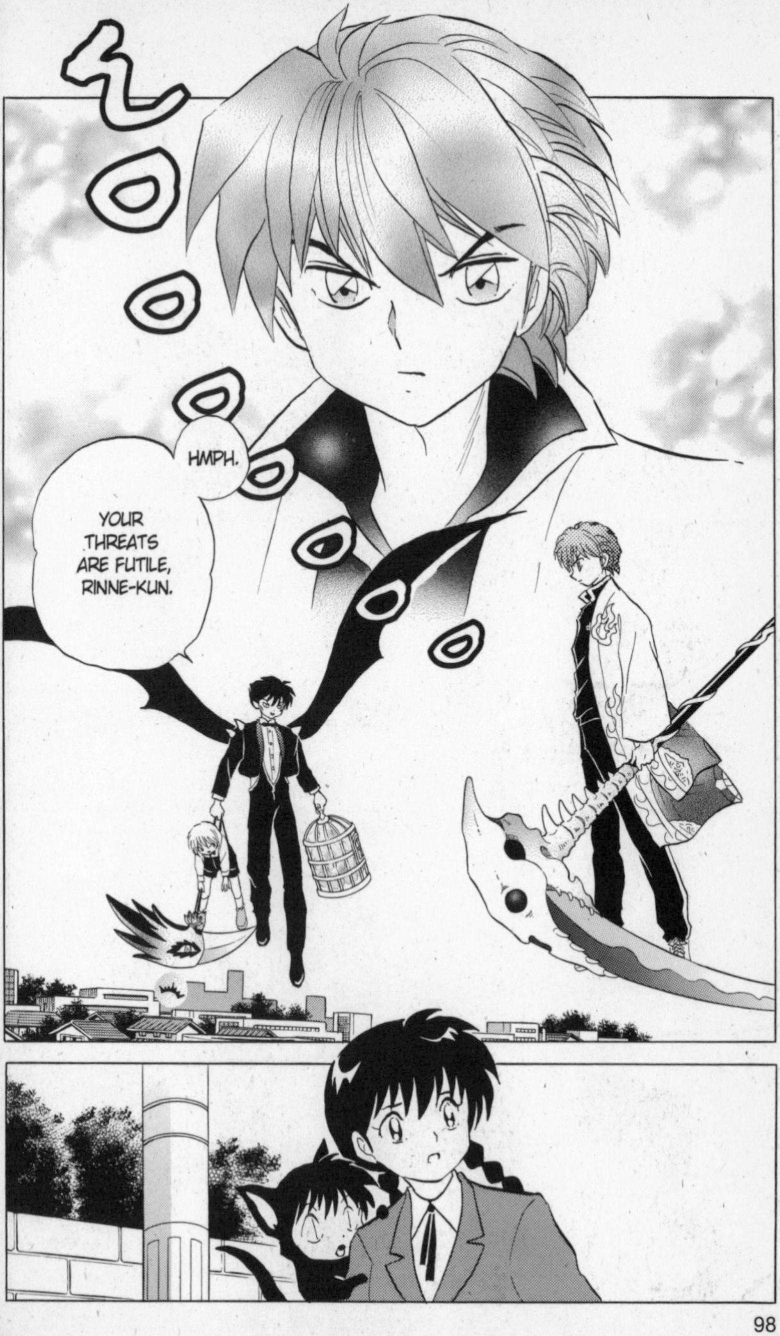
HMPH.
YOUR THREATS ARE FUTILE, RINNE-KUN.

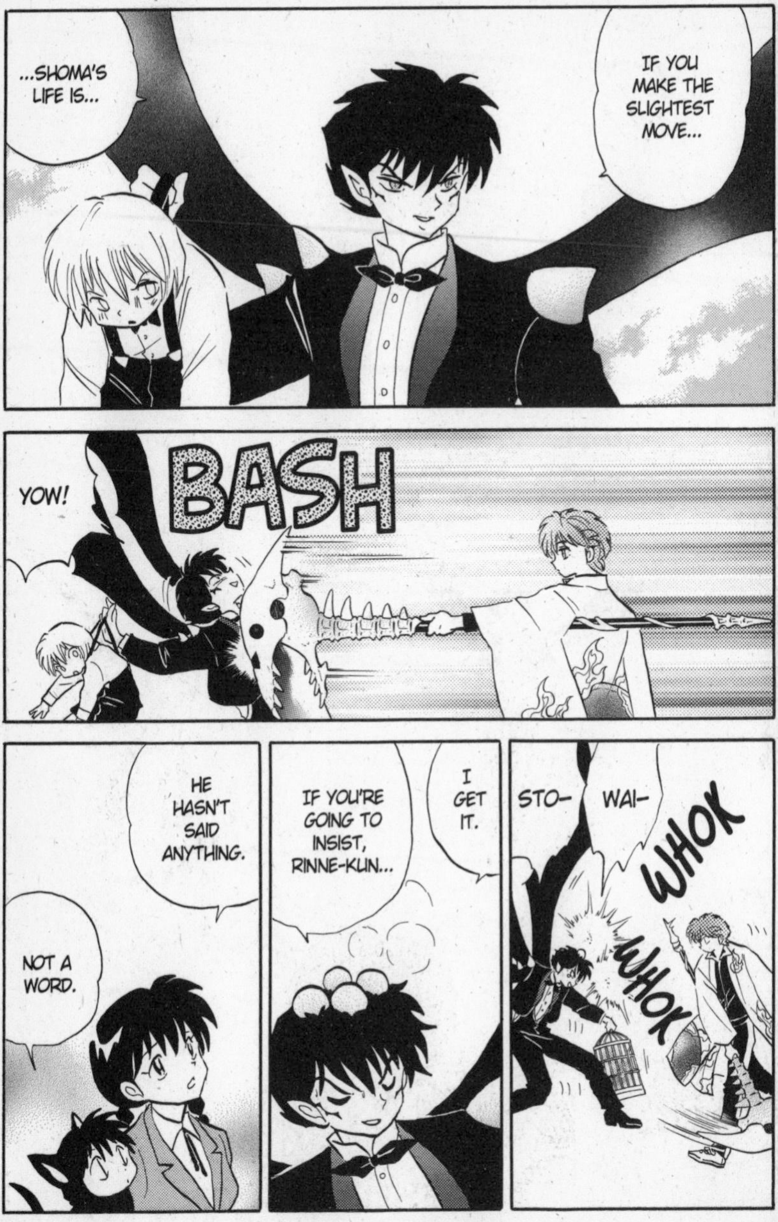
IF YOU MAKE THE SLIGHTEST MOVE...
...SHOMA'S LIFE IS...
BASH
YOW!
WAI-
STO-
WHOK
WHOK
I GET IT.
IF YOU'RE GOING TO INSIST, RINNE-KUN...
HE HASN'T SAID ANYTHING.
NOT A WORD.

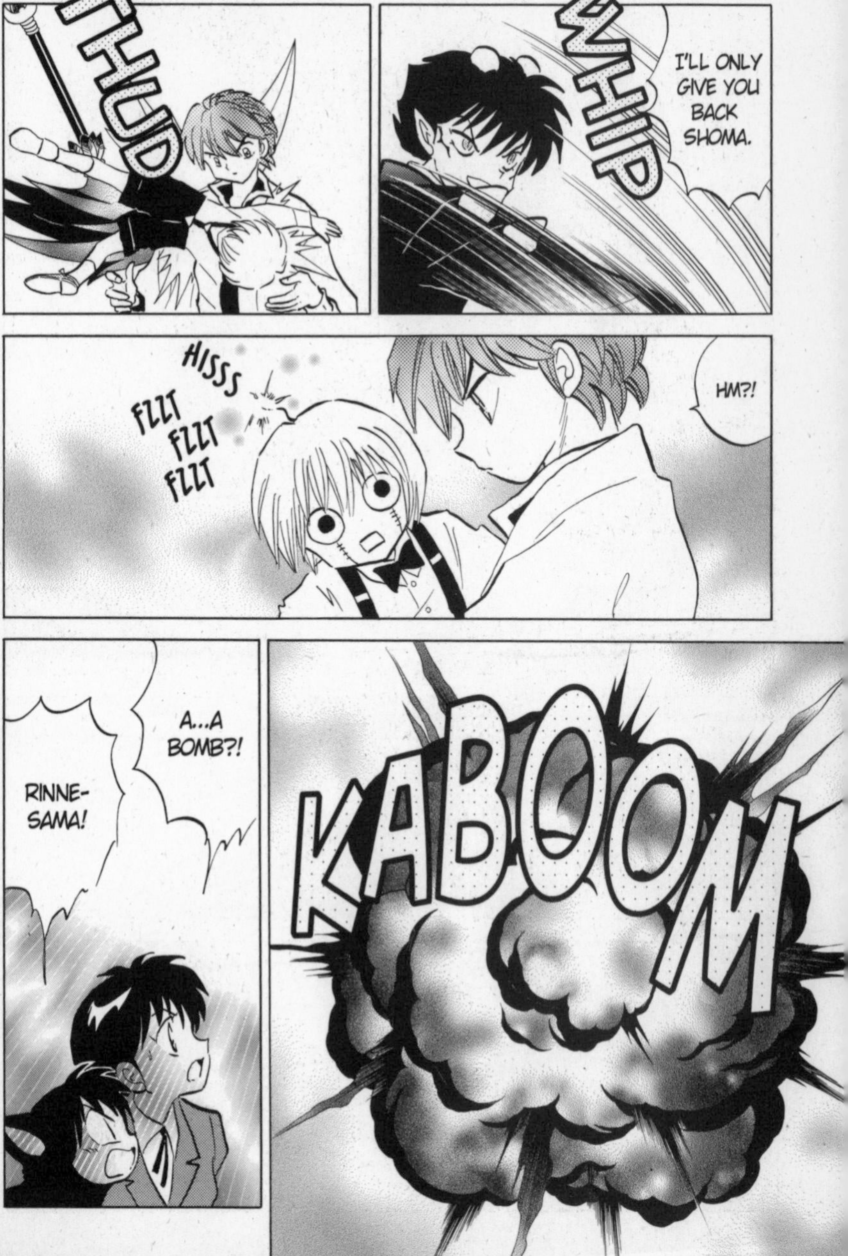
WHIP
I'LL ONLY GIVE YOU BACK SHOMA.
THUD
HM?!
HISSS
FZZT FZZT FZZT
KABOOM
A...A BOMB?!
RINNE-SAMA!

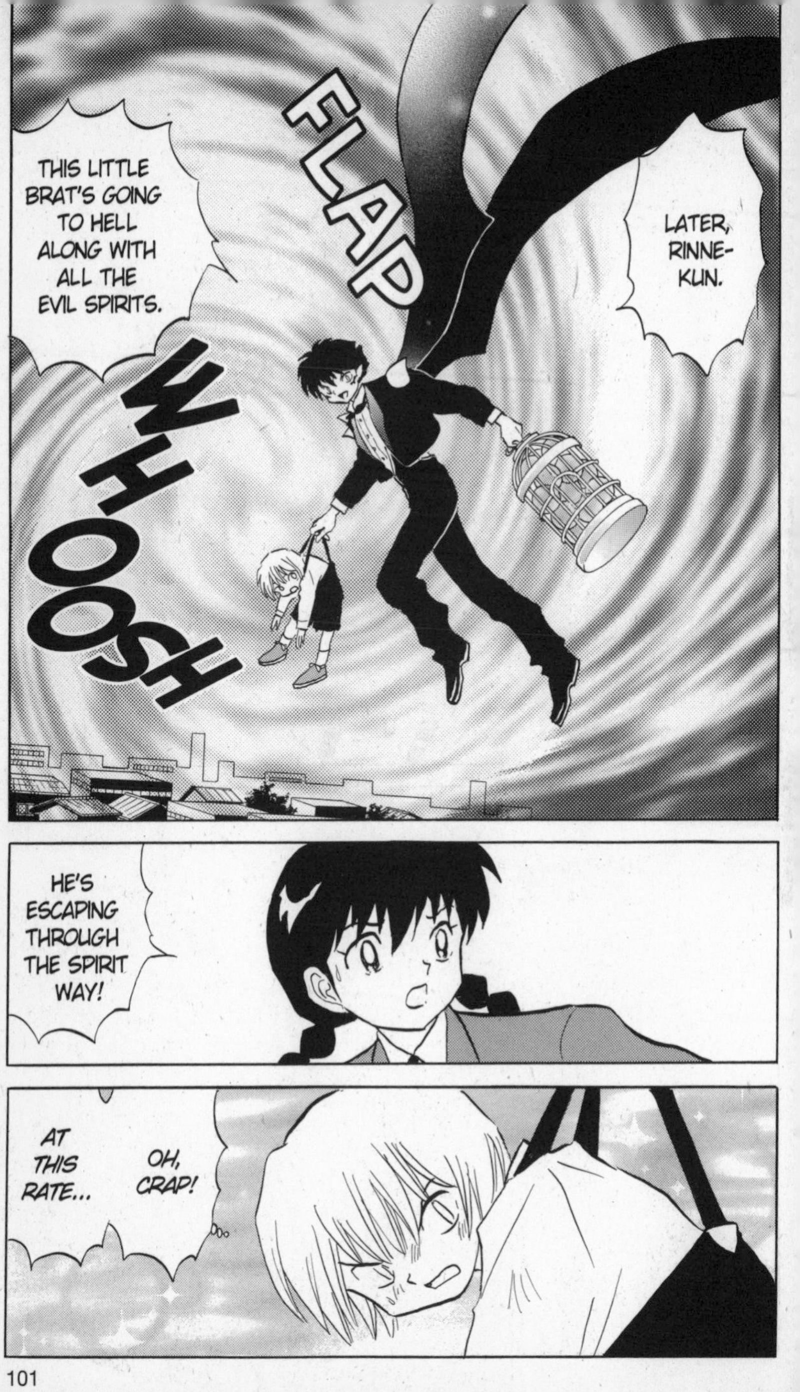
LATER, RINNE-KUN.
FLAP
THIS LITTLE BRAT'S GOING TO HELL ALONG WITH ALL THE EVIL SPIRITS.
WHOOSH
HE'S ESCAPING THROUGH THE SPIRIT WAY!
OH, CRAP!
AT THIS RATE...

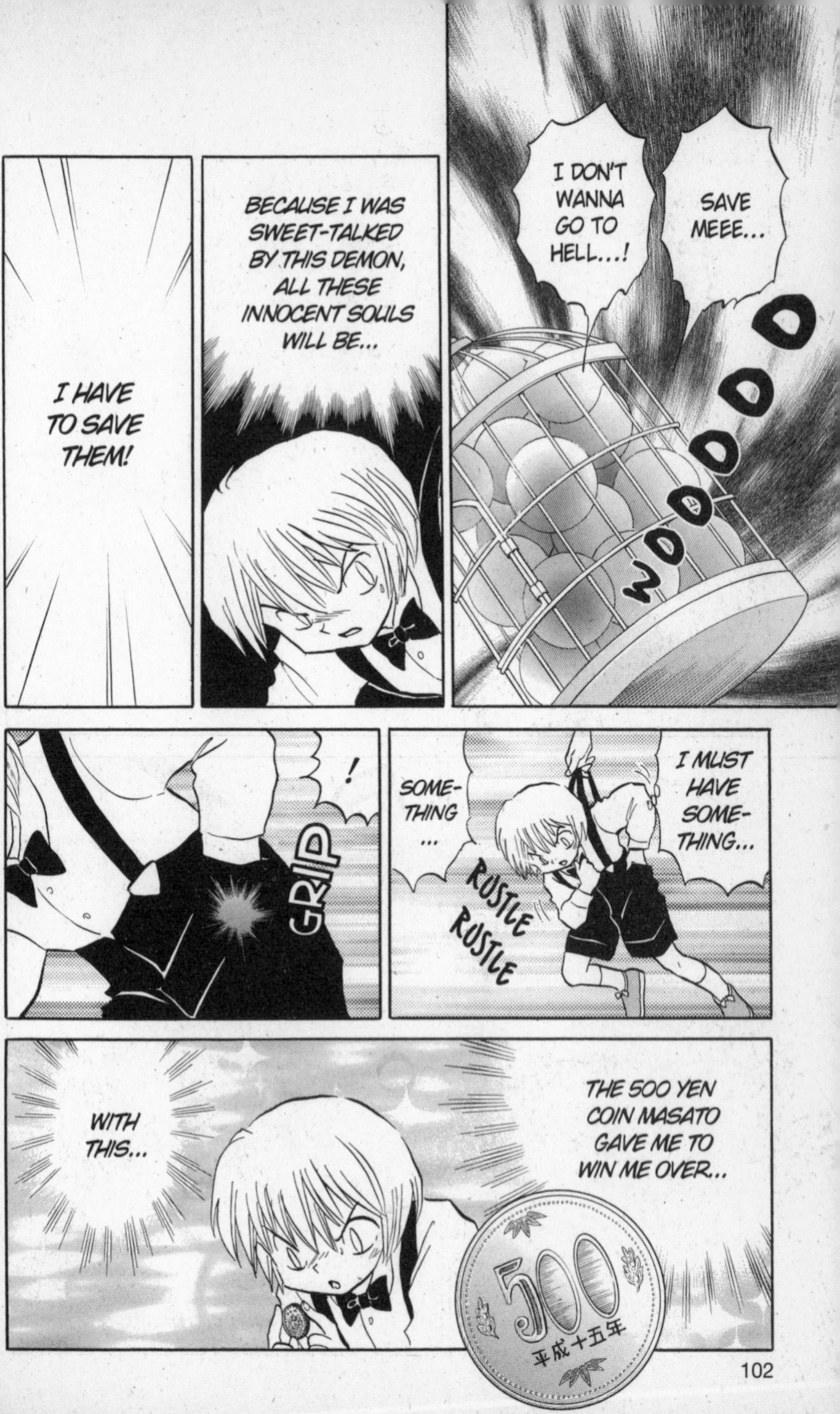
SAVE MEEE...
I DON'T WANNA GO TO HELL...!
WDDDDD
BECAUSE I WAS SWEET-TALKED BY THIS DEMON, ALL THESE INNOCENT SOULS WILL BE...
I HAVE TO SAVE THEM!
I MUST HAVE SOME-THING...
SOME-THING...
RUSTLE RUSTLE
!
GRIP
THE 500 YEN COIN MASATO GAVE ME TO WIN ME OVER...
WITH THIS...
500
平成十五年

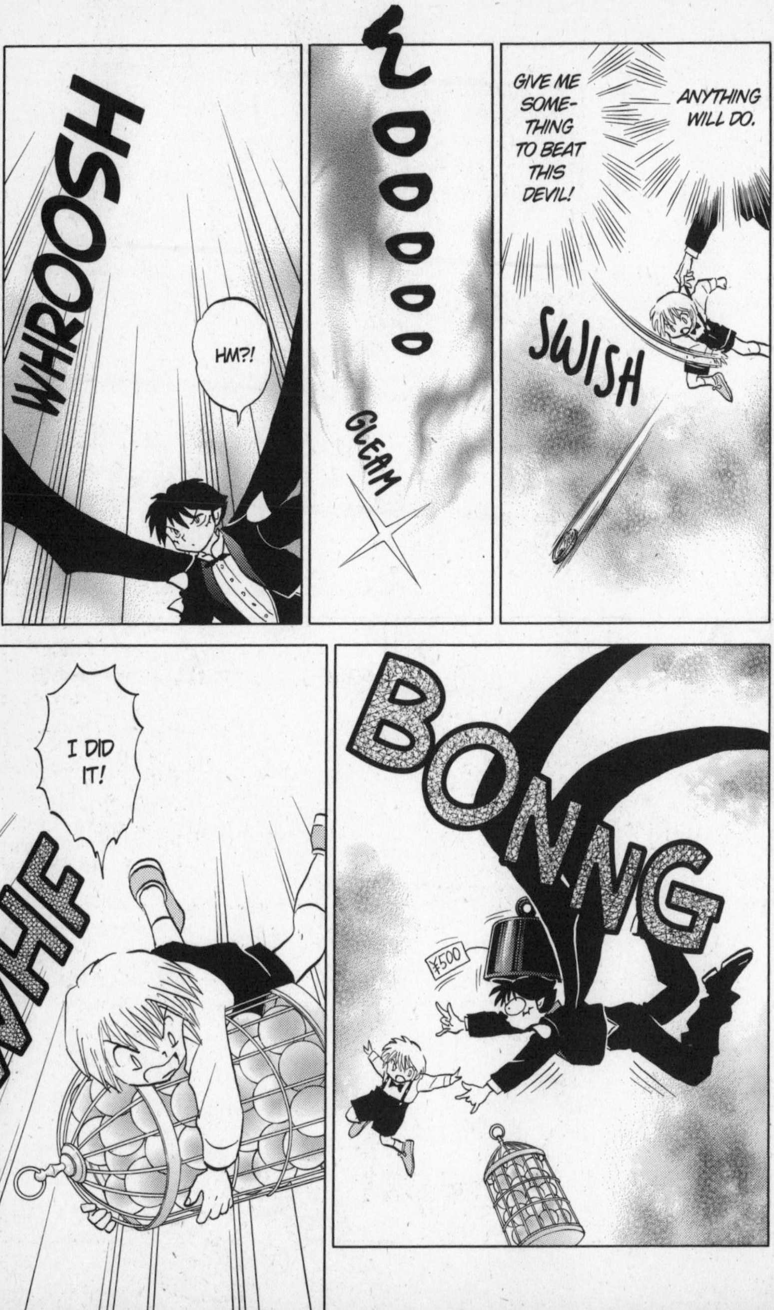

ANYTHING WILL DO.
GIVE ME SOME-THING TO BEAT THIS DEVIL!
SWISH
WOOOOOO
GLEAM
WHROOSH
HM?!
BONNG
¥500
I DID IT!
WHIF

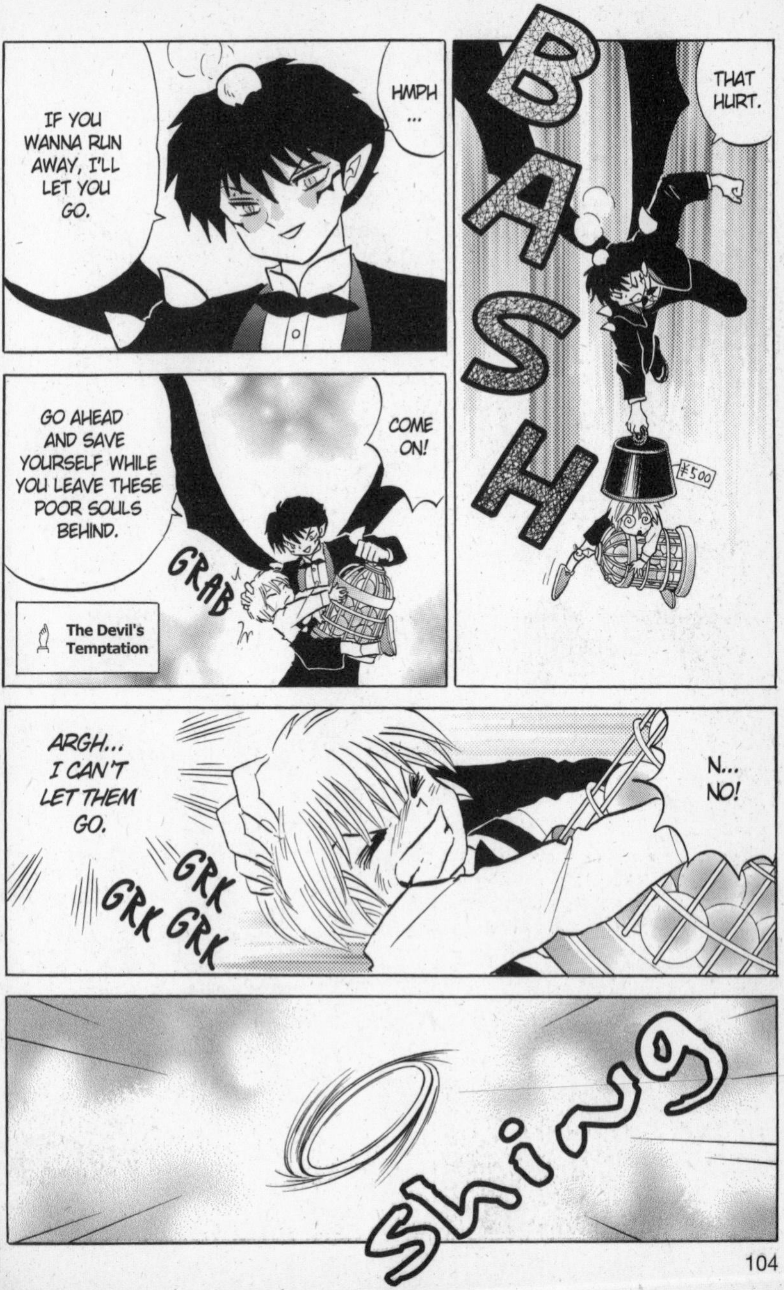
THAT HURT.
BASH
¥500
HMPH ...
IF YOU WANNA RUN AWAY, I'LL LET YOU GO.
COME ON!
GO AHEAD AND SAVE YOURSELF WHILE YOU LEAVE THESE POOR SOULS BEHIND.
GRAB
The Devil's Temptation
N... NO!
ARGH... I CAN'T LET THEM GO.
GRK GRK GRK
Shing

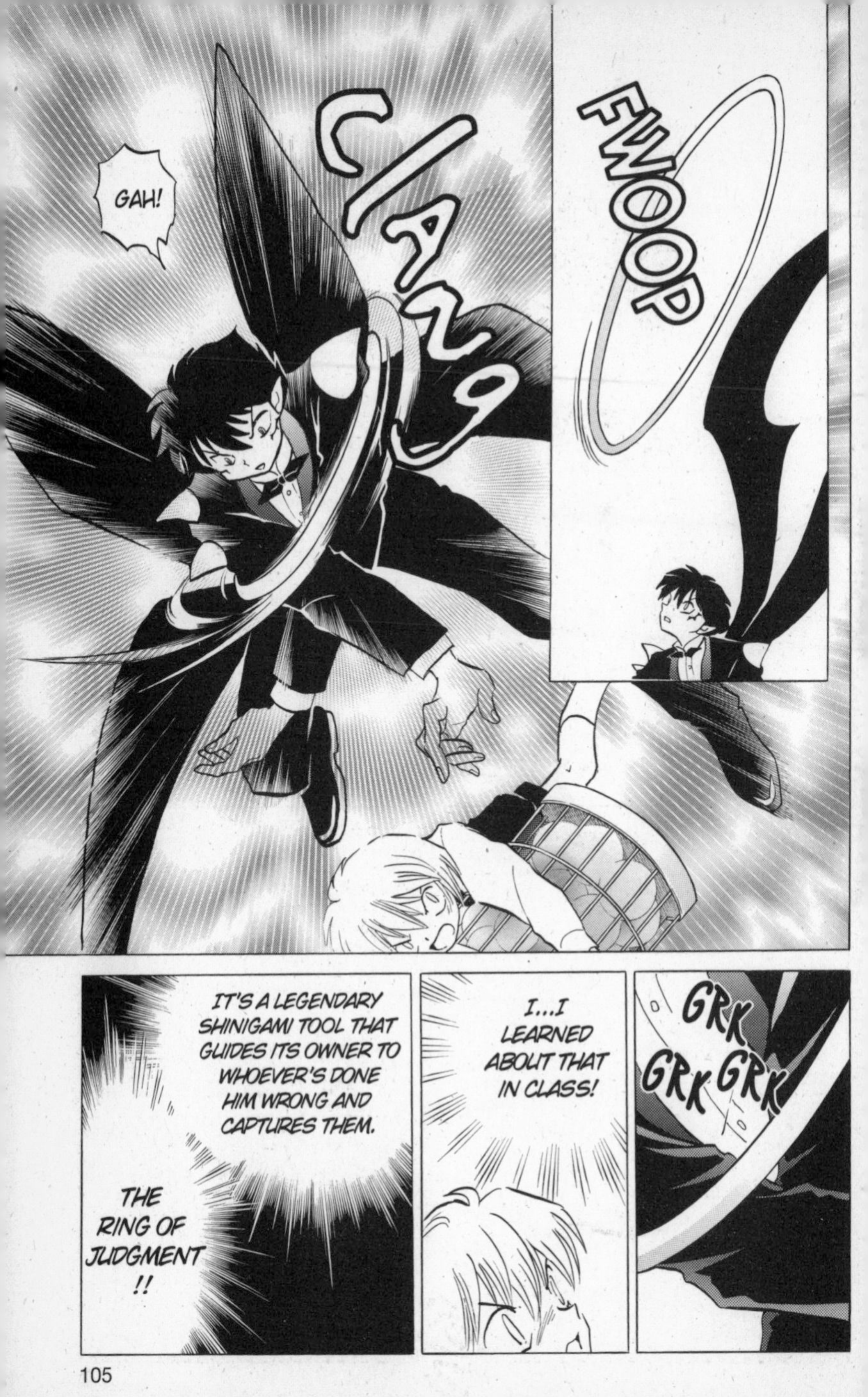
FWOOP
CLANG
GAH!
GRK GRK GRK GRK
I...I LEARNED ABOUT THAT IN CLASS!
IT'S A LEGENDARY SHINIGAMI TOOL THAT GUIDES ITS OWNER TO WHOEVER'S DONE HIM WRONG AND CAPTURES THEM.
THE RING OF JUDGMENT!!

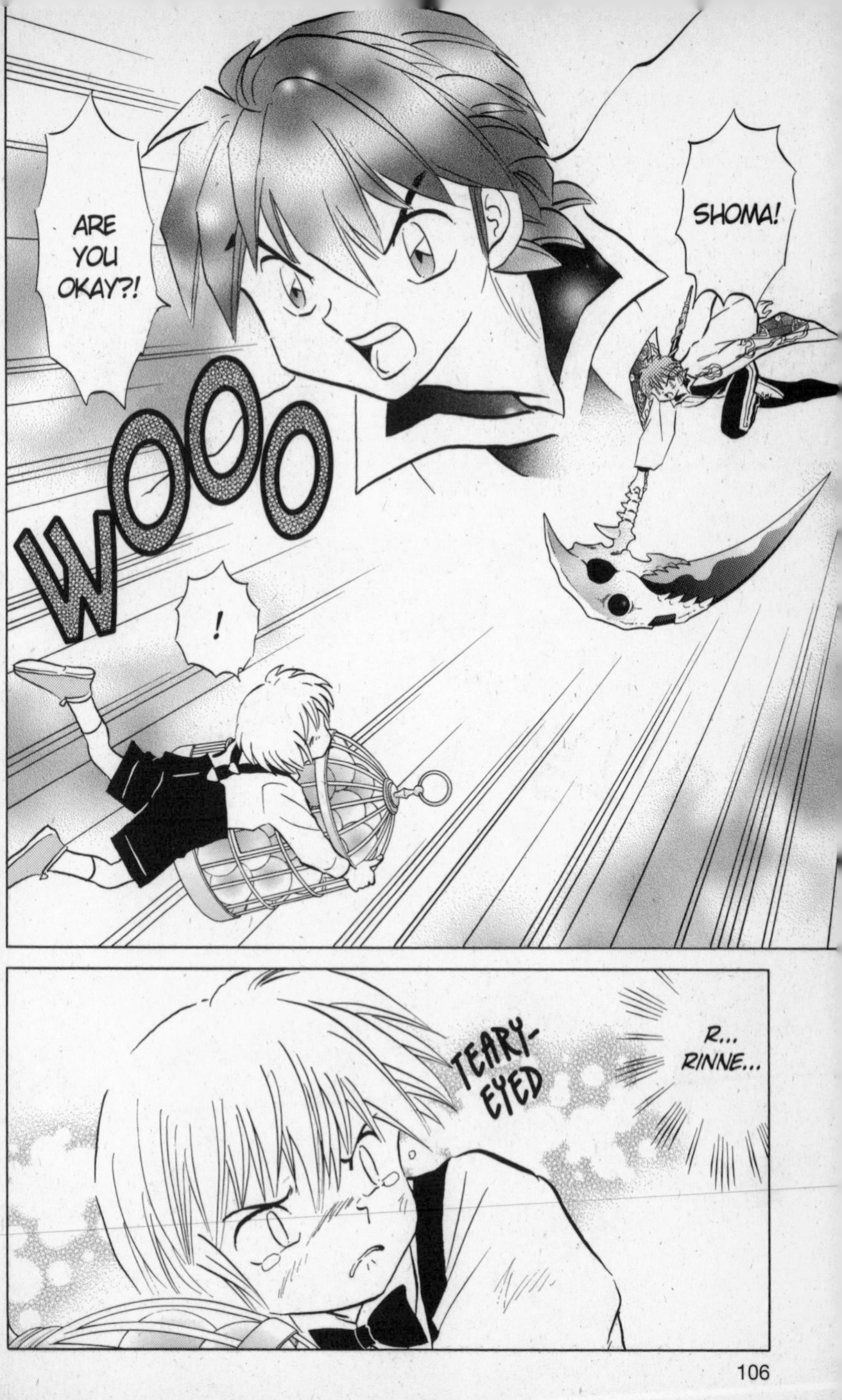
SHOMA!
ARE YOU OKAY?!
WOOO
!
R... RINNE...
TEARY-EYED

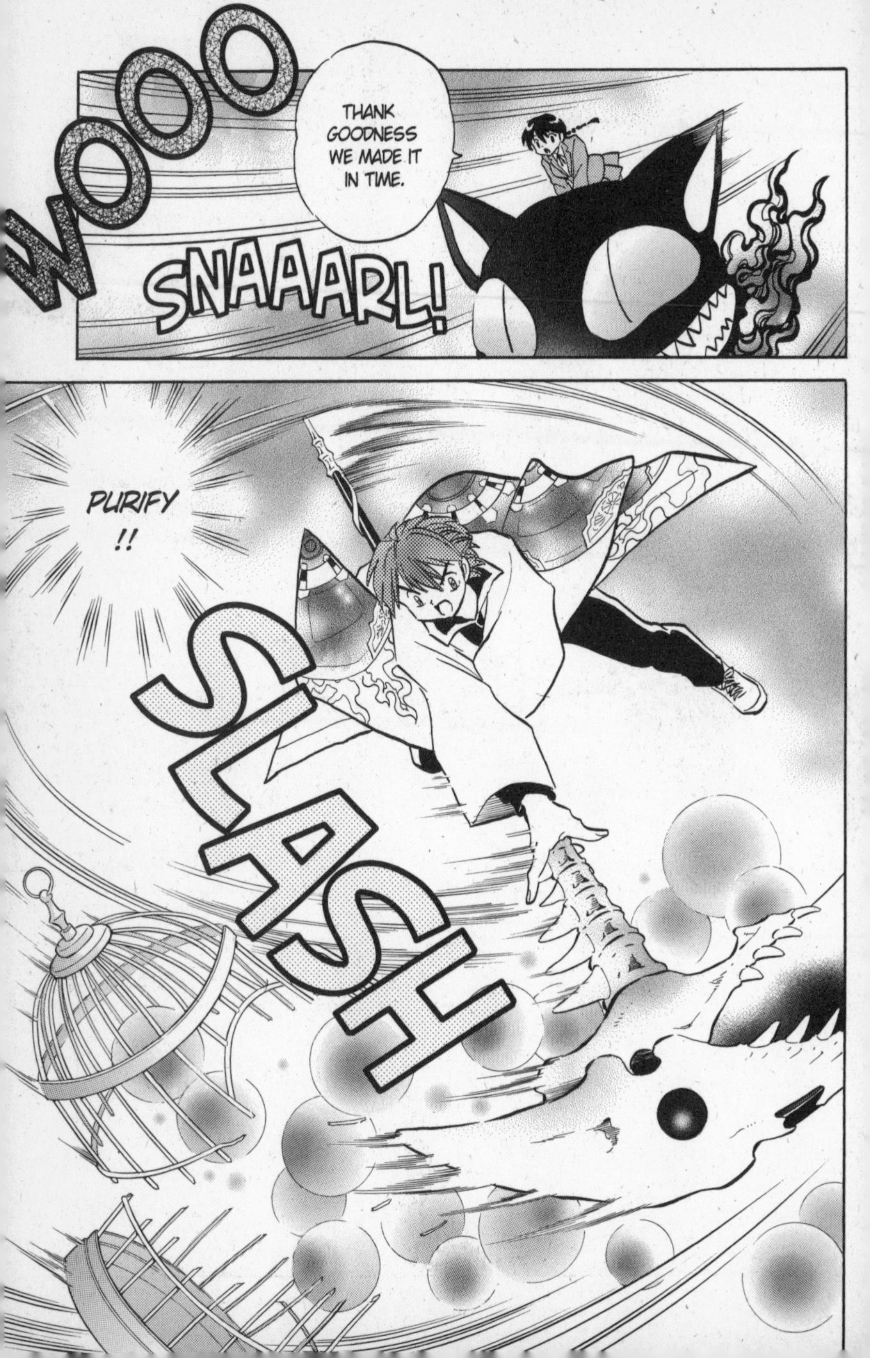

THANK GOODNESS WE MADE IT IN TIME.
WOOOO
SNAAARL!
PURIFY !!
SLASH

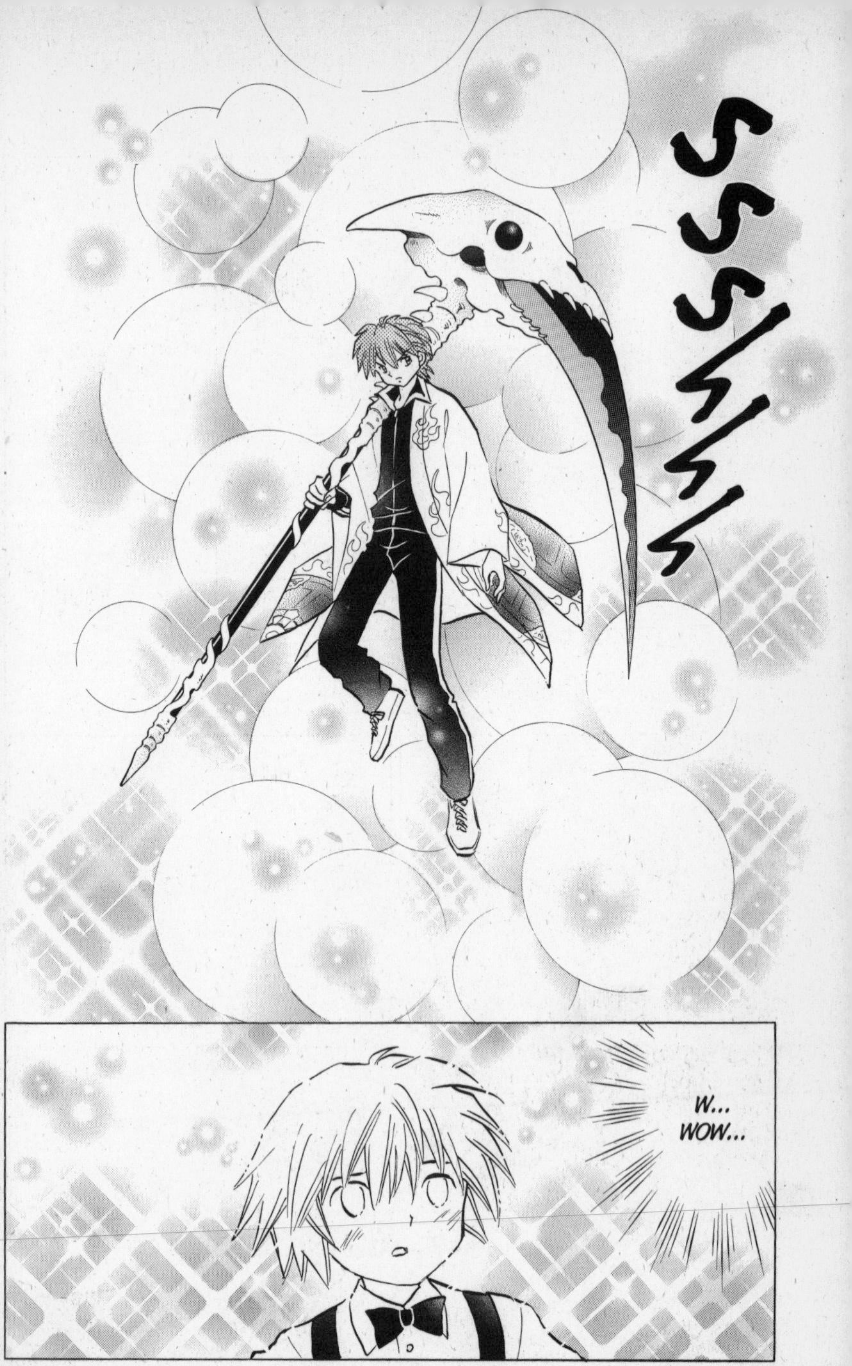
SSSHHHH
W... WOW...

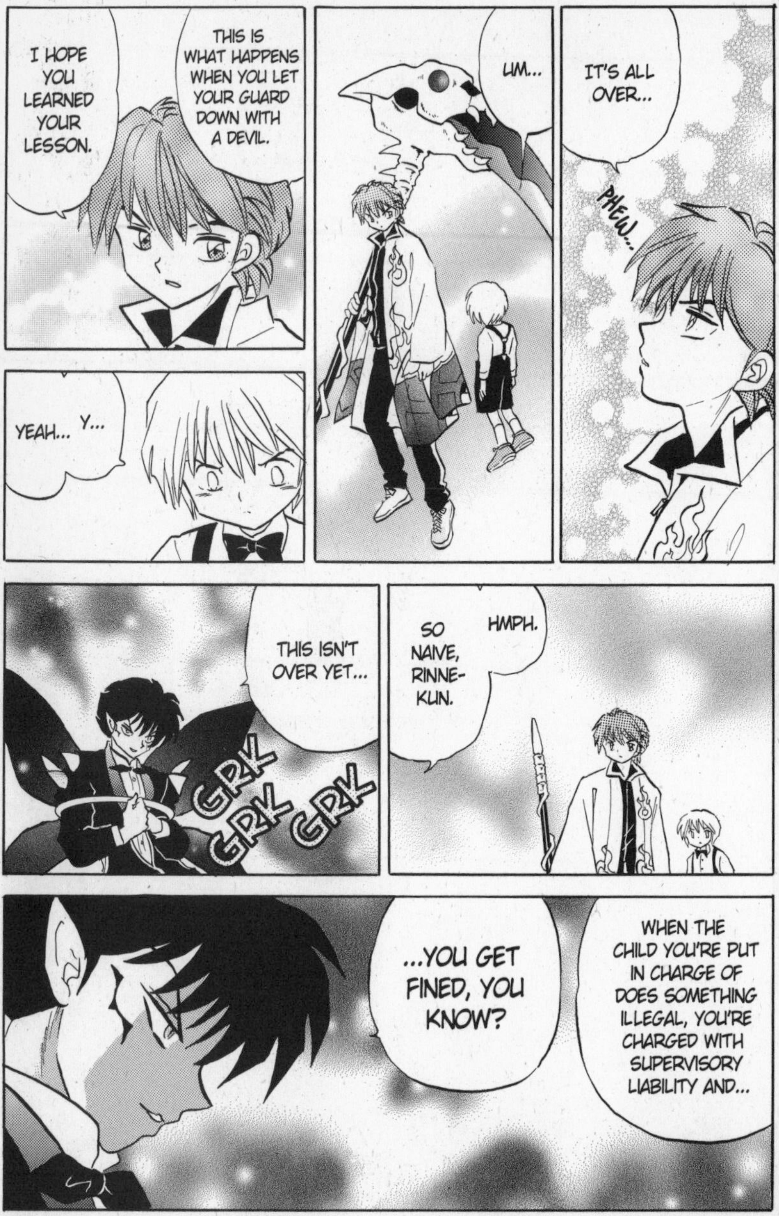
IT'S ALL OVER...
PHEW...
UM...
THIS IS WHAT HAPPENS WHEN YOU LET YOUR GUARD DOWN WITH A DEVIL.
I HOPE YOU LEARNED YOUR LESSON.
YEAH... Y...
HMPH.
SO NAIVE, RINNE-KUN.
THIS ISN'T OVER YET...
GRK GRK GRK
WHEN THE CHILD YOU'RE PUT IN CHARGE OF DOES SOMETHING ILLEGAL, YOU'RE CHARGED WITH SUPERVISORY LIABILITY AND...
...YOU GET FINED, YOU KNOW?

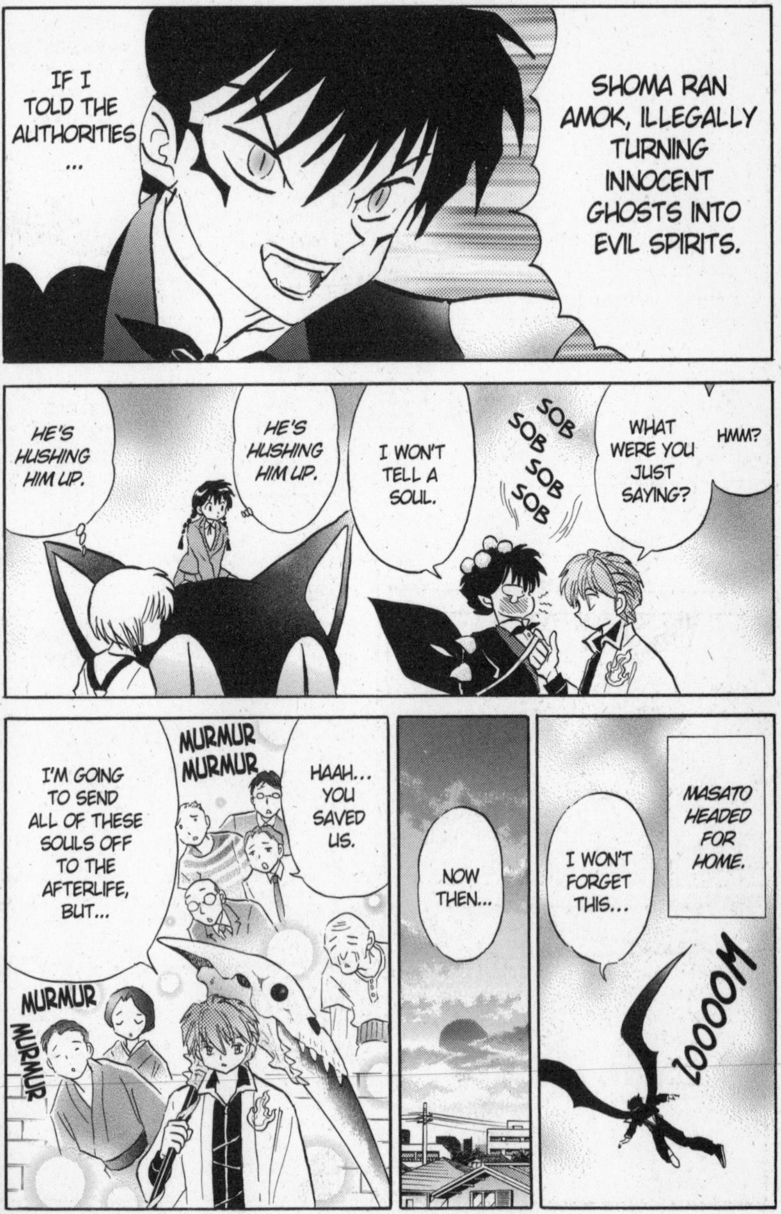
SHOMA RAN AMOK, ILLEGALLY TURNING INNOCENT GHOSTS INTO EVIL SPIRITS.
IF I TOLD THE AUTHORITIES ...
HMM?
WHAT WERE YOU JUST SAYING?
SOB SOB SOB SOB SOB
I WON'T TELL A SOUL.
HE'S HUSHING HIM UP.
HE'S HUSHING HIM UP.
MASATO HEADED FOR HOME.
I WON'T FORGET THIS...
ZOOOOM
NOW THEN...
HAAH... YOU SAVED US.
MURMUR MURMUR
I'M GOING TO SEND ALL OF THESE SOULS OFF TO THE AFTERLIFE, BUT...
MURMUR
MURMUR

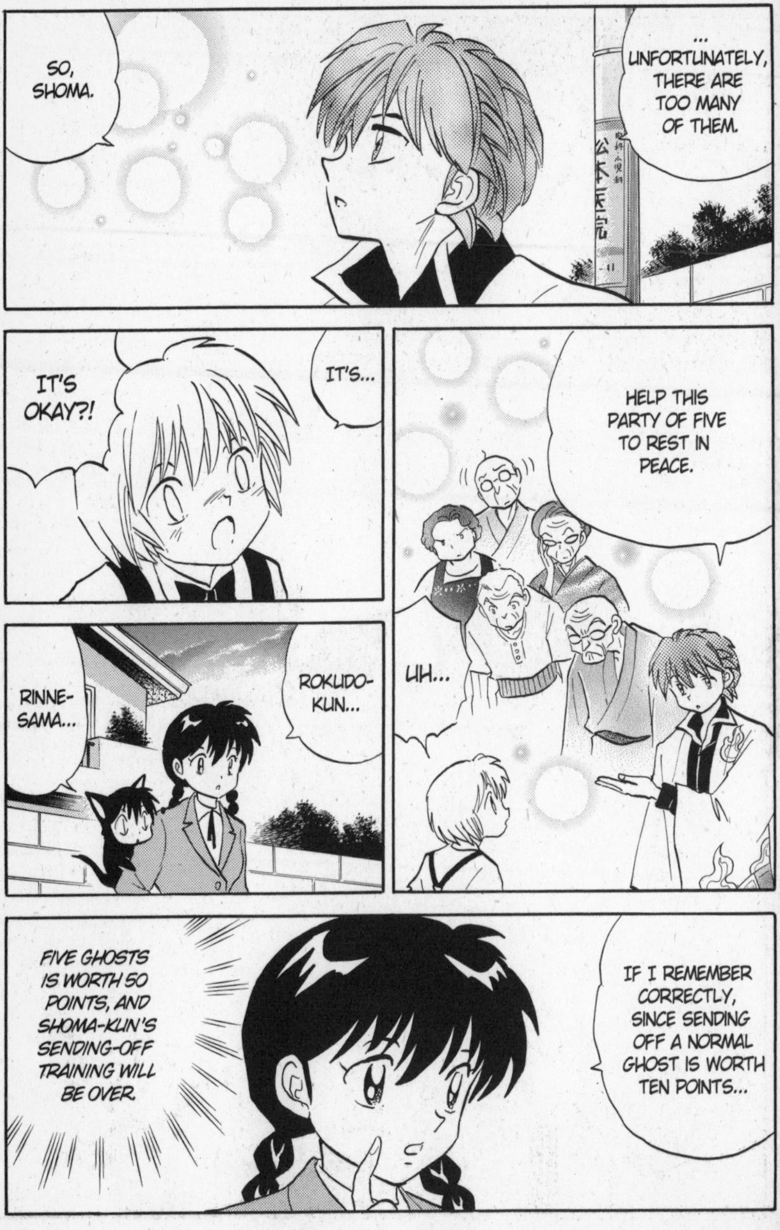

... UNFORTUNATELY, THERE ARE TOO MANY OF THEM.
SO, SHOMA.
HELP THIS PARTY OF FIVE TO REST IN PEACE.
UH...
IT'S...
IT'S OKAY?!
ROKUDO-KUN...
RINNE-SAMA...
IF I REMEMBER CORRECTLY, SINCE SENDING OFF A NORMAL GHOST IS WORTH TEN POINTS...
FIVE GHOSTS IS WORTH 50 POINTS, AND SHOMA-KUN'S SENDING-OFF TRAINING WILL BE OVER.

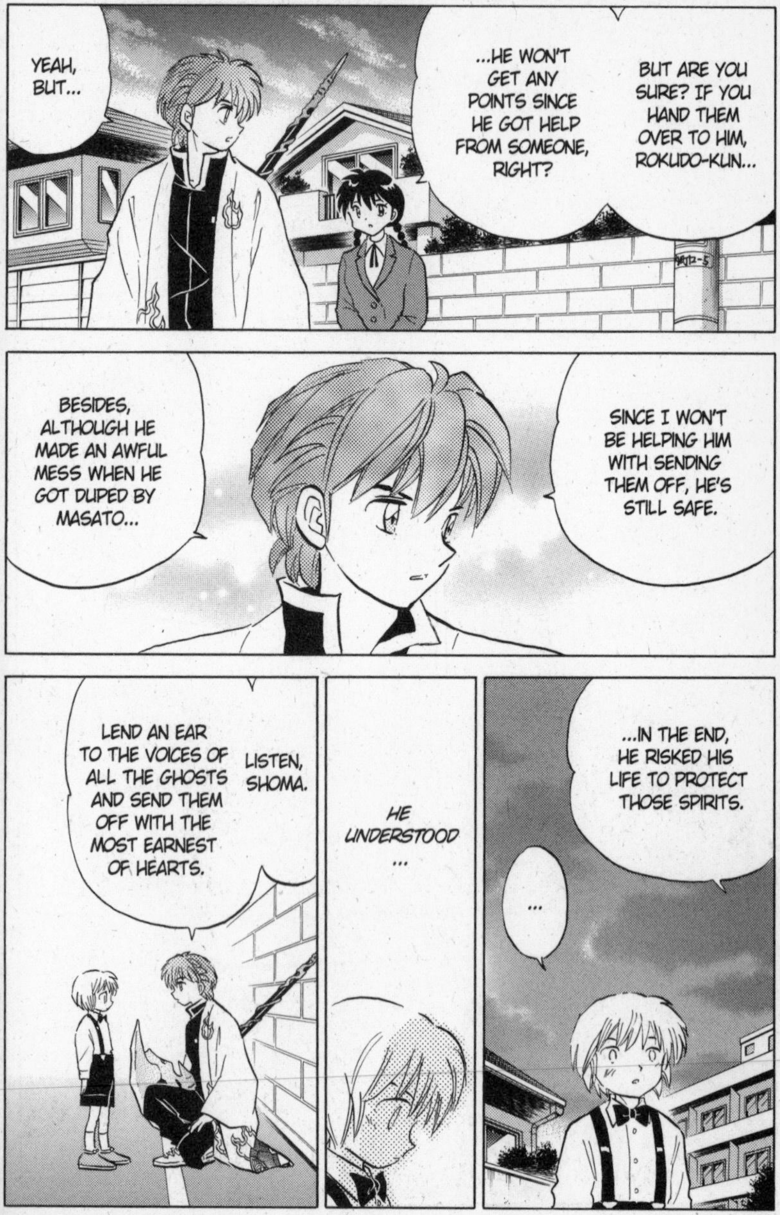
BUT ARE YOU SURE? IF YOU HAND THEM OVER TO HIM, ROKUDO-KUN...
...HE WON'T GET ANY POINTS SINCE HE GOT HELP FROM SOMEONE, RIGHT?
YEAH, BUT...
SINCE I WON'T BE HELPING HIM WITH SENDING THEM OFF, HE'S STILL SAFE.
BESIDES, ALTHOUGH HE MADE AN AWFUL MESS WHEN HE GOT DUPED BY MASATO...
...IN THE END, HE RISKED HIS LIFE TO PROTECT THOSE SPIRITS.
...
HE UNDERSTOOD...
LISTEN, SHOMA.
LEND AN EAR TO THE VOICES OF ALL THE GHOSTS AND SEND THEM OFF WITH THE MOST EARNEST OF HEARTS.

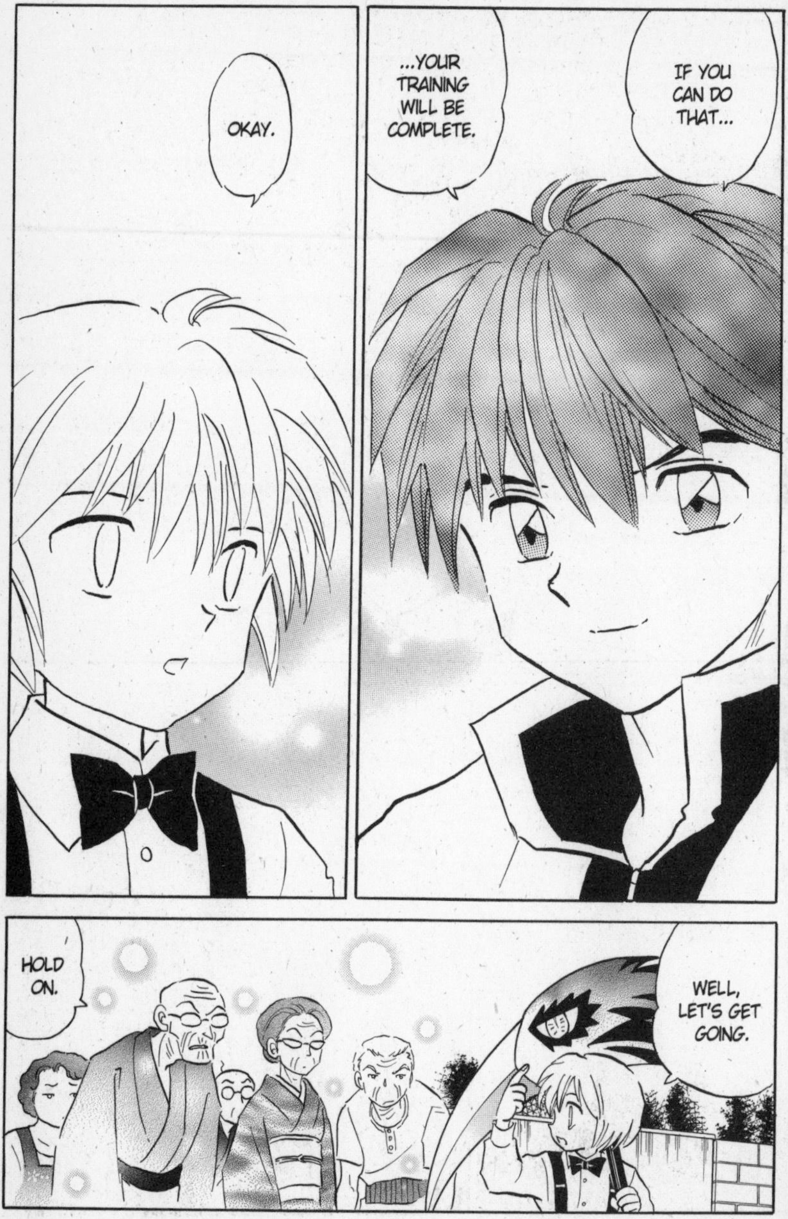
IF YOU CAN DO THAT...
...YOUR TRAINING WILL BE COMPLETE.
OKAY.
WELL, LET'S GET GOING.
HOLD ON.

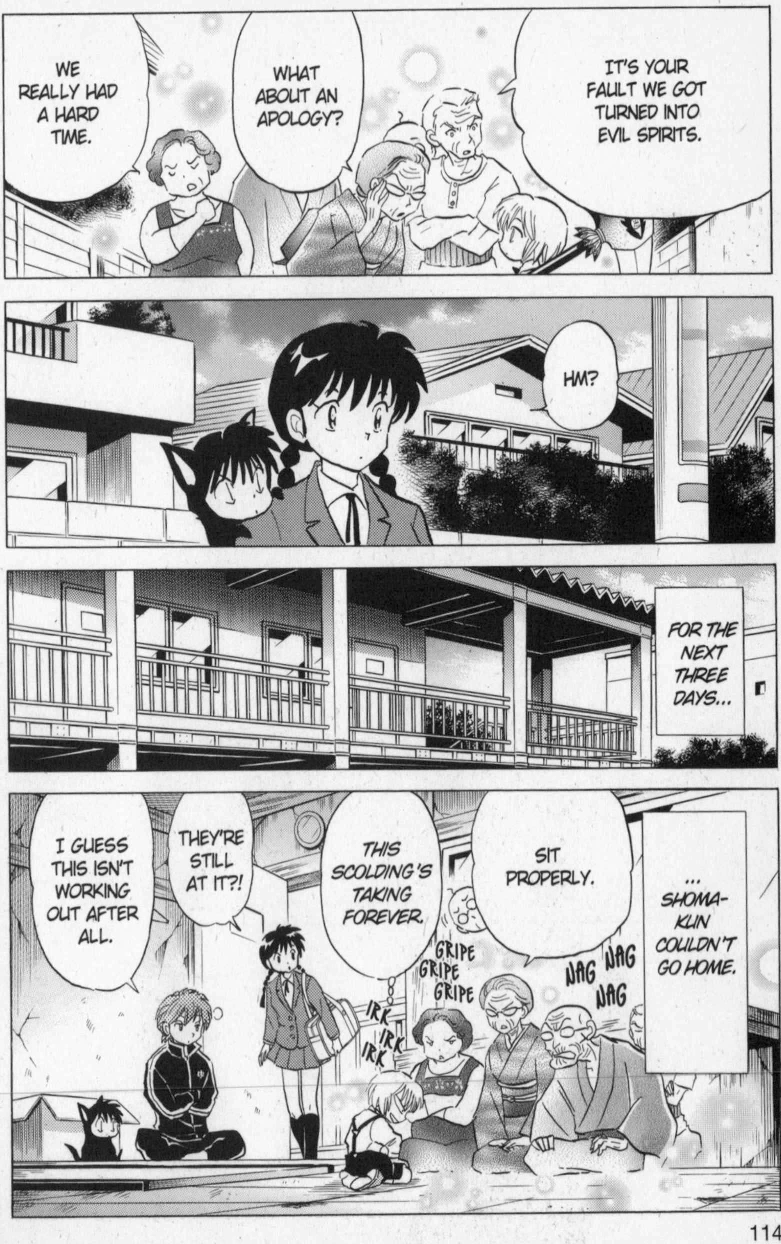

IT'S YOUR FAULT WE GOT TURNED INTO EVIL SPIRITS.
WHAT ABOUT AN APOLOGY?
WE REALLY HAD A HARD TIME.
HM?
FOR THE NEXT THREE DAYS...
... SHOMA-KUN COULDN'T GO HOME.
SIT PROPERLY.
NAG NAG NAG
THIS SCOLDING'S TAKING FOREVER.
GRIPE GRIPE GRIPE
IRK IRK IRK
THEY'RE STILL AT IT?!
I GUESS THIS ISN'T WORKING OUT AFTER ALL.

CHAPTER 75: THE FRIENDLY SQUARE

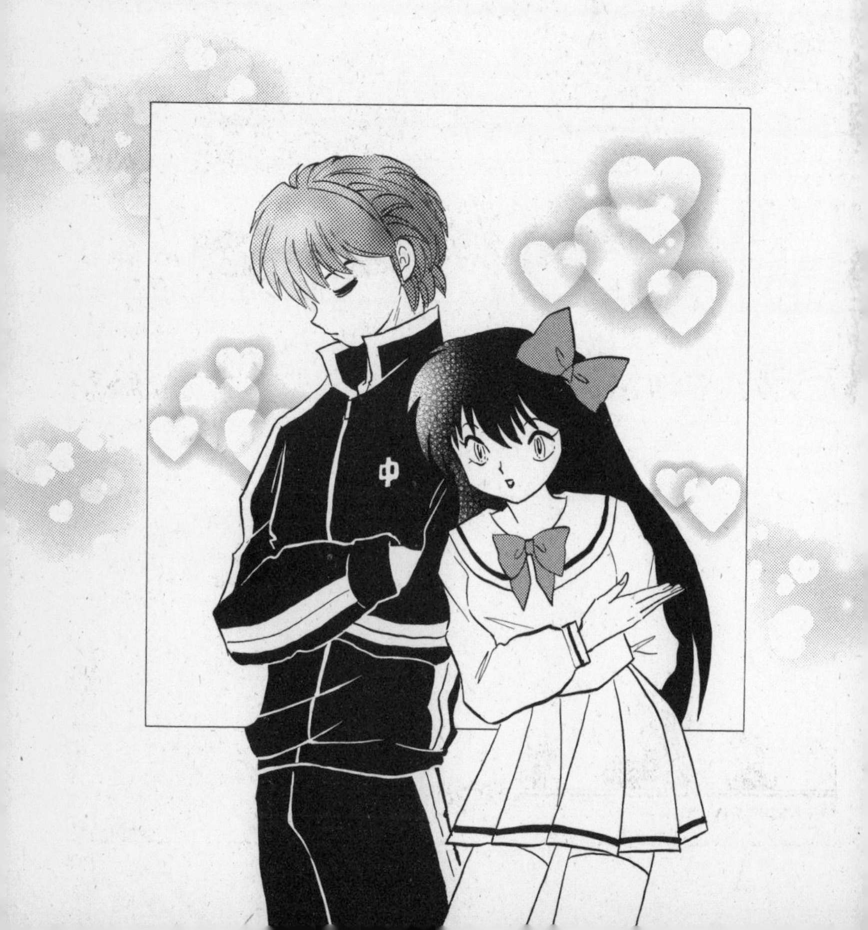

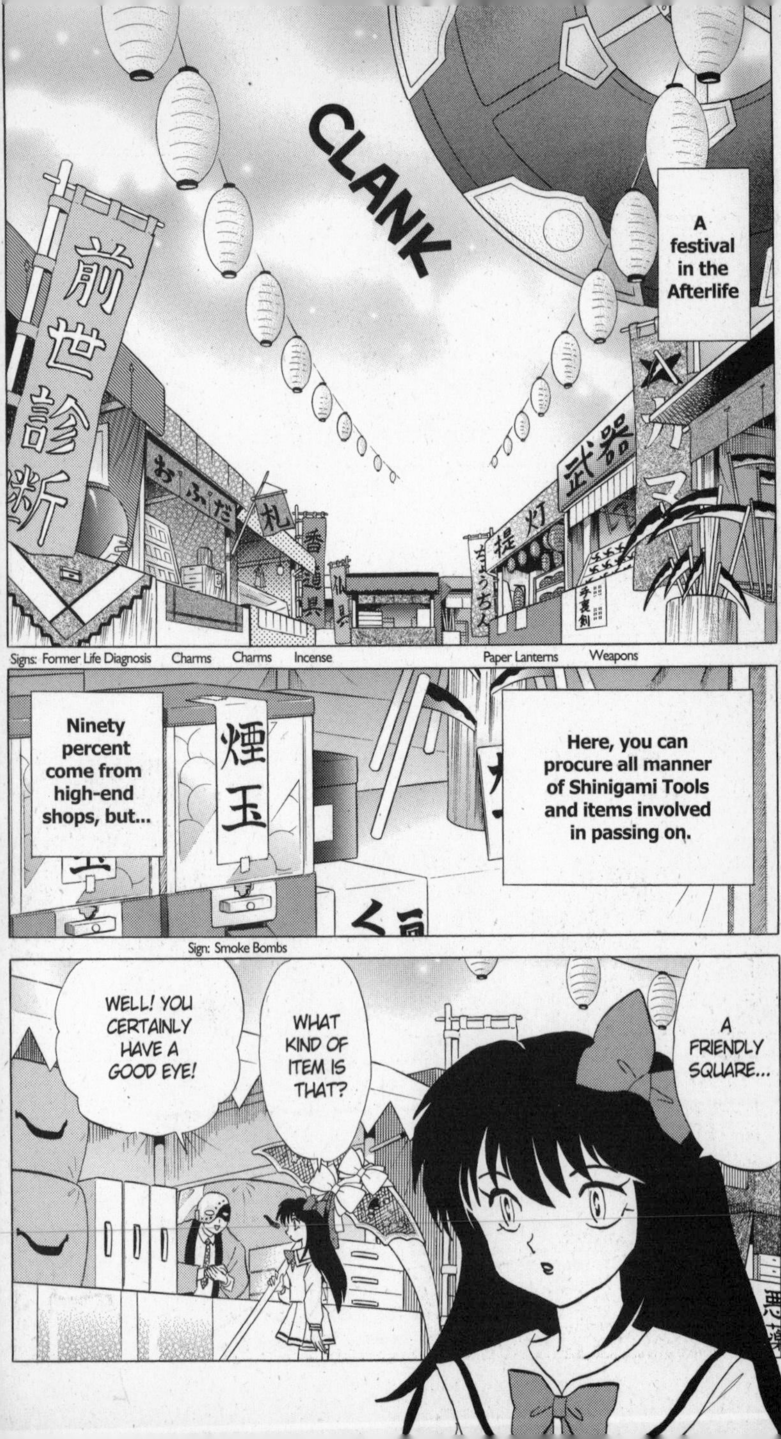
A festival in the Afterlife
CLANK
武器
提灯
札
前世診断
おふだ
Signs: Former Life Diagnosis Charms Charms Incense Paper Lanterns Weapons
Here, you can procure all manner of Shinigami Tools and items involved in passing on.
煙玉
Ninety percent come from high-end shops, but...
Sign: Smoke Bombs
A FRIENDLY SQUARE...
WHAT KIND OF ITEM IS THAT?
WELL! YOU CERTAINLY HAVE A GOOD EYE!

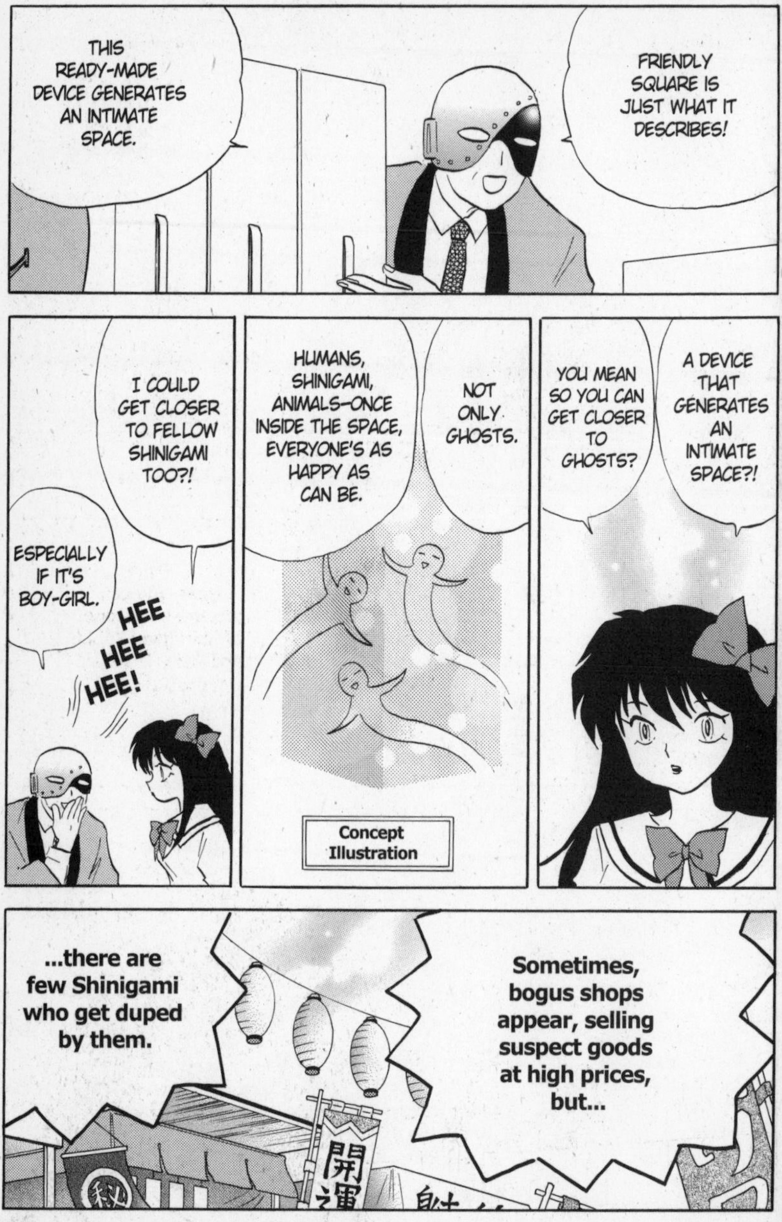
FRIENDLY SQUARE IS JUST WHAT IT DESCRIBES!
THIS READY-MADE DEVICE GENERATES AN INTIMATE SPACE.
A DEVICE THAT GENERATES AN INTIMATE SPACE?!
YOU MEAN SO YOU CAN GET CLOSER TO GHOSTS?
NOT ONLY GHOSTS.
HUMANS, SHINIGAMI, ANIMALS—ONCE INSIDE THE SPACE, EVERYONE'S AS HAPPY AS CAN BE.
Concept Illustration
I COULD GET CLOSER TO FELLOW SHINIGAMI TOO?!
ESPECIALLY IF IT'S BOY-GIRL.
HEE HEE HEE!
Sometimes, bogus shops appear, selling suspect goods at high prices, but...
...there are few Shinigami who get duped by them.

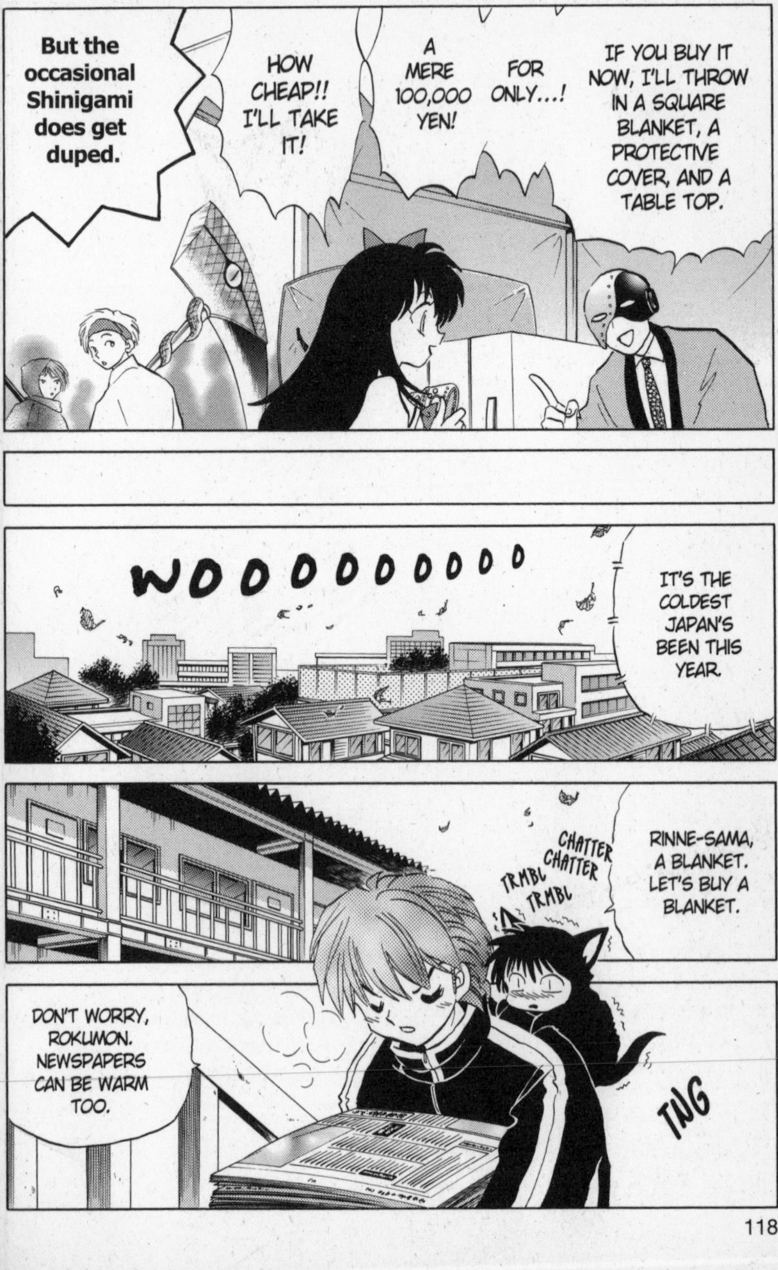
IF YOU BUY IT NOW, I'LL THROW IN A SQUARE BLANKET, A PROTECTIVE COVER, AND A TABLE TOP.
FOR ONLY...!
A MERE 100,000 YEN!
HOW CHEAP!! I'LL TAKE IT!
But the occasional Shinigami does get duped.
IT'S THE COLDEST JAPAN'S BEEN THIS YEAR.
WOOOOOOOOO
RINNE-SAMA, A BLANKET. LET'S BUY A BLANKET.
CHATTER CHATTER
TRMBL TRMBL
DON'T WORRY, ROKUMON. NEWSPAPERS CAN BE WARM TOO.
TNG

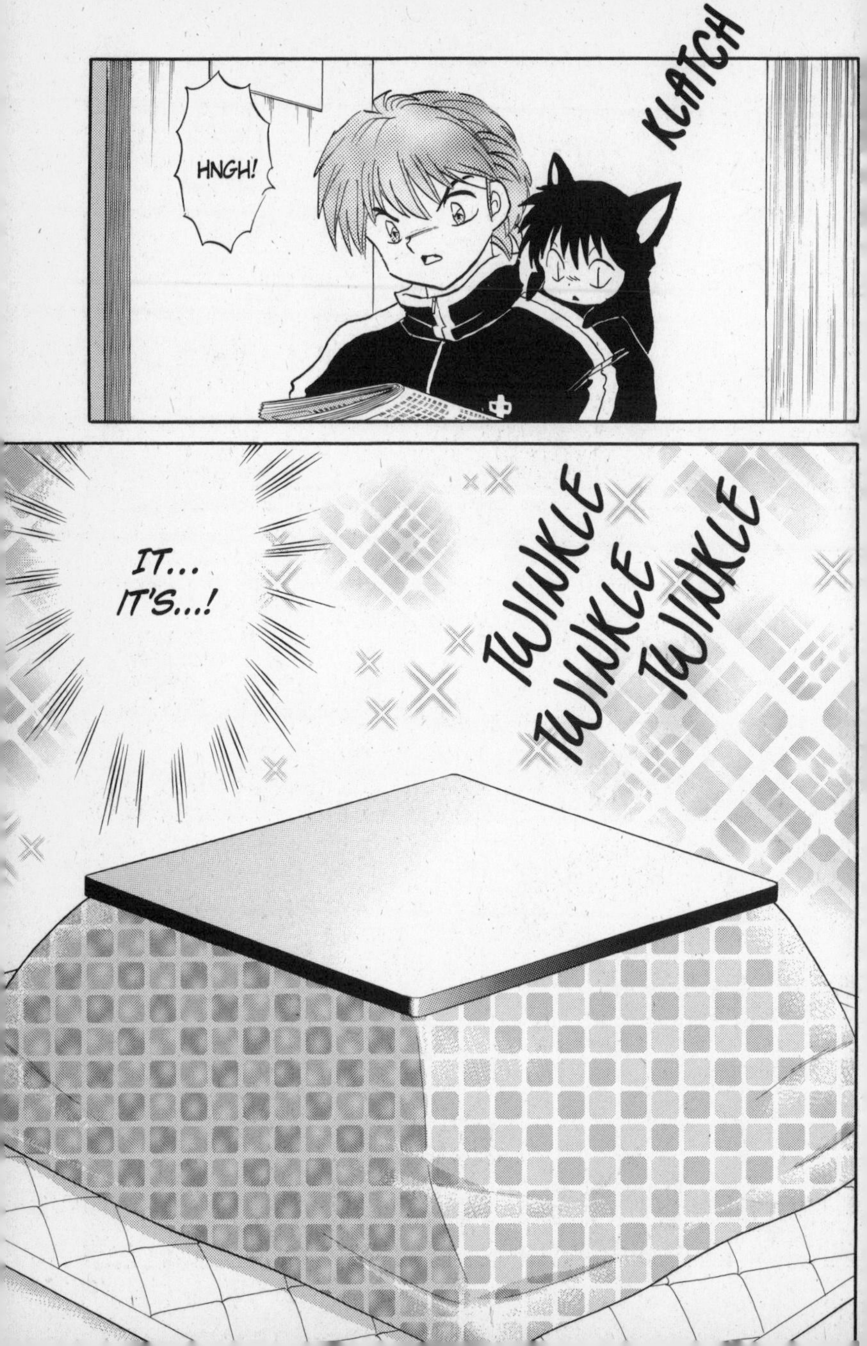
KLATCH
HNGH!
TWINKLE TWINKLE TWINKLE
IT... IT'S...!

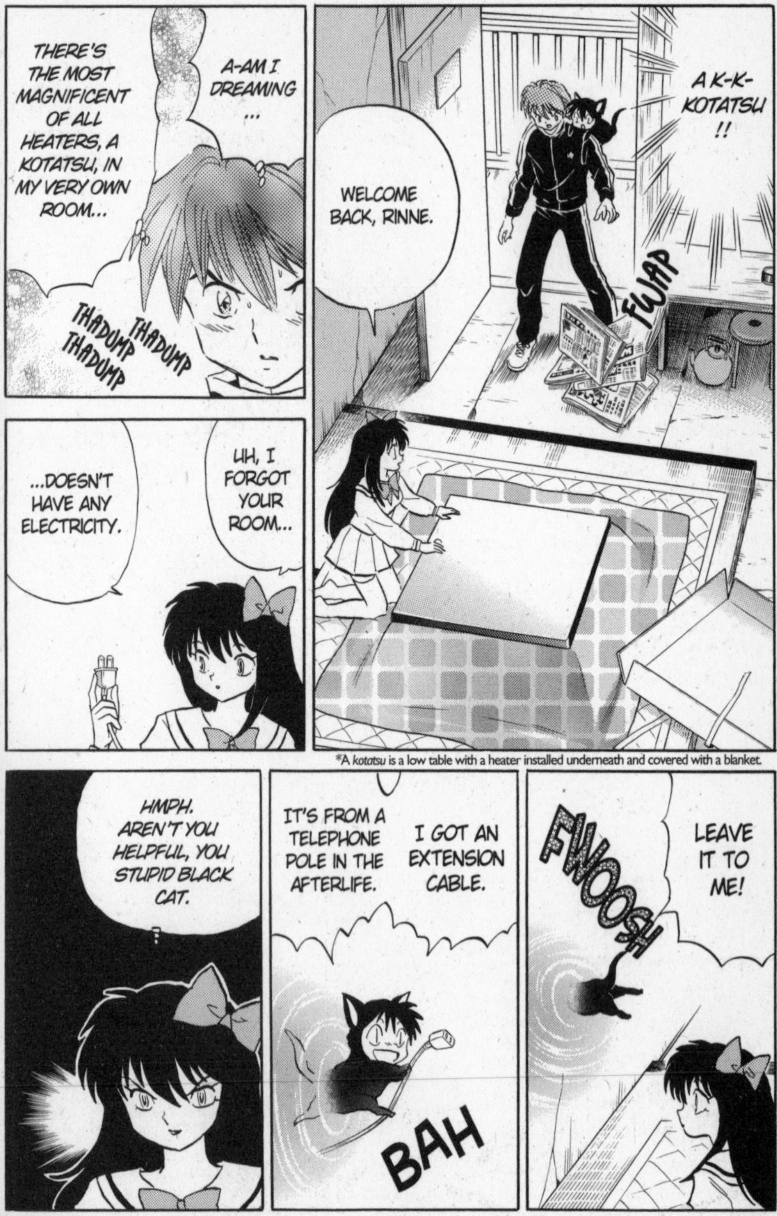
A K-K-KOTATSU!!
FWAP
WELCOME BACK, RINNE.
A-AM I DREAMING...
THERE'S THE MOST MAGNIFICENT OF ALL HEATERS, A KOTATSU, IN MY VERY OWN ROOM...
THADUMP THADUMP THADUMP
UH, I FORGOT YOUR ROOM...
...DOESN'T HAVE ANY ELECTRICITY.
FWOOSH
LEAVE IT TO ME!
I GOT AN EXTENSION CABLE.
IT'S FROM A TELEPHONE POLE IN THE AFTERLIFE.
BAH
HMPH. AREN'T YOU HELPFUL, YOU STUPID BLACK CAT.

*A *kotatsu* is a low table with a heater installed underneath and covered with a blanket.

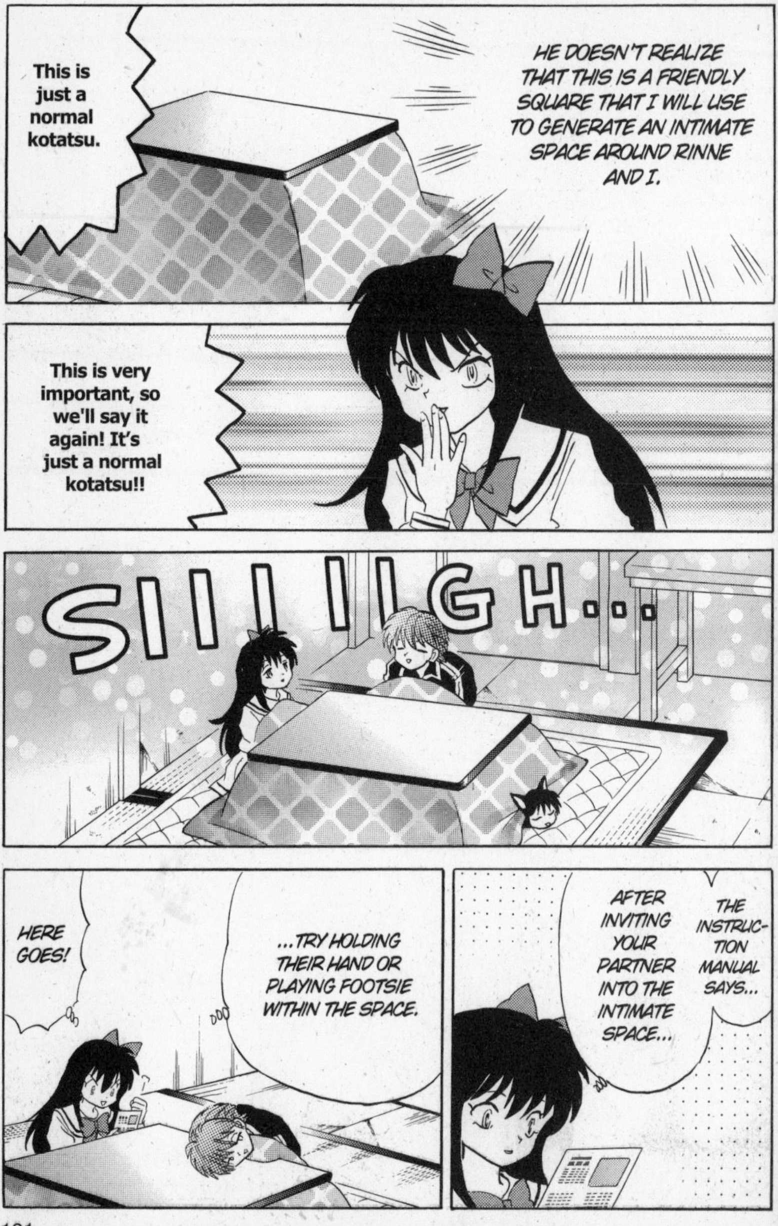
HE DOESN'T REALIZE THAT THIS IS A FRIENDLY SQUARE THAT I WILL USE TO GENERATE AN INTIMATE SPACE AROUND RINNE AND I.
This is just a normal kotatsu.
This is very important, so we'll say it again! It's just a normal kotatsu!!
SIIIIGH...
THE INSTRUCTION MANUAL SAYS...
AFTER INVITING YOUR PARTNER INTO THE INTIMATE SPACE...
...TRY HOLDING THEIR HAND OR PLAYING FOOTSIE WITHIN THE SPACE.
HERE GOES!

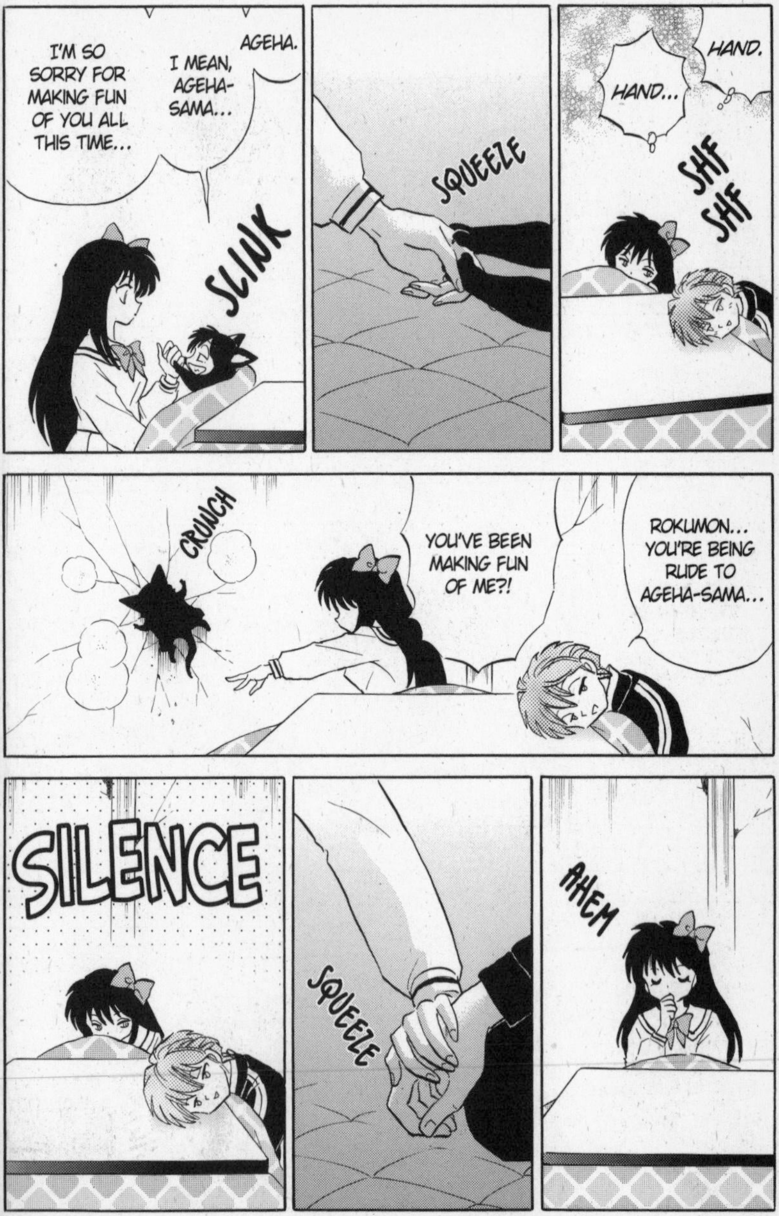
HAND.
HAND...
SHF SHF
SQUEEZE
AGEHA.
I MEAN, AGEHA-SAMA...
I'M SO SORRY FOR MAKING FUN OF YOU ALL THIS TIME...
SLINK
ROKUMON... YOU'RE BEING RUDE TO AGEHA-SAMA...
YOU'VE BEEN MAKING FUN OF ME?!
CRUNCH
AHEM
SQUEEZE
SILENCE

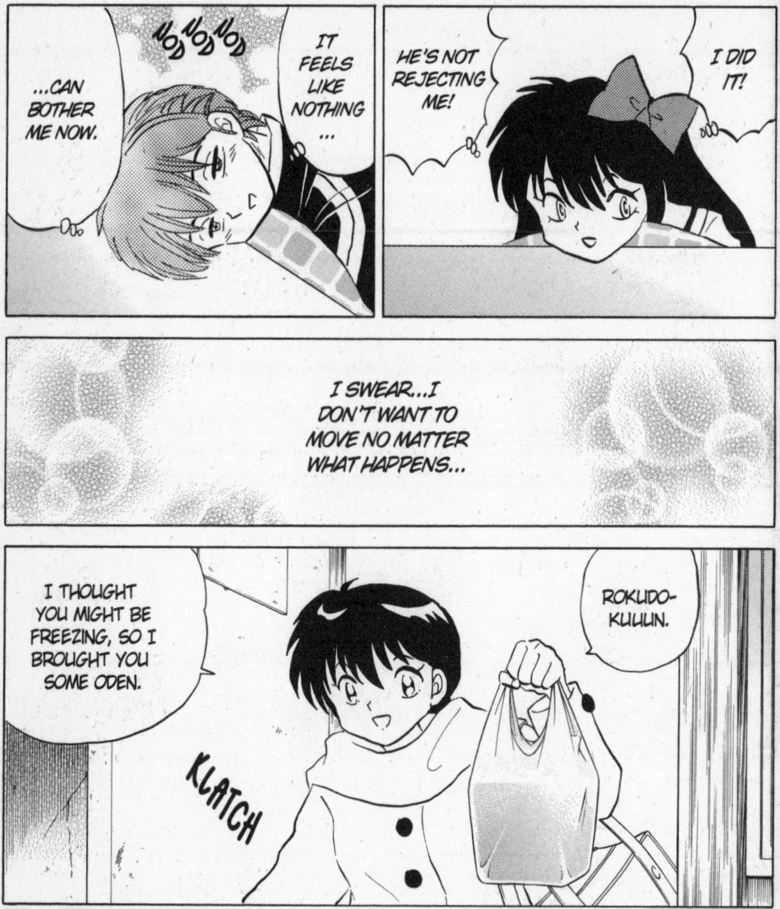
I DID IT!
HE'S NOT REJECTING ME!
IT FEELS LIKE NOTHING...
NOD NOD NOD
...CAN BOTHER ME NOW.
I SWEAR...I DON'T WANT TO MOVE NO MATTER WHAT HAPPENS...
ROKUDO-KUUUN.
I THOUGHT YOU MIGHT BE FREEZING, SO I BROUGHT YOU SOME ODEN.
KLATCH

*Oden is a kind of stew often served during the winter.

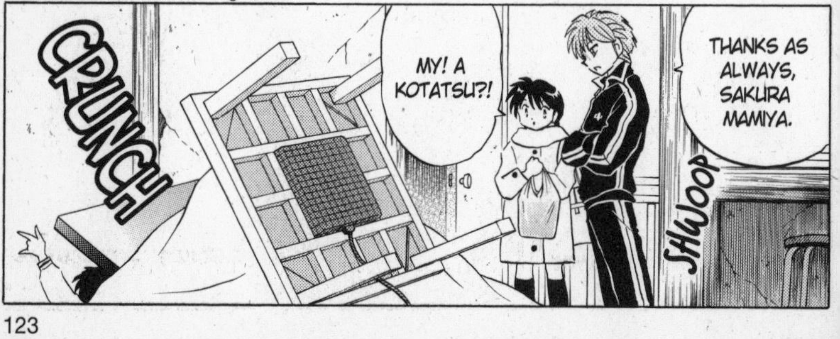
THANKS AS ALWAYS, SAKURA MAMIYA.
SHWOOP
MY! A KOTATSU?!
CRUNCH

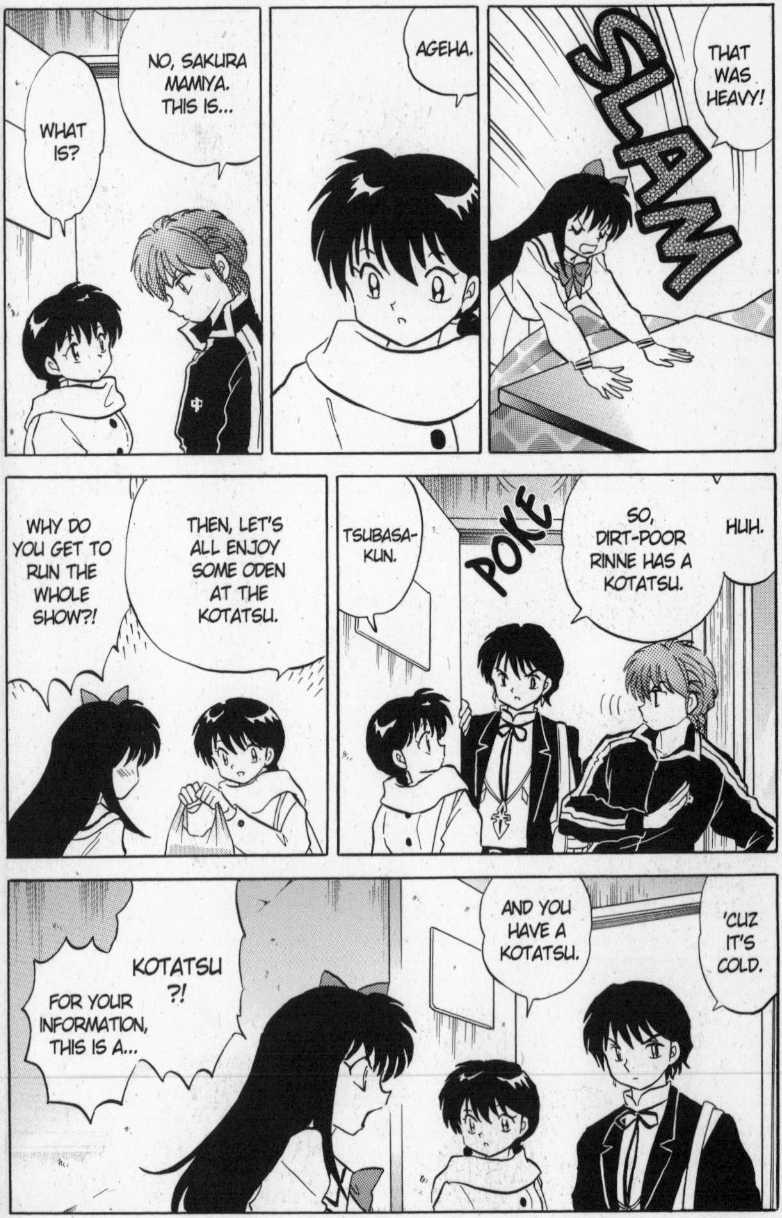
SLAM
THAT WAS HEAVY!
AGEHA.
NO, SAKURA MAMIYA. THIS IS...
WHAT IS?
HUH.
SO, DIRT-POOR RINNE HAS A KOTATSU.
POKE
TSUBASA-KUN.
THEN, LET'S ALL ENJOY SOME ODEN AT THE KOTATSU.
WHY DO YOU GET TO RUN THE WHOLE SHOW?!
'CUZ IT'S COLD.
AND YOU HAVE A KOTATSU.
KOTATSU ?!
FOR YOUR INFORMATION, THIS IS A...

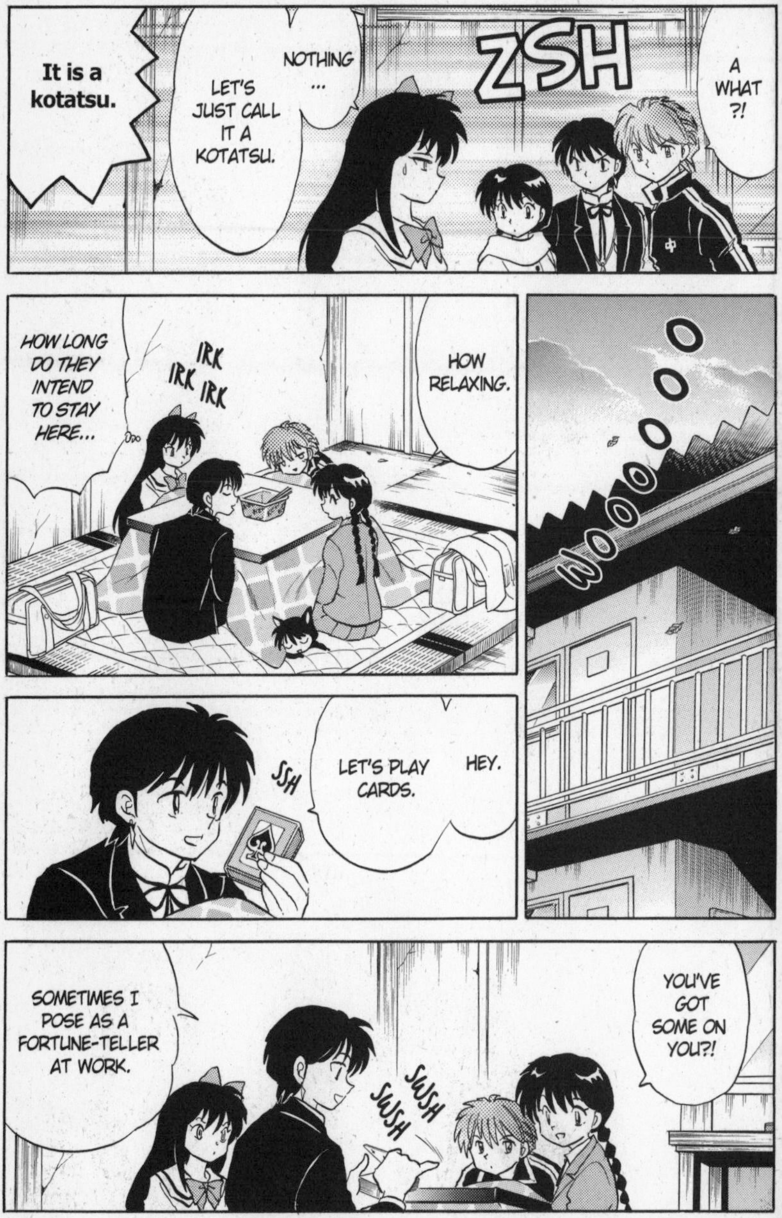
A WHAT ?!
ZSH
NOTHING ...
LET'S JUST CALL IT A KOTATSU.
It is a kotatsu.
WOOOOOOO
HOW RELAXING.
IRK IRK IRK
HOW LONG DO THEY INTEND TO STAY HERE...
HEY.
LET'S PLAY CARDS.
SSH
YOU'VE GOT SOME ON YOU?!
SWISH SWISH
SOMETIMES I POSE AS A FORTUNE-TELLER AT WORK.

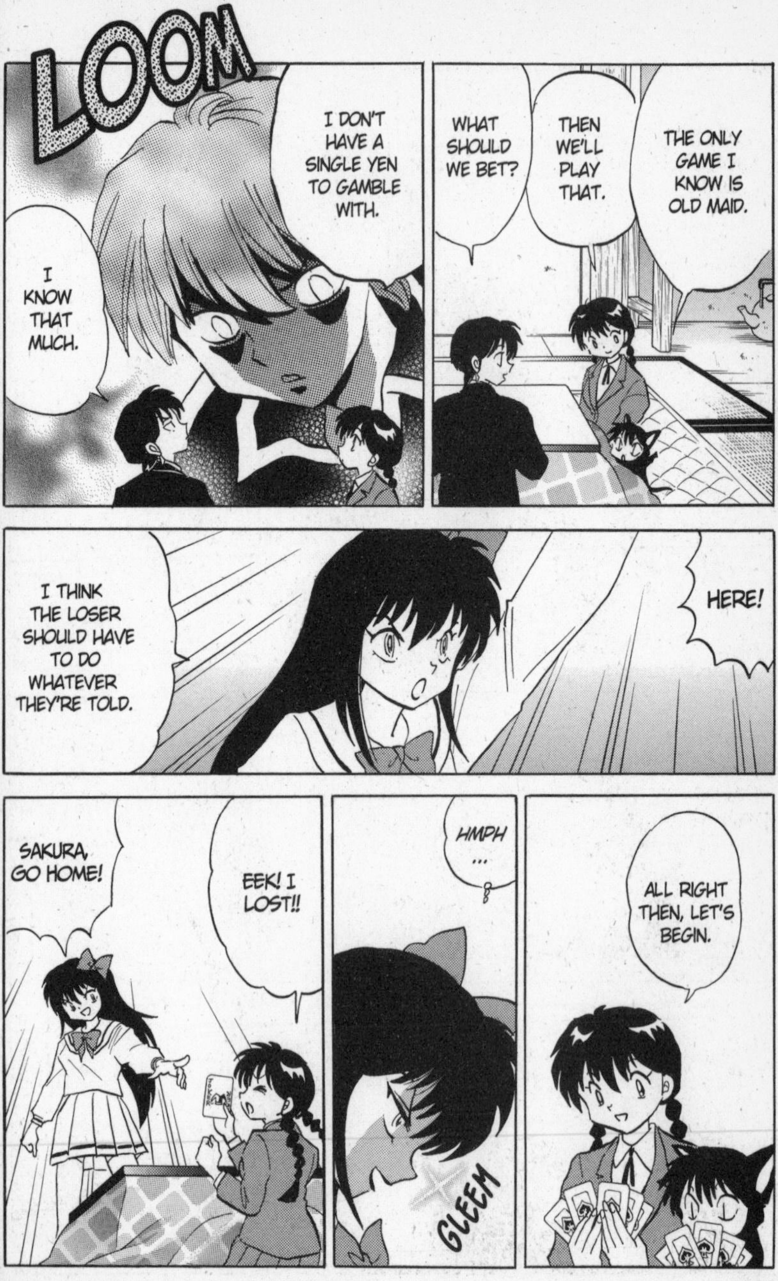
THE ONLY GAME I KNOW IS OLD MAID.
THEN WE'LL PLAY THAT.
WHAT SHOULD WE BET?
I DON'T HAVE A SINGLE YEN TO GAMBLE WITH.
LOOM
I KNOW THAT MUCH.
HERE!
I THINK THE LOSER SHOULD HAVE TO DO WHATEVER THEY'RE TOLD.
ALL RIGHT THEN, LET'S BEGIN.
HMPH ...
GLEEM
EEK! I LOST!!
SAKURA, GO HOME!

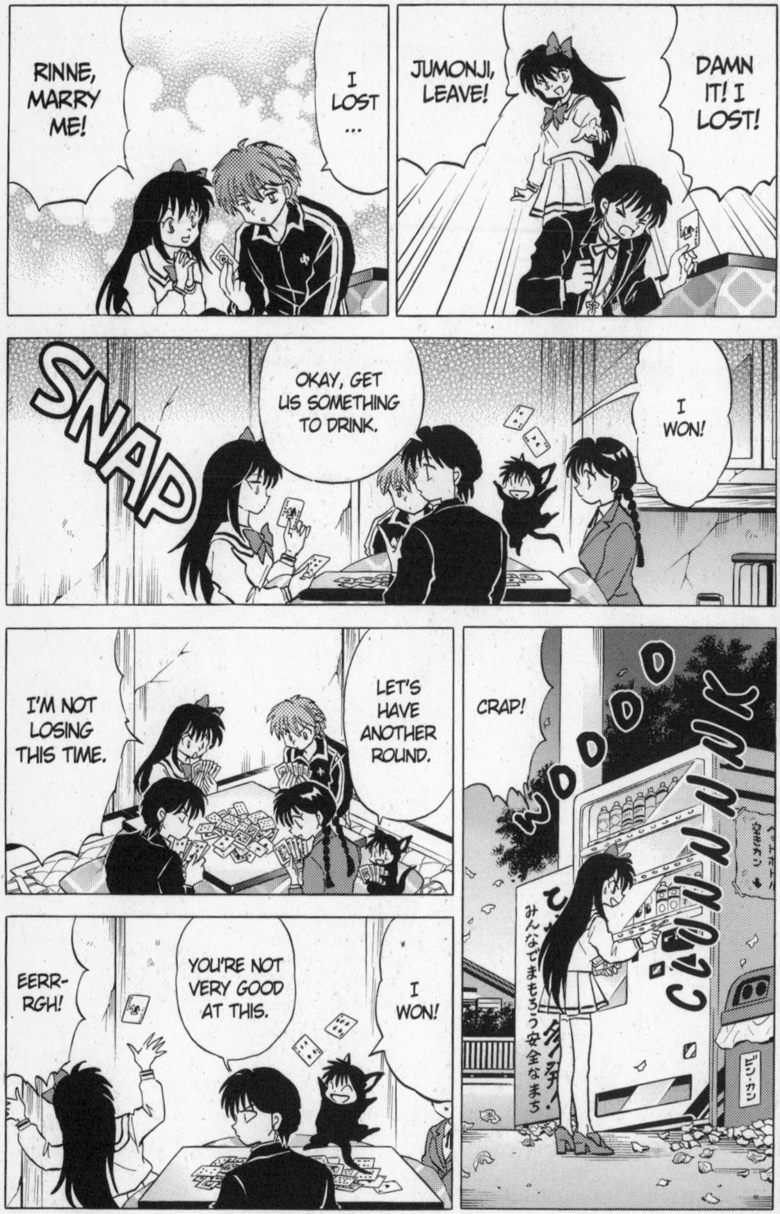
DAMN IT! I LOST!
JUMONJI, LEAVE!
I LOST ...
RINNE, MARRY ME!
I WON!
OKAY, GET US SOMETHING TO DRINK.
SNAP
CRAP!
CLUNK
みんなでまもろう安全なまち
ビン・カン
LET'S HAVE ANOTHER ROUND.
I'M NOT LOSING THIS TIME.
I WON!
YOU'RE NOT VERY GOOD AT THIS.
EERR-RGH!

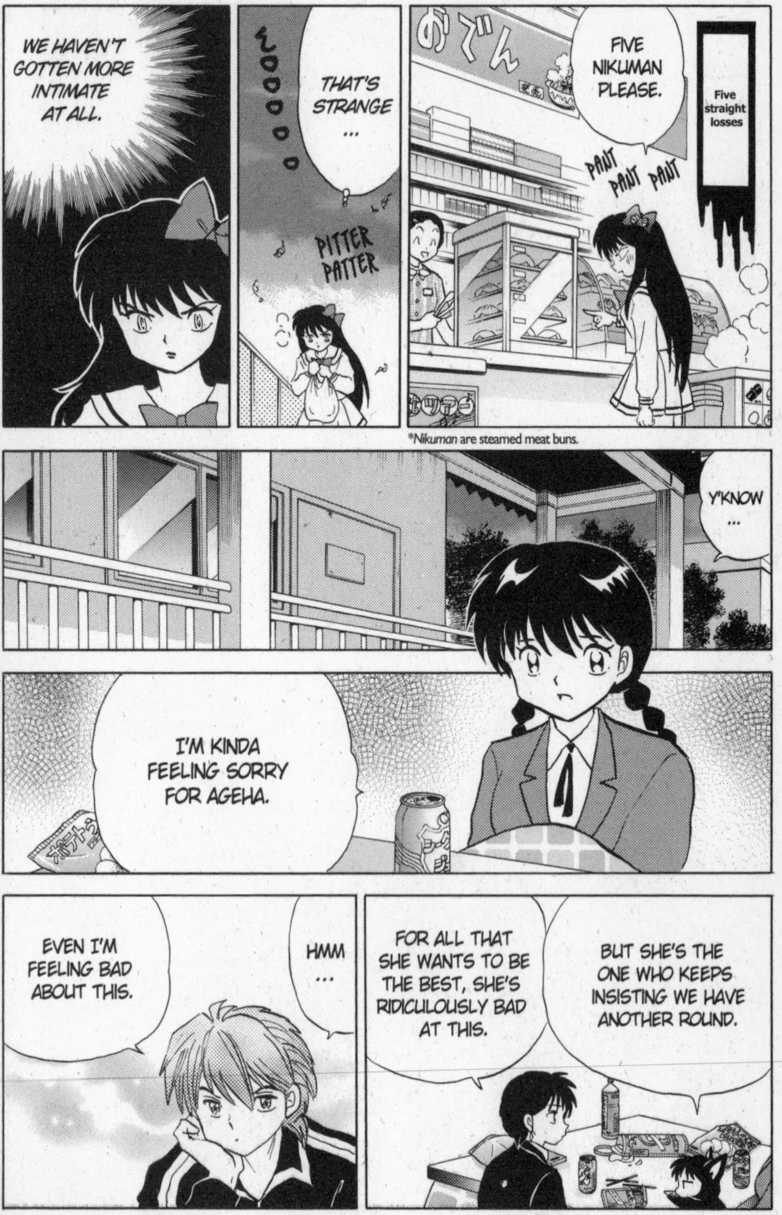
Five straight losses
FIVE NIKUMAN PLEASE.
PANT PANT PANT
THAT'S STRANGE ...
PITTER PATTER
WE HAVEN'T GOTTEN MORE INTIMATE AT ALL.
Y'KNOW ...
I'M KINDA FEELING SORRY FOR AGEHA.
BUT SHE'S THE ONE WHO KEEPS INSISTING WE HAVE ANOTHER ROUND.
FOR ALL THAT SHE WANTS TO BE THE BEST, SHE'S RIDICULOUSLY BAD AT THIS.
HMM ...
EVEN I'M FEELING BAD ABOUT THIS.

*Nikuman are steamed meat buns.

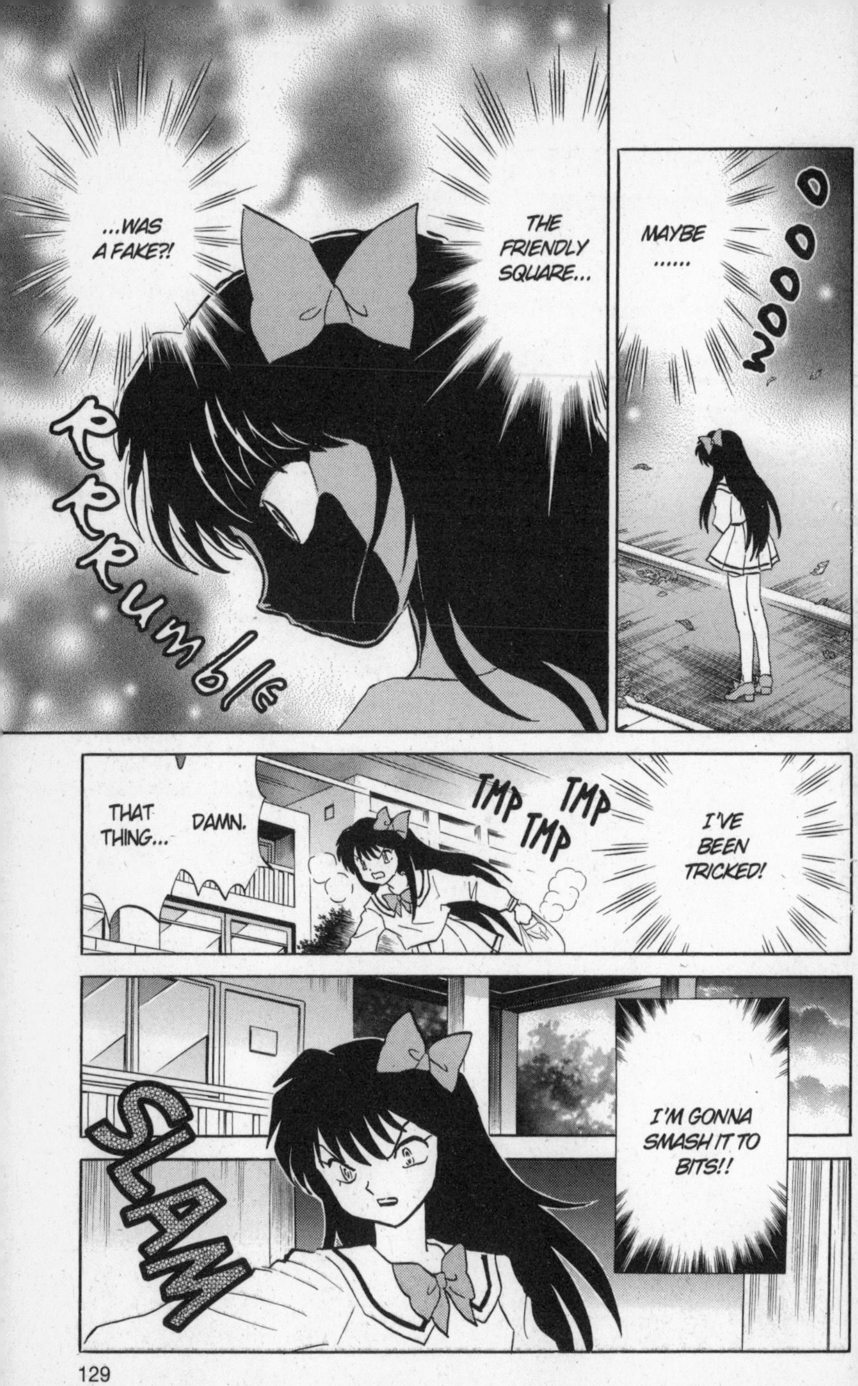
MAYBE ......
WOOOO
THE FRIENDLY SQUARE...
...WAS A FAKE?!
RRRumble
I'VE BEEN TRICKED!
TMP TMP TMP
DAMN.
THAT THING...
I'M GONNA SMASH IT TO BITS!!
SLAM

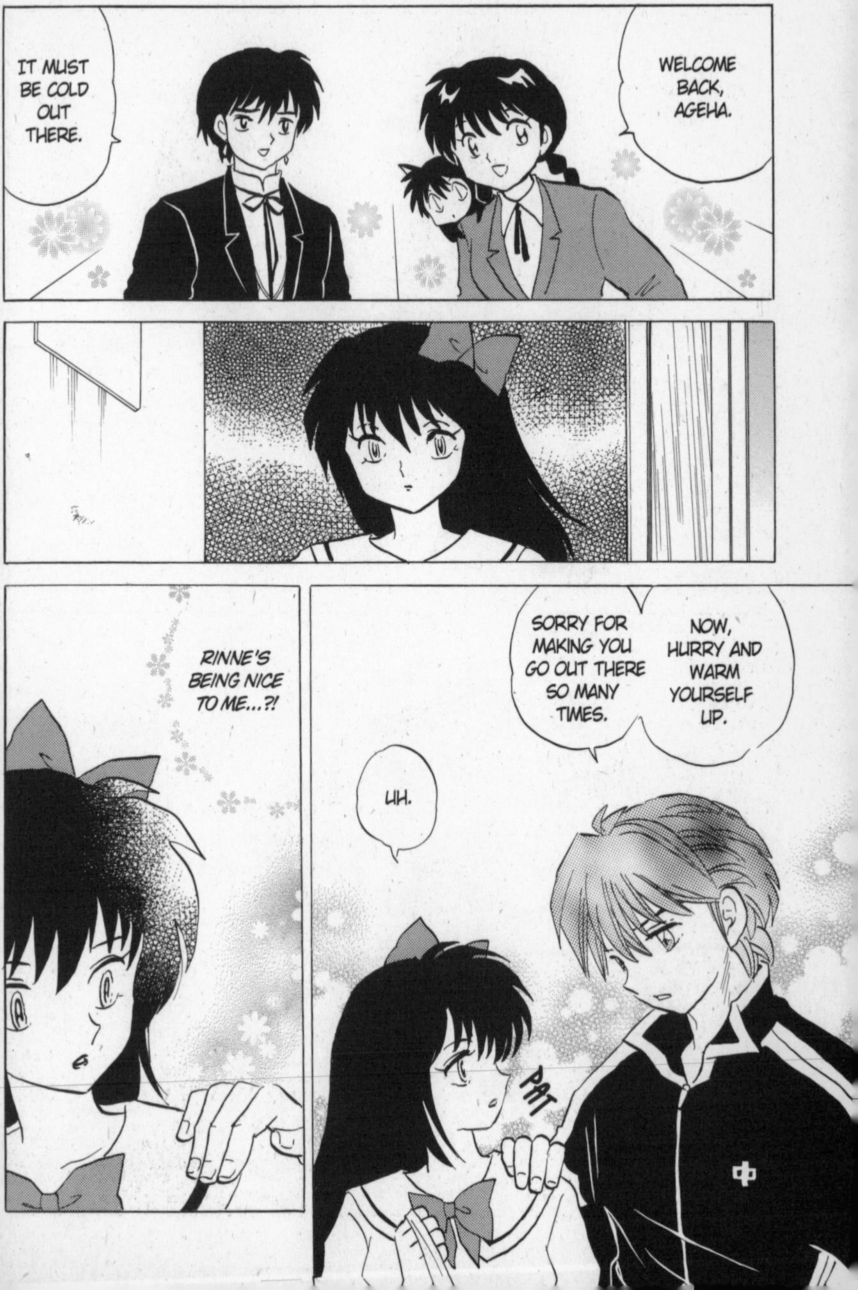
WELCOME BACK, AGEHA.
IT MUST BE COLD OUT THERE.
NOW, HURRY AND WARM YOURSELF UP.
SORRY FOR MAKING YOU GO OUT THERE SO MANY TIMES.
UH.
PAT
RINNE'S BEING NICE TO ME...?!

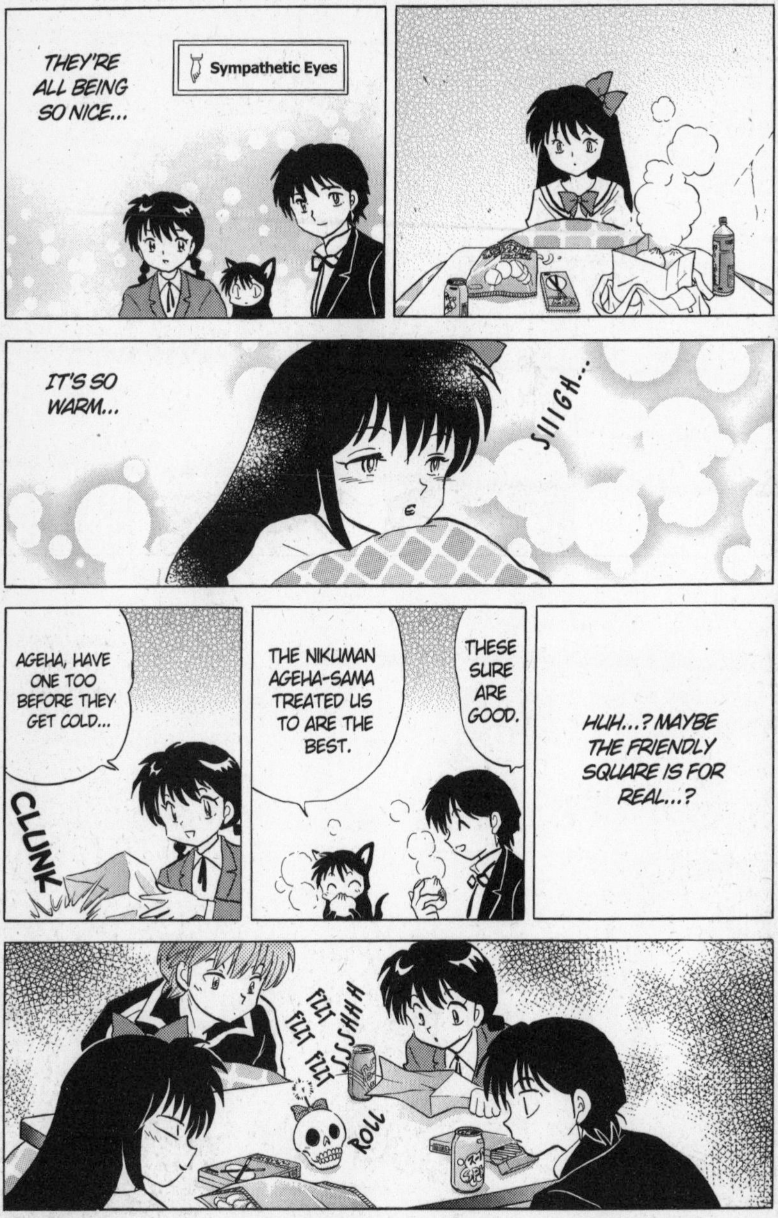
Sympathetic Eyes
THEY'RE ALL BEING SO NICE...
IT'S SO WARM...
SIIIGH...
HUH...? MAYBE THE FRIENDLY SQUARE IS FOR REAL...?
THESE SURE ARE GOOD.
THE NIKUMAN AGEHA-SAMA TREATED US TO ARE THE BEST.
AGEHA, HAVE ONE TOO BEFORE THEY GET COLD...
CLUNK
SSSHHH
FZZT FZZT FZZT
ROLL

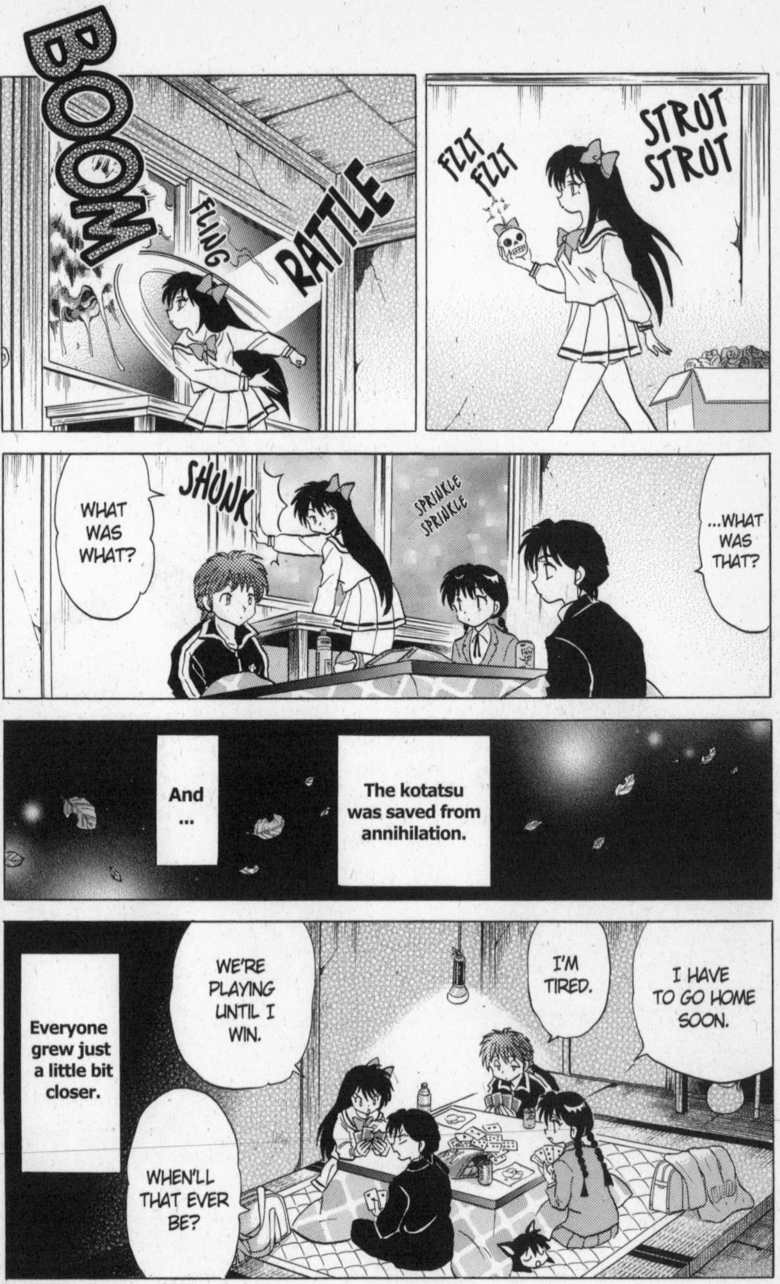
STRUT STRUT
FZZT FZZT
BOOM
RATTLE
FLING
...WHAT WAS THAT?
SPRINKLE SPRINKLE
SHUNK
WHAT WAS WHAT?
And ...
The kotatsu was saved from annihilation.
I HAVE TO GO HOME SOON.
I'M TIRED.
WE'RE PLAYING UNTIL I WIN.
WHEN'LL THAT EVER BE?
Everyone grew just a little bit closer.

CHAPTER 76: THE CURSE OF THE KITCHEN COUNTER

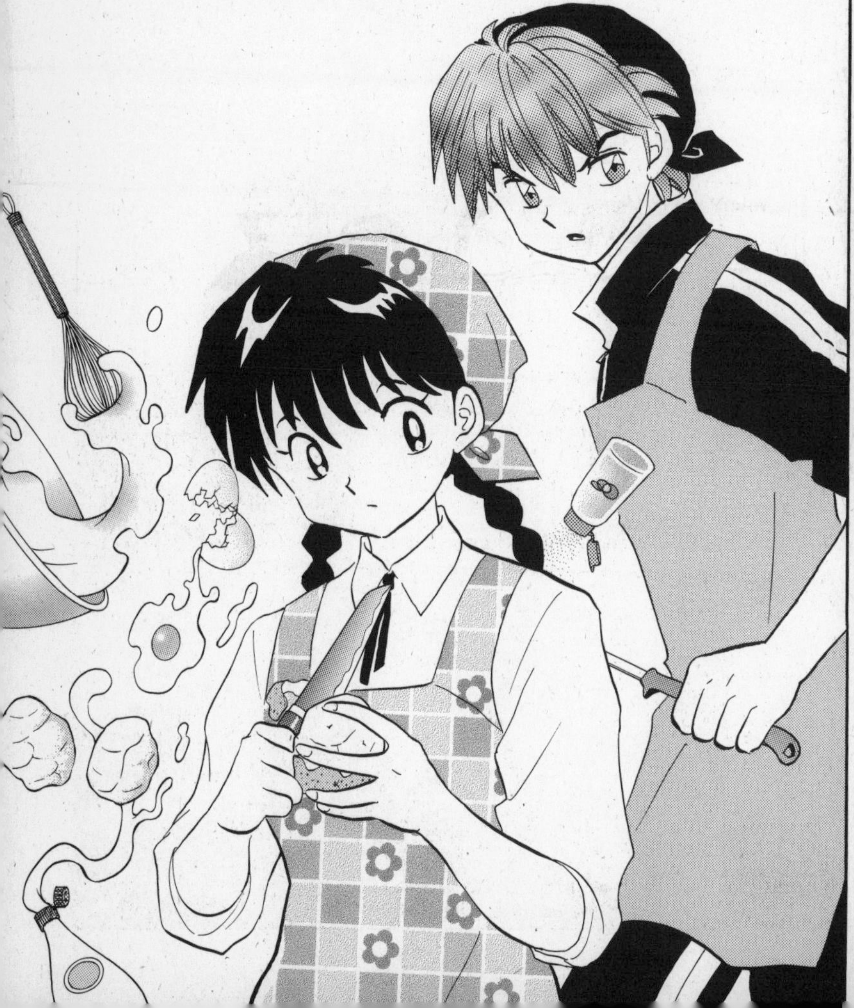

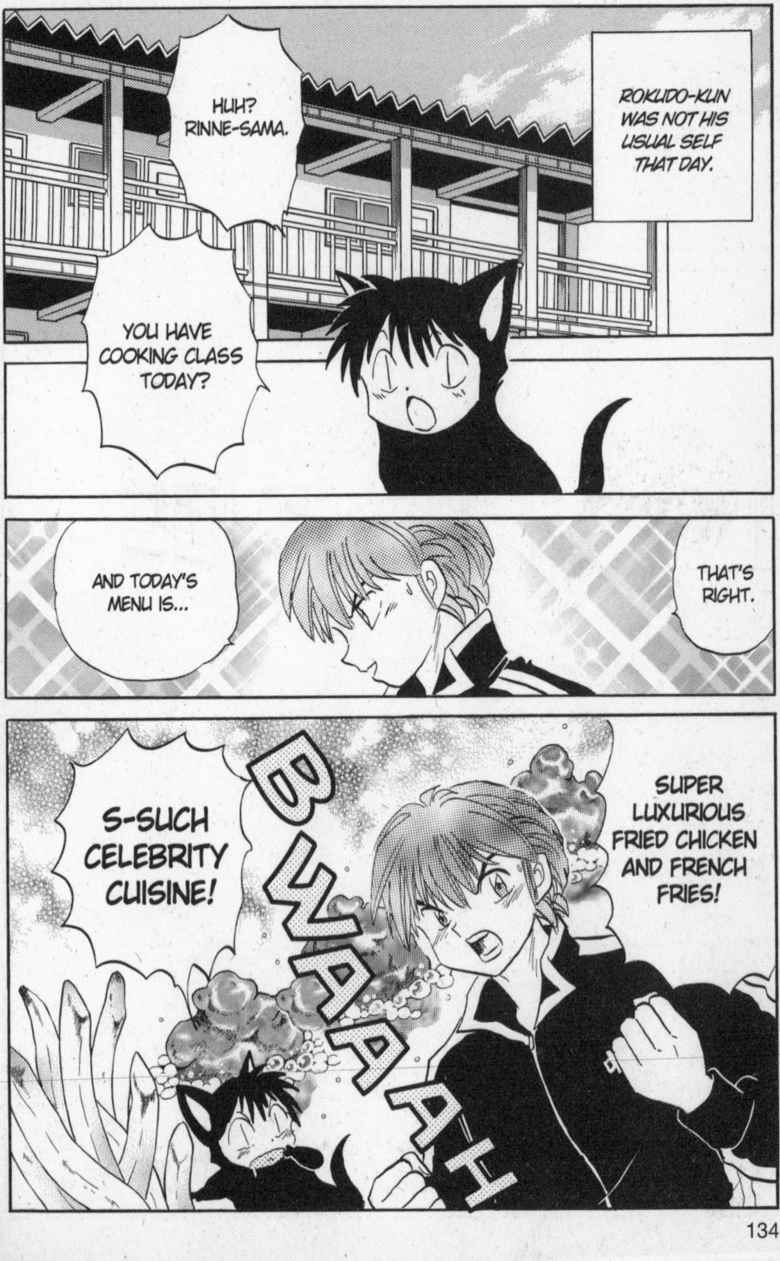
ROKUDO-KUN WAS NOT HIS USUAL SELF THAT DAY.
HUH? RINNE-SAMA.
YOU HAVE COOKING CLASS TODAY?
THAT'S RIGHT.
AND TODAY'S MENU IS...
SUPER LUXURIOUS FRIED CHICKEN AND FRENCH FRIES!
BWAAAH
S-SUCH CELEBRITY CUISINE!

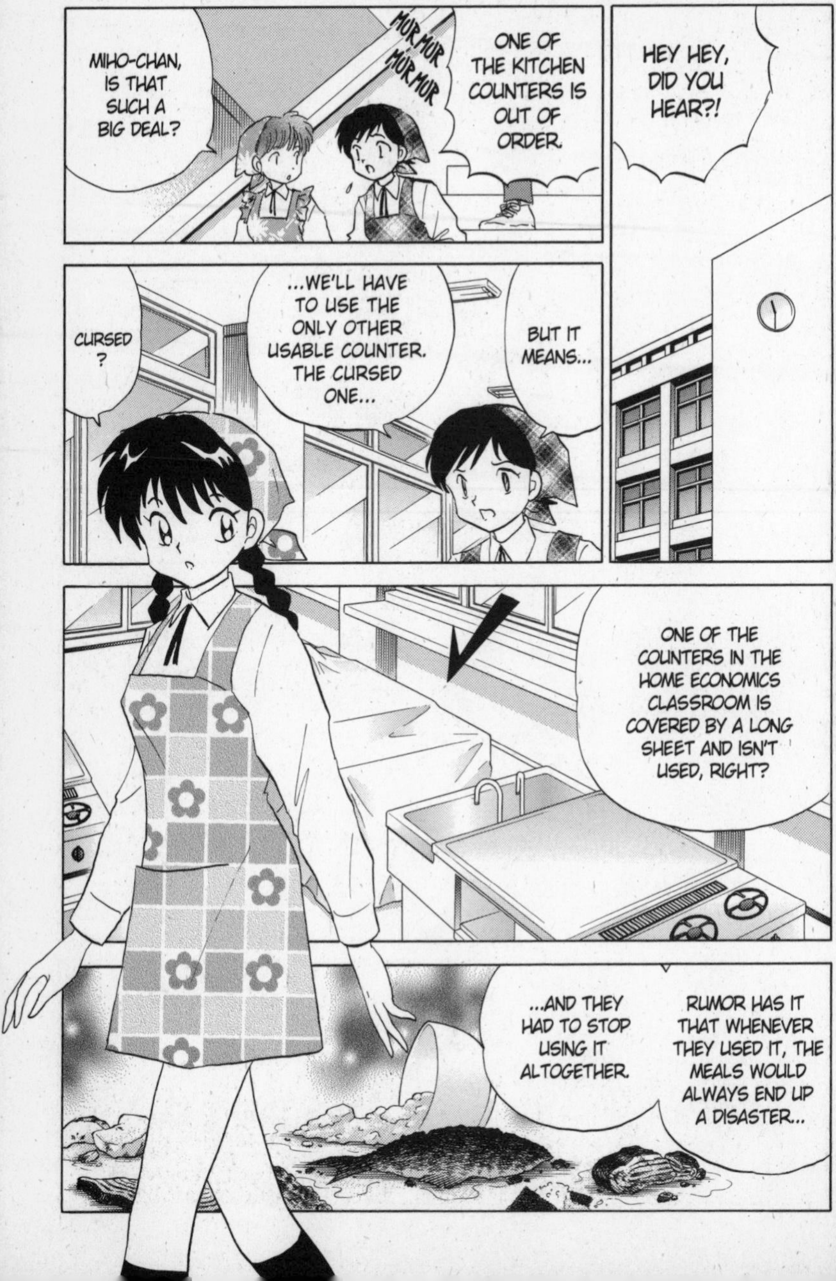
HEY HEY, DID YOU HEAR?!
ONE OF THE KITCHEN COUNTERS IS OUT OF ORDER.
MUR MUR MUR MUR
MIHO-CHAN, IS THAT SUCH A BIG DEAL?
BUT IT MEANS...
...WE'LL HAVE TO USE THE ONLY OTHER USABLE COUNTER. THE CURSED ONE...
CURSED?
ONE OF THE COUNTERS IN THE HOME ECONOMICS CLASSROOM IS COVERED BY A LONG SHEET AND ISN'T USED, RIGHT?
RUMOR HAS IT THAT WHENEVER THEY USED IT, THE MEALS WOULD ALWAYS END UP A DISASTER...
...AND THEY HAD TO STOP USING IT ALTOGETHER.

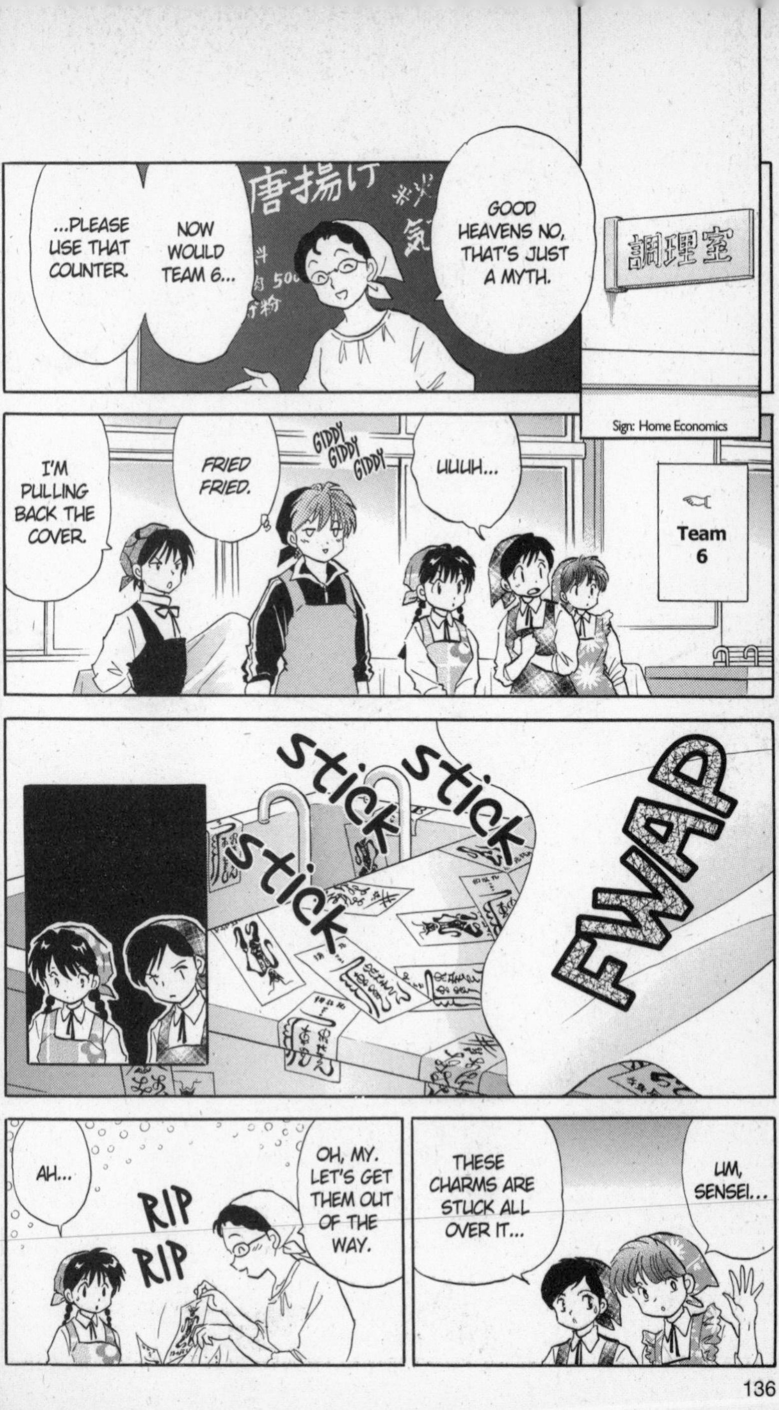

調理室
Sign: Home Economics
GOOD HEAVENS NO, THAT'S JUST A MYTH.
NOW WOULD TEAM 6...
...PLEASE USE THAT COUNTER.
Team 6
UUUH...
GIDDY GIDDY GIDDY
FRIED FRIED.
I'M PULLING BACK THE COVER.
FWAP
stick stick stick
UM, SENSEI...
THESE CHARMS ARE STUCK ALL OVER IT...
OH, MY. LET'S GET THEM OUT OF THE WAY.
RIP RIP
AH...

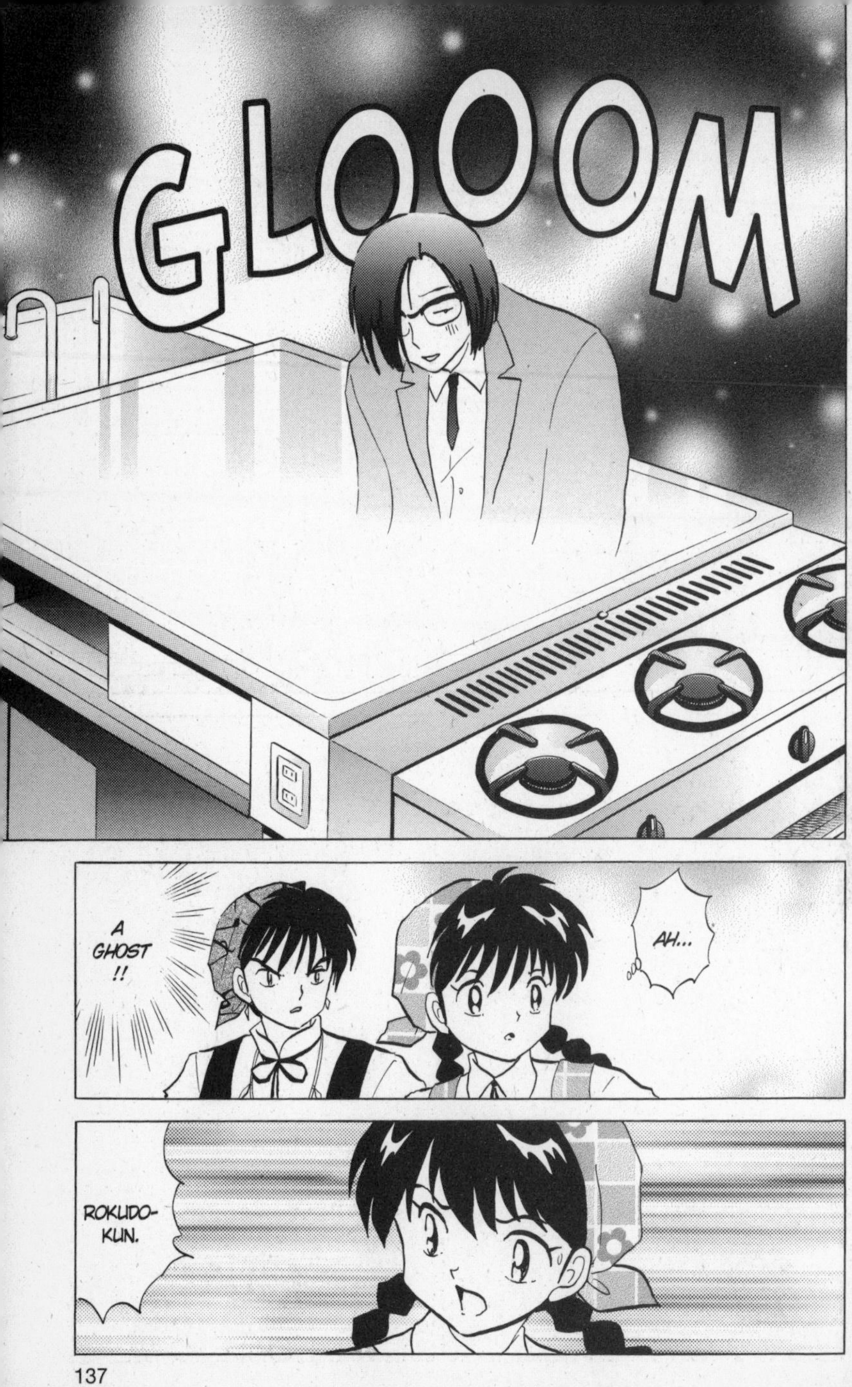
GLOOOM
AH...
A GHOST !!
ROKUDO-KUN.

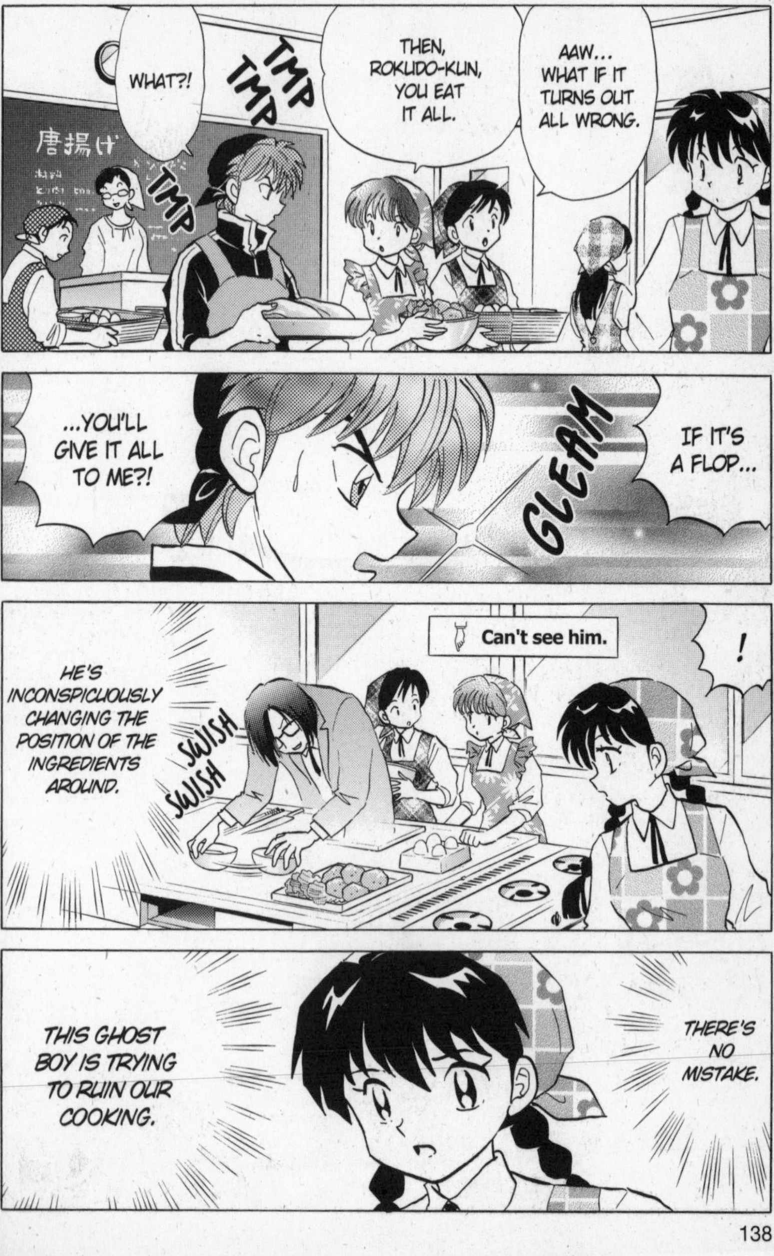
AAW... WHAT IF IT TURNS OUT ALL WRONG.
THEN, ROKUDO-KUN, YOU EAT IT ALL.
TMP TMP
TMP
WHAT?!
唐揚げ
IF IT'S A FLOP...
GLEAM
...YOU'LL GIVE IT ALL TO ME?!
!
Can't see him.
SWISH SWISH
HE'S INCONSPICUOUSLY CHANGING THE POSITION OF THE INGREDIENTS AROUND.
THERE'S NO MISTAKE.
THIS GHOST BOY IS TRYING TO RUIN OUR COOKING.

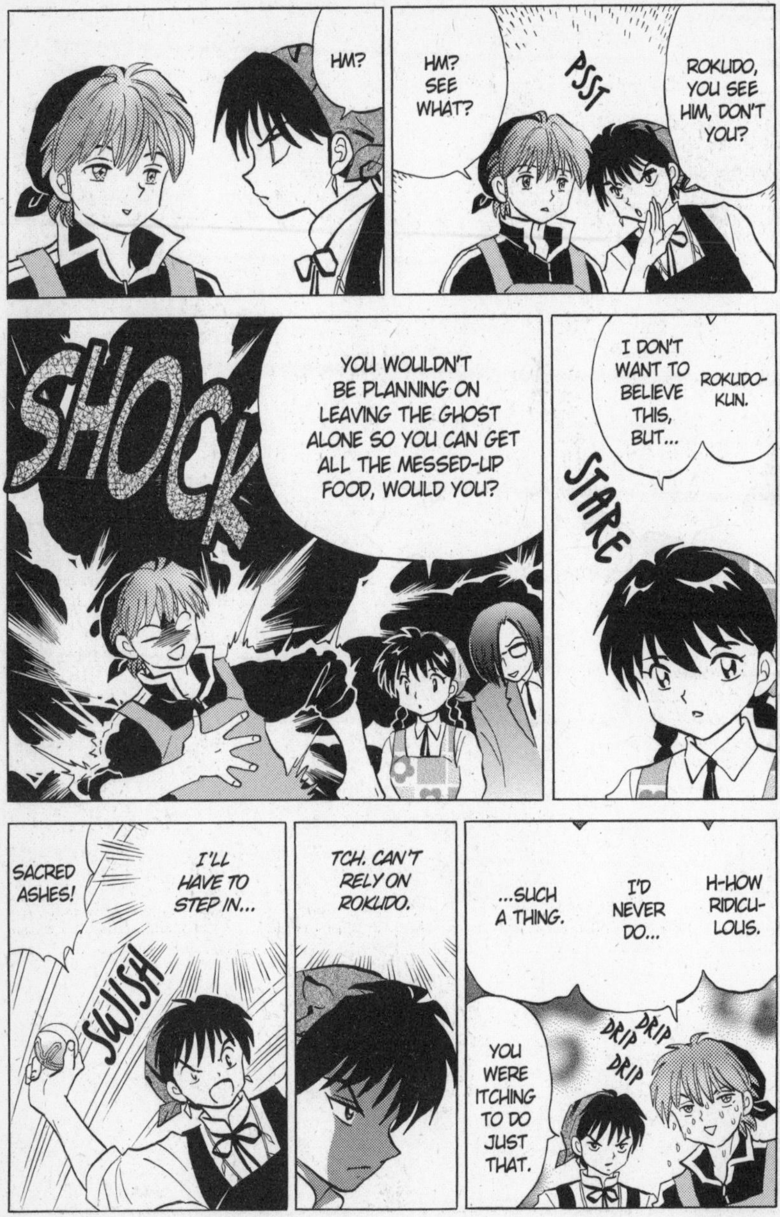
ROKUDO, YOU SEE HIM, DON'T YOU?
PSST
HM? SEE WHAT?
HM?
ROKUDO-KUN.
I DON'T WANT TO BELIEVE THIS, BUT...
STARE
YOU WOULDN'T BE PLANNING ON LEAVING THE GHOST ALONE SO YOU CAN GET ALL THE MESSED-UP FOOD, WOULD YOU?
SHOCK
H-HOW RIDICULOUS.
I'D NEVER DO...
...SUCH A THING.
DRIP
DRIP
DRIP
DRIP
YOU WERE ITCHING TO DO JUST THAT.
TCH. CAN'T RELY ON ROKUDO.
I'LL HAVE TO STEP IN...
SACRED ASHES!
SWISH

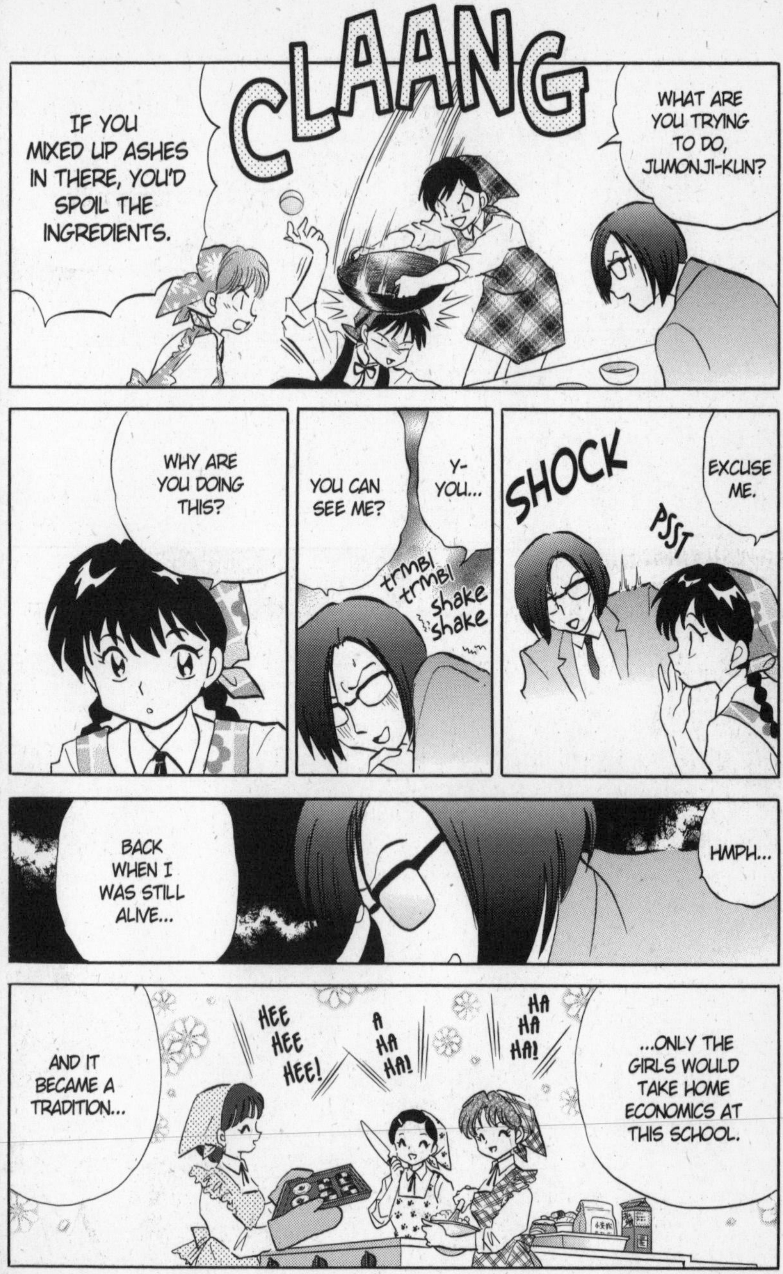
CLAANG
WHAT ARE YOU TRYING TO DO, JUMONJI-KUN?
IF YOU MIXED UP ASHES IN THERE, YOU'D SPOIL THE INGREDIENTS.
EXCUSE ME.
SHOCK
PSST
Y- YOU...
YOU CAN SEE ME?
trmbl trmbl
shake shake
WHY ARE YOU DOING THIS?
HMPH...
BACK WHEN I WAS STILL ALIVE...
...ONLY THE GIRLS WOULD TAKE HOME ECONOMICS AT THIS SCHOOL.
HA HA HA!
A HA HA!
HEE HEE HEE!
AND IT BECAME A TRADITION...

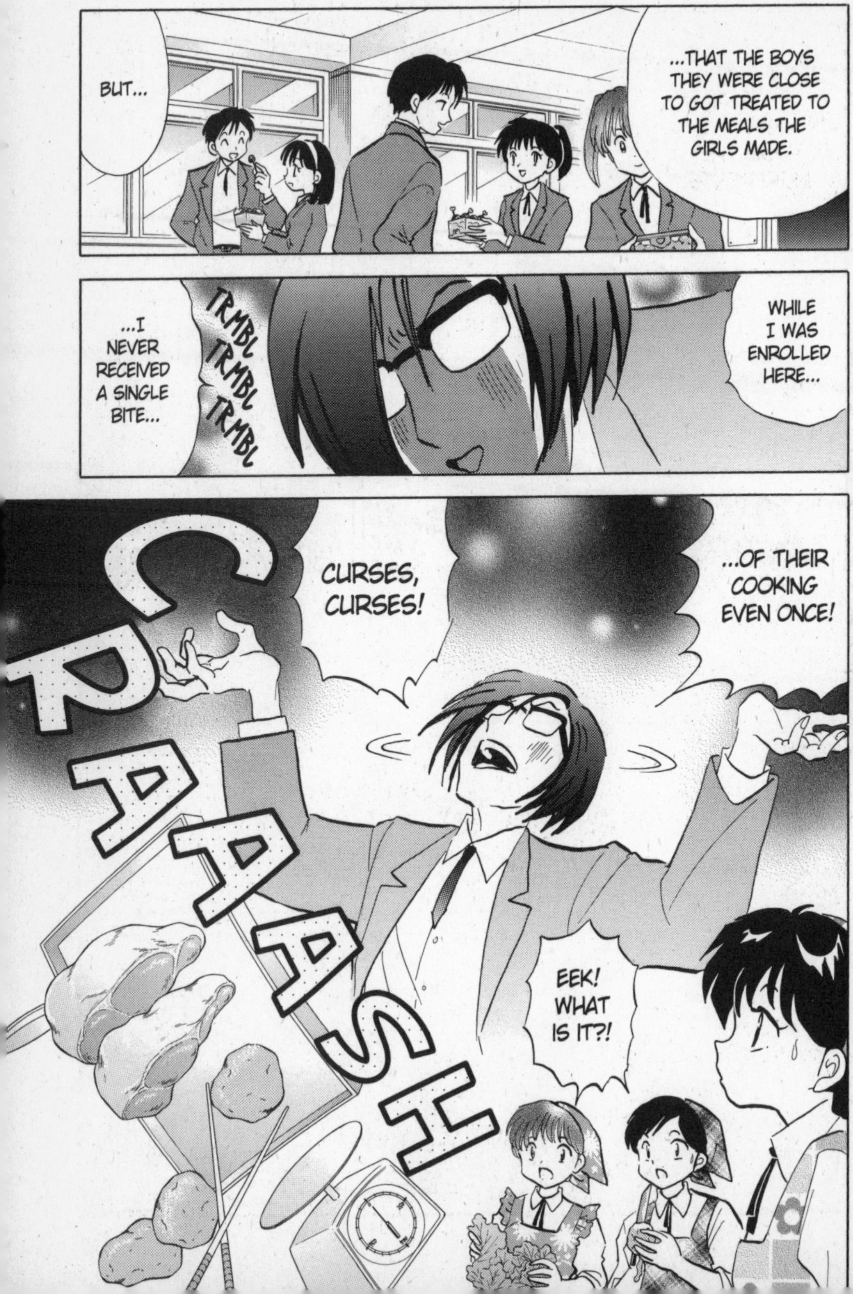
...THAT THE BOYS THEY WERE CLOSE TO GOT TREATED TO THE MEALS THE GIRLS MADE.
BUT...
WHILE I WAS ENROLLED HERE...
...I NEVER RECEIVED A SINGLE BITE...
TRMBL TRMBL TRMBL
...OF THEIR COOKING EVEN ONCE!
CURSES, CURSES!
CRAAASH
EEK! WHAT IS IT?!

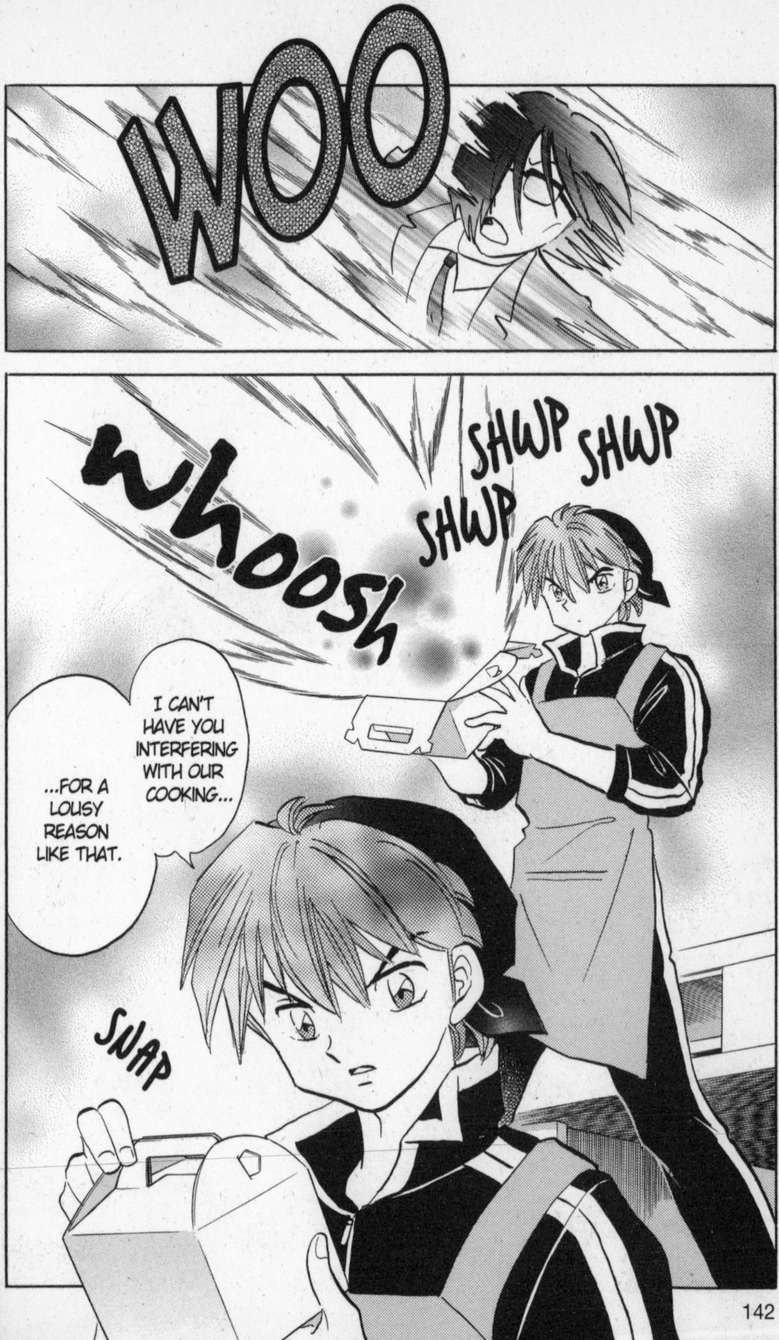
WOO
SHWP SHWP SHWP
WHOOSH
I CAN'T HAVE YOU INTERFERING WITH OUR COOKING...
...FOR A LOUSY REASON LIKE THAT.
SNAP

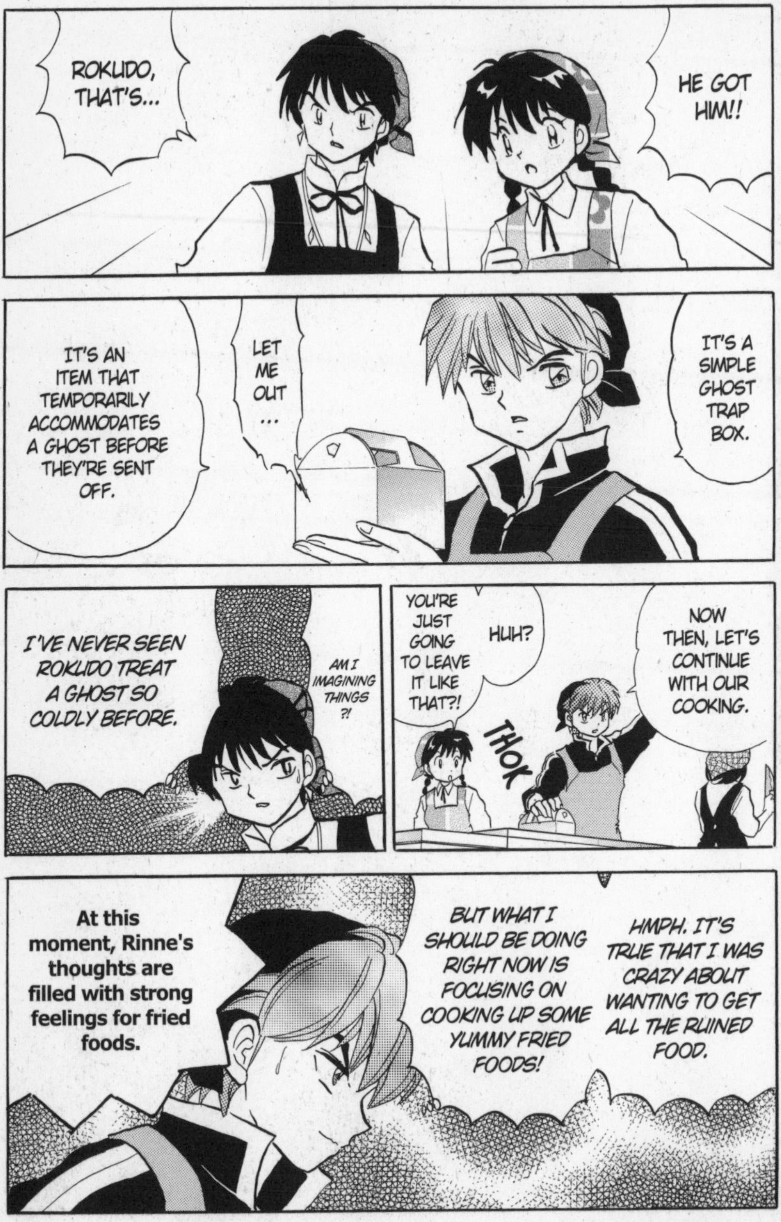
HE GOT HIM!!
ROKUDO, THAT'S...
IT'S A SIMPLE GHOST TRAP BOX.
LET ME OUT ...
IT'S AN ITEM THAT TEMPORARILY ACCOMMODATES A GHOST BEFORE THEY'RE SENT OFF.
NOW THEN, LET'S CONTINUE WITH OUR COOKING.
THOK
HUH?
YOU'RE JUST GOING TO LEAVE IT LIKE THAT?!
AM I IMAGINING THINGS ?!
I'VE NEVER SEEN ROKUDO TREAT A GHOST SO COLDLY BEFORE.
HMPH. IT'S TRUE THAT I WAS CRAZY ABOUT WANTING TO GET ALL THE RUINED FOOD.
BUT WHAT I SHOULD BE DOING RIGHT NOW IS FOCUSING ON COOKING UP SOME YUMMY FRIED FOODS!
At this moment, Rinne's thoughts are filled with strong feelings for fried foods.

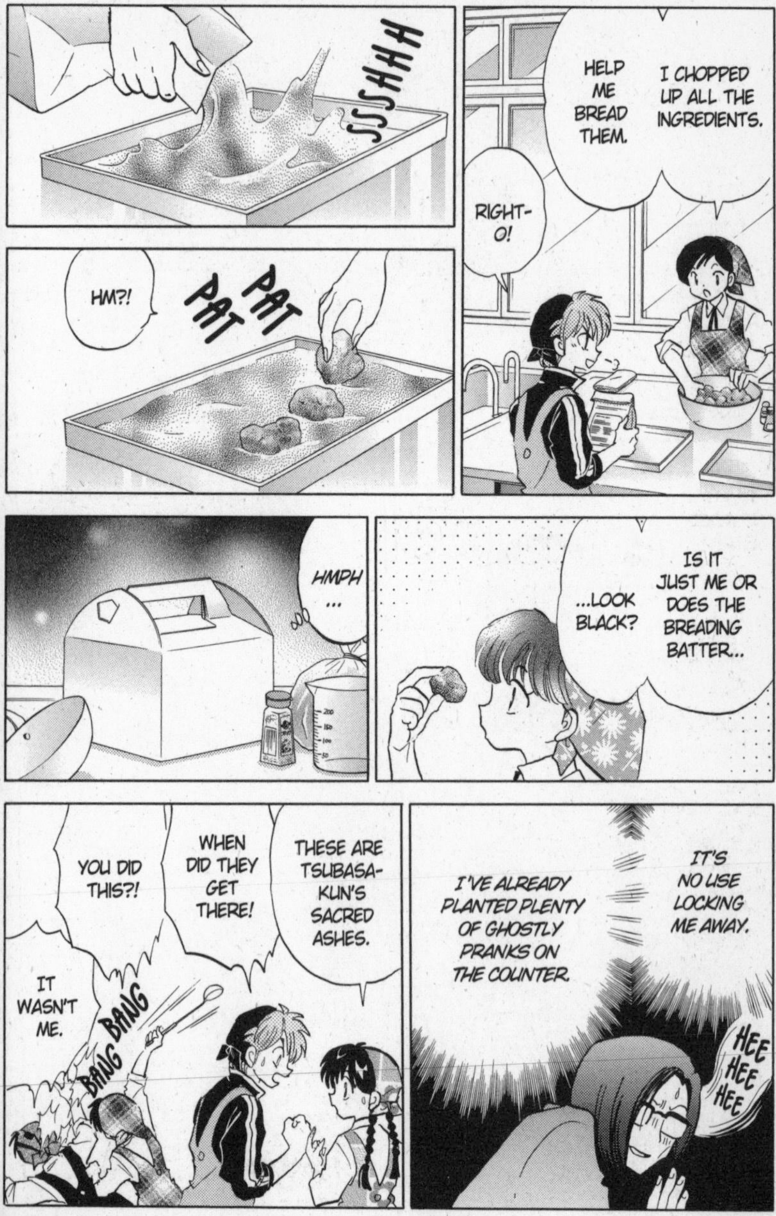
I CHOPPED UP ALL THE INGREDIENTS.
HELP ME BREAD THEM.
RIGHT-O!
SSSHHHH
HM?!
PAT PAT
IS IT JUST ME OR DOES THE BREADING BATTER...
...LOOK BLACK?
HMPH...
IT'S NO USE LOCKING ME AWAY.
I'VE ALREADY PLANTED PLENTY OF GHOSTLY PRANKS ON THE COUNTER.
HEE HEE HEE
THESE ARE TSUBASA-KUN'S SACRED ASHES.
WHEN DID THEY GET THERE!
YOU DID THIS?!
BANG BANG
IT WASN'T ME.

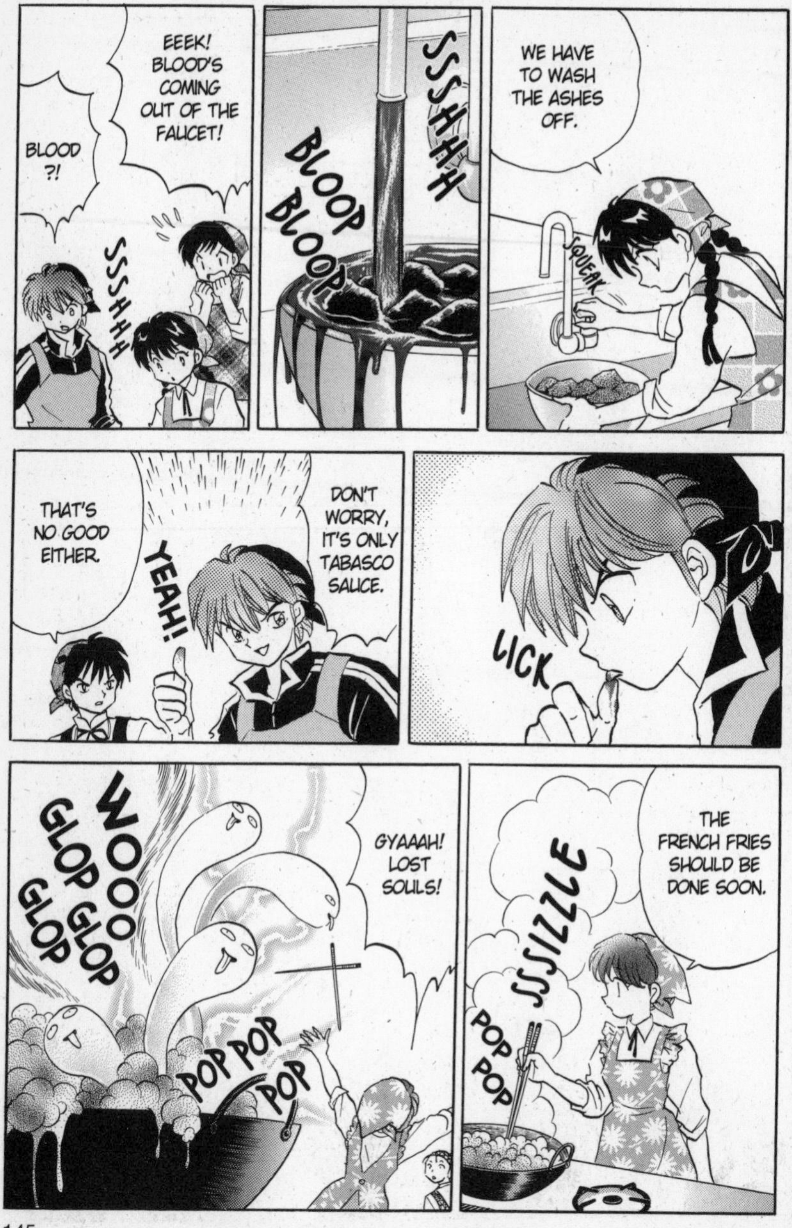
WE HAVE TO WASH THE ASHES OFF.
SQUEAK
SSSHHHH
BLOOP BLOOP
EEEK! BLOOD'S COMING OUT OF THE FAUCET!
BLOOD ?!
SSSHHH
LICK
DON'T WORRY, IT'S ONLY TABASCO SAUCE.
YEAH!
THAT'S NO GOOD EITHER.
THE FRENCH FRIES SHOULD BE DONE SOON.
SSSIZZLE
POP POP
GYAAAH! LOST SOULS!
WOOOO
GLOP GLOP GLOP
POP POP POP

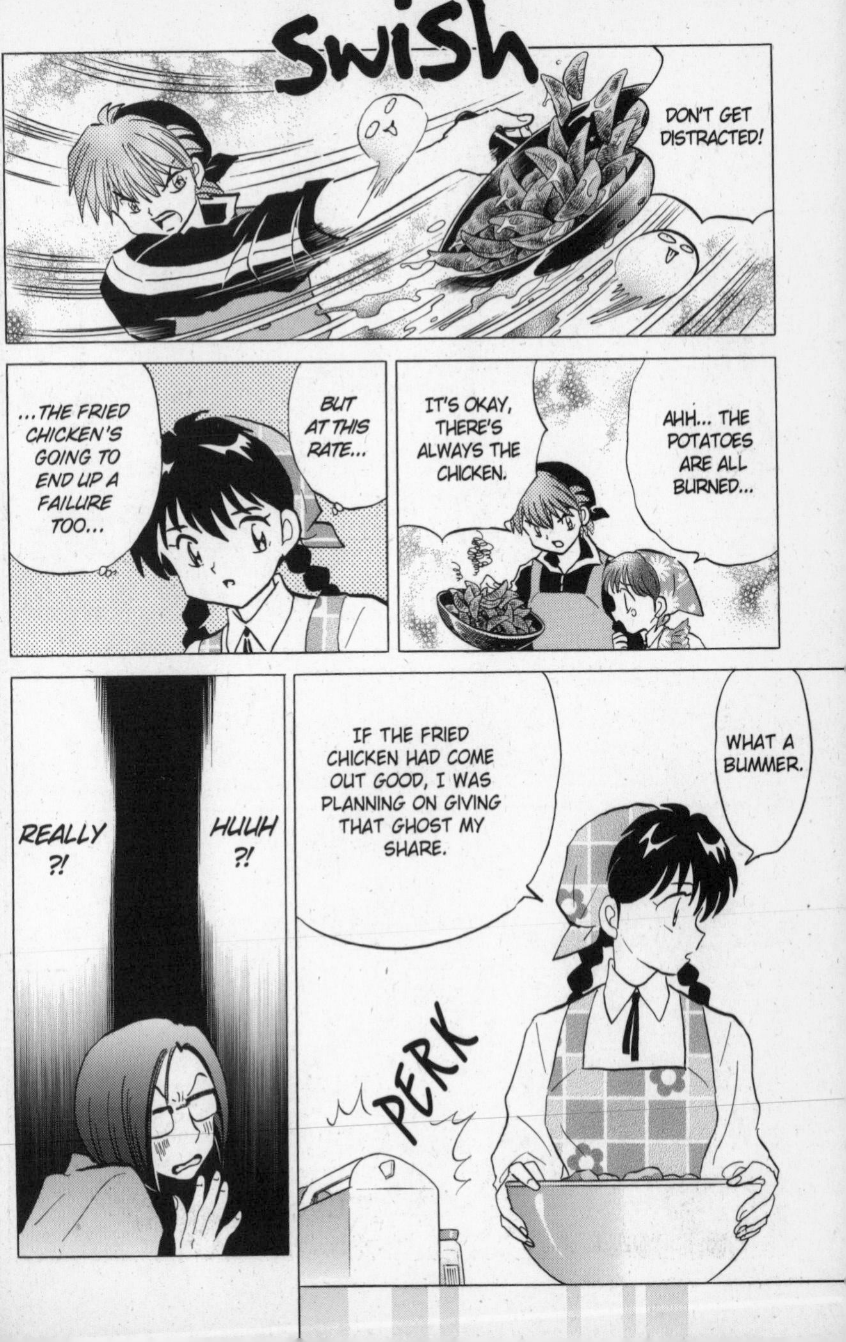
SWISH
DON'T GET DISTRACTED!
AHH... THE POTATOES ARE ALL BURNED...
IT'S OKAY, THERE'S ALWAYS THE CHICKEN.
BUT AT THIS RATE...
...THE FRIED CHICKEN'S GOING TO END UP A FAILURE TOO...
WHAT A BUMMER.
IF THE FRIED CHICKEN HAD COME OUT GOOD, I WAS PLANNING ON GIVING THAT GHOST MY SHARE.
PERK
HUUH ?!
REALLY ?!

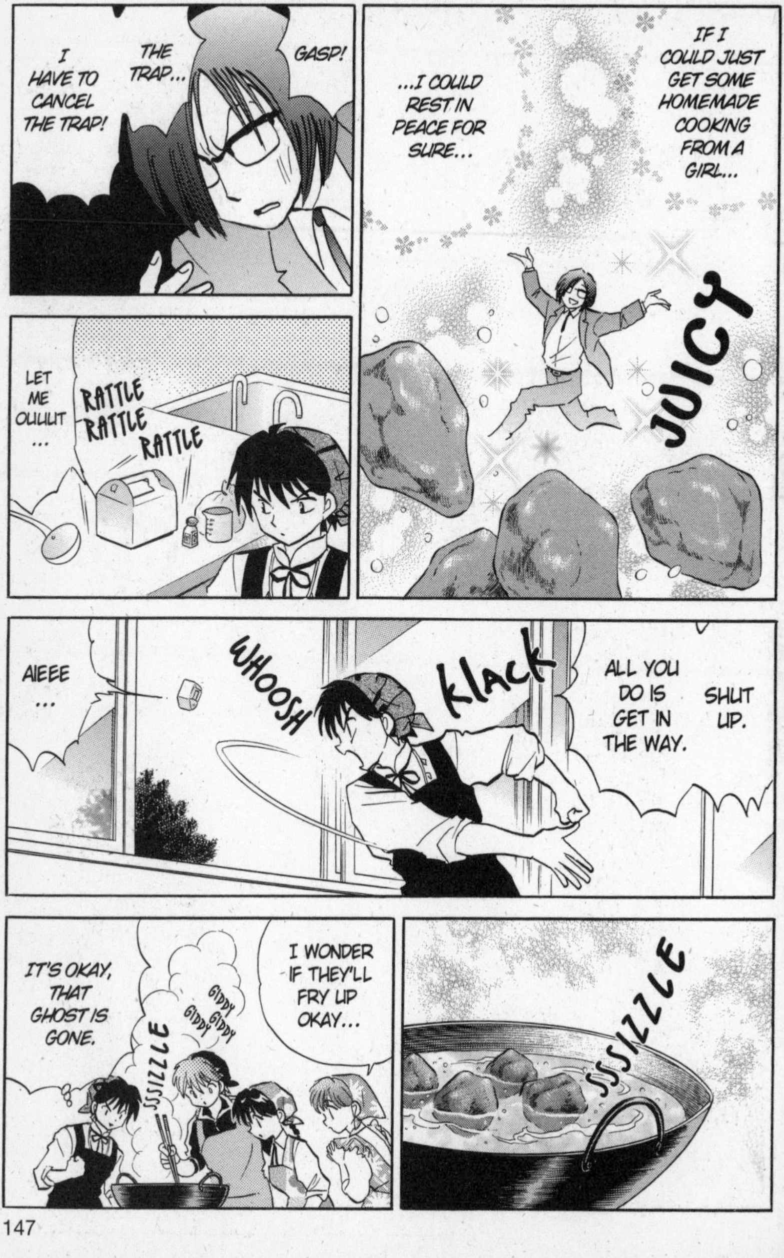

IF I COULD JUST GET SOME HOMEMADE COOKING FROM A GIRL...
...I COULD REST IN PEACE FOR SURE...
JUICY
GASP!
THE TRAP...
I HAVE TO CANCEL THE TRAP!
RATTLE RATTLE RATTLE
LET ME OUUUT ...
SHUT UP.
ALL YOU DO IS GET IN THE WAY.
KLACK
WHOOSH
AIEEE ...
SSSIZZLE
I WONDER IF THEY'LL FRY UP OKAY...
GIDDY GIDDY GIDDY GIDDY
SSSIZZLE
IT'S OKAY, THAT GHOST IS GONE.

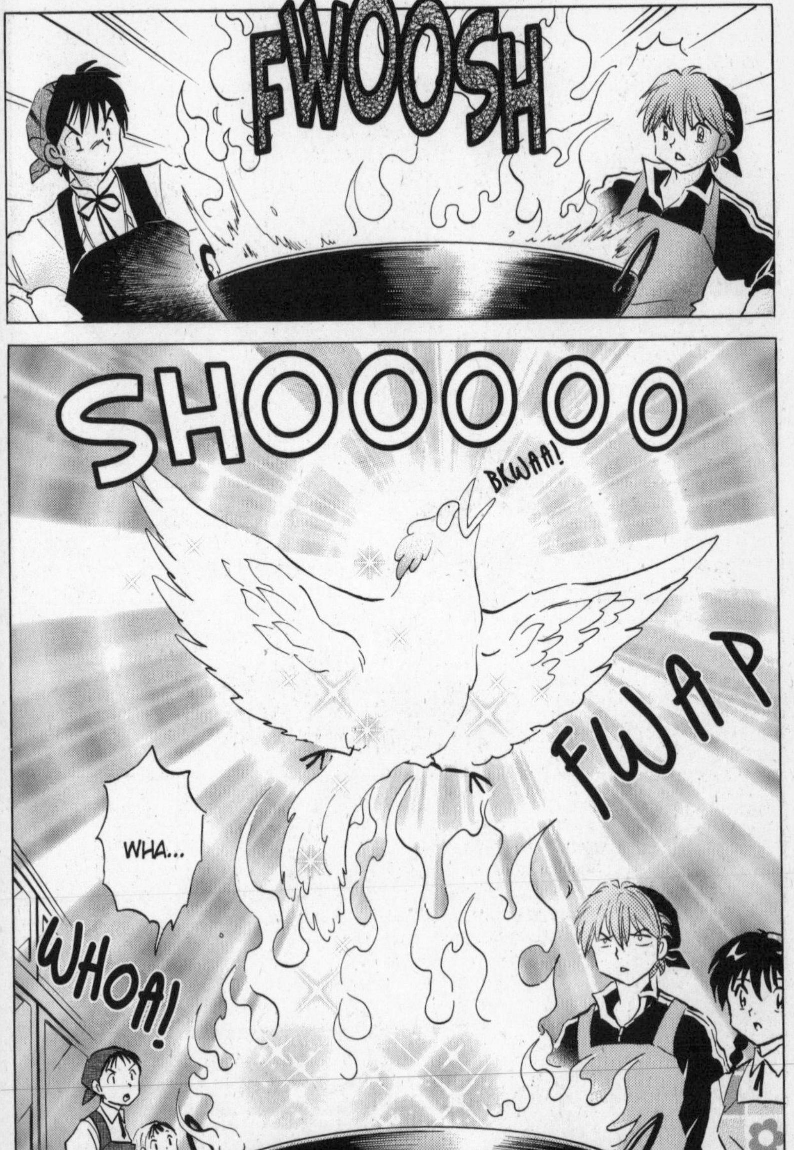
FWOOSH
SHOOOOO
BKWAA!
FWAP
WHA...
WHOA!

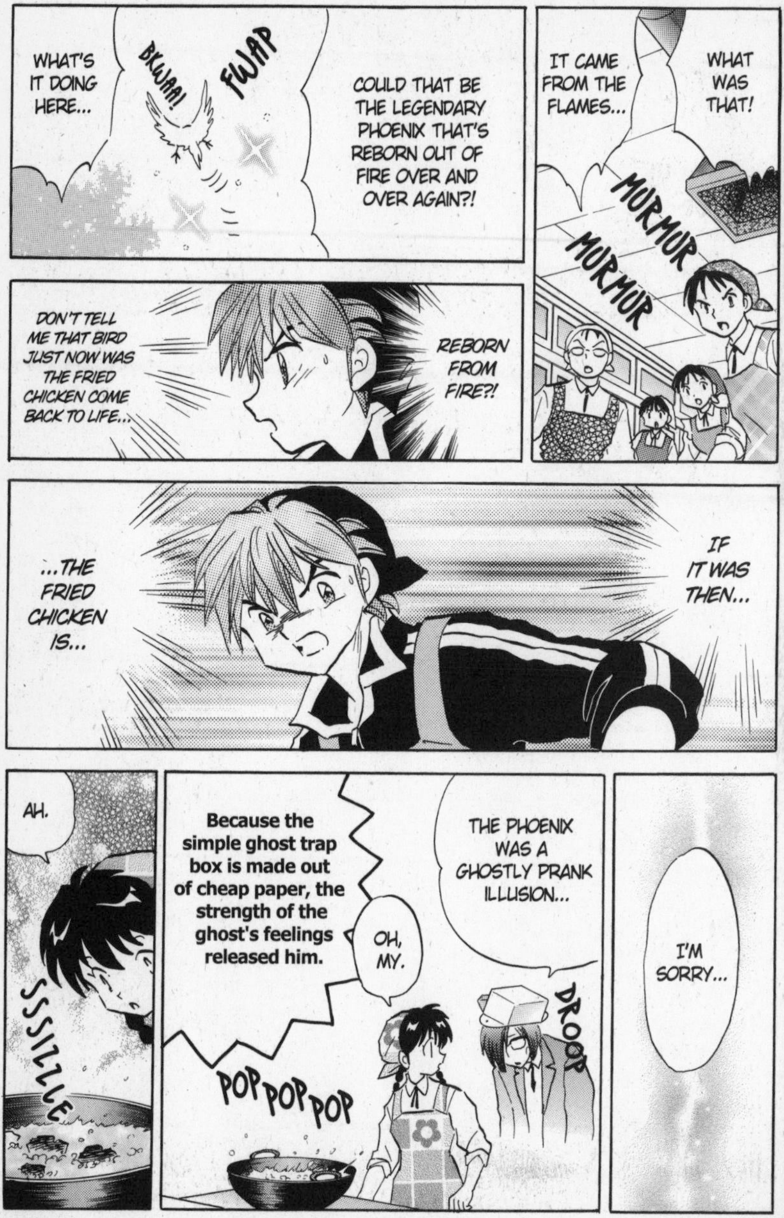
WHAT WAS THAT!
IT CAME FROM THE FLAMES...
MURMUR
MURMUR
COULD THAT BE THE LEGENDARY PHOENIX THAT'S REBORN OUT OF FIRE OVER AND OVER AGAIN?!
FWAP
BKWAA!
WHAT'S IT DOING HERE...
REBORN FROM FIRE?!
DON'T TELL ME THAT BIRD JUST NOW WAS THE FRIED CHICKEN COME BACK TO LIFE...
IF IT WAS THEN...
...THE FRIED CHICKEN IS...
I'M SORRY...
THE PHOENIX WAS A GHOSTLY PRANK ILLUSION...
DROOP
OH, MY.
Because the simple ghost trap box is made out of cheap paper, the strength of the ghost's feelings released him.
POP POP POP
AH.
SSSIZZLE

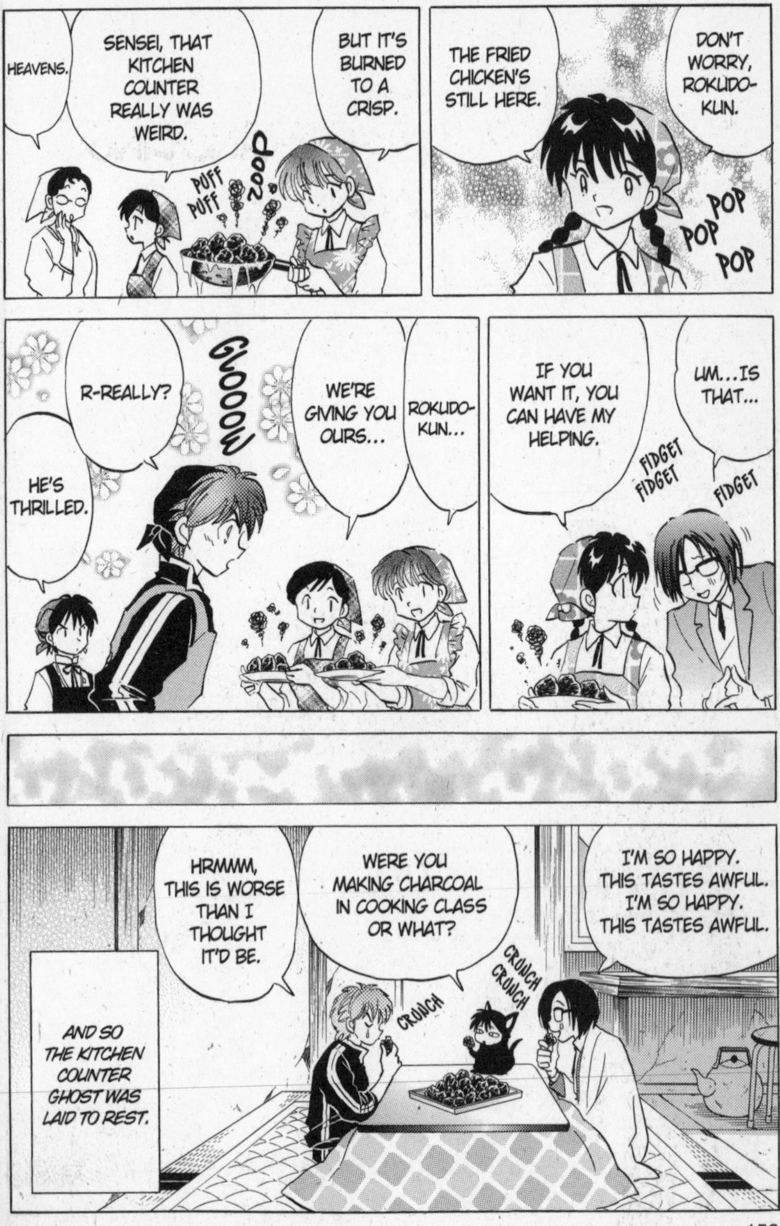
DON'T WORRY, ROKUDO-KUN.
THE FRIED CHICKEN'S STILL HERE.
POP POP POP POP
BUT IT'S BURNED TO A CRISP.
SENSEI, THAT KITCHEN COUNTER REALLY WAS WEIRD.
HEAVENS.
ZOOOP
PUFF PUFF
UM...IS THAT...
IF YOU WANT IT, YOU CAN HAVE MY HELPING.
FIDGET
FIDGET FIDGET
ROKUDO-KUN...
WE'RE GIVING YOU OURS...
GLOOOOW
R-REALLY?
HE'S THRILLED.
I'M SO HAPPY. THIS TASTES AWFUL. I'M SO HAPPY. THIS TASTES AWFUL.
WERE YOU MAKING CHARCOAL IN COOKING CLASS OR WHAT?
HRMMM, THIS IS WORSE THAN I THOUGHT IT'D BE.
CRUNCH CRUNCH
CRUNCH
AND SO THE KITCHEN COUNTER GHOST WAS LAID TO REST.

CHAPTER 77: THE STRANGLING SCARF

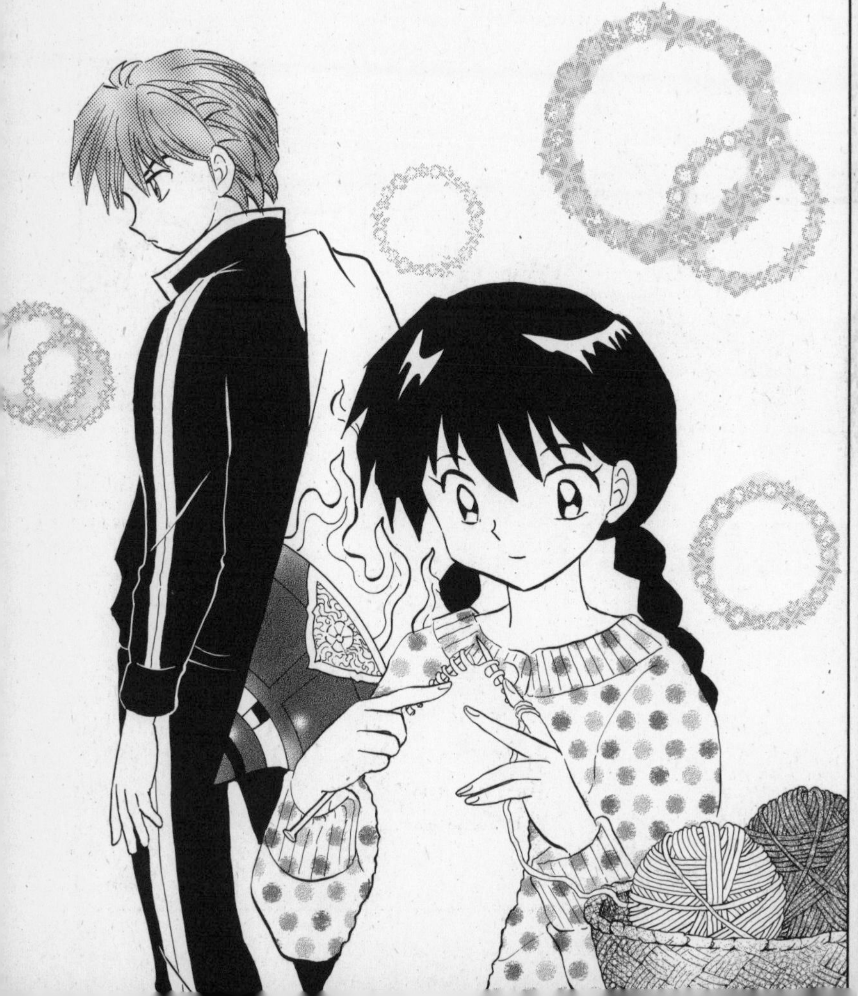

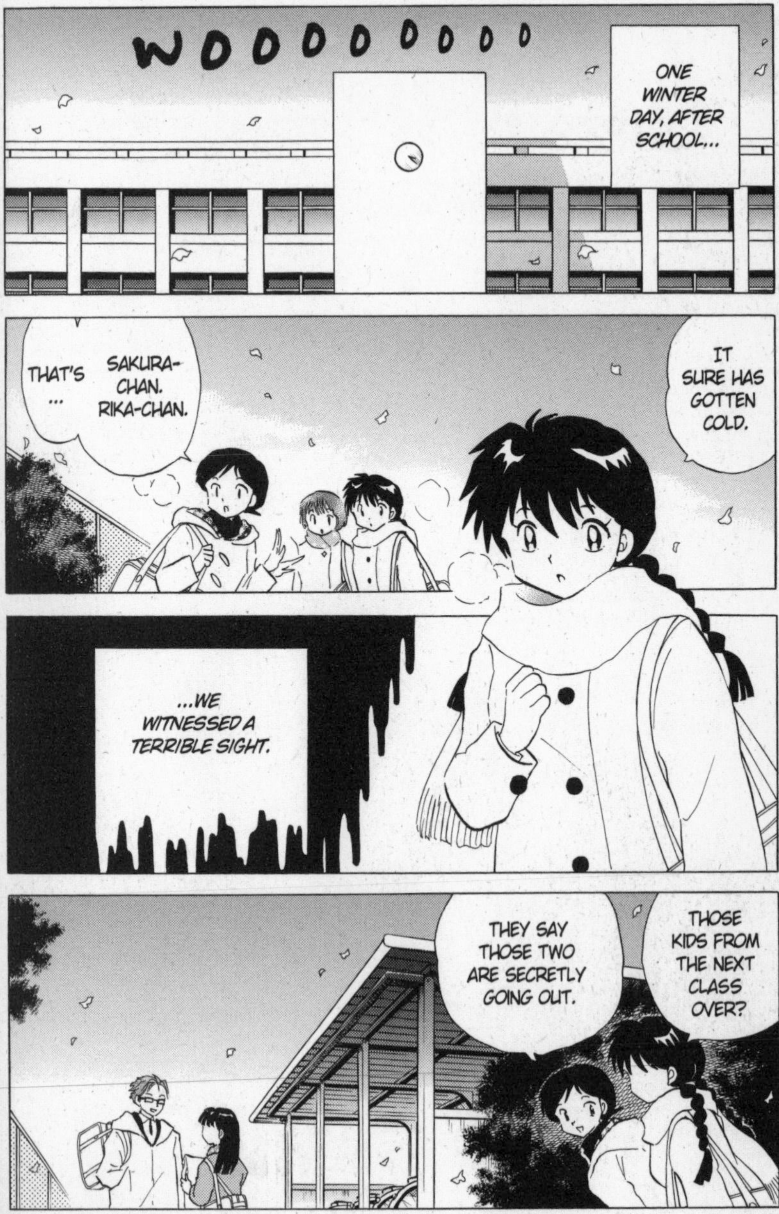
ONE WINTER DAY, AFTER SCHOOL...
WOOOOOOOO
IT SURE HAS GOTTEN COLD.
THAT'S ... SAKURA-CHAN. RIKA-CHAN.
...WE WITNESSED A TERRIBLE SIGHT.
THOSE KIDS FROM THE NEXT CLASS OVER?
THEY SAY THOSE TWO ARE SECRETLY GOING OUT.

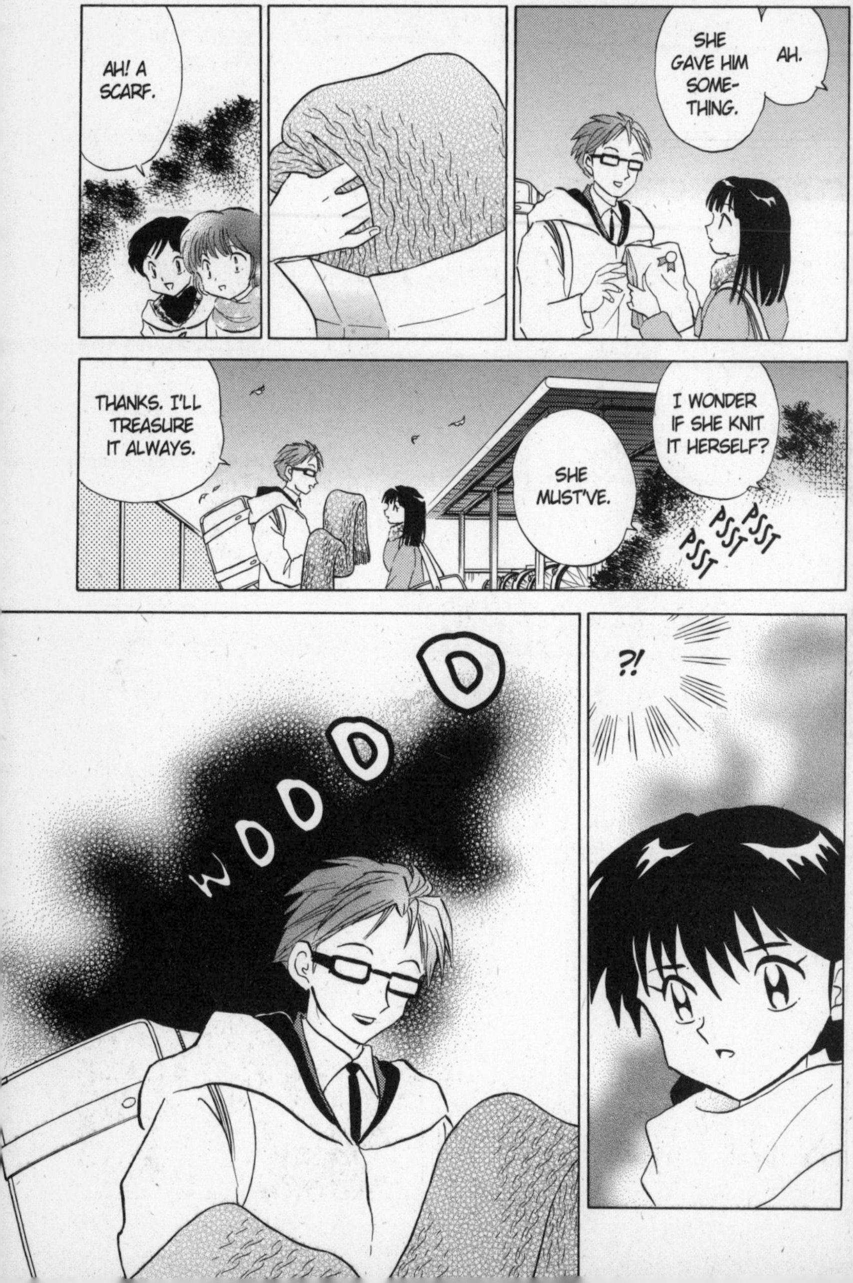
AH.
SHE GAVE HIM SOME-THING.
AH! A SCARF.
I WONDER IF SHE KNIT IT HERSELF?
PSST PSST PSST
SHE MUST'VE.
THANKS. I'LL TREASURE IT ALWAYS.
?!
WOODD

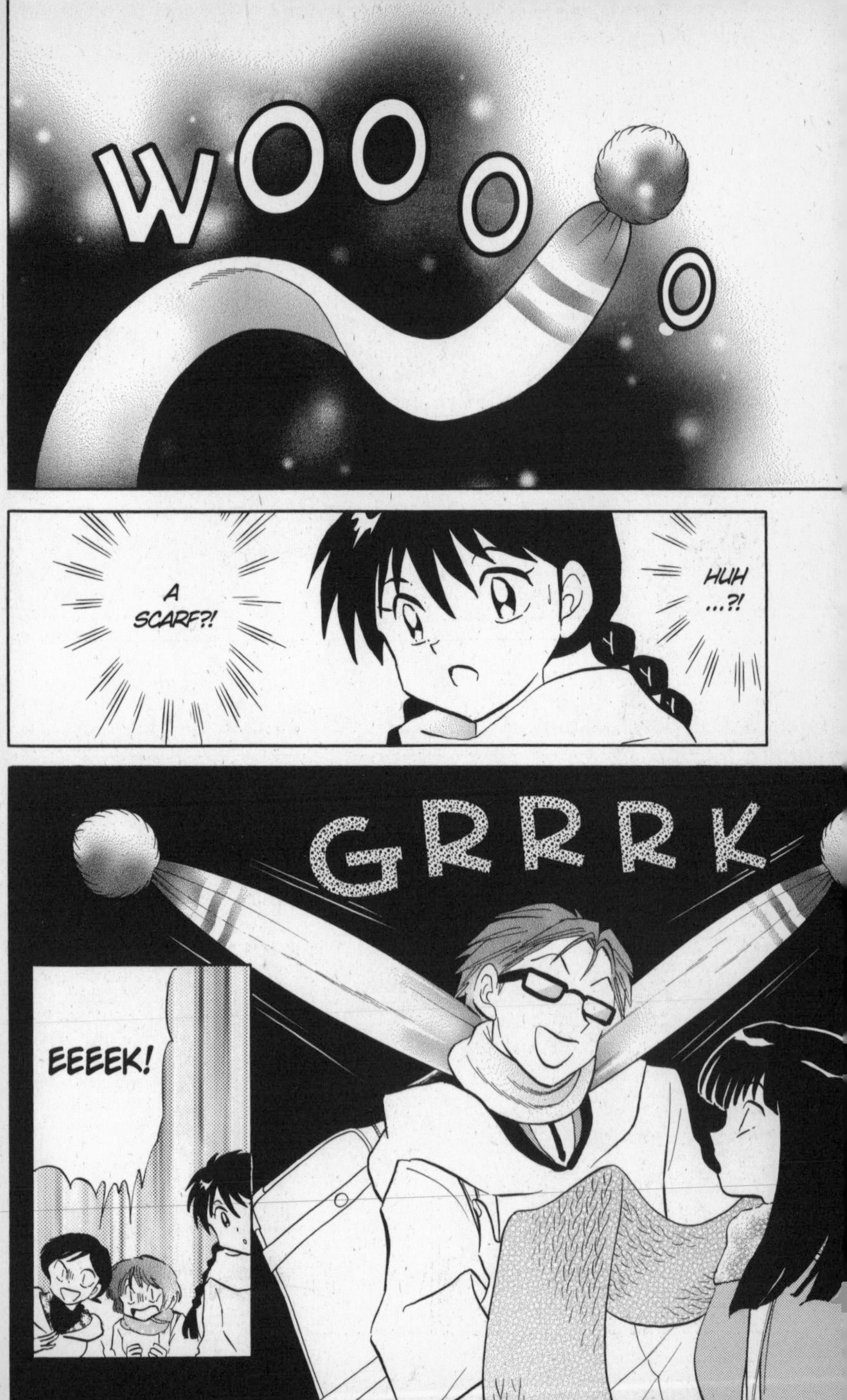
WOOOO
HUH ...?!
A SCARF?!
GRRRK
EEEEK!

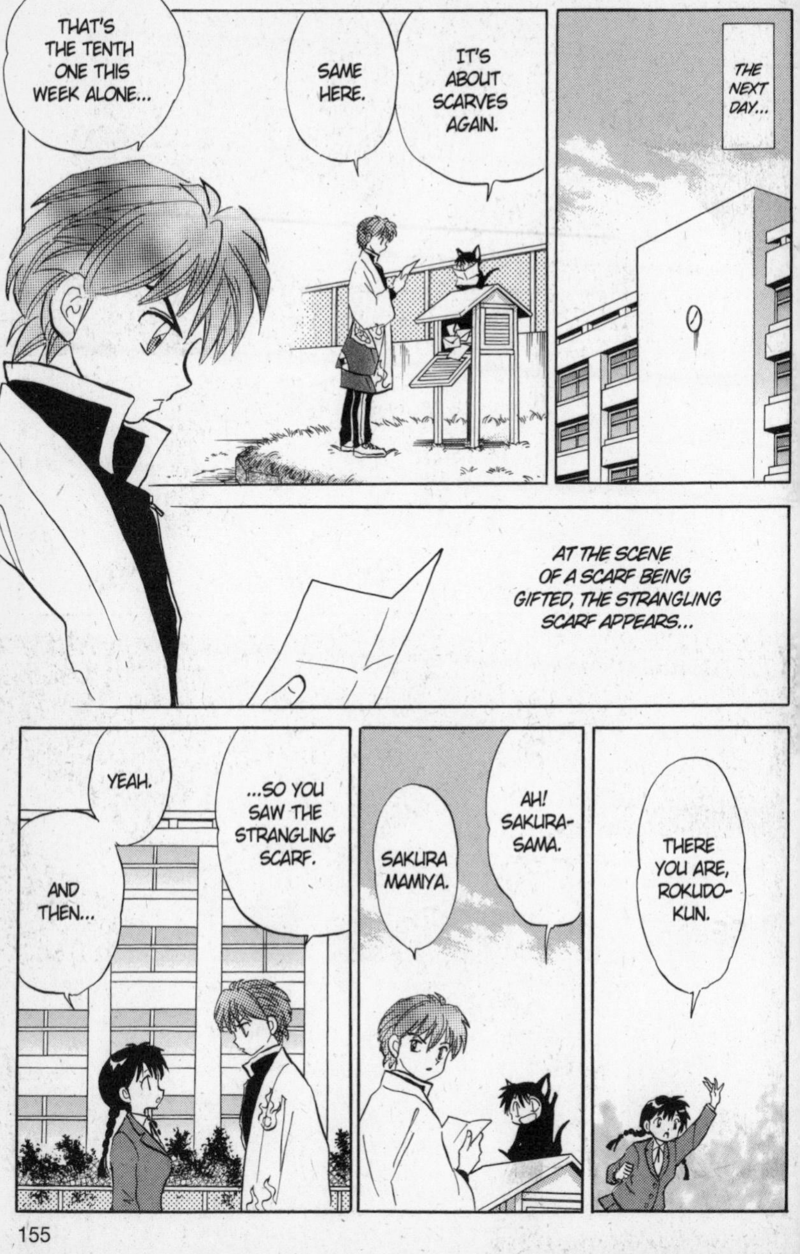
THE NEXT DAY...
IT'S ABOUT SCARVES AGAIN.
SAME HERE.
THAT'S THE TENTH ONE THIS WEEK ALONE...
AT THE SCENE OF A SCARF BEING GIFTED, THE STRANGLING SCARF APPEARS...
THERE YOU ARE, ROKUDO-KUN.
AH! SAKURA-SAMA.
SAKURA MAMIYA.
...SO YOU SAW THE STRANGLING SCARF.
YEAH.
AND THEN...

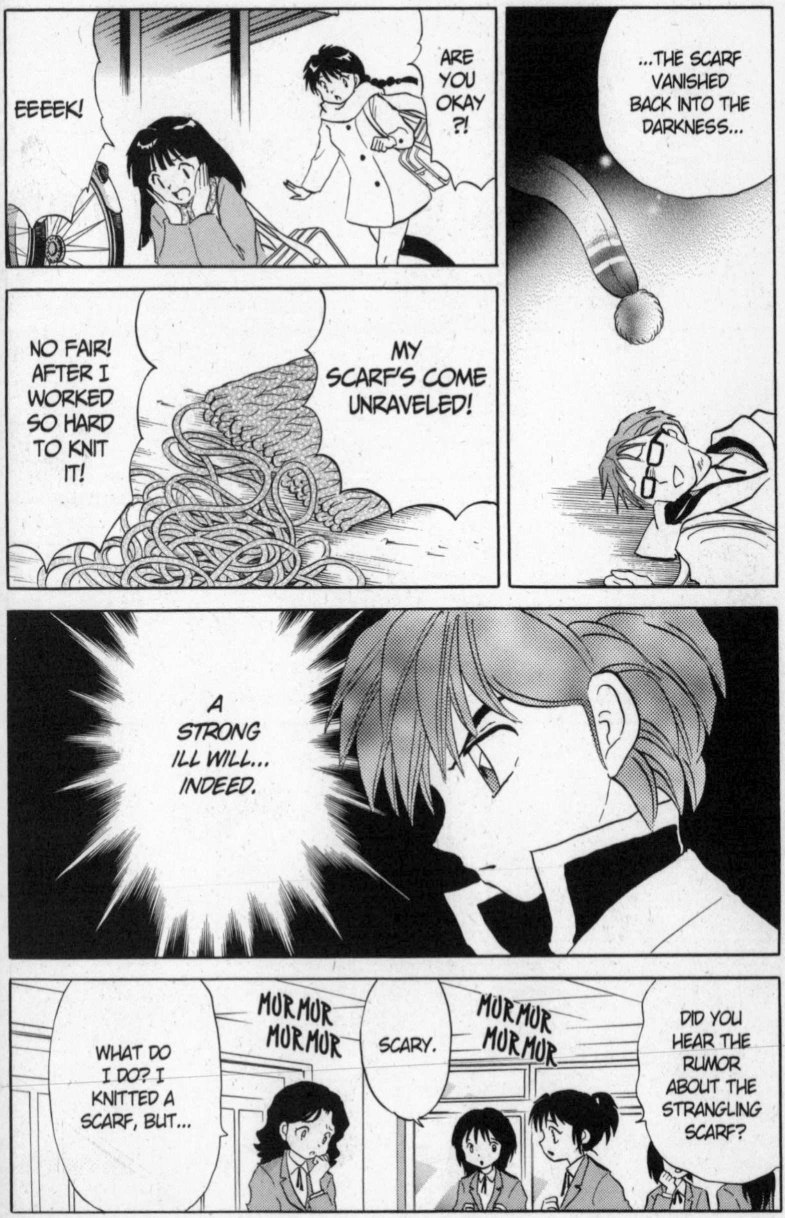
...THE SCARF VANISHED BACK INTO THE DARKNESS...
ARE YOU OKAY ?!
EEEEK!
MY SCARF'S COME UNRAVELED!
NO FAIR! AFTER I WORKED SO HARD TO KNIT IT!
A STRONG ILL WILL... INDEED.
DID YOU HEAR THE RUMOR ABOUT THE STRANGLING SCARF?
MURMUR MURMUR
SCARY.
MURMUR MURMUR
WHAT DO I DO? I KNITTED A SCARF, BUT...

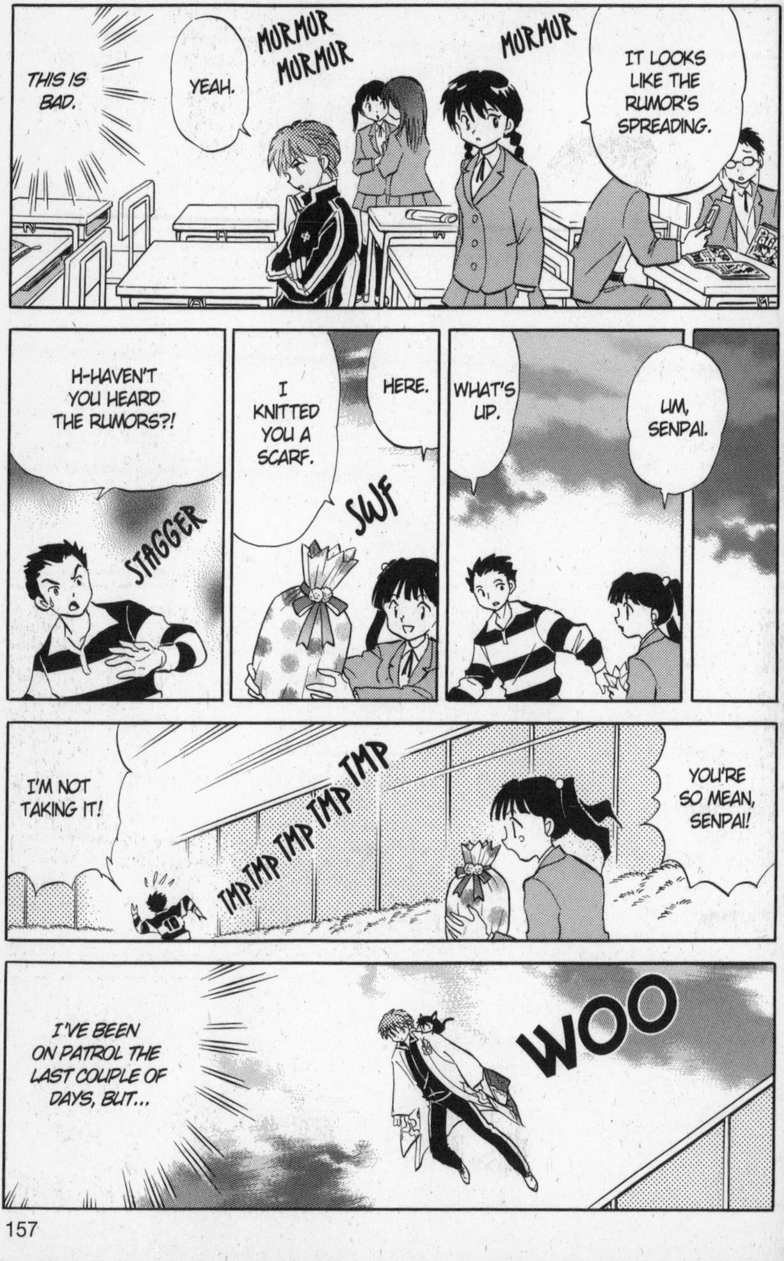
IT LOOKS LIKE THE RUMOR'S SPREADING.
MURMUR
MURMUR MURMUR
YEAH.
THIS IS BAD.
UM, SENPAI.
WHAT'S UP.
HERE.
I KNITTED YOU A SCARF.
SWF
H-HAVEN'T YOU HEARD THE RUMORS?!
STAGGER
YOU'RE SO MEAN, SENPAI!
TMP TMP TMP TMP TMP
I'M NOT TAKING IT!
WOO
I'VE BEEN ON PATROL THE LAST COUPLE OF DAYS, BUT...

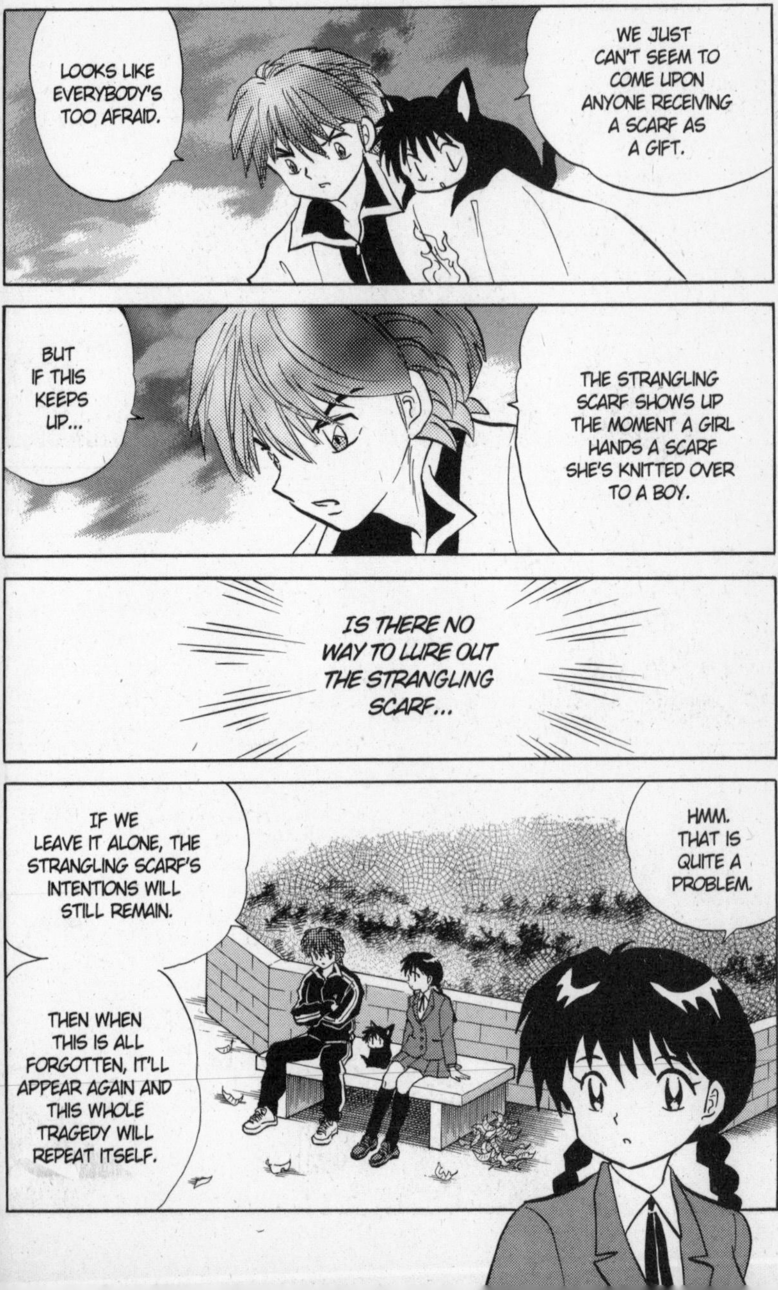
WE JUST CAN'T SEEM TO COME UPON ANYONE RECEIVING A SCARF AS A GIFT.
LOOKS LIKE EVERYBODY'S TOO AFRAID.
THE STRANGLING SCARF SHOWS UP THE MOMENT A GIRL HANDS A SCARF SHE'S KNITTED OVER TO A BOY.
BUT IF THIS KEEPS UP...
IS THERE NO WAY TO LURE OUT THE STRANGLING SCARF...
HMM. THAT IS QUITE A PROBLEM.
IF WE LEAVE IT ALONE, THE STRANGLING SCARF'S INTENTIONS WILL STILL REMAIN.
THEN WHEN THIS IS ALL FORGOTTEN, IT'LL APPEAR AGAIN AND THIS WHOLE TRAGEDY WILL REPEAT ITSELF.

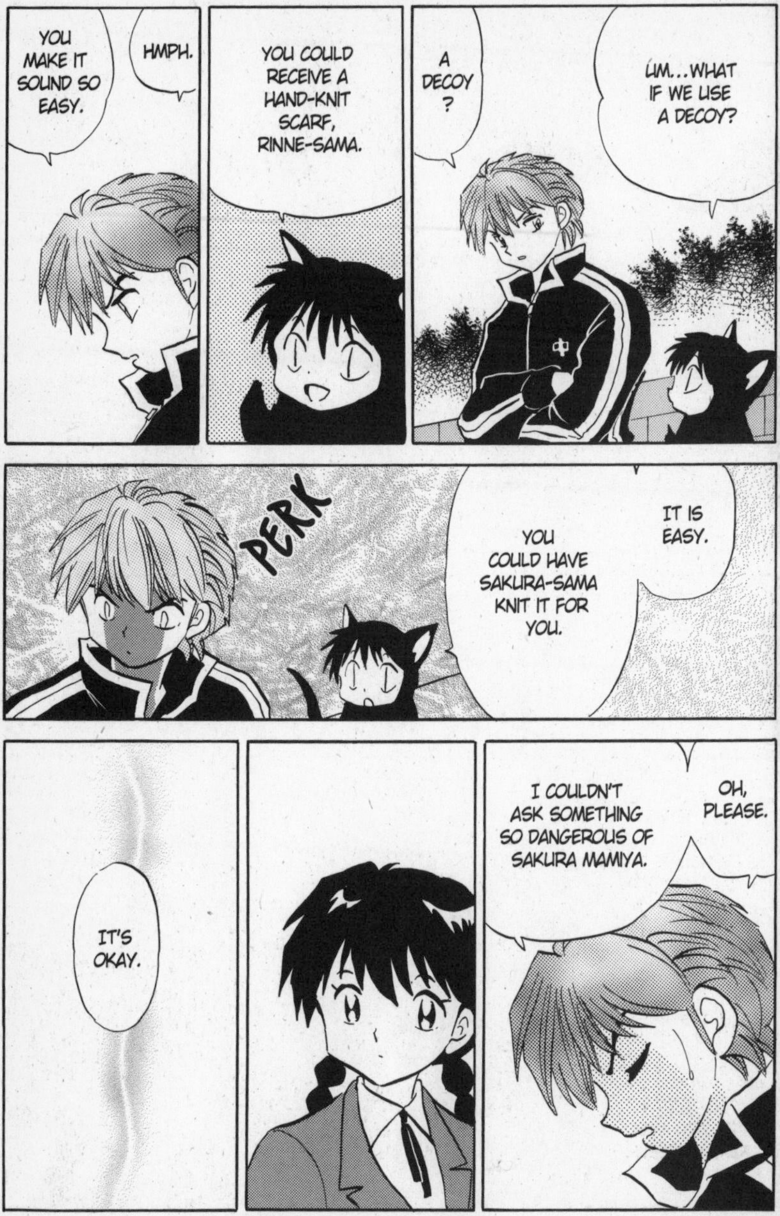
UM...WHAT IF WE USE A DECOY?
A DECOY ?
YOU COULD RECEIVE A HAND-KNIT SCARF, RINNE-SAMA.
HMPH.
YOU MAKE IT SOUND SO EASY.
IT IS EASY.
YOU COULD HAVE SAKURA-SAMA KNIT IT FOR YOU.
PERK
OH, PLEASE.
I COULDN'T ASK SOMETHING SO DANGEROUS OF SAKURA MAMIYA.
IT'S OKAY.

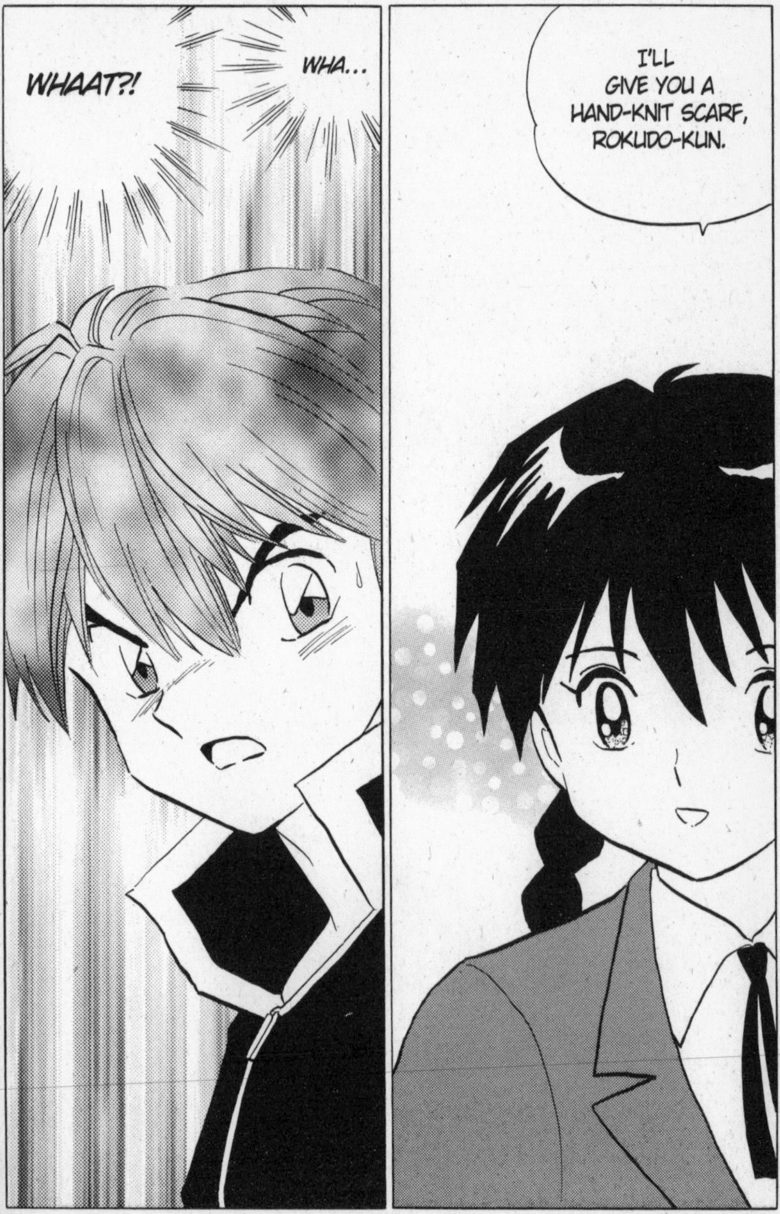
I'LL GIVE YOU A HAND-KNIT SCARF, ROKUDO-KUN.
WHA...
WHAAT?!

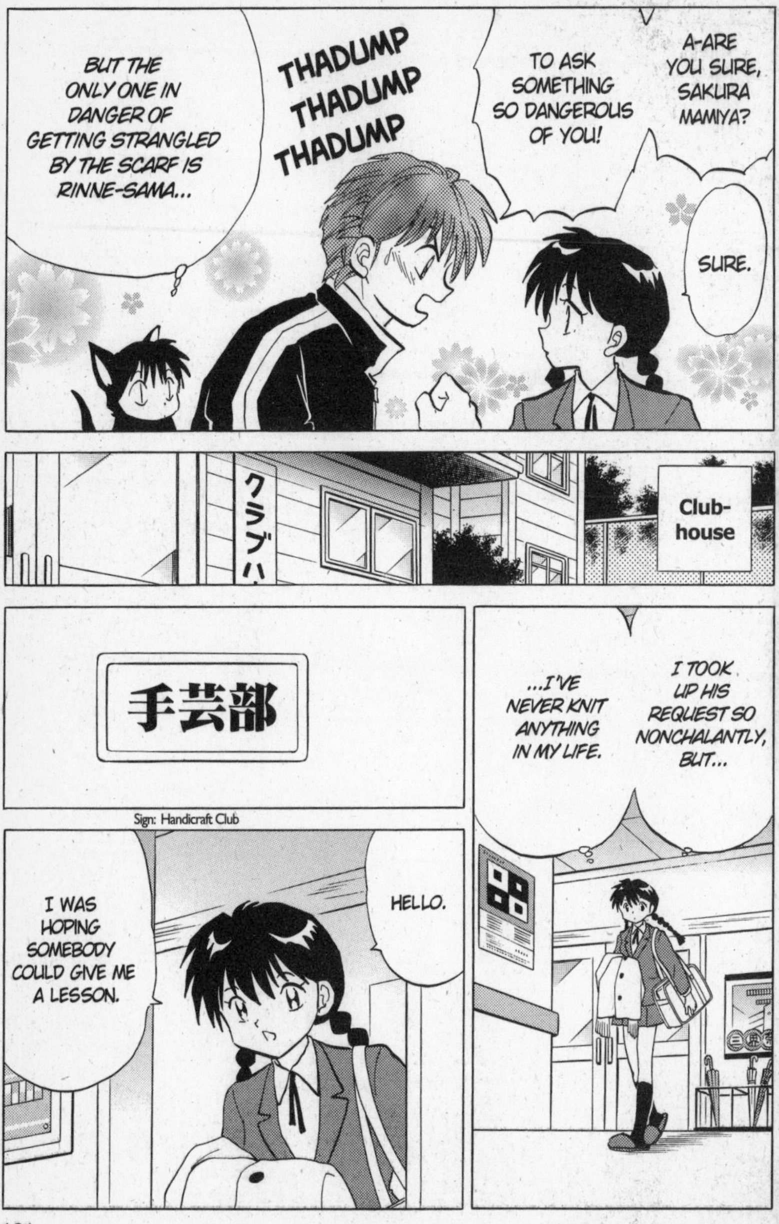
A-ARE YOU SURE, SAKURA MAMIYA?
TO ASK SOMETHING SO DANGEROUS OF YOU!
SURE.
THADUMP THADUMP THADUMP
BUT THE ONLY ONE IN DANGER OF GETTING STRANGLED BY THE SCARF IS RINNE-SAMA...
クラブハ
Club-house
I TOOK UP HIS REQUEST SO NONCHALANTLY, BUT...
...I'VE NEVER KNIT ANYTHING IN MY LIFE.
手芸部
HELLO.
I WAS HOPING SOMEBODY COULD GIVE ME A LESSON.

Sign: Handicraft Club

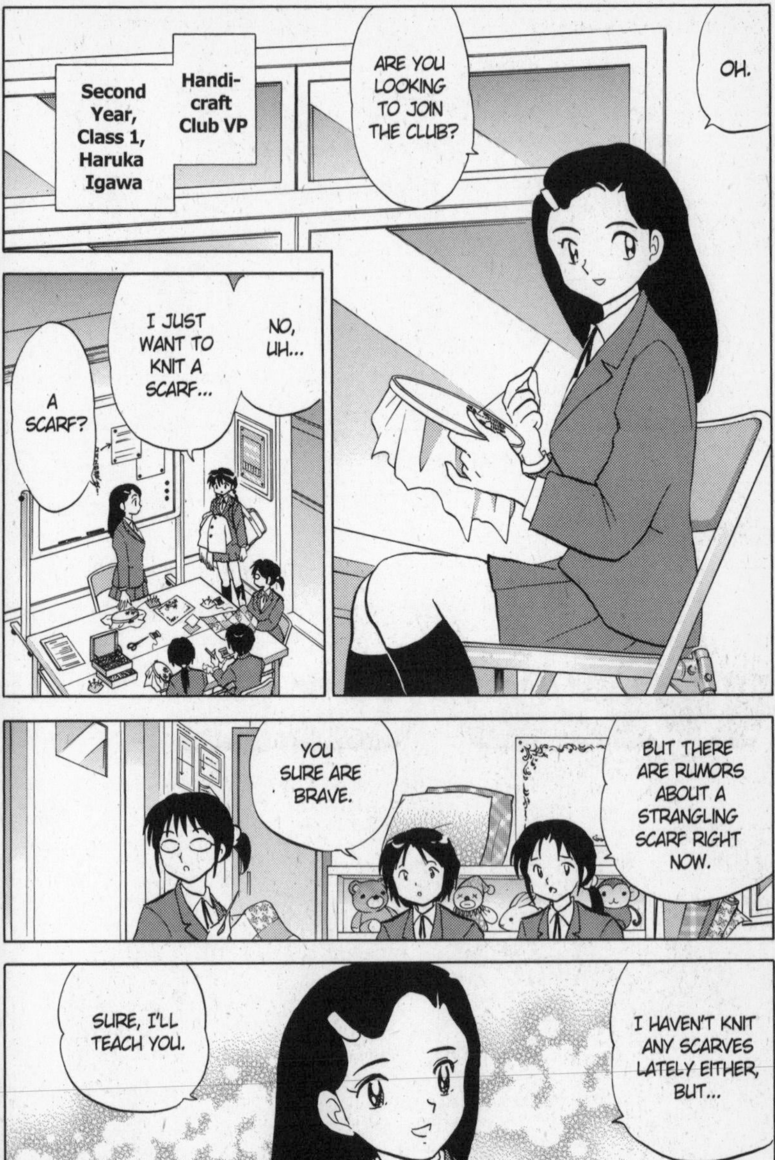
OH.
ARE YOU LOOKING TO JOIN THE CLUB?
Handi-craft Club VP
Second Year, Class 1, Haruka Igawa
NO, UH...
I JUST WANT TO KNIT A SCARF...
A SCARF?
BUT THERE ARE RUMORS ABOUT A STRANGLING SCARF RIGHT NOW.
YOU SURE ARE BRAVE.
I HAVEN'T KNIT ANY SCARVES LATELY EITHER, BUT...
SURE, I'LL TEACH YOU.

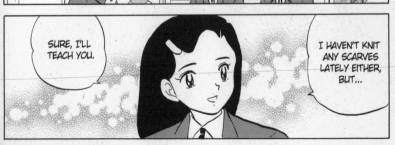

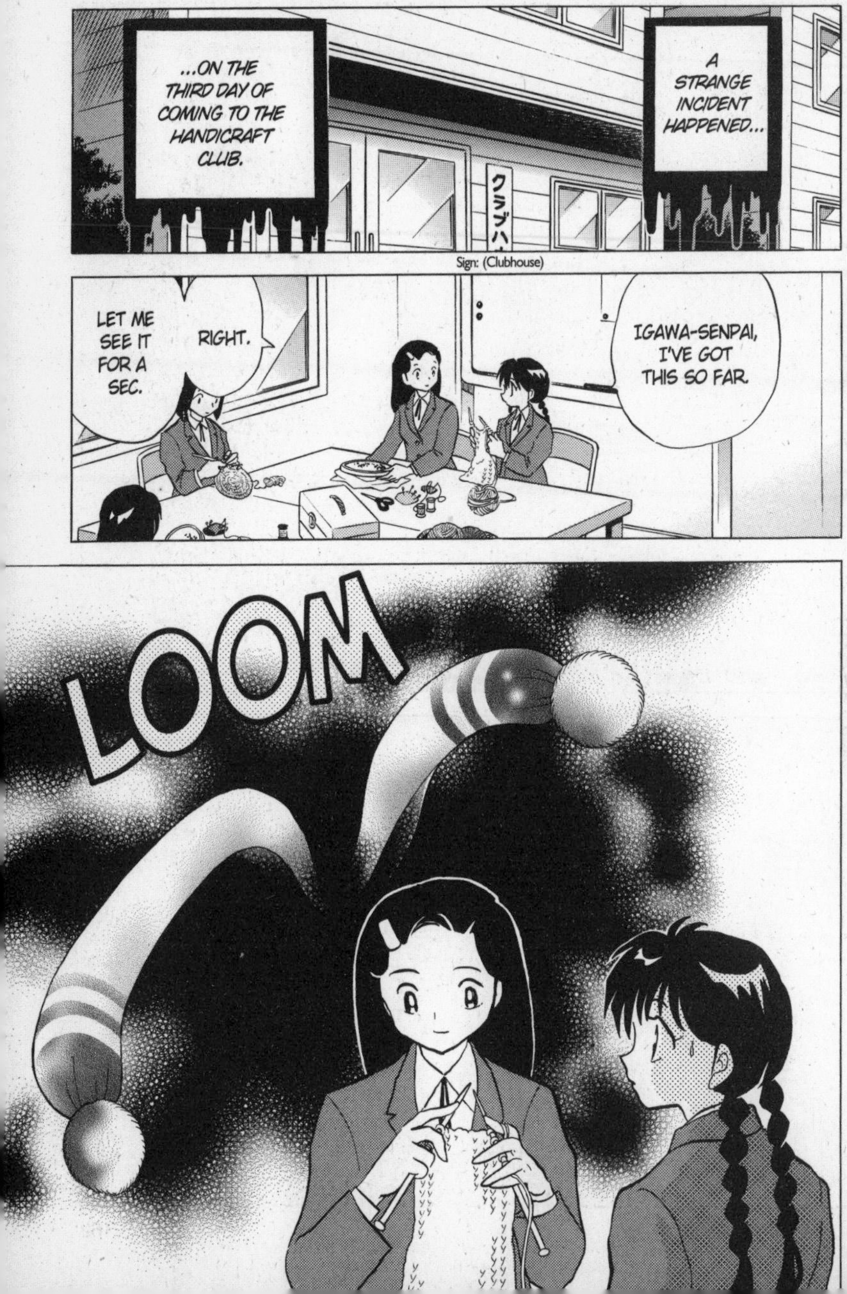
A STRANGE INCIDENT HAPPENED...
...ON THE THIRD DAY OF COMING TO THE HANDICRAFT CLUB.
クラブハ
Sign: (Clubhouse)
IGAWA-SENPAI, I'VE GOT THIS SO FAR.
RIGHT.
LET ME SEE IT FOR A SEC.
LOOM

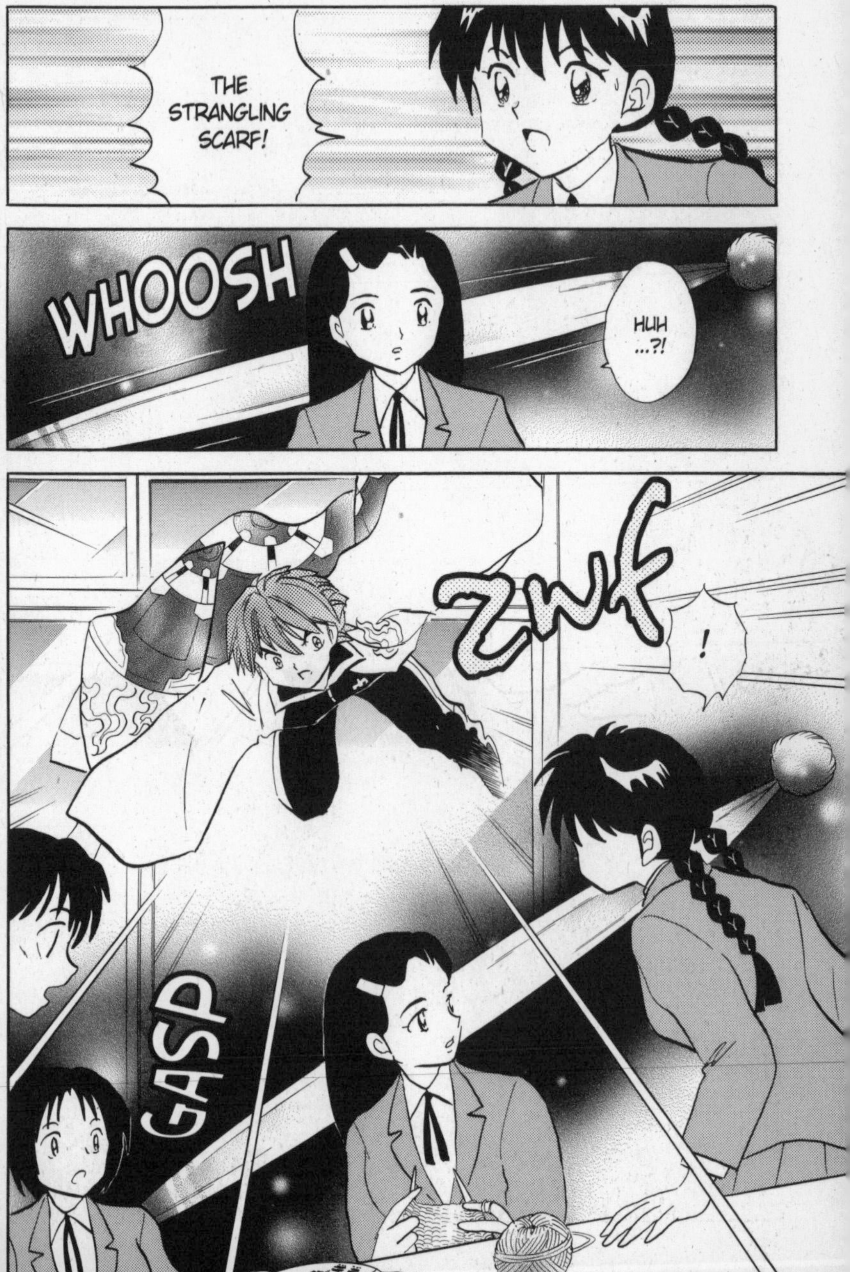
THE STRANGLING SCARF!
HUH ...?!
WHOOSH
!
ZWF
GASP

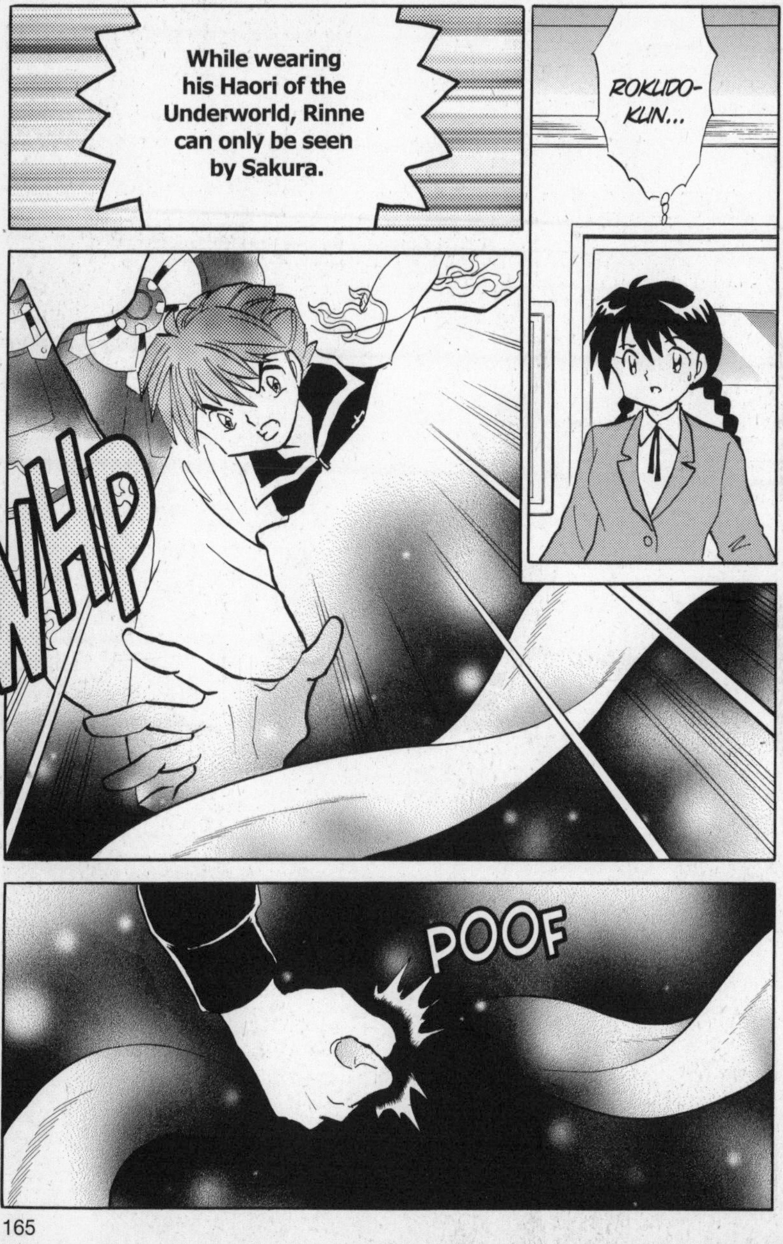
ROKUDO-KUN...
While wearing his Haori of the Underworld, Rinne can only be seen by Sakura.
WHP
POOF

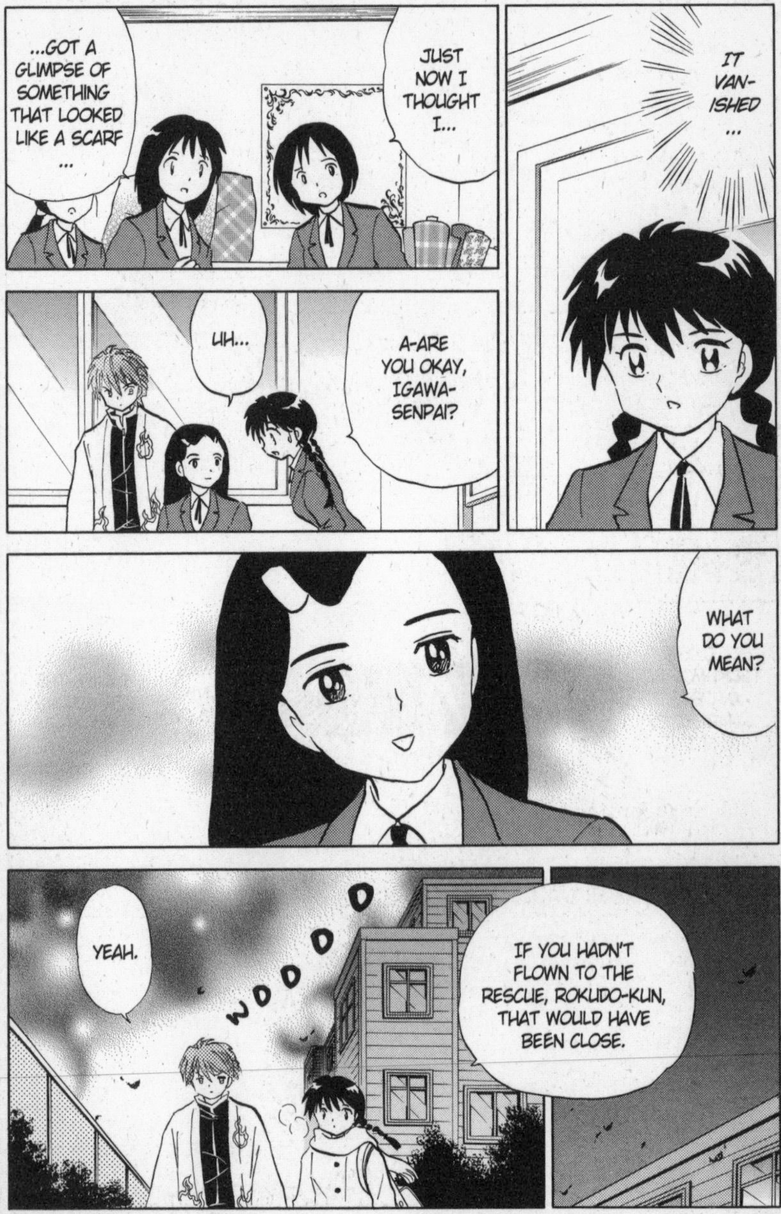
IT VAN-ISHED ...
JUST NOW I THOUGHT I...
...GOT A GLIMPSE OF SOMETHING THAT LOOKED LIKE A SCARF ...
A-ARE YOU OKAY, IGAWA-SENPAI?
UH...
WHAT DO YOU MEAN?
IF YOU HADN'T FLOWN TO THE RESCUE, ROKUDO-KUN, THAT WOULD HAVE BEEN CLOSE.
WDDDD
YEAH.

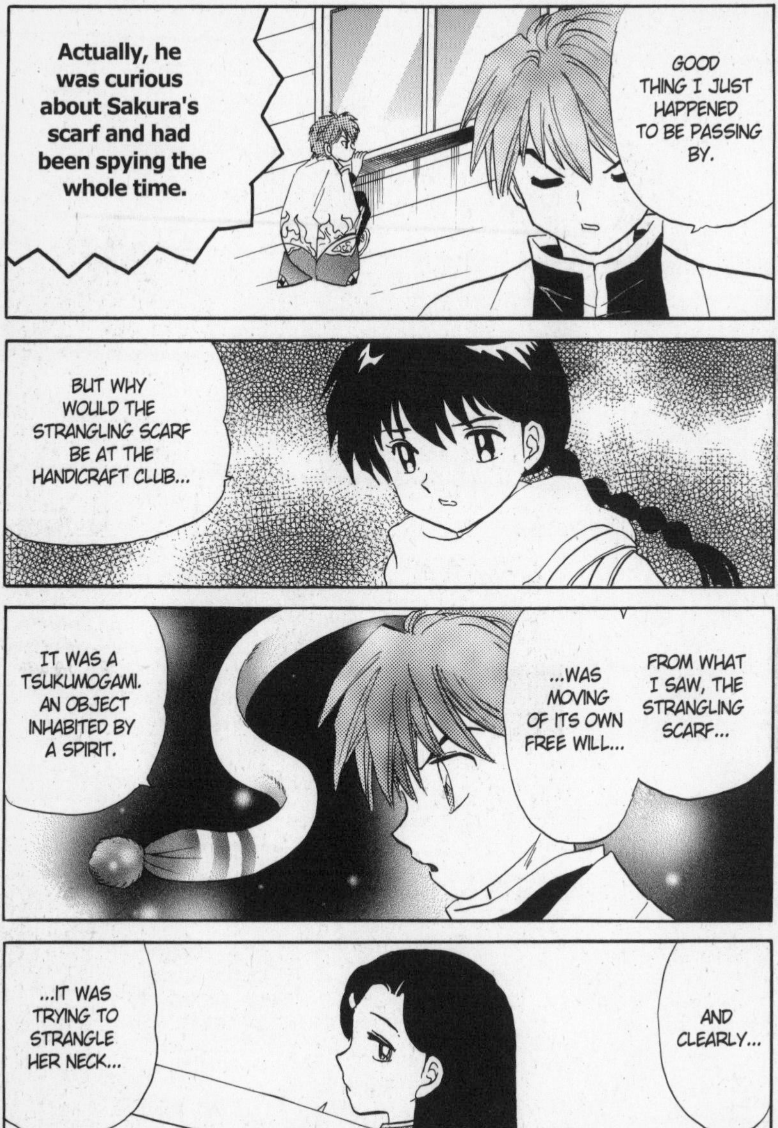
GOOD THING I JUST HAPPENED TO BE PASSING BY.
Actually, he was curious about Sakura's scarf and had been spying the whole time.
BUT WHY WOULD THE STRANGLING SCARF BE AT THE HANDICRAFT CLUB...
FROM WHAT I SAW, THE STRANGLING SCARF...
...WAS MOVING OF ITS OWN FREE WILL...
IT WAS A TSUKUMOGAMI. AN OBJECT INHABITED BY A SPIRIT.
AND CLEARLY...
...IT WAS TRYING TO STRANGLE HER NECK...

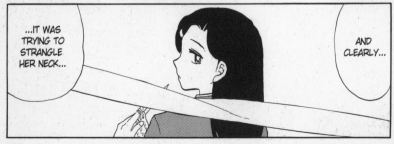

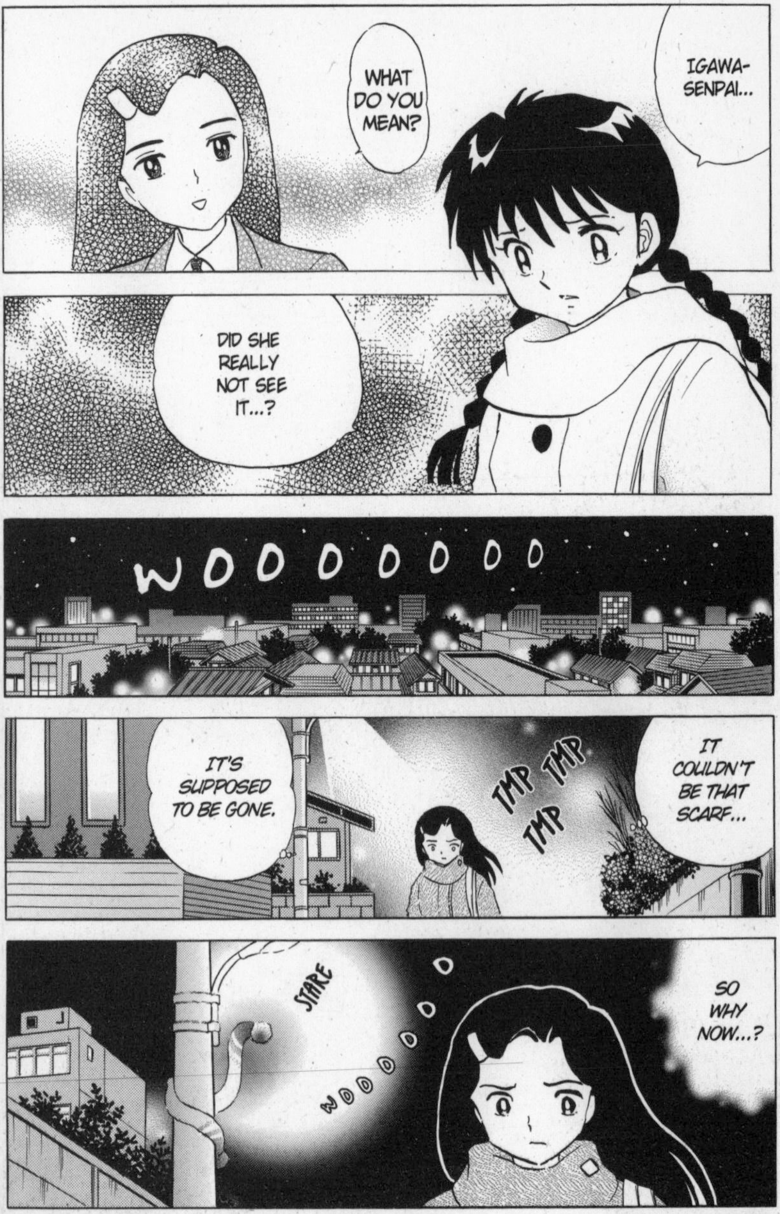
IGAWA-SENPAI...
WHAT DO YOU MEAN?
DID SHE REALLY NOT SEE IT...?
WOOOOOOO
IT COULDN'T BE THAT SCARF...
TMP TMP TMP
IT'S SUPPOSED TO BE GONE.
SO WHY NOW...?
WOOOOOOO
STARE

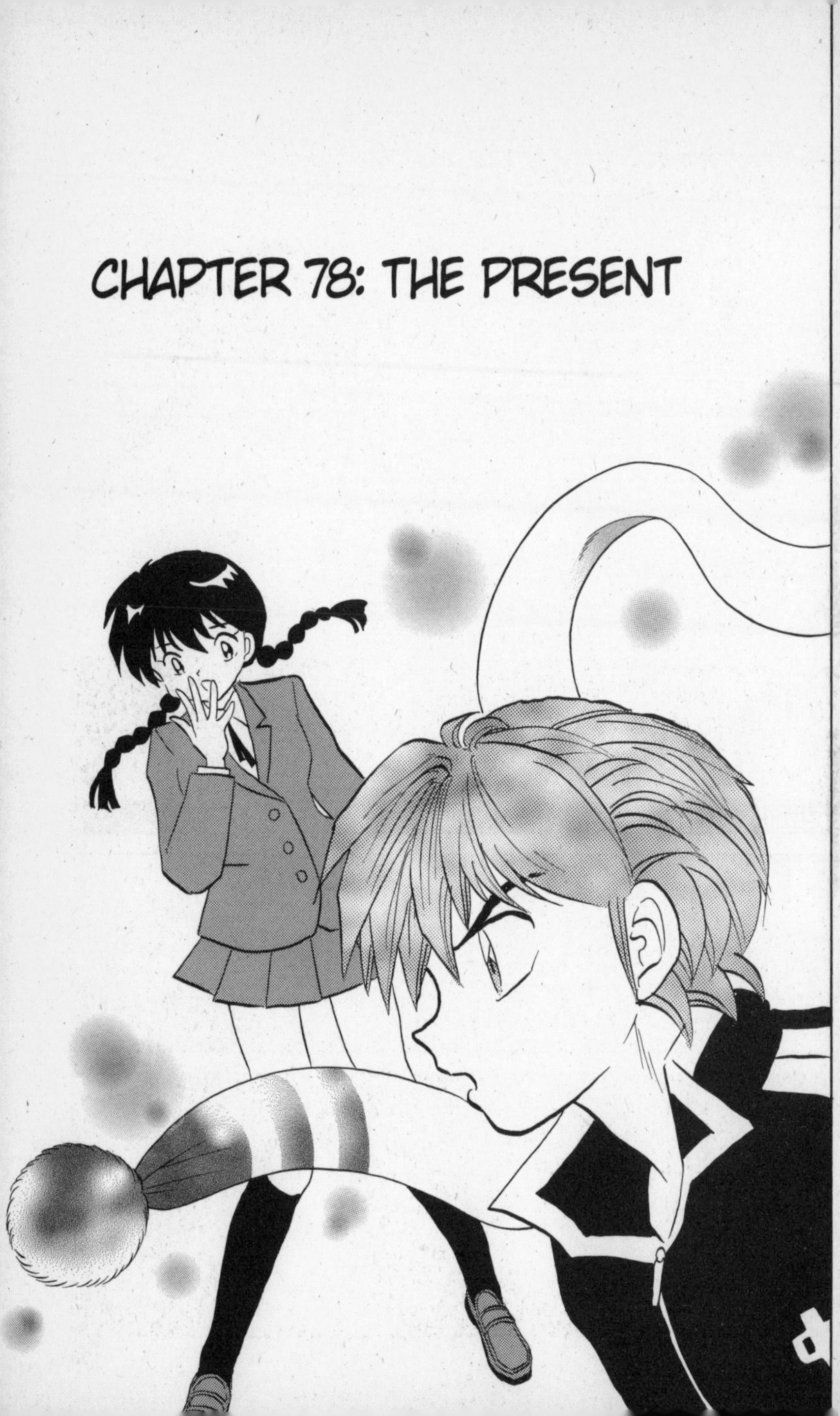
CHAPTER 78: THE PRESENT

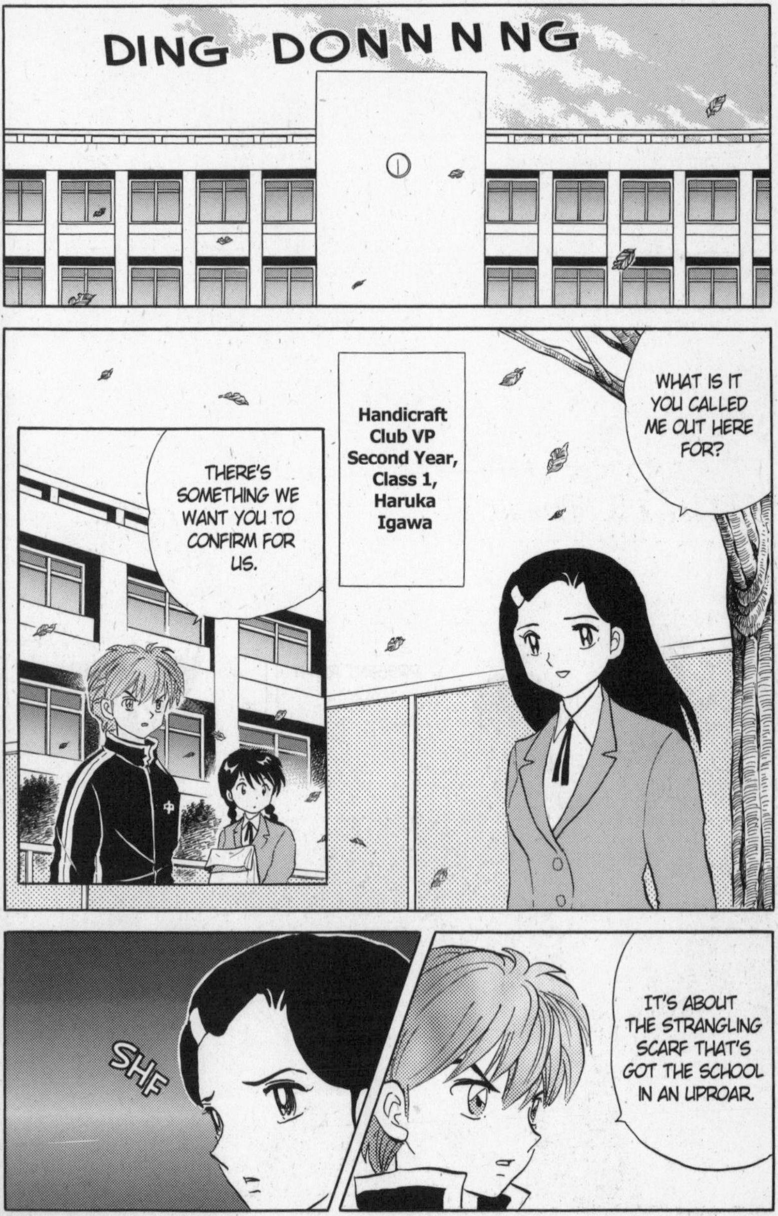
DING DONNNNG
WHAT IS IT YOU CALLED ME OUT HERE FOR?
Handicraft Club VP Second Year, Class 1, Haruka Igawa
THERE'S SOMETHING WE WANT YOU TO CONFIRM FOR US.
IT'S ABOUT THE STRANGLING SCARF THAT'S GOT THE SCHOOL IN AN UPROAR.
SHF

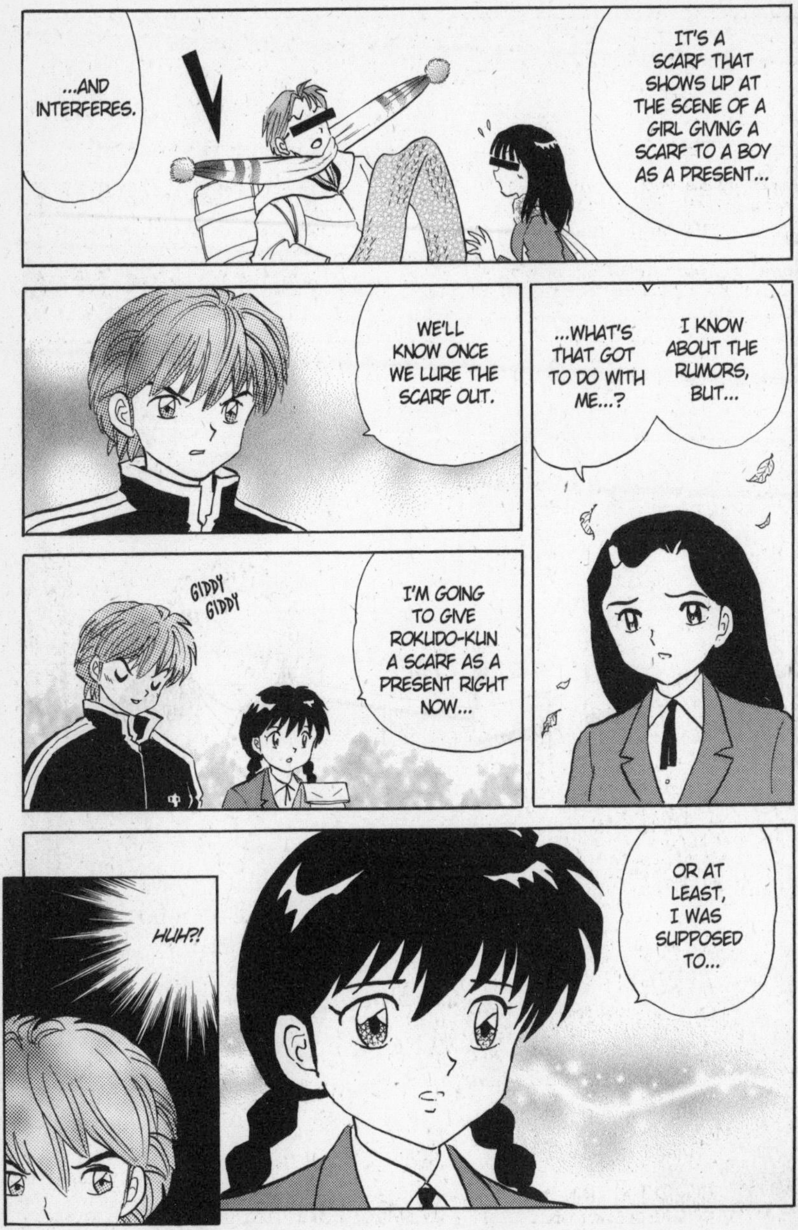
IT'S A SCARF THAT SHOWS UP AT THE SCENE OF A GIRL GIVING A SCARF TO A BOY AS A PRESENT...
...AND INTERFERES.
I KNOW ABOUT THE RUMORS, BUT...
...WHAT'S THAT GOT TO DO WITH ME...?
WE'LL KNOW ONCE WE LURE THE SCARF OUT.
I'M GOING TO GIVE ROKUDO-KUN A SCARF AS A PRESENT RIGHT NOW...
GIDDY GIDDY
OR AT LEAST, I WAS SUPPOSED TO...
HUH?!

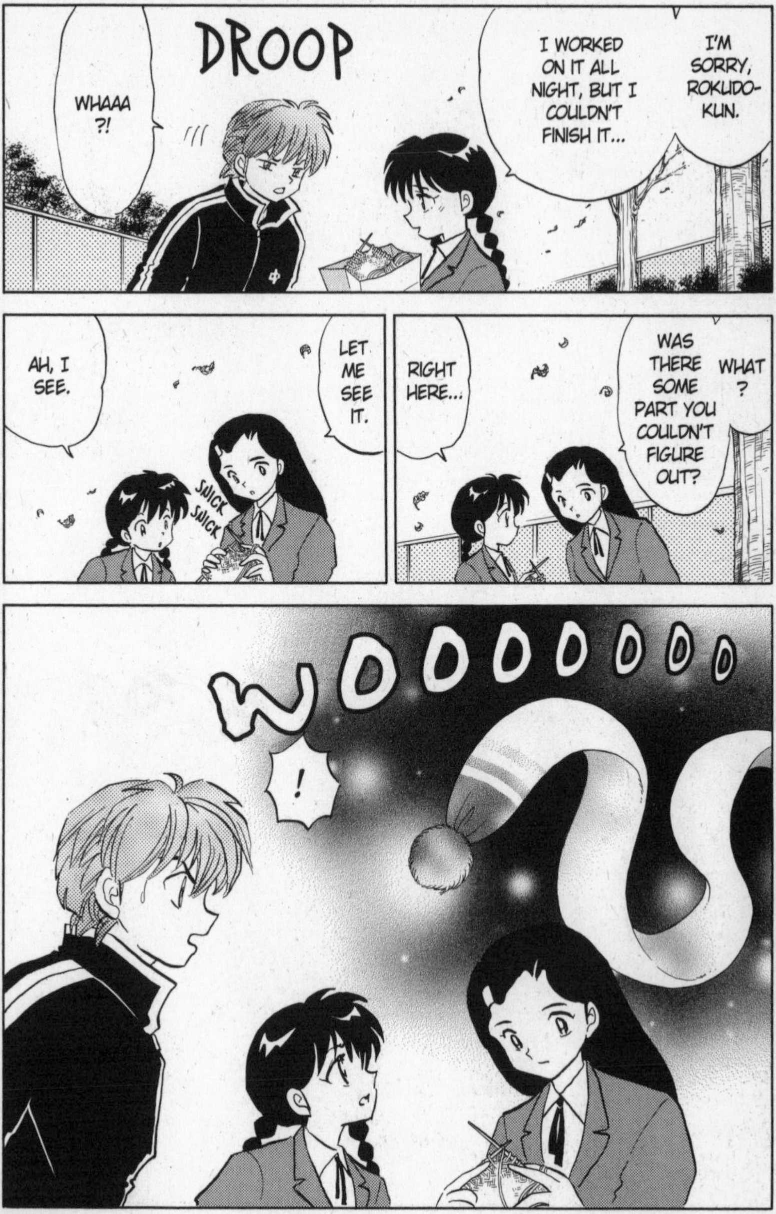
I'M SORRY, ROKUDO-KUN.
I WORKED ON IT ALL NIGHT, BUT I COULDN'T FINISH IT...
DROOP
WHAAA ?!
WHAT ?
WAS THERE SOME PART YOU COULDN'T FIGURE OUT?
RIGHT HERE...
LET ME SEE IT.
SWICK SWICK
AH, I SEE.
WOOOOOOO
!

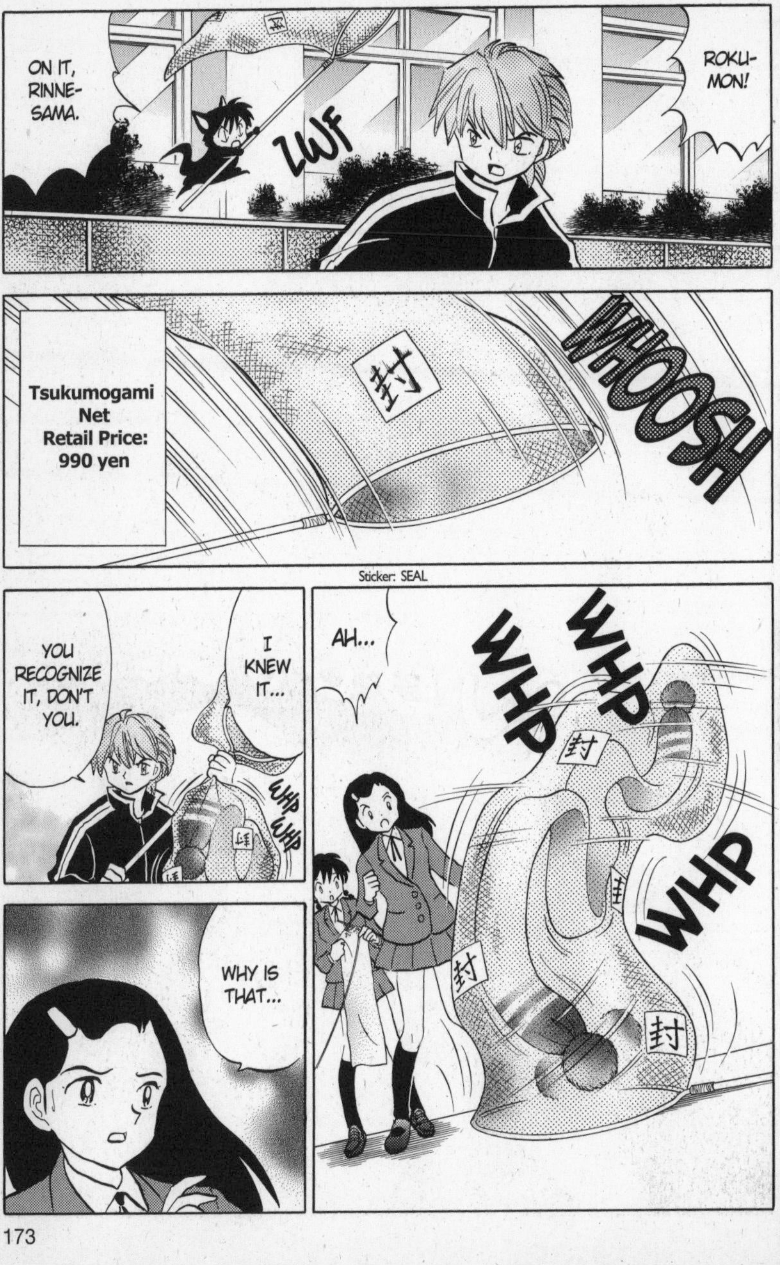
ROKU-MON!
ON IT, RINNE-SAMA.
ZUF
WHOOSH
Tsukumogami Net Retail Price: 990 yen
Sticker: SEAL
AH...
WHP
WHP
WHP
I KNEW IT...
YOU RECOGNIZE IT, DON'T YOU.
WHP WHP
WHY IS THAT...

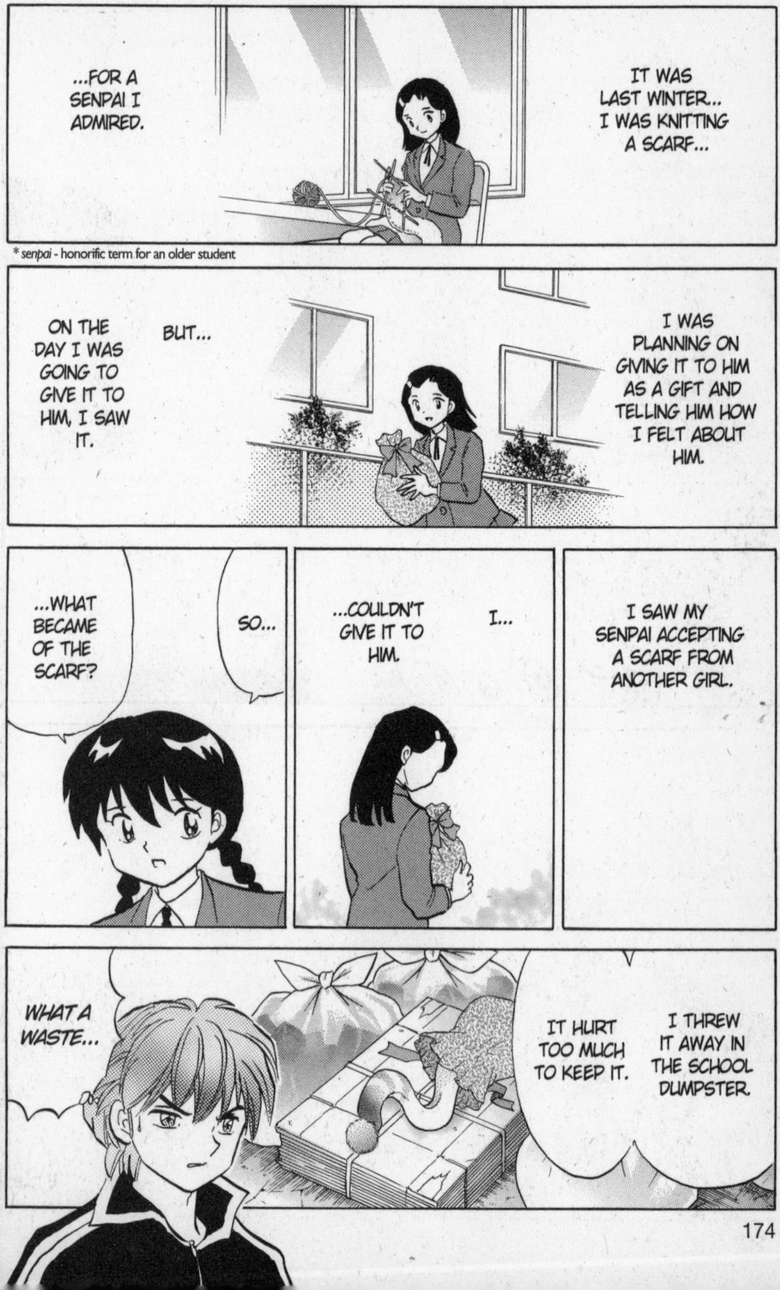
IT WAS LAST WINTER... I WAS KNITTING A SCARF...
...FOR A SENPAI I ADMIRED.
I WAS PLANNING ON GIVING IT TO HIM AS A GIFT AND TELLING HIM HOW I FELT ABOUT HIM.
BUT...
ON THE DAY I WAS GOING TO GIVE IT TO HIM, I SAW IT.
I SAW MY SENPAI ACCEPTING A SCARF FROM ANOTHER GIRL.
I...
...COULDN'T GIVE IT TO HIM.
SO...
...WHAT BECAME OF THE SCARF?
I THREW IT AWAY IN THE SCHOOL DUMPSTER.
IT HURT TOO MUCH TO KEEP IT.
WHAT A WASTE...

* *senpai* - honorific term for an older student

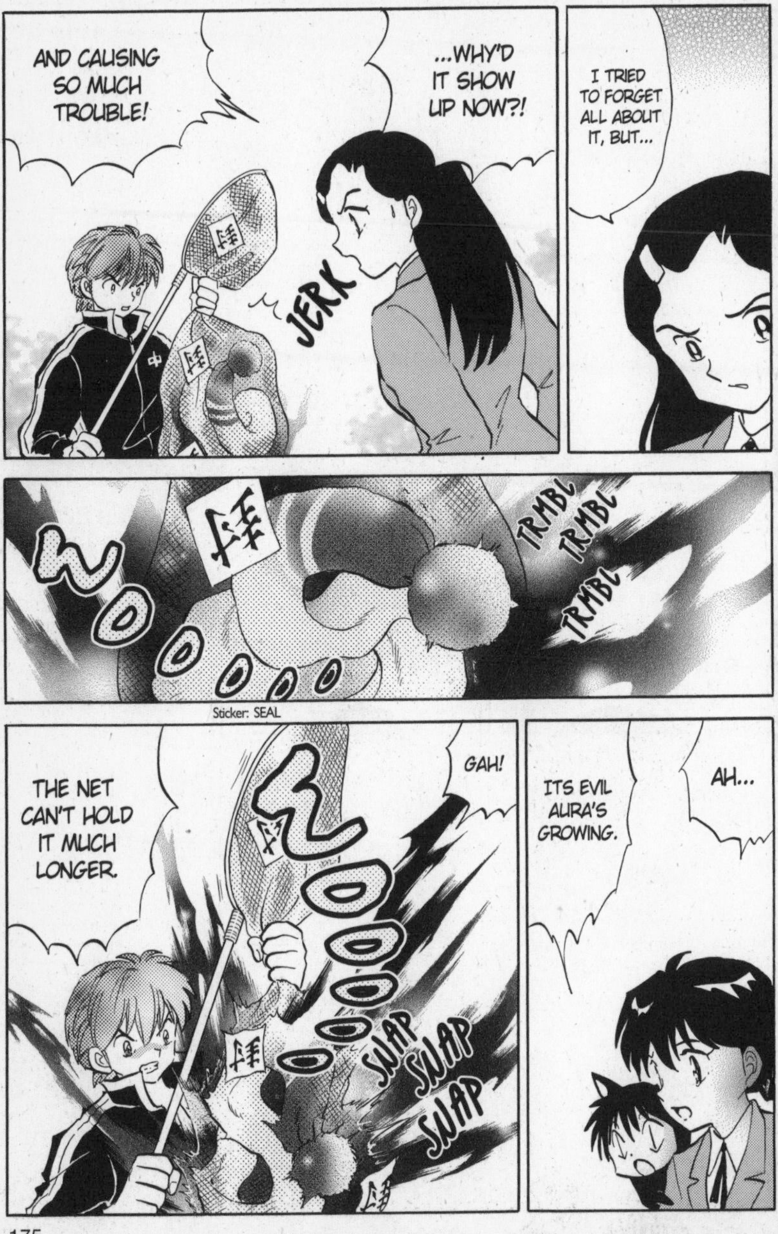
I TRIED TO FORGET ALL ABOUT IT, BUT...
...WHY'D IT SHOW UP NOW?!
AND CAUSING SO MUCH TROUBLE!
JERK
TRMBL TRMBL TRMBL
WOOOOOOO
Sticker: SEAL
AH...
ITS EVIL AURA'S GROWING.
GAH!
THE NET CAN'T HOLD IT MUCH LONGER.
WOOOOOOO
SNAP SNAP SNAP

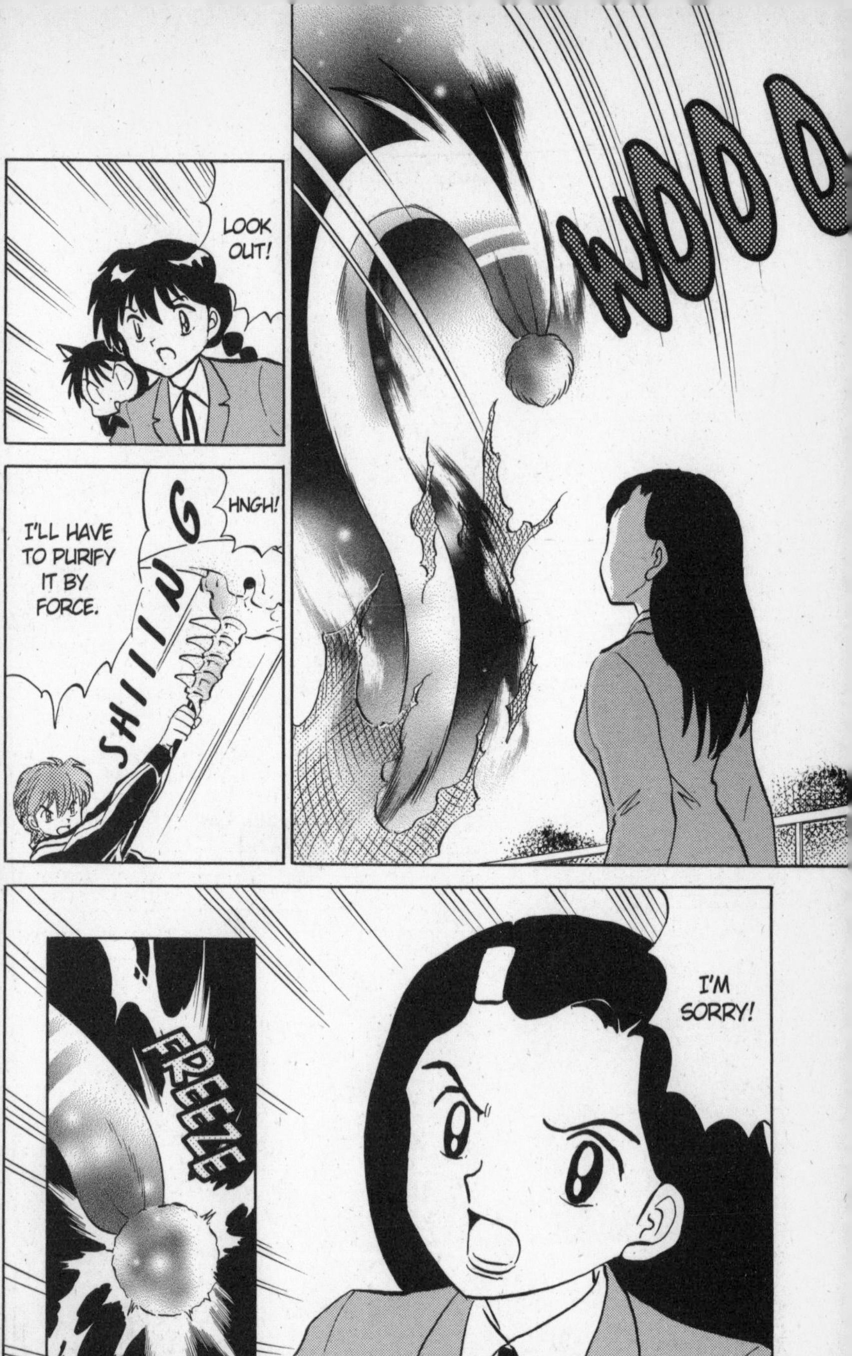
WOOOO
LOOK OUT!
HNGH!
I'LL HAVE TO PURIFY IT BY FORCE.
SHIIING
I'M SORRY!
FREEZE

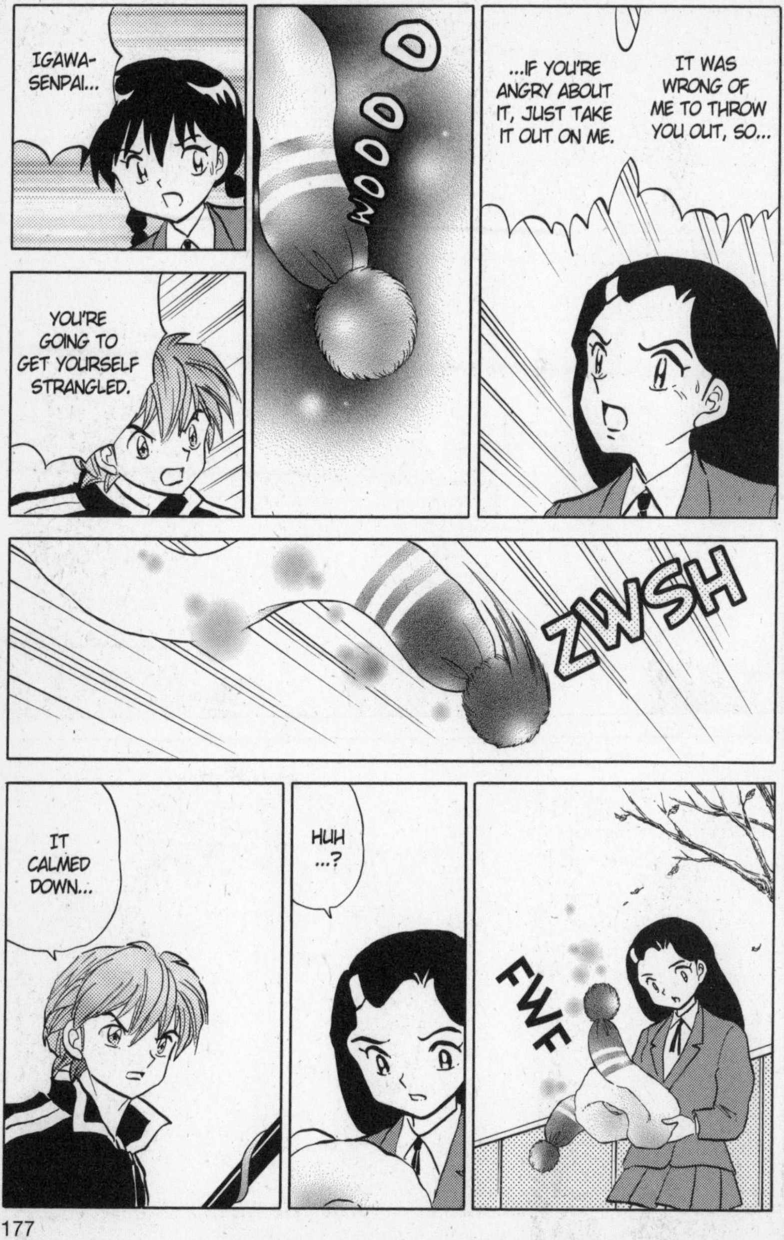
IT WAS WRONG OF ME TO THROW YOU OUT, SO...
...IF YOU'RE ANGRY ABOUT IT, JUST TAKE IT OUT ON ME.
DOOOOM
IGAWA-SENPAI...
YOU'RE GOING TO GET YOURSELF STRANGLED.
ZWSH
FWF
HUH ...?
IT CALMED DOWN...

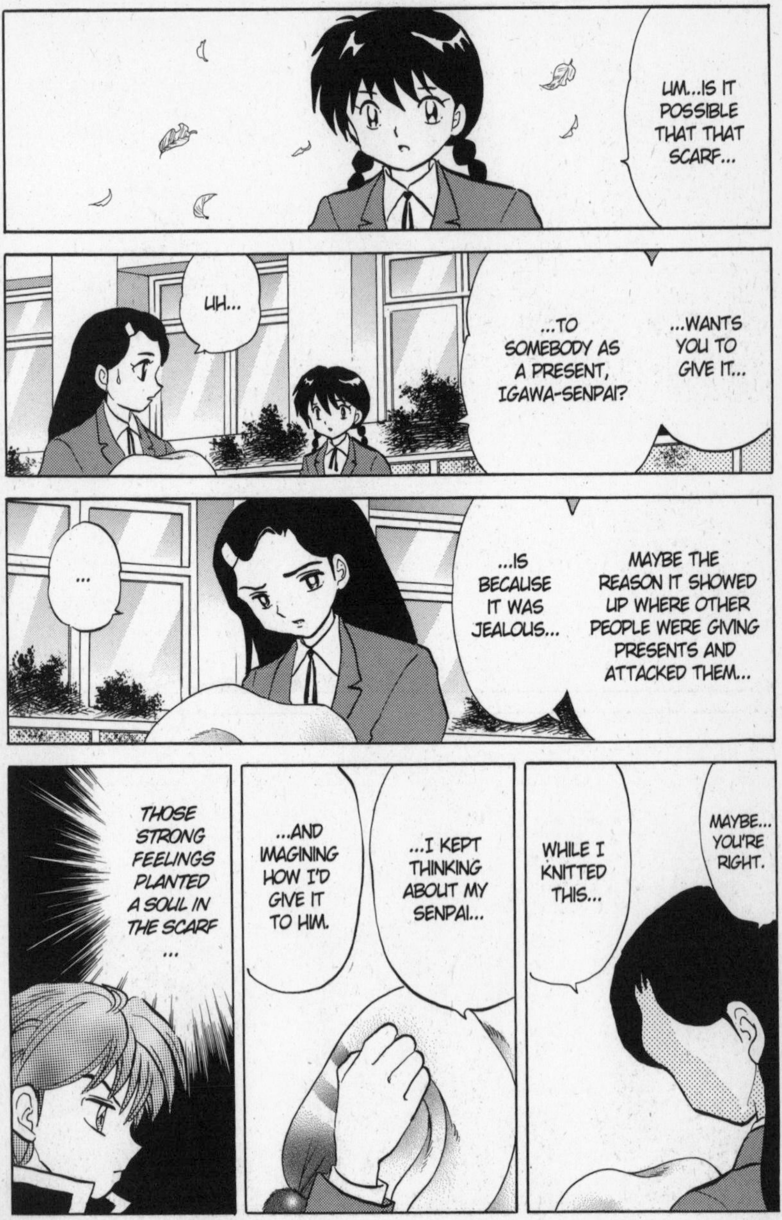
UM...IS IT POSSIBLE THAT THAT SCARF...
...WANTS YOU TO GIVE IT...
...TO SOMEBODY AS A PRESENT, IGAWA-SENPAI?
UH...
MAYBE THE REASON IT SHOWED UP WHERE OTHER PEOPLE WERE GIVING PRESENTS AND ATTACKED THEM...
...IS BECAUSE IT WAS JEALOUS...
...
MAYBE... YOU'RE RIGHT.
WHILE I KNITTED THIS...
...I KEPT THINKING ABOUT MY SENPAI...
...AND IMAGINING HOW I'D GIVE IT TO HIM.
THOSE STRONG FEELINGS PLANTED A SOUL IN THE SCARF...

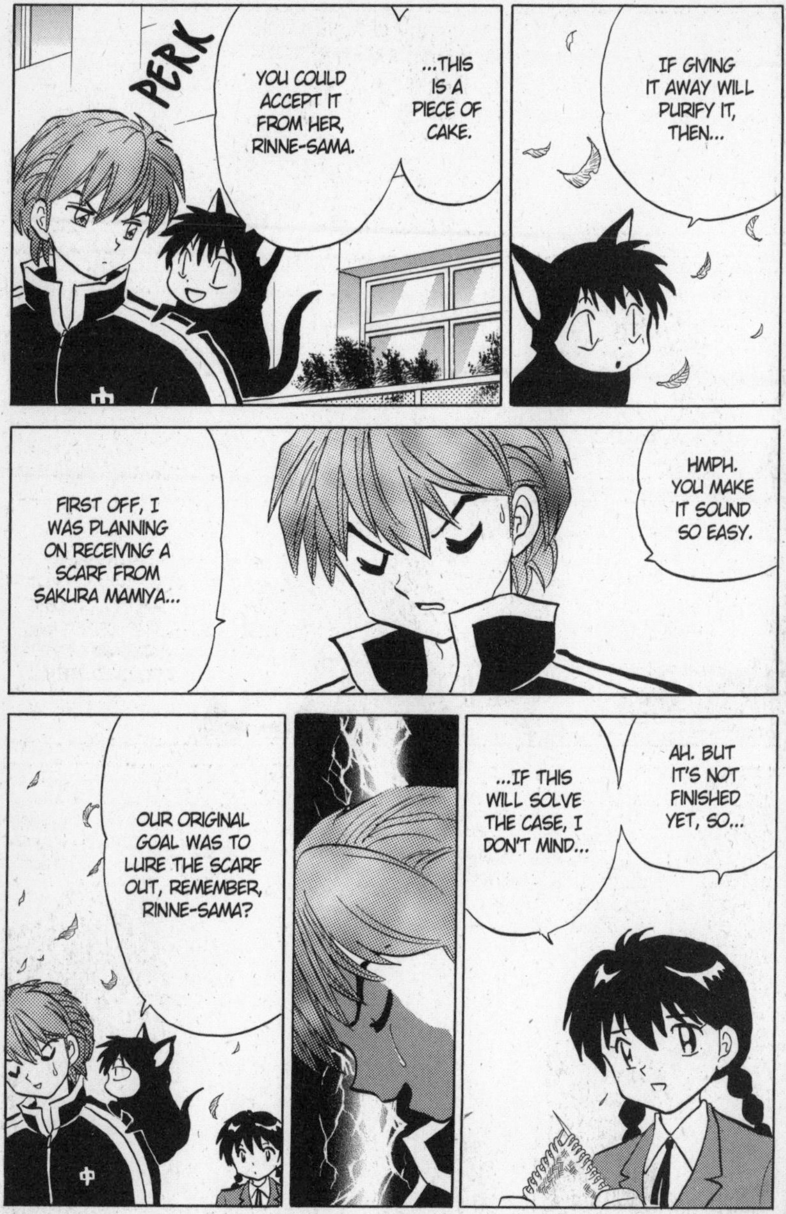
IF GIVING IT AWAY WILL PURIFY IT, THEN...
...THIS IS A PIECE OF CAKE.
YOU COULD ACCEPT IT FROM HER, RINNE-SAMA.
PERK
HMPH. YOU MAKE IT SOUND SO EASY.
FIRST OFF, I WAS PLANNING ON RECEIVING A SCARF FROM SAKURA MAMIYA...
AH. BUT IT'S NOT FINISHED YET, SO...
...IF THIS WILL SOLVE THE CASE, I DON'T MIND...
OUR ORIGINAL GOAL WAS TO LURE THE SCARF OUT, REMEMBER, RINNE-SAMA?

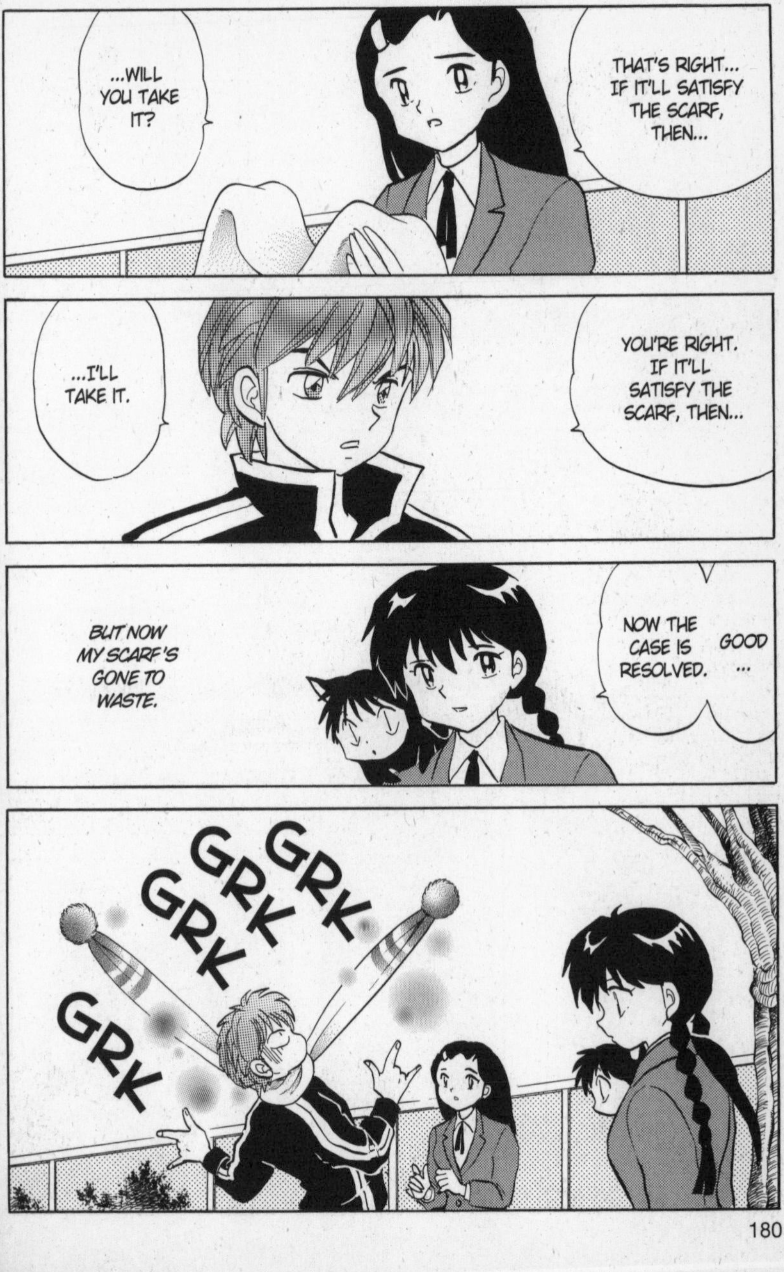
THAT'S RIGHT... IF IT'LL SATISFY THE SCARF, THEN...
...WILL YOU TAKE IT?
YOU'RE RIGHT. IF IT'LL SATISFY THE SCARF, THEN...
...I'LL TAKE IT.
GOOD...
NOW THE CASE IS RESOLVED.
BUT NOW MY SCARF'S GONE TO WASTE.
GRK
GRK
GRK
GRK

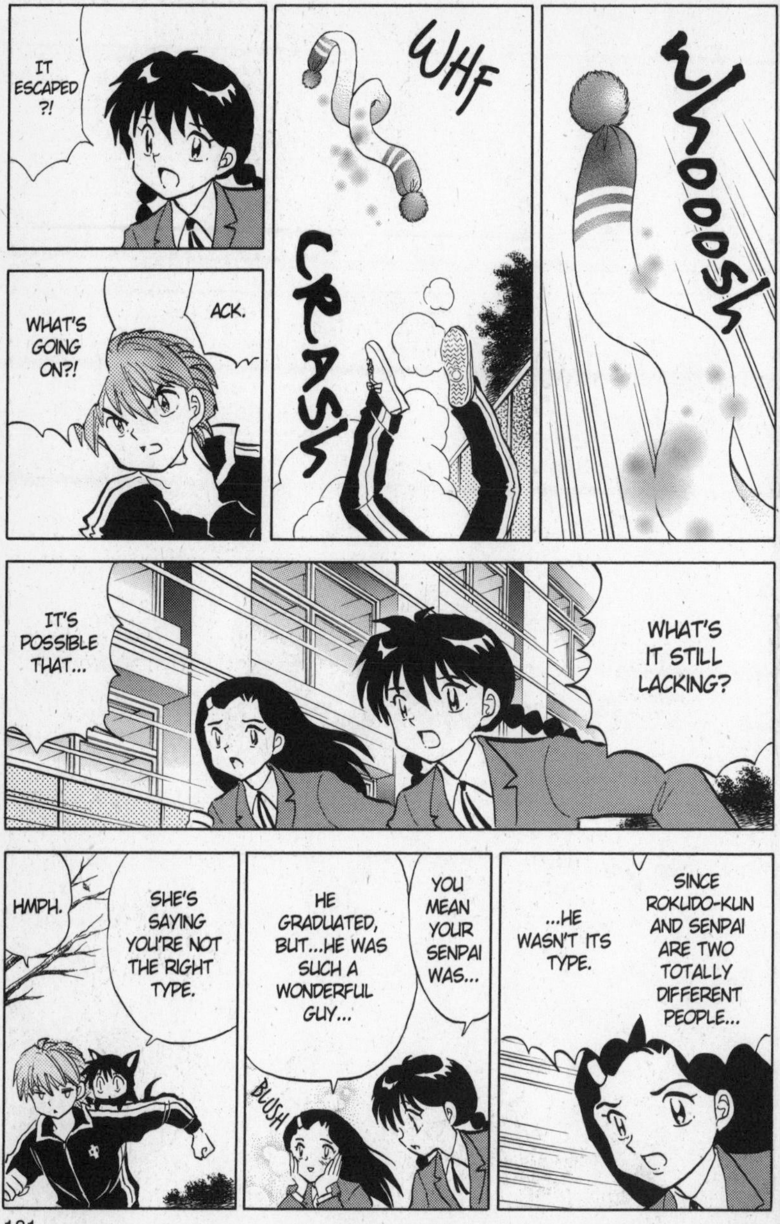
WHOOOSH
WHF
CRASH
IT ESCAPED?!
ACK.
WHAT'S GOING ON?!
WHAT'S IT STILL LACKING?
IT'S POSSIBLE THAT...
SINCE ROKUDO-KUN AND SENPAI ARE TWO TOTALLY DIFFERENT PEOPLE...
...HE WASN'T ITS TYPE.
YOU MEAN YOUR SENPAI WAS...
HE GRADUATED, BUT...HE WAS SUCH A WONDERFUL GUY...
BLUSH
SHE'S SAYING YOU'RE NOT THE RIGHT TYPE.
HMPH.

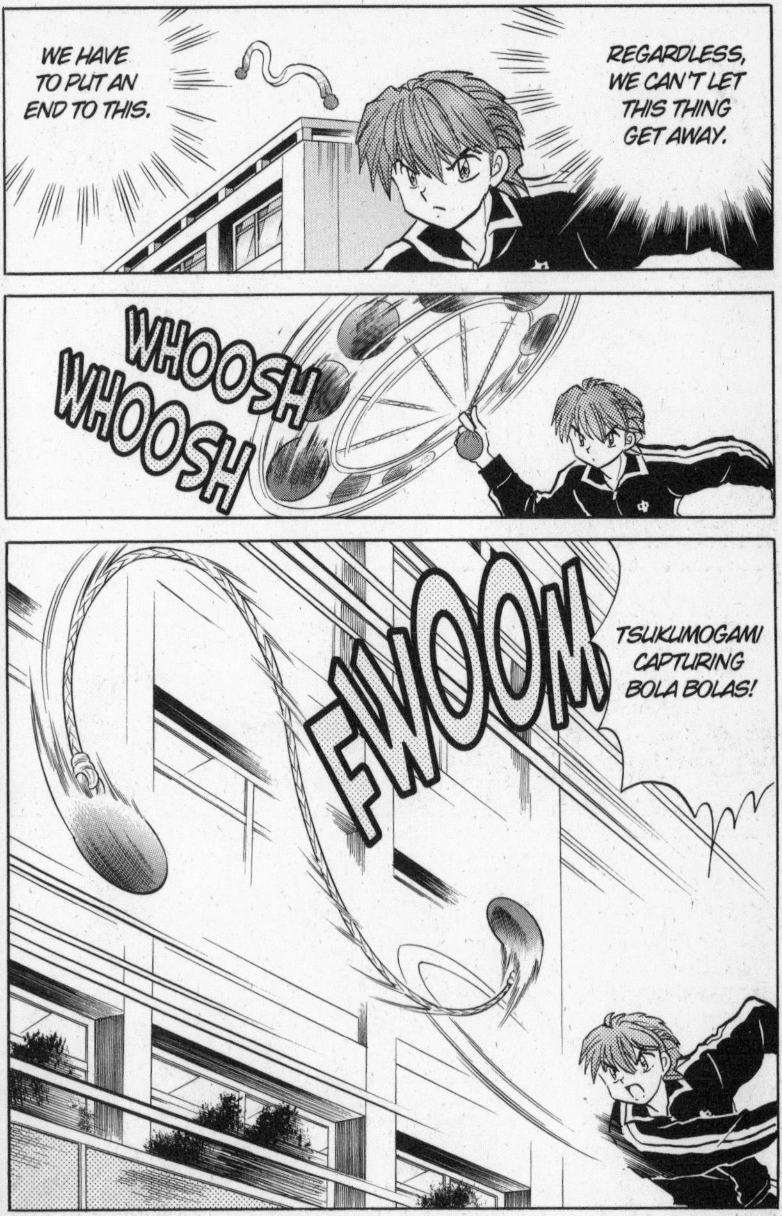
REGARDLESS, WE CAN'T LET THIS THING GET AWAY.
WE HAVE TO PUT AN END TO THIS.
WHOOSH WHOOSH
TSUKUMOGAMI CAPTURING BOLA BOLAS!
FWOOM

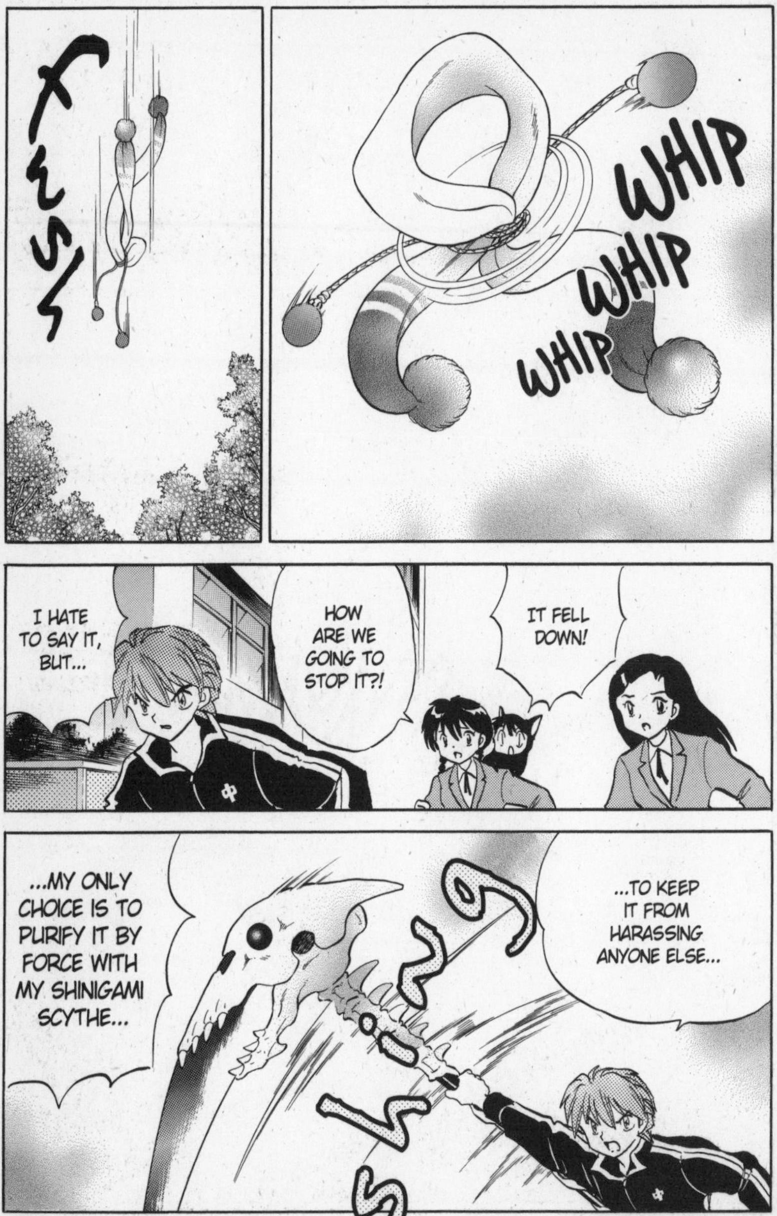
WHIP
WHIP
WHIP
IT FELL DOWN!
HOW ARE WE GOING TO STOP IT?!
I HATE TO SAY IT, BUT...
...TO KEEP IT FROM HARASSING ANYONE ELSE...
...MY ONLY CHOICE IS TO PURIFY IT BY FORCE WITH MY SHINIGAMI SCYTHE...
shing

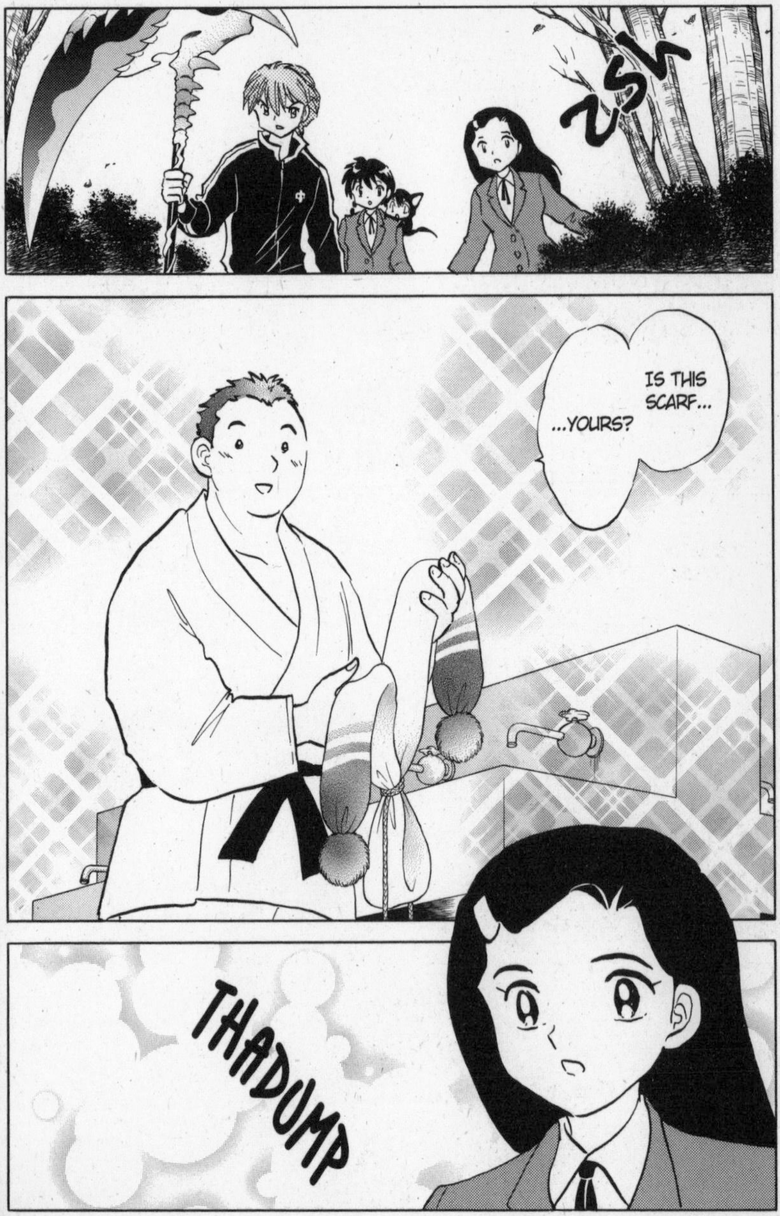
ZSH
IS THIS SCARF...
...YOURS?
THADUMP

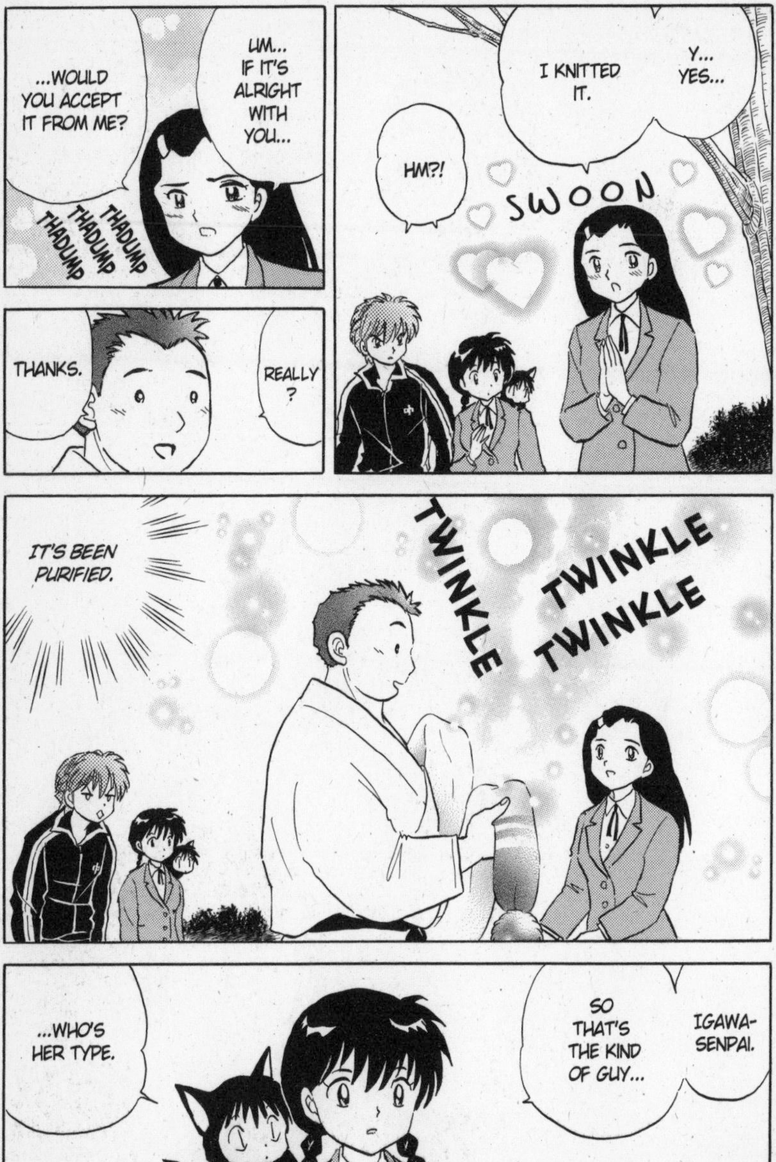
Y... YES...
I KNITTED IT.
HM?!
SWOON
UM... IF IT'S ALRIGHT WITH YOU...
...WOULD YOU ACCEPT IT FROM ME?
THADUMP THADUMP THADUMP
REALLY?
THANKS.
TWINKLE TWINKLE
TWINKLE
IT'S BEEN PURIFIED.
IGAWA-SENPAI.
SO THAT'S THE KIND OF GUY...
...WHO'S HER TYPE.

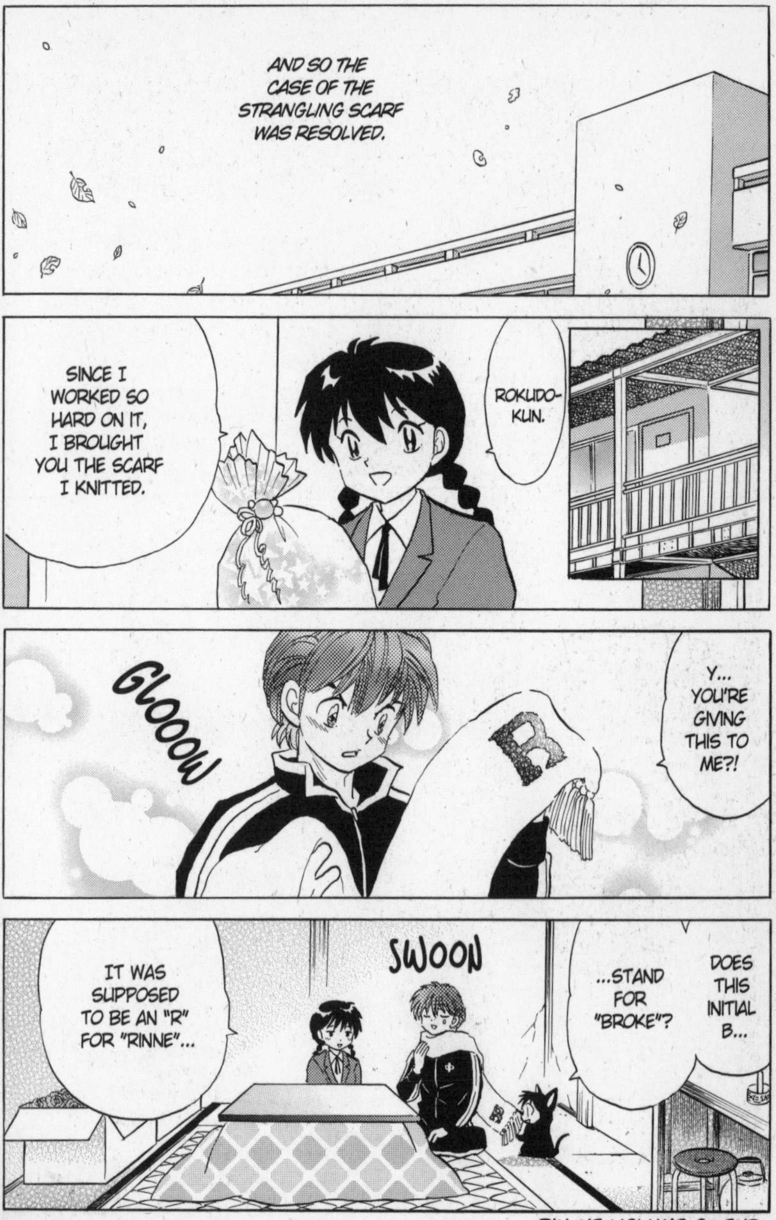
AND SO THE CASE OF THE STRANGLING SCARF WAS RESOLVED.
ROKUDO-KUN.
SINCE I WORKED SO HARD ON IT, I BROUGHT YOU THE SCARF I KNITTED.
Y... YOU'RE GIVING THIS TO ME?!
GLOOOW
DOES THIS INITIAL B...
...STAND FOR "BROKE"?
SWOON
IT WAS SUPPOSED TO BE AN "R" FOR "RINNE"...

RIN-NE VOLUME 8 -END-

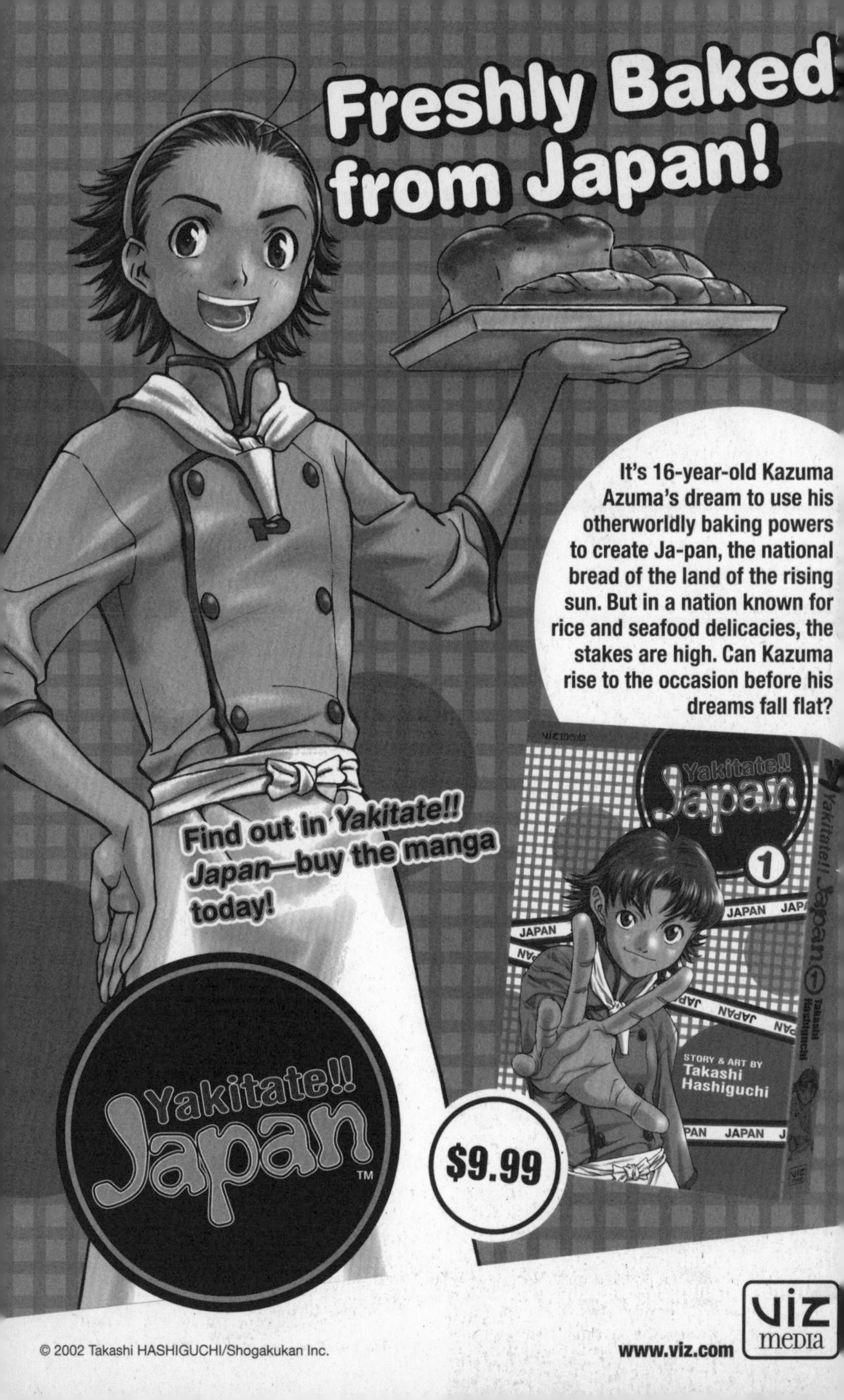

Freshly Baked from Japan!
It's 16-year-old Kazuma Azuma's dream to use his otherworldly baking powers to create Ja-pan, the national bread of the land of the rising sun. But in a nation known for rice and seafood delicacies, the stakes are high. Can Kazuma rise to the occasion before his dreams fall flat?
Find out in Yakitate!! Japan—buy the manga today!
Yakitate!! Japan™
$9.99
Yakitate!! Japan 1
STORY & ART BY Takashi Hashiguchi
© 2002 Takashi HASHIGUCHI/Shogakukan Inc.
www.viz.com
VIZ MEDIA

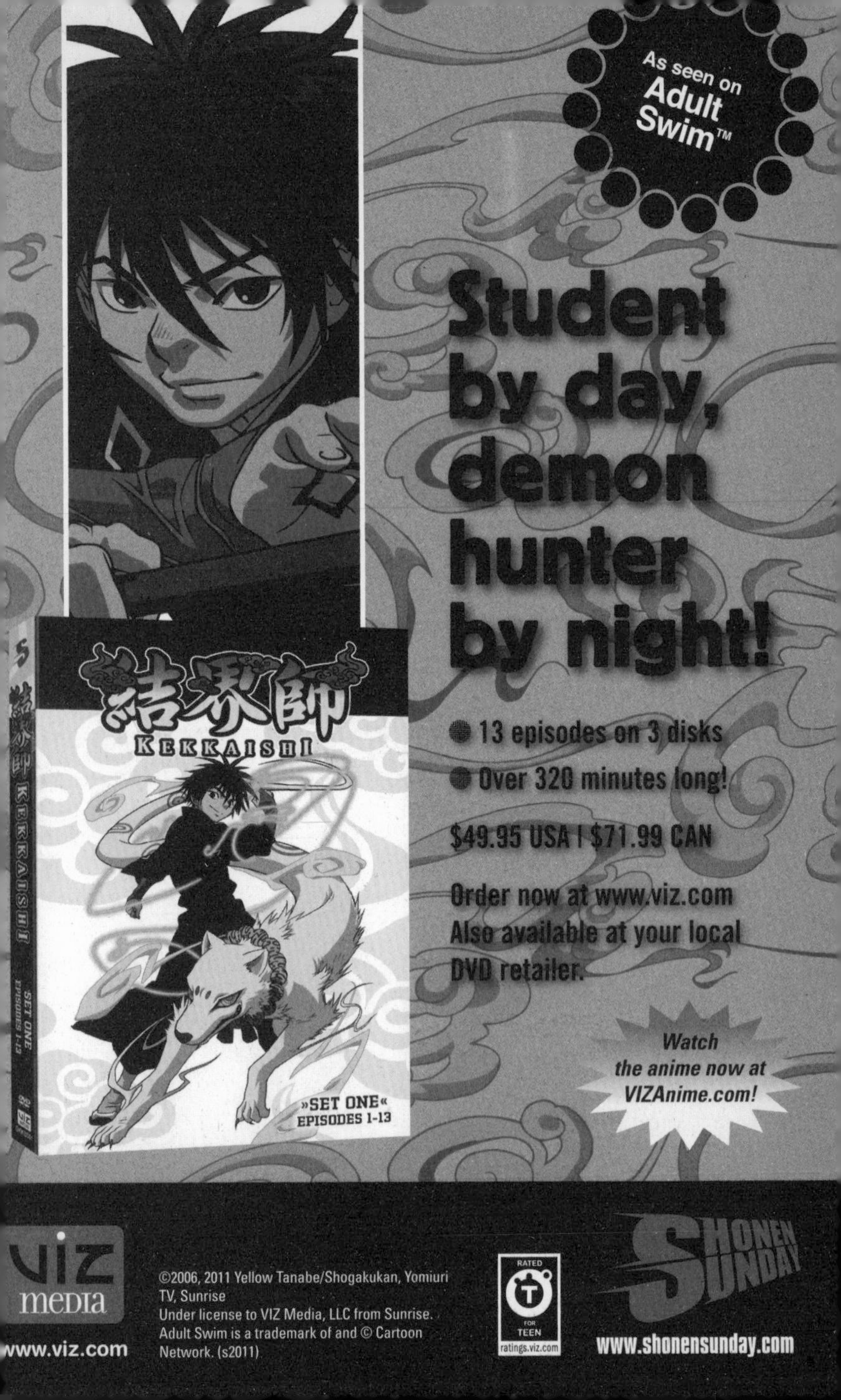
As seen on Adult Swim™
Student by day, demon hunter by night!
結界師 KEKKAISHI
»SET ONE« EPISODES 1-13
13 episodes on 3 disks
Over 320 minutes long!
$49.95 USA | $71.99 CAN
Order now at www.viz.com
Also available at your local DVD retailer.
Watch the anime now at VIZAnime.com!
VIZ media
www.viz.com
©2006, 2011 Yellow Tanabe/Shogakukan, Yomiuri TV, Sunrise
Under license to VIZ Media, LLC from Sunrise.
Adult Swim is a trademark of and © Cartoon Network. (s2011)
RATED T FOR TEEN
ratings.viz.com
SHONEN SUNDAY
www.shonensunday.com